MERGERS & ACQUISITIONS

The Art of Science

Ashish Patil

Published by:- SAAA Capital Pte. Ltd

Copy editing: MAP Systems Ltd (Thanks to Mr. Sam and Mr. Krishna)

Acknowledgement

Dedicated

Parents, Spouse, and kids

Thanks

Family, friends, well-wishers, and students

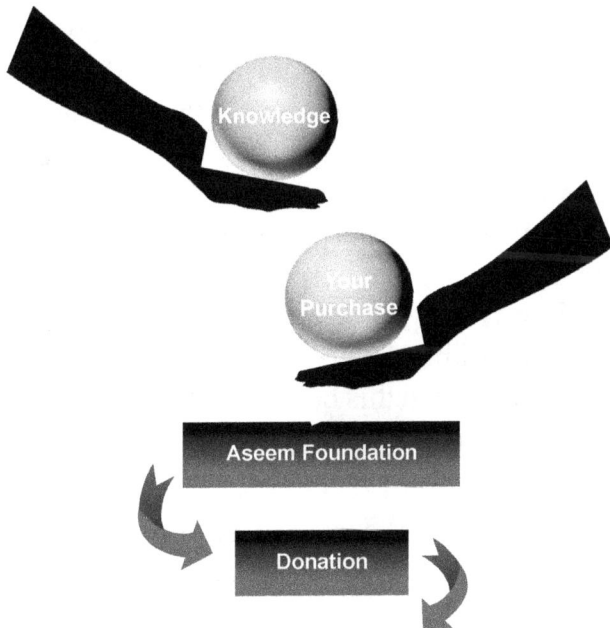

Foreword

Foreword from my boss @ Nalanda Capital, which has been the temple of learning wherein I learnt and unlearnt lot of things at professional and personal level. I am what I am today is due to my employer.

Books don't write themselves. And so if I were you, I would want to understand why *this* author is better than many others who have written extensively on the complex and critical subject of M&A. And a detailed resume wouldn't do for me. A resume can succinctly describe what the person has done, but not what he *is*. And in this short foreword, my objective is exactly this: to share with you the Ashish I know, and who, I believe, is the best person to have written this book.

Here is how highly I think of Ashish—I offered him a job without ever meeting him! No, this is a not a reflection of my impetuous nature; I am actually quite risk-averse and deliberate a lot over big decisions. I offered a job to him because while I had not met Ashish, I had *heard* him a lot over the years. I used to work for a private equity firm in India in early 2000s, and in this relatively "new" asset class, the M&A environment was either not transparent or was changing rapidly. I also believed that our advisors—lawyers, bankers, accountants—frequently gave us poor advice. None of us at this private equity firm had any formal M&A training. And on these occasions, my team and me inevitably turned to just one person—Ashish—for practical advice. In a majority of these calls, Ashish was neither on the buy or the sell side. He was just a good samaritan helping fellow professionals navigate the morass of the Indian M&A environment. I have been in the corporate world for 27 years, and to assert that this is a rare quality would be a huge understatement. Ashish is not the one to hoard his knowledge. He is an active and willing disseminator of his lifelong learnings, and this book is just another step in that direction.

I have now closely worked with Ashish for almost a decade, and while his official designation is that of CFO, he is much more than that. He is an active participant in *investment* decisions at our fund and is also our conscience keeper. Nothing that we do at Nalanda in the field of investing or otherwise is without Ashish's approval.

His career at Merrill Lynch gave him a perspective of M&A from the trenches, and his decade-long association with Nalanda has helped him evaluate the same issues as an intelligent observer. I haven't come across professionals who have developed this unique understanding of the M&A phenomenon from diametrically opposite points of view. This book is a great testament to Ashish's keen intellect, world-class expertise, and long experience. And so I have one word for you before you begin the book. Enjoy.

Pulak Prasad

Preface

The choice of "Eagle pose" of yoga for cover will be befuddling. First, it signifies the need for eagle instincts in M&A and ride the M&A like an eagle to become spacious, stable, and steady with least resistance.

Second, this "Eagle pose" is an extremely difficult pose needing stillness of mind, unwavering concentration along with flexibility, strength, and endurance to eventually bring about alignment and balance leading to a graceful pose. Flexibility in joints and strength in arms, shoulders, core, hips, and legs is the key to this pose.

As also, when doing M&A, it requires enormous strength, flexibility, endurance, and unwavering concentration to bring about alignment and balance allowing acquisition, assimilation, and accretion, thereby riding the acquisition in a stable and steady manner.

M&A has come to acquire centrepiece of corporate strategies and M&A as a tool for value creation. However, given the high risk–high return strategy, the failure rates of M&A are also very high and have led to enormous value destruction. Unfortunately, the risk involved in high return M&A is least understood.

The book emphasizes on understanding the risk involved followed with right approach and discipline. Given the increasing reliance on M&A, the book in general tries to make us understand the dynamics of the M&A and intends to marry it with sensible analysis to understand and practise this art of science to enhance value and/or prevent destruction.

Credits

My sincere thanks to my friends and well wishers, who helped me with the soft launch and their inputs.

My due acknowledgement to Mr Amit Chandra and Mr Sanjay Sharma for initiating me into world of Investment banking.

My due regards and thanks to Mr Rajeev Gupta from whom I learnt this art of M&A Science.

Note:

The content of the book has been based on publicly available information, annual reports, press releases, and company websites.

The book also uses Indian notations like crores, lakhs etc. The below table gives the conversion:

10,000,000	1 crore
100,000	1 lakh

Contents

Merger & Acquisition Origination

Contents

1.1 Introduction

Origination is a term, which is not dealt in academic books on finance or Merger & Acquisition (M&A), but is part of lingua franca of the deal making world of investment banking.

Origination, in very simple terms, means conceiving an idea on M&A. It can be of any type like buy, sell, restructure, spin-off, or capitalization. It represents the initial phase of M&A deal and is the most important part of the entire cycle. The later part of the M&A cycle comprises the execution to origination, thereby completing the M&A deal cycle. Origination is credited the most in investment banking because it represents the sourcing of deal and eventual revenues for the firm.

In M&A, the academic literature focuses only on acquisitions and not much is explained about the selling side of M&A or restructuring or divestures. This has contributed to lopsided understanding of the term M&A as acquisitions only. It has been restricted toward explaining the buyer's intent or acquisitions only. The term "SYNERGY" is commonly used to describe the intent for acquisitions. It is not the only element but one of the elements to drive M&A deals. There are a lot of elements that interplay to create deals encompassing buy, sell, restructure, spin-off, divestures etc.

These origination elements have not received much attention in M&A textbooks, so as to enable junior bankers or students of Corporate Finance to understand the nuances of the deal origination.

The chapter seeks to explore these elements and presents a much broader picture of M&A in context of "Origination."

1.2 Origination

A classical M&A origination would involve defining M&A strategy based on the gap assessment a particular client is facing and may wish to pursue that M&A strategy to achieve growth and create value for the shareholders.

The gap assessment could be of following nature:

- Product gap
- Market gap
- Geography gap
- Distribution gap
- Skill/expertise gap

Origination to Acquisition

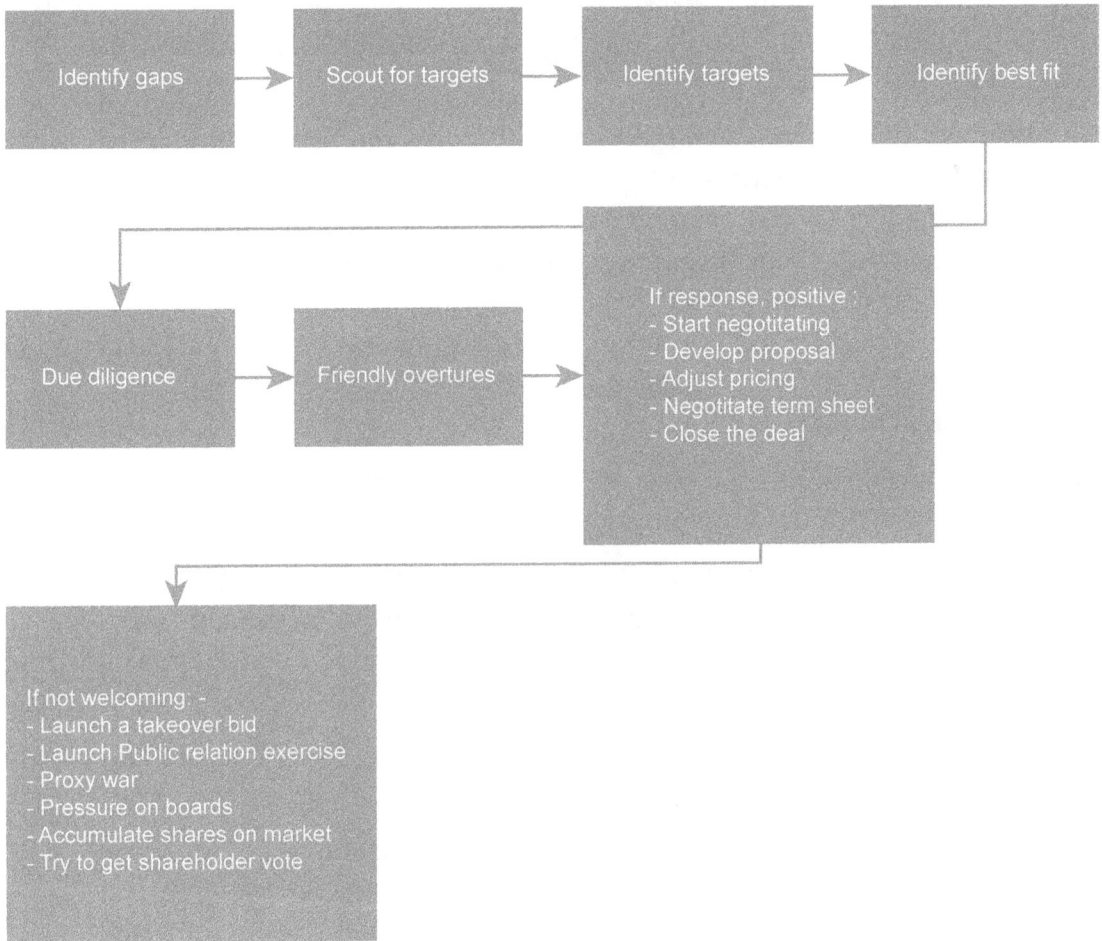

```
[Identify gaps] → [Scout for targets] → [Identify targets] → [Identify best fit]

[Due diligence] → [Friendly overtures] → [If response, positive :
                                          - Start negotitating
                                          - Develop proposal
                                          - Adjust pricing
                                          - Negotitate term sheet
                                          - Close the deal]

[If not welcoming: -
- Launch a takeover bid
- Launch Public relation exercise
- Proxy war
- Pressure on boards
- Accumulate shares on market
- Try to get shareholder vote]
```

A company having tried and failed in its endeavor to build the gap organically by investing resources and time may rely on M&A to fill up the gap. Here, the origination of deal starts to take shape. The deal is conceived by investment bankers in the preliminary form for the client.

The next step in the process of origination is to build on the conception and would involve the following:

- Initiate scouting for the targets which carry these gaps;
- Identify the best fit among the targets;

  Best fits can be further categorized into:

  - Gap fit;
  - Probability of the management/shareholders agreeing to sell;
  - Scouting for the share-holder base and possible sellers;

- - Figuring out kinks in the targets armor (leverage, inefficient management, disgruntled shareholder, growth challenges);
- - Whether the price justifies the gap it builds and thereby creates shareholder value.

- Carry out due diligence on the target and figure out the preliminary valuation;
- Initiate friendly overtures to figure out possibility of a deal;
- In case the response is positive, start negotiating and develop a proposal;
- If the response is not positive, work through the possibility of hostile bid or provide bear hug and assess the probability of success;
- Arriving at price based on due diligence results, synergy assessment, and controlling or non-controlling stake;
- Negotiate and close.

Subsequent integration is the post-acquisition activity, which will eventually determine the success of the acquisition.

The eventual value creation will be determined by the ability of the acquirer to put their arms around the target taking expeditious decision on human resources, closing or divesting unproductive assets, and raising capital to finance the acquisition, if funded through debt etc.

The assumptions which lead to the acquisition will now be tested and assessed. The robustness of the same will determine the eventual outcome.

The above can be highlighted with the following case study.

Case study 1.1: Kraft Foods Acquisition of Cadbury

Details

Kraft Foods, renamed as Mondelez International, was predominantly a North America-based food and confectionary company. The major items manufactured by them include cheese, biscuits, crackers, and sauce and grocery items. Kraft had minimal presence in the domain of chocolate and confectionary products. Although it had some presence in Europe, it depicted minimal presence in emerging markets like India and South America.

Kraft had a ~5% global market share in chocolate and candy industries. Kraft was facing a saturated market in North America with evident product gaps. At the same time, it was competing with Nestle, Kelloggs, and General Mills in the confectionery market.

Despite being a packaged food company, Kraft was not so strong in the chocolate and confectionary; rather, it can be said to be virtually absent in the market for these products. Kraft represented its presence only in North America and lacked

European and Asian/emerging market exposure. Cadbury was a perfect fit for the complementary product and market fit. On contrary, Cadbury was not present in the US market and had overall underperformed on the stock market with disgruntled shareholders.

Origination–Execution–Completion

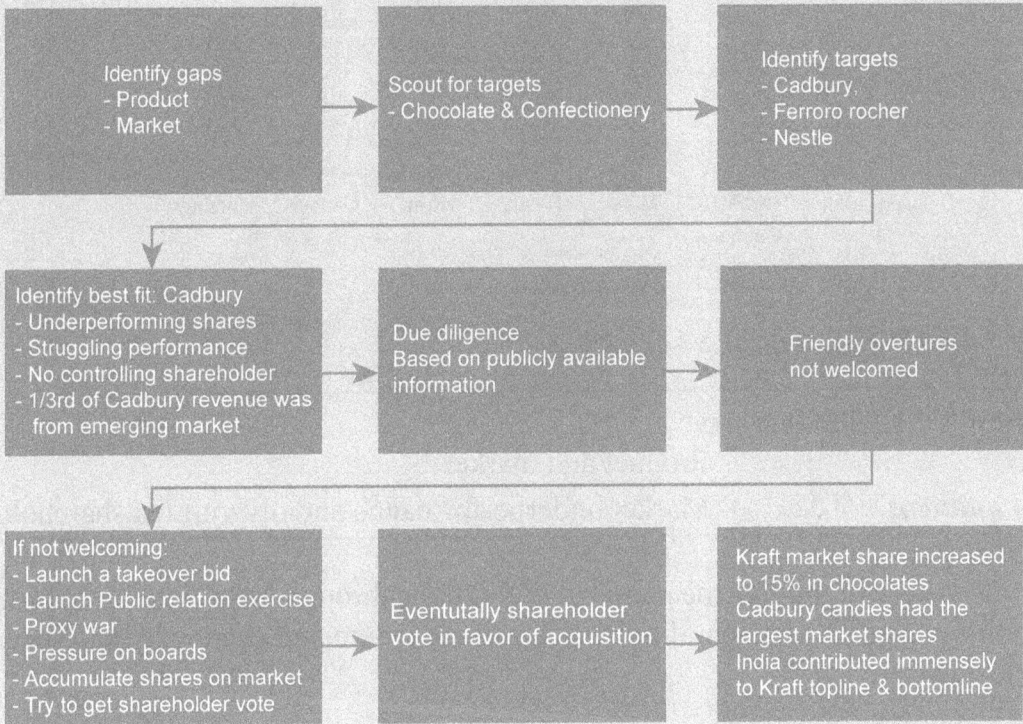

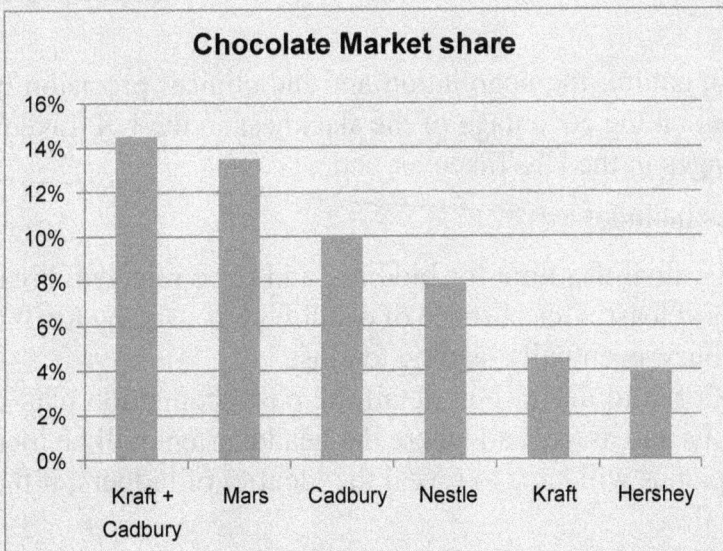

Identify gaps
- Product
- Market

→

Scout for targets
- Chocolate & Confectionery

→

Identify targets
- Cadbury
- Ferroro rocher
- Nestle

Identify best fit: Cadbury
- Underperforming shares
- Struggling performance
- No controlling shareholder
- 1/3rd of Cadbury revenue was from emerging market

→

Due diligence
Based on publicly available information

→

Friendly overtures
not welcomed

If not welcoming:
- Launch a takeover bid
- Launch Public relation exercise
- Proxy war
- Pressure on boards
- Accumulate shares on market
- Try to get shareholder vote

→

Eventutally shareholder vote in favor of acquisition

→

Kraft market share increased to 15% in chocolates
Cadbury candies had the largest market shares
India contributed immensely to Kraft topline & bottomline

Chocolate Market share

Category	Market Share
Kraft + Cadbury	~14.5%
Mars	~13.5%
Cadbury	~10%
Nestle	~8%
Kraft	~4.6%
Hershey	~4.2%

Source: Annual reports and company data

Confectionery Market share

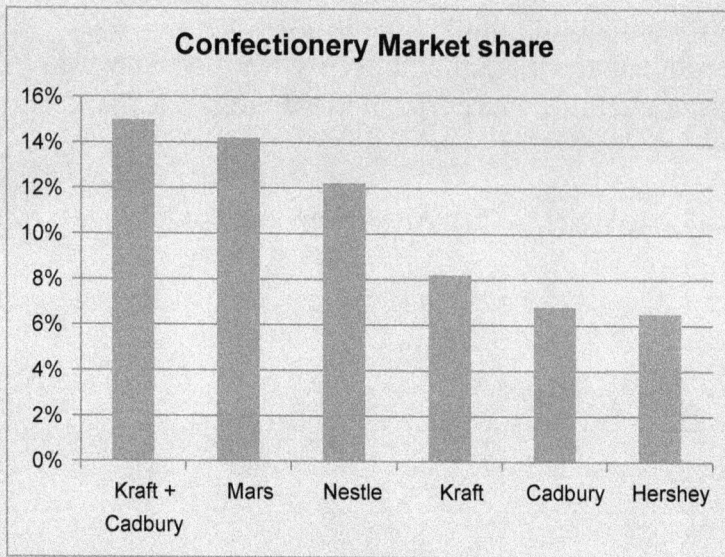

Source: Annual reports and company data

Key Learning

Origination elements	
Gaps	Product and market
Deal quotient	Market underperformance and disgruntled shareholders

The above case highlights the classical M&A done through identification of product and market gap. The launch of bid was hostile in nature and eventually had successful closing.

The acquisition was successful for Kraft. It was demonstrated by Kraft's eventual acquisition of 15% market share and becoming the number one player in the market of candy.

Due to hostile nature, the negotiation and the clinical precision by which Kraft executed the deal taking advantage of the slackness in the UK Takeover code led to subsequent changes in the UK Takeover code.

The key changes include:

* There will be final deadline for bidding, and once rejected, it cannot be re-bid for 6 months at least. This absence of deadline was used by Kraft to create a bear hug on Cadbury, eventually leading to close.
* The bidders need to disclose in detail the post-acquisition plan especially with respect to jobs and assets and where the headquarters will be located.
* Target companies will have to reveal the identity of bidders, if they receive take over proposal.
* Employees can make a view about the bid.
* No anti-competitive tools like inducement fee were permitted.

It is important to understand the above elements. Though the changes were made to the UK law, the manner of exploiting the slackness represents the learning tools for future takeovers in any geography. Such learning allows the acquirers to make clean and clinical bid for their targets.

1.3 Examples of Classical Origination in M&A

P&G Acquisition of Gillette:

Origination elements	
Gaps	Product
Deal quotient	Under-marketed products of seller and ability to roll-out Gillette products onto existing distribution set-up

P&G portfolio had personal care products, but it lacked the product in Men's category such as shaving type of personal category; thus, it was a complementary product for P&G. The product gap was further complemented by geographical spread that could be achieved for Gillette's product on the existing distribution setup of P&G.

Google Acquisition of Motorola Mobile Phone Business

Origination elements	
Gaps	Brand and technology
Deal quotient	Motorola had already split its handphone business there by indicating it's intention to sell

Google has an ambition to rule every domain in the world of technology. As it could not make headway through Nexus, it lacked presence in the field of smartphones unlike Apple. Thus, acquiring Motorola patents and brands was imperative for it to pursue this particular business.

Facebook Acquisition of Whatsapp and Instagram

Origination elements	
Gaps	Product gap
Deal quotient	Start-up companies who will eventually sell out at price

Facebook presents a classical example in the field of social media which will try to keep plugging in product gaps and keep rivals from emerging to maintain its supremacy. Thus, Instagram and WhatsApp being incidental to its business and obvious product gaps represent a classical origination.

Diageo's Acquisition of United Breweries

Origination elements	
Gaps	Market gap
Deal quotient	The seller under distress will eventually sell-off

For a long duration, Diageo was sitting on the sidelines of the Indian market, while its rival like Pernod-Ricard had already made headway. Thus, the vulnerability of the seller due to problems in Kingfisher business presented an opportunity to seize the market through M&A.

Tech Mahindra's Acquisition of Satyam

Origination elements	
Gaps	Product gap and client concentration
Deal quotient	The seller under-distress and up for sell

Satyam was hit by on accounting scandal by its founder, sending the Company into tailspin. Tech Mahindra was largely a telecom software service provider as well as had client concentration. Tech Mahindra sensed it as the perfect opportunity to diversify product and diversify clients as Satyam was dominant in banking and financial sectors.

Etihad's Acquisition of Jet Airways

Origination elements	
Gaps	Market gap
Deal quotient	Leveraged balance sheet, change in foreign carrier investment regulations

Indian aviation markets with its size and growth potential has been an attractive market for the foreign carriers. M&A represents an attractive entry option given the regulatory framework of the sector, wherein foreign carriers can own only 49% of the venture. The change brought about in the foreign investment guidelines in aviation sector coupled with the leveraged balance sheet of Jet Airways represented a perfect opportunity for foreign carriers like Etihad to set up M&A of Jet Airways.

The above examples explain the concept of origination and how deal making originates. The origination as a concept is built on the classical objectives of M&A as listed below:

- Growth
- Economics scale
- Monopoly power
- Increased market valuation

- Reduced uncertainty
- Opportunity
- Asset stripping
- Empire building
- Learn and develop new capabilities
- Re-shape firm's competitive scope
- Increase diversification
- Lower risk compared to developing new products
- Increase speed to market
- Overcome entry barriers
- Increase market power

The above listed objectives focus only on the motivations of the buyer, but fall short of explaining how the buyer and seller motivations are matched by match-making investment bankers to originate deal. We will look into other origination elements on both the acquirer and the target side to originate deals and generate revenues.

Before we dig deeper into the origination elements, we need to understand what is M&A banking.

1.4 What is Merger & Acquisition Banking: M&A deal life cycle

What is M&A Banking?

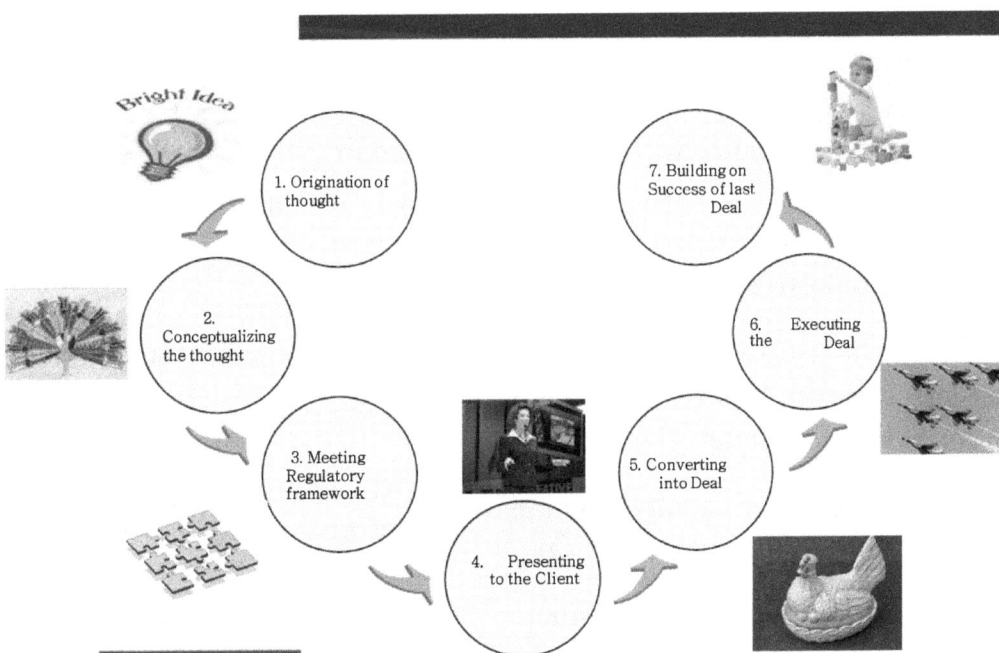

- **Step-1: Origination of thought:** This step essentially involves the conceptualization of M&A idea. This could be path breaking or following a classical M&A thought depending on the buy-side or sell-side analysis or could be just jumping onto a particular M&A bandwagon.

- **Step-2: Conceptualizing the thought:** What's the use of an idea, if it's not packaged into concept that is presentable to the client.

- **Step-3: Meeting regulatory framework:** The ideas that are great at times push the envelope on the regulatory framework. Thus, it is very essential to have the t's crossed and i's dotted before taking the idea to the client. Ideas that are not practically possible will end up eating into the credibility of the banker.

- **Step-4: Presenting to the client:** Presenting the deal in complete detail with an end-to-end solution to the situation. The complete presentation makes it easy to bag the mandate.

- **Step-5: Converting into deal:** Once having bagged the mandate, it is the onus on the banker to convert it into deal.

- **Step-6: Executing the deal:** This represents a very critical stage of the deal requiring near perfect orchestra to be played so that there are no hiccups and enables us to cut the deal like a hot knife through the butter.

- **Step-7: Building on the last deal:** Use the successfully executed deal to build future mandates with the same client or showcase it to other clients to bag their mandates.

Case Study 1.2: Vedanta's Acquisition of Cairn India

Details

Vedanta Resources promoted by Mr. Agarwal started in 1988 as Sterlite Industries. The history and background of Vedanta Resources is as under:

1986	Sterlite Industries	Engaged in copper smelting and making copper cables.
1988	Sterlite Industries	Listed on Bombay Stock Exchange.
1992	Sterlite Industry makes hostile bid for Indian Aluminum Company	The bid fails.
1995	Sterlite Industries acquires Madras Aluminum Company (MALCO)	MALCO was sick-government run enterprise which was turned into profit making venture.
1999	Acquires copper mines in Tasmania	First International acquisition.

(Continued)

2001	Acquires Bharat Aluminum Company (BALCO)	BALCO was sick government run enterprise which was transformed to a profit making venture.
2002	Acquires Hindustan Zinc Ltd.	Hindustan Zinc was also government run loss making enterprise but, with largest zinc mines.
2003	Gets listed on London Stock Exchange	First Indian company to be listed on LSE.
2004	Buys Konkola Copper engaged in copper mining in Zambia	Konkola Copper is the biggest copper miner in Zambia.
2007	Sterlite Industries is listed on NYSE	Raises $2 billion.
2007	Acquires Sesa Goa for $ one billion	Enters iron ore sector.
2009	Buys Dempo iron ore mines	Building on success of Sesa Goa Acquisition.

Around 2008, Vedanta made a bid for Arasco, a copper miner and smelter in America. It was a high-pitched battle that was eventually won by Vedanta for US $2.4 billion. Besides the deal frenzy and on back of record commodity prices, the stock was doing well which enabled fund raising to the tune of $5 billion by Vedanta.

The high commodity prices precluded further in buying metal commodity as well as there was dearth of good buys. So, the question was:

What next?

Vedanta Group was on a high with string of successful acquisitions and successful capital raising vaulting onto the top of the market capitalization.

So, the question to be answered is WHAT will be the NEXT on the plate of the group. It had virtually established its presence in all metals, namely iron ore, aluminium, copper, and zinc. There was ambition to grow further and also cash pile, but there was no target in the metal space them.

Origination of Thought

However, canny banker realized that here was an Acquirer who was ambitious, cash rich, and would be willing to look beyond metals as long as it was big bang and transformational acquisition.

Conceiving the Thought

Cairn Plc, the parent of Cairn India, after having stuck oil was looking at exit, as it had no business interest in refining oil. Thus, the banker thought that makes sense as a shareholder wanted to exit and an acquirer was willing to buy as long as the acquisition was a big bang.

Meeting Regulatory Framework and Presenting to the Client

Since it was an oil industry and government of India involved, it meant that there would be regulatory issues. Part of it were met by reps and indemnities from the buyer and seller as there were contentious issues with Cairn India pricing of oil and payment of cess and royalty to government of India and ONGC.

Converting into Deal

Ironing out the differences between the buyer and seller the mandate got converted into deal. Vedanta announced the acquisition of Cairn India Ltd. for $9bn.

Executing the Deal

As highlighted earlier, the execution of deal is considered to be the most crucial step of the cycle where origination sets the ball rolling, execution gets the ball pass the goal post. The execution in this case was bit weak and could have been better executed, given the heady mix of big bang, ambitious group, oil industry, competition, and foreign seller. After considerable delay and adjustments, the deal was finally executed and Vedanta Resources became the new owner of Cairn India.

Building On Success of Last Deal

Further deals that originated from this deal:

- Merger of Sesa Goa, Sterlite into Vedanta
- Buyback by Cairn India to buy back residual stake of Cairn Plc
- Merger of Vedanta Resources and Cairn India.

Key Learning

The originality of thought of getting a metal player like Vedanta to buy into another target operating in commodity resource, sensing the ambition and the ability of the acquirer. This represents how not only deep thinking but also the originality of thought can lead to origination of a deal with minimal competition. Further, such idea got the eyes and ears of the clients much more easily then it would do in a routine deal.

The above also leads to much better fees and apart from revenue builds up the M&A banking capability of the bank which in turn allows them a comparatively better access with the same and the next client.

Banks with origination capability will lead the pack in terms of league tables and fee tables.

In the next section, we will look into the capabilities within the bankers of the bank to get the origination and closing of such originated deals.

To summarize, the origination elements in this case will be:

Origination elements	
Gaps	Product gap in the commodity spread
Deal quotient	Willing seller, cash rich willing and ambitious buyer

The successful closing of large acquisitions spawns smaller deals, which keeps the revenues rolling and the client relationship going.

1.5 M&A banking

Case Study 1.3: Making of Aditya Birla Nuvo Ltd.

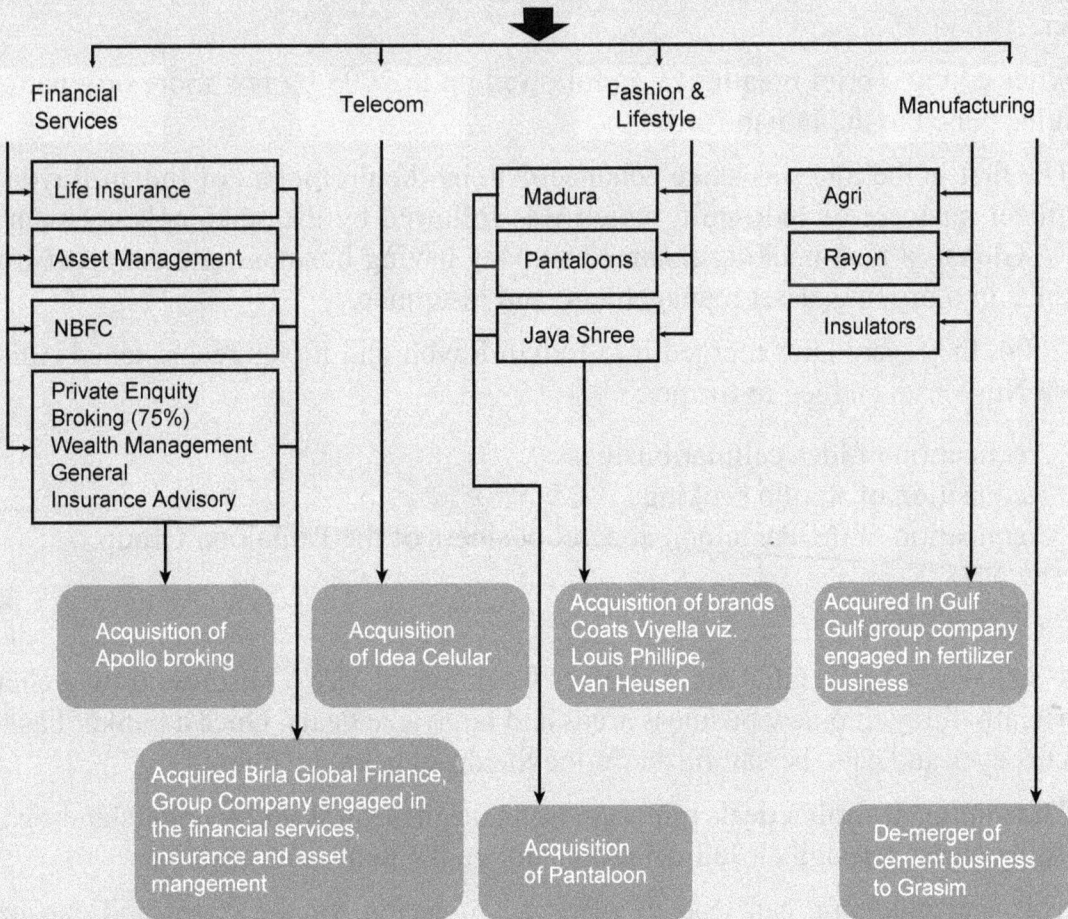

Details

The above chart depicts the series of M&A deals that can be done with a single client and how origination plays a key role.

Aditya Birla Nuvo was formerly known as Indian Rayon Limited having business interests in cement, textiles, and carbon black and may be for exigency reasons went onto make foray into telecom. On taking over of the reign of Aditya Birla group, the chairman Mr Kumarmangalam Birla announced venture into new age business that took the group ahead from commodities to a leading player in the knowledge business as well.

"Globalisation is a way of life. We'll see much more global character coming forth in the next few years" - Kumar Mangalam Birla, Chairman, Aditya Birla Group

Thus, in 1998 the demerger of cement business by Indian Rayon to pure play Cement Company of the group viz. Grasim took place. This was followed up in 1999–2000 by the acquisition of apparel brands Coats Viyella viz. Louis Phillipe, Van Heusen, Peter England from Coats Viyella Plc, UK-based apparel manufacturer.

After taking a brief breath, it was followed up in 2003 by few more originations that happened in the Indian Rayon.

The first in the line was stake enhancement by the promoters of Indian Rayon in fertilizer business of Indo-gulf, which was followed by the stake enhancement in Birla Global, a Non-banking finance company having business interest apart from finance into broking, asset management, and insurance.

In 2004, they were later merged into Indian Rayon and it was rechristened Aditya Birla Nuvo Ltd. and led to further:

- Acquisition of Idea cellular business
- Acquisition of Apollo broking
- Acquisition of the Pantaloon apparel business of the Pantaloon Group.

Key Learning

The statements of the CEO are harbinger for potential M&A business from a client, especially foray into new business areas and large size deals. Once a banker has the clients eyes and ears, he can further mine the deals from the client.

The mining of further deals requires strong origination skills by understanding the client business through close interaction and good client relationships.

This understanding can lead to stringing of pearls for the client and can help achieve their business objectives through right shaping of their corporate strategies.

1.6 Becoming a Rainmaker

Traits of Successful M&A Banker

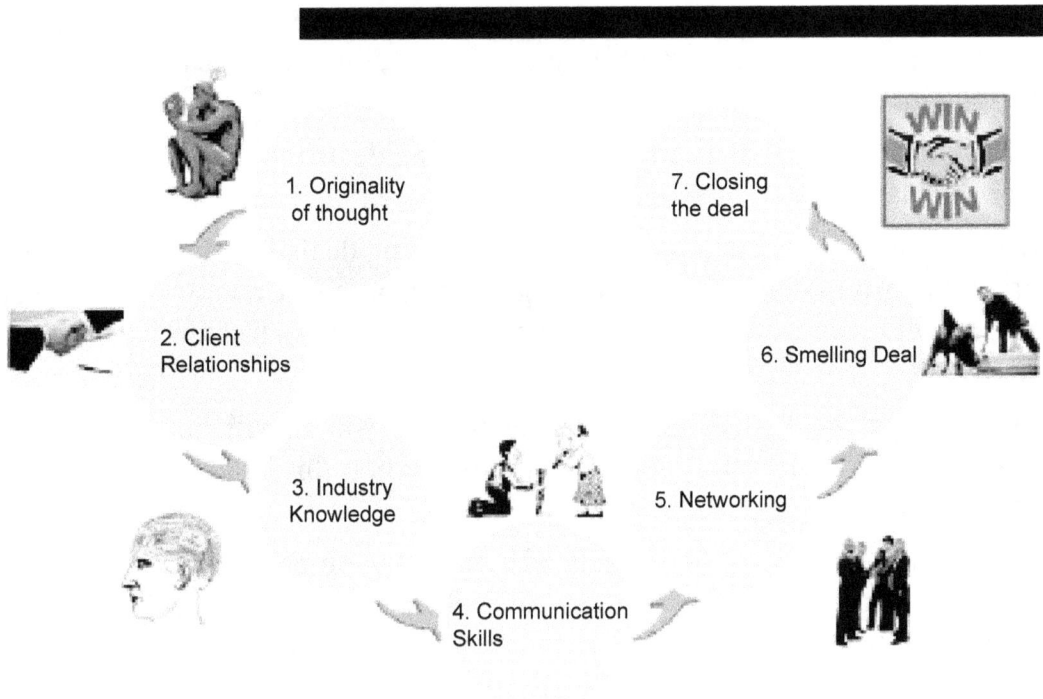

M&A Bankers who wish to be rainmakers need to have the above traits. They can be labelled as: -

Originality of thought: Innovative ideas, which are different from the competing bankers, would earn client respect. Thus, it would require a deep focus on the client needs and solutions to craft original ideas.

Client relationships: The ability to call client and make the client receptive to ideas is the hallmark of M&A banking.

Industry knowledge: This would provide the impetus to understand the clients' need and solutions for the same.

Communication skills: Knowledge, thoughts, etc., would be rudderless unless excellent communication skills are used to wrap them and conclude the deals.

Networking and Smelling the deal: The ability to be clued into the banking ecosystem proves to smell deals.

Closing the deal: Ability to close the deal will only make the M&A banker a rain maker. Thus, all the above traits can only help in the closing deals and emerge as a rainmaker.

Rainmaking: In Asia, there are various tycoons leading business empire and leading business groups. Notable among them are the Hutchison led by Li-Ka Shing, Tata Group, the Maxis group from Malaysia, Alibaba, Dalian Wanda, and Fosun. They have led various deals within their group to expand businesses at home and abroad. To be a banker with such group will enable to be a rainmaker. There are reports that the Li-Ka Shing group has generated fees in excess of US $1 billion since 2000.

Li-Ka Shing Empire has been one of the prolific deals making entity. Not only it buys or sells large ticket, but every deal enables to gather some more deals.

Over the past year, it has undertaken the following deals which included restructuring of the group companies involving Hutchison and Cheung Kong Holdings Besides, it has gone on to buy assets in telecom, infrastructure, and financial services.

It has bought the British telecom operator O2 which will be combined with Hutchison 3G. It will be followed by sale of the one third stakes to pension and sovereign funds.

The purchase of O2 will be roughly $20 bn and is on back of other acquisitions such as the takeovers of a British train-car maker, a Dutch drugstore chain, and an Irish air-craft leasing firm.

While in last year, it has divested a 25% stake for US $5.7 billion in retailer A.S. Watson Co. Tema Holdings Pte. Ltd.

From the mentioned facts, it is evident how clients focus and understand M&A needs to deliver big bucks and credits to the banks.

Instincts of a Successful M&A Banker

Apart from the traits of being a successful M&A banker, the banker also needs to possess certain instincts not only to successfully originate a deal but also to execute and conclude it successfully as well. These instincts are necessary because origination does not get credit unless the deal is successfully executed and concluded. These parts of lifecycle are very demanding and instincts are needed to protect the deal, ward-off competition, and craft a value creating situation for their client.

- **Cunning as fox:** To strategize the acquisitions
- **Sharp as an eagle:** To be able to see prey as well as predator
- **Fast like a cheetah:** To be able to conclude in expeditious manner an originated deal.
- **Eye on rear view:** To be on alert and do not get complacent. To work toward safe and accident-free journey.

Case study 1.4: Lafarge–DLF–Gujarat Ambuja Deal

Details

DLF Cement owned by the DLF group was based in Rajasthan with accumulated losses. Lafarge, the French cement giant, had just entered the Indian cement market in 1999 with the acquisition of Tata Steels cement capacity. Lafarge was vigilant in search of further acquisition of the capacities. DLF Cement not being one of the core businesses of DLF group was bleeding and was up for sale. Lafarge was in negotiation and at the verge of acquiring DLF Cement with only signing-off the deal remaining due to the weekend and scheduled it for Monday.

Gujarat Ambuja, which was one of the leading cement manufacturers got the whiff of the impending deal and to thwart competition from MNC Cement giant took immediate steps by deputing its CFO on flight to Delhi on Saturday, concluded meeting with the promoters of DLF Cement offered 5% more than Lafarge and arranged a banker's cheque to the promoters on the weekend from Bank of America by yanking their bankers off from an off-site retreat in Mumbai, which was hand delivered in Delhi on public holiday. The deal was signed and delivered in flat 2 non-working days, leaving the French cement major Lafarge high and dry, who failed to keep an eye on the rear view mirror and got complacent and lost the deal.

Key Learning

This case highlights the key traits and instincts needed for M&A deal making. It highlights client relationships, networking, protecting, and closing the deal on trait side. While on the instinct side it emphasis being eagle-eyed, cunning, swift, and keeping rear view on.

The above case also highlights how to marry the traits and instincts to create a successful rainmaker. This would mean being a cunning fox to smell deal and be smart at closing the deals. Be a cheetah to have the speed of execution. How the deal is to be protected, giving no leeway even during weekend. Be a bald eagle to keep a sharp eye on the deal and the industry. Last, but not the least, to always have eye on the rear view mirror to monitor, if anybody is pulling over or out-speeding.

Thus, we can conclude that instinct to traits is like what icing is to cake.

1.7 Origination Principles

Before we leap into the elements of origination, the principles of origination need to be understood.

The principle states:

NO to NO

    a.   Never say No: Be ever optimistic about the origination and closing
    b.   Never take No: Be forever persistent with clients or the opposite party
    c.   Nothing is free in life: Basically, we need to know what's the straw that will break the camel's back and you will know the way forward.

Case Study 1.5: Murdoch Finally Acquires Dow Jones

Details

The above case represents the origination principles discussed earlier. The Rupert Mudroch group, which had interest in the news properties such as Fox Network and Times of London, made a bid for Dow Jones, the publisher of the famous financial daily "The Wall Street Journal." The Rupert Mudroch group is popularly known for its sensational journalism. The bid for Dow Jones was made at 67% premium to the unaffected price.

Dow Jones was owned and run since 1902 by the Bancroft Family, a large and fragmented family spread across three dozen adult members and operating its interest in Dow Jones through trusts and their trustees. Being the most famous for its properties, it was a family silver for the Bancroft's.

While Dow Jones was owned by the Bancroft's, it was independently run by journalists and the family had stayed aloof from the management. With no dominant shareholder within the family, Dow Jones was more focussed on the journalism than the business economics quotient. Dow Jones was suffering from dwindling advertisement revenues and falling stock price.

Thus, the bid by the aggressive Rupert Mudroch created immediate revulsion not only from the management of Dow Jones, but also from the Bancroft family which feared the muzzling of the journalistic tradition of Dow Jones.

How the Origination Principles were Applied

Given the facts of the case, it is now pretty evident that NO was written all over the place. This case highlights how not to take a NO, not to say NO as well as how to figure out the price for not saying NO.

- The family was dyed in wool about the paper being more about journalism rather than economics. The huge premium got their attention to think about whether it made sense to abandon the journalistic pursuit and think about the economics.
- Mr Mudroch committed to holding standards of journalism at Dow Jones. He invited a family member to be a part of the Board and agreed to form a committee to overlook the journalistic standards and independence.
- It is also reported that Rupert Mudroch personally called on the members of family who were more vocal or who control a large portion of the voting shares. It is also reported that he offered to pay the legal and banking fees in return for their YES vote.
- The management was worked upon as well as made to work upon its shareholders to agree to the deal.

Key Learning

This case highlights the application of no to NO. It also elucidates how much attention is needed to be paid to the elements such as:

- Competition: There was no hostile bid.
- Management: They could see the economics and convey to family.
- Employees: A potent opposition could not manage to rustle a competitive bid.

This case study also highlights the use of non-monetary inducement like personal telephonic calls and formation of committees to uphold journalistic tradition. He also used softeners such as upholding journalistic traditions, offering to pick up the legal and banking tabs that would eventually close the deal.

1.8 Origination Elements

Having seen some cases of M&A deal origination in the previous chapter, we will now dwell into the elements in detail. Each origination element mentioned in the table below can be attributed to either the potential buyer "buy-side" or the potential seller "sell-side" of an asset or company. Understanding the rationale behind each origination element is essential for M&A bankers because it is the crux of mandate in one industry than others. Once identified, bankers should leverage the situation in order to secure a mandate either on the buy-side or on the sell-side.

Buy-side	Sell-side
1. Cash rich	1. Distressed
2. Noveau CEO	2. Conglomerate/non-core business
3. Outpace Darwin	3. Frothy valuations
4. Tax incentives	4. Lack of focus/company succession
5. Opportunistic	5. Minority stakes
6. Consolidation play	6. Growth greater than cash flows
7. Peer pressure	7. Inferior growth
8. Cheap financing	8. Leverage issues
9. Inward and outward	9. Financial engineering
10. Hidden equity/sleeping beauties	10. Investment book
11. Serial acquirers	11. Management/litigation issues
12. Chasing growth	12. Arbitrage players

1.9 Buy-side aspects

1. Cash rich

Some companies have accumulated large cash balance on their balance sheet and are not so much interested in distributing the cash back to shareholders. So the next course for utilization of cash is to do acquisitions. The reason being acquisitions do take up big pile of cash against capital expenditure which is a slow grind over 3–5 years.

- Wipro sitting on $2-billion war chest eyes more acquisitions
- Ranbaxy promoters having divested their stake in Ranbaxy and sitting on cash will look to deploy that cash. Thus, we saw spate of acquisition like Fortis and Religare.

2. Noveau CEO or Chairman

When a new CEO or chairman get in one word charge, he or she outlines his or her vision. In many cases, that vision needs to be captured to serve the M&A plate either on the buy-side or on the sell-side.

Therefore, their statements can be of particular interest for the banker. If keenly watched, they can help shape origination ideas:

"Globalisation is a way of life. We'll see much more global character coming forth in the next few years" - *Kumar Mangalam Birla, Chairman, Aditya Birla Group*

"We want to be a group catering to the larger part of income pyramid in India and overseas " - *Ratan Tata, Chairman, TATA group*

Cyrus Mistry's Vision 2025: Tata Group to be in Global 25

3. Outpace Darwin/Chasing growth

There are certain companies who want to speed up on the evolution curve and outpace Darwin's theory of evolution. Such companies generally try to grow at frenetic pace, generating no free cash flow which makes them reliable on external financing. The initial fast growth is financed by equity, but as they start faltering on growth, they need to resort to debt to support financing. Eventually, many of them get caught in a tangle of fast growth, inadequate return on capital, and disappointed share and debtholders. These companies present an opportunity for sell side origination, although may not be easy to close due to the high level of liabilities.

4. Tax incentives

There are companies which seek lower tax payments through merging with other companies carrying accumulated losses. In other cases when there is lot of intra-group sales, there is the chance to avoid transaction taxes by merging the respective group companies.

The merging of ITC and ITC Bhadrachalam (loss making paper business) as well as that of Reliance and Reliance Petroleum are a case in point.

The wave of tax inversions driven mergers happening between US corporates and non-US headquartered corporates in order to minimize the tax impact of high US tax rate is a good example.

The data below give a glimpse of companies which might be considering tax inversion:

US Organization	Proposed new incorporation
Applied Materials Inc.	Netherlands
Burger King Worldwide Inc.	Canada
C&J Energy Services Ltd.	Bermuda
Civeo Corp.	Canada
Cyberonics Inc.	England
Medtronic Inc.	Ireland
Mylan Inc.	Netherlands
Steris Corp.	England
Wright Medical Group Inc.	Netherlands

There are also a couple of cancelled deals such as Monsanto, the US agribusiness company's bid for the Swiss company Syngenta. The transaction was structured as an inversion which would allow it to move its headquarters to the UK. A number of others, including drugmakers Pfizer and AbbVie, also launched but ultimately failed bids at tax inversion deals.

Another case of tax-driven M&A are tax-neutral spin-offs. An example is Yahoo Inc.'s spin-off of a 15% stake in Alibaba Group. The successful spin-off is contingent on it being tax neutral.

5. Opportunistic players

These are savvy players, who look at treasury gains through M&A and are willing to acquire minority stakes either to build up later or to just hold on for a flip that might come from potential acquirer later. This could include players who may join hostile bid as well to push the price for the acquirer and then liquidate their holding.

Reliance is one of the very opportunistic player in this space. L&T, IPCL, East India Hotels are examples of such opportunistic acquisitions.

6. Consolidation play

This is generally applicable in cases wherein the industry has come out of high growth and a lot of players. Eventually, this will result in the stronger players buying out the weaker or marginal players.

The telecom industry is one good example wherein many M&A has happened by stronger players acquiring marginal ones.

Pharma is a another industry seeing consolidation driven by factors such as tax inversion or cutting down on R&D costs (by acquiring companies with drugs patents in the pipeline). In 2015, these type of deals crossed $300 billion.

Pfizer's itself has attempted takeover of AstraZeneca and Glaxo Smithklime in the UK and has now made an attempt for Allergan.

Teva's ended up purchasing Allergan's generics business for $40.5 billion post rejection of its $43 billion bid for rival Mylan.

Shire recently made a $30 billion unsolicited bid for Baxalta, the new biotech spin-off from Baxter, and AbbVie bought out Pharmacyclics for $21 billion.

While the above represents acquisition cases of companies such as Merck & Co, which divested its consumer health business to Bayer as well as GlaxoSmithKline and Novartis, which swapped oncology and vaccines portfolios for a deal worth over $20 billion. GlaxoSmithKline has been on selling spree, notable being meningitis vaccines to Pfizer, Perrigo a OTC brand, Ribena to Suntroy, and its Australian opiates business to Sun Pharma.

7. Peer pressure

Mittal acquiring Arcellor was followed by Tata's acquisition of Corus, which then was followed by Hindalco acquiring Novellis. The aforesaid represents a peer pressure dynamic which can lead competitors to believe in the strategy of their peers and get them onto acquisition bandwagon.

- Arcelor Mittal deal opened a lot of ideas about acquisitions in steel industry on cross-border and expanding in the global market. Tata's got carried away by the consolidation theme and made a bid for Corus catapulting them from rank 16th to rank 5th steel producer.
- The Tata-Corus deal created peer pressure for the Birla group as well to make a billion dollars splash and the bid for Novelis was offshoot of the pressure.

8. Cheap financing

Since 2007, many major economies decided to pursue an ultra-lose monetary policy in order to get economic growth back on its past phase. This political move offset a wave of mega mergers across the globe where abundant leverage is available at near zero interest rates. The financing of acquisition by leverage provides opportunities for financial engineering (please refer the EPS accretion section in "Chapter Valuation") as the yield required on the purchase of target became very low and thus EPS accretive. These types of acquisitions are usually not driven by growth objectives but by cost reduction where the combined entity covers the interest on leverage.

The phenomenon is further driven by the fact that large-sized corporates which are naturally growing at a slower pace are further slowed by the slow economic recovery in Europe and the United/states The synergies realized through cost savings on thumb rule basis without accounting for the cost of risk of the acquisition make it an attractive proposition to buy companies through leverage at low interest rates.

Low interest rates and liquidity also permit leverage buyout funds to be a more active player in the acquisition game, primarily driven by financial engineering.

9. Inward or Outward M&A

Inward and outward M&A deals are cross-border transactions into developed and emerging markets. When emerging markets were at a low and the developed markets were doing well (2000–2005), there was this phase of global corporates acquiring companies in emerging markets in India and China.

When the emerging markets started doing well post-2006, there were companies from India and China acquiring companies abroad. While, in the current phase wherein the emerging markets are down and corporates who have long-term plans will take advantage of depressed currencies in emerging markets and asset prices to acquire assets in emerging markets.

Chinese companies such as Alibaba, Fosun, and Dalian Wanda have been on buying spree at home and abroad. As also companies such as Lenovo who recently acquired the server business of IBM and handphone business of Google. All the aforesaid companies are sitting on cash and want to diversify from Mainland geography.

Reports indicate that the outbound acquisitions from China have been in excess of $ 70 bn in last year.

Examples:

- Inward M&A: Acquisition by Holcim of ACC and Gujarat Ambuja will represent Inward M&A.
- Outward M&A: Acquisition of Corus by Tata's or of Novellis by Hindalco represent Outward M&A.

10. Hidden equity/sleeping beauties

There are certain corporates which are trading at a price lower than its intrinsic value or simpliciter lower than their book value. Such cases represent an attractive opportunity for hostile takeovers as these candidates allow for quick arbitrage gains. Sometimes, certain assets on the balance sheet like real estate can be significantly worth more than their book value, representing an easy kill.

Cases such as Bombay Dyeing, Great Eastern now known as Mahindra Holiday's, and Forbes Gokak represent few examples of this type of origination.

11. Serial Acquirer

These are players, who have a track record of building companies through acquisitions and could be on the lookout for their next target.

A great example of a serial acquirer is Valeant Pharma (Canada). Since 2008, the company has made more than 140 acquisitions. Below is a selection of major transactions.

Year	Target	Value ($ bn)
2012	Medicis Pharmaceutical	3
2013	Bausch & Lomb	9
2014	Allergan	53
2015	Salix Pharmaceuticals	15
2015	Addyi	1

12. Chasing Growth

It can be seen into two categories:

- First, being the companies trading at peak valuations and management in aggressive mode to expand the footprint. Many times, they would have publicly stated their intent to chase growth through acquisitions.

  - Example: Godrej Consumers acquisition of companies in the emerging markets.

- Second, the companies which have slowed down and are facing strong headwinds in their core business and look to shore up growth through acquisitions.
- Example: Airtel acquisition of Zain can fall into this category.

Case Study 1.6: Asian Paints–Choksey–Akzo Noble

Details

The British major ICI's (now Akzo Noble) acquisition of 9.1% stake in the Asian Paints raised heat and dust as it was an MNC seen as predator acquiring Indian company in repercussion of the liberalization of the Indian economy.

Asian Paints is the #1 Indian paints company having a dominant market share with a strong marketing and distribution network (14,000 dealers as compared to ICI's 4000).

Asian Paints was managed and controlled by four families. One of the family viz. Atul Chokseys decided to sell his stake and approached Merrill Lynch regarding the proposal.

Merrill Lynch approached Foreign Institutional Investors for the bid and firm bids were placed. However, when the news became public, there was huge protest from the rest of the three families who were not willing to take risk of the sizeable portion of the company's shareholding falling in the hands of possible bidders for the company.

The Foreign Investor backed-off from the bids claiming they were not aware that this was one of the controlling stakes. Immediately after the failure of this bid, the Seller, Atul Choksey got in touch with Kotak Mahindra Capital Company (KMCC). Kotak in principle bought out Choksey's holding (3.66 lakh shares) for Rs.127.1 crore and within hours of signing another deal with British paints major ICI Plc., selling the block for Rs.128.4 Crore.

ICI, desperate to increase its meager 7% market share in India, was quick to cash in. For ICI, Kotak's offer could not have come at a better time. ICI saw this as a God given chance to acquire one word share in an illiquid Company and increase its presence. In the event of any of the family members selling stake in future, the presence of ICI Ltd with its 10% shareholding will act as deterrent to others.

Key Learning

The case highlights how origination elements come into play. The elements involve the disgruntled shareholder, opportunistic buyer, and the speed at which investment bank needs to close the deal.

It also highlights the thought and consideration that needs to go into selling a dominant shareholding stake. How dominant shareholder stake should not be sold, how to be fast in decision-making, how to find right fit buyer in right time, and how to conclude deal expeditiously.

The issues reflect legal agreements as well as whether it is the right price for such a dominant stake in #1 Paint Company of India. Haste makes waste. Thus, M&A situations need a thorough appraisal and find the right buyer for the even more right price.

1.10 Sell-side aspects

1. Distressed

There are companies or their promoters who get distressed for a variety of reasons. This circumstance can trigger them to sell assets or their shareholdings in the respective companies.

Examples of distressed M&A

- Sale of United Spirits to Diageo
- Sale of Deccan Airlines to Kingfisher airlines
- Sale of Jaypee Hydropower assets to Reliance

- Sale of Pantaloon retail to Aditya Birla Nuvo
- Sale of Ranbaxy to Daiichi Sankyo

2. Conglomerate/non-core business

The origination in this type of M&A is to attack conglomerate discount. Conglomerate discount arises because investors are not able to clearly ascertain the value of a business. This can be the case when a large variety of businesses are aggregated or when the company has become too big to manage so that it requires a trimming of its asset portfolio.

As a legacy issue, especially in India, there are business houses having aggregation of too many disparate businesses with one cross-subsidizing the other business. This normally leads to valuation discount and presents an opportunity for bankers to recommend selling opportunities and to improve valuations.

- Larsen & Toubro is probably one of the best conglomerate discount examples when they eventually decided to sell their cement business.

There are other situations wherein certain businesses are defined as core and non-core over passage of time. This definition allows the banker to originate sell-side opportunities for the non-core business.

- The divesture of parts of the TATA portfolio such as Tata Oil Mills, Lakme, Hitech etc. can be partially considered as an example of trimming off non-core businesses.

3. Frothy valuation

When markets are at high (say, based on long-term PE multiple or margins), the valuations get exorbitant, making it right time to exit. Sale of Hutch telecom assets by Hutchison is an example of such M&A.

4. Lack of focus/company succession

When the division or business is not in the area of focus for the management or where the founder/promoter has grown old and the next generation is not interested in the business or where the family itself has lost interest in the business.

- Sale of Bank of Madura by its founder to ICICI.

5. Minority stakes

These are situations in which minority stakes are available and the minority share holder no longer intends pursuing it for consolidation. Thus, somebody may be willing to take over the baton from the minority shareholder.

- Sale by Reliance of its minority stake in L&T to Grasim.

6. Growth greater than cash flow

These are train wreck companies, having grown at fast pace not generating enough free cash and when the capital market access in form of equity or debt is cut off and offer themselves to vultures.

- Koutons, Shubiksha, Air Deccan are examples of such situation.

7. Inferior growth

Companies struggling for growth in matured industry or companies which are showing inferior growth compared to its peers, thus, intensifying pressure on the company to either sell out or getting preyed by acquirer

- Sale of Henkel to Jyothy Laboratories
- Sale of Zandu to Emami

8. Leverage issues

Companies which are having high debt equity and facing pressure to deleverage or can be facing demerger situation to improve market valuations or sell its family silver to finance loss in other division

- Sale of Pantaloon to Aditya Birla De Nuvo. Sale of United Spiritis to Diageo by UB Group.

9. Financial engineering

Companies can use accounting ploy to restructure its operations or financial statements. This could involve revaluation or transfer of assets between group companies or refinancing of the loans or valuing brands or issue of bonus debentures or writing off goodwills or losses or assets against reserves of the company.

- Issue of bonus debentures by Unilver, Valuation of Infosys brand by Infosys, Merging group companies such as ICICI and ICICI Bank.

10. Investment book

Companies may have legacy minority investment on the book, which may be used to either generate liquidity or look profits in rosy market conditions. Loss of interest of the management in that investment including failed attempt at control of the target company.

- Selling of Reliance stake in L&T to Grasim. L&T's stake in Satyam.

11. Management/litigation issues

Foreign acquirers get too hassled by management or litigation issues, which is a drag on the performance. Thus, they become willing sellers even at discount.

12. Arbitrage players

This represents sellers who have no expertise of running the core business but have access into those business through licenses mining rights or quotas.

- The sale of Times Bank by the owners of Times of India to HDFC. Sale of Spice telecom by B K Modi to Idea during the hot times of telecom industry will give a flavor of arbitrage players.

Case Study1.7: Ranbaxy–Daiichi Sankyo-Sun Pharma deal

Details

June 2008: Daiichi acquires majority stake in Ranbaxy to become a powerhouse in the generic drug manufacturing.

About Daiichi Sankyo Company, Limited

Daiichi Sankyo Company, Limited, established in 2005 after the merger of two leading century-old Japanese pharmaceutical companies, is continuously generating innovative drugs that enrich the quality of life for patients around the world. The company uses its cumulative knowledge and expertise in the fields of cardiovascular disease, cancer, metabolic disorders, and infection as a foundation for developing an abundant product line-up and R&D pipeline.

About Ranbaxy Laboratories Limited

Ranbaxy Laboratories Limited, India's largest pharmaceutical company, is an integrated, research-based, international pharmaceutical company producing a wide range of quality, affordable generic medicines, trusted by healthcare professionals and patients across geographies. The company is serving its customers in over 125 countries and has an expanding international portfolio of affiliates, joint ventures and alliances, ground operations in 49 countries, and manufacturing operations in 11 countries.

Origination elements:

Buy-side:

Origination elements	Outward M&A, Chasing growth, Peer pressure
	April 2008: Takeda Japan's largest Pharma company to Acquire Millennium valued at $8.8 Billion.

(Continued)

Daiichi Sankyo which is the second largest Pharma Company was looking for the growth outside saturated Japanese market and the Takeda deal hastened the process to acquire Ranbaxy at astounding valuation.

Sell-side:

Origination elements	Frothy valuation, leverage issue, and litigation .
	Ranbaxy also is facing challenges as it tries to join the drug making big leagues. It had to contend with the ongoing legal battles brought by rivals such as Pfizer (PFE), which has challenged Ranbaxy's right to make generic versions of Lipitor. At the same time, it has also faced more competition in the generics, and the company has also struggled with its new-drug discovery operation.

The Deal

Ranbaxy Laboratories Limited ("Ranbaxy"), among the top 10 generic companies in the world, is India's largest pharmaceutical company and Daiichi Sankyo Company, Limited ("Daiichi Sankyo"), one of the largest pharmaceutical companies in Japan, announced that a binding Share Purchase and Share Subscription Agreement (the "SPSSA") was entered into between Daiichi Sankyo, Ranbaxy, and the Singh family, the largest and controlling shareholders of Ranbaxy (the "Sellers"), pursuant to which Daiichi Sankyo will acquire the entire shareholding of the Sellers in Ranbaxy and further seek to acquire the majority of the voting capital of Ranbaxy at a price of Rs. 737 per share with the total transaction value expected to be between US $3.4 to US $4.6 billion (currency exchange rate: US $1= Rs. 43). On the post-closing basis, the transaction would value Ranbaxy at US $8.5 billion.

The SPSSA has been unanimously approved by the Boards of Directors of both companies. Daiichi Sankyo is expected to acquire the majority of equity stakes in Ranbaxy by a combination of:

i.   Purchase of shares held by the Sellers,
ii. Preferential allotment of equity shares,
iii. An open offer to the public shareholders for 20% of Ranbaxy's shares, as per Indian regulations, and
iv. Daiichi Sankyo's exercise of a portion or all of the shares warrants to be issued on a preferential basis. All the shares/warrants will be acquired / issued at a price of Rs. 737 per share.

This purchase price represents a premium of 53.5% to Ranbaxy's average daily closing price on the National Stock Exchange for the three months ending on June 10, 2008, and 31.4% to such closing price on June 10, 2008.

The Aftermath

Daiichi Sankyo after stepping into Ranbaxy got a taste of "buyers beware," it claimed that it was not made aware of the FDA-related manufacturing problems that Ranbaxy was facing. Soon after took over, it was exposed to warning letters, import bans, a consent decree, and a $500 million settlement with US authorities.

After the settlement, the company said it had been misled by "certain former shareholders of Ranbaxy" before the deal about the troubles the company has faced. It claimed to take legal action to wrest back some of the $4.6 billion it has shelled out on the deal.

It does not appear that there was any indemnity for Daiichi Sankyo for "such eventualities." The Japanese drug maker has found it daunting to turn problems around at its Indian subsidiary.

These legal wrangles and reputational issue with FDA made Daiichi put Ranbaxy on the selling block in just 5 years time. The Company never stabilized during this period of 5 years.

Key Learning

The above scenario elucidates how peers pressure as well as hunger for growth led to the hasty acquisition by Daiichi Sankyo. The acquisition was rapidly cobbled up leaving gaps in due diligence as well as the valuation not discounting the risk of acquiring an emerging market company.

On sell side, we can see how combination of attractive valuation in the face of potential issues can entice the holder to sell the company.

PART II

Daiichi Sankyo–Sun Pharma Deal

Billionaire Dilip Shanghvi Inks $4 Billion Deal with Daiichi Sankyo to buy rival Ranbaxy

Buy-side

Origination elements	Serial acquirer, discounted price, opportunistic buyer

Sell-side

Origination elements	Management issue and litigation

Details

Sun Pharmaceutical Industries announced that it will acquire Delhi-headquartered rival Ranbaxy Laboratories from Japanese firm Daiichi Sankyo in an all-stock deal valued at $4 billion, including debt.

The transaction values Ranbaxy at 2.2 times its $1.8 billion revenues for 2013 or about Rs. 457 per share. Shareholders of Ranbaxy, including Daiichi which owns a 63.5% stake, will get 0.8 shares of Sun for every share they hold. Post-deal, Daiichi will be Sun Pharma's single largest shareholder after promoters Shanghvi himself, with a 9% stake and a seat on the company's board. The seller taking advantage of the high valuation of Sun Pharma later exited the stock and netted approximately $3.5 billion in the process.

Shanghvi has established a solid track record as a turnaround specialist which included the string of acquisitions—16 including Israel's Taro Pharmaceuticals for which Shanghvi fought a hard-won battle to take control that were successfully integrated with the mother ship.

Key Learning

It is observed that how Japanese owner facing management and litigation issues was a willing seller lapped up by the serial acquirer Sun Pharma which has 16 acquisitions to its credit with a track record of turning around company facing issues. Further, the use of high value shares of Sun Pharma being offered as currency to acquire the target at discount of 38% to Daiichi's earlier buy price for Ranbaxy created incentive enough for it to bite the bullet.

Apart from the origination elements, the Part I of the case demonstrates how not to acquire a company, the flip side of it being how to sell a company when not exactly in a rosy situation.

On contrary, the Part II demonstrates how to make acquisition in a win–win manner for both buyer and seller. The buyer with expertise in turnaround gets a good company at a good price, while the seller gets honourable exit and uses shares as currency to cut its losses.

1.11 Executive Summary

The chapter provides a deeper understanding of the deal making world of M&A banking. It highlights the deal making life cycle as well as the traits and instincts required to make M&A deals successful.

"Origination" is the central theme of this chapter and explains the elements involved in M&A deal making even beyond the usual academic coverage. The origination elements are further explained with elements which determine "acquirer" and the "target."

Thus, we see the concept of origination that applies to the real world of M&A and how idea generation can be systematically put into a framework to originate M&A.

2

Effective Acquisitions

Contents

2.1 Introduction

"Successful deals involve finding the right seller at the right price, with the right approach."

Various studies would suggest that organic growth would have paid bigger dividend than inorganic growth. The acquisition path to growth has been a bed of thorns rather than a bed of roses for the acquirers. Three-fourths of the acquisitions have failed to create any value. Despite the high failure rate of acquisition, the appetite for Merger & Acquisitions (M&A) is on the rise. In fact, most corporates now have M&A departments or team. It has become an essential part of their corporate finance or growth strategy.

Does this make the M&A evaluation a complex job given the low success rate? Is there a better way or strategy to execute successful M&A? This chapter stresses on the importance of simple matrix to gauge the success probability of M&A. Unfortunately, the most cited academic attribution focuses on the integration and culture issues for failure of acquisition. There has been very less discussions about the risk evaluation of acquisition and the price paid for acquisition and whether it discounts the risk begin undertaken.

The present chapter intends to educate the least covered aspect of failure of M&As. The chapter focuses on the risk evaluation of the success of acquisition and tries to stress on the maxim that *"Everything Is In Price."*

The aforesaid issues are being highlighted through various case studies to drive home the points which drive effective acquisition.

Thus, endeavoring to understand effective acquisitions and improve the success ratio to reduce the destruction of shareholder value.

2.2 Ground Rules for Effective Acquisition

Let us have a deeper understanding of ground rules to have effective acquisition. The point that is being re-emphasized is the acquisition price, and the consequent discounting of risk will be the single biggest determining factor in the success or failure of the acquisition. The point to be remembered is that it is the single biggest but not the only reason to determine success rate.

There emerges a need to understand whether the price discounts the risk being undertaken. This is the single most differentiator between successful and non-successful deals. Whether, the price discounts synergy risk, integration risk, cross-border risk, or culture risk remains to be understood.

There is also a critical need to understand the amount of risk being undertaken relative to the size of the company. The size in relation to the acquirer company being assessed in terms of revenue, asset base, market cap etc., as also the probability of loss of capital and its adverse impact on the Company's net-worth, profile and morale also need to be understood.

Whether, the acquisition is following the fundamental rule of buying low and selling high or the other way round. Often people laugh at this rule as preposterous or impractical and useless advice, because one can know the highs and lows only in the hindsight. The tip of the peak or bottom of the trough cannot be predicted in advance; however basic analysis could easily show if the deal period/deal assumptions fall under the broad range of highs or lows. Though this is a subjective analysis, let us look at one of many approaches on this task.

A simple analysis of historical averages involving key business and valuation metrics over long term can be carried out. For example, on the business/product side, one can consider revenue growth rate, capacity utilization, operating margin, net margin of the companies involved and the overall industry. On the valuation aspect, one can look at PE ratio and EBITDA multiple of companies/industry involved and overall market. Historical data points on each of these variables over long term, say 10 to 20 years, can be plotted on individual graphs. The actual historical line graph over years can be observed with the help of a median line for the entire period. In addition to the median line, one can have few bands, say high range and highest range above the median band and low range and lowest range below the median band. This would help to further understanding of the magnitudes of highs and lows in the past vis-a-vis the deal period/assumption.

Getting a priori macrosense of high range or low range may not be difficult, while accuracy as to how high or how low may depend on fineness of the analysis, which is difficult most of the times on a priori basis. The focus of the discussion is on the need to be aware of the historical highs and lows vis-a-vis the deal, instead of the need to predict perfectly, which anyway is impossible.

Unfortunately, lot of deal activity happens in the upmarket or peak markets when the general market sentiment is bullish, which results in obtaining companies at peak or high valuations, and lot many times, it is bought with the aid of leverage. The combination of high valuations and leverage results in distress due to downturn in markets, and thus end up selling at trough or low valuations and violating the fundamental rule of buying low and selling high. Thus, M&A's done in trough market have higher probability of success than deals done at the peak of cycle.

The simple explanation for the failure of peak cycle deals is the inflated valuation. Peak market means peak profits and possibly peak multiple, which results in the overpaid price not discounting the risks enough, thereby leading to failure.

This would mean at peak markets, forward growth is not likely to be sustained, and hence the growth rates would come down and disturb the future discounting done on the excel spreadsheets. The below case study highlights the virtues of trough market.

Case Study 2.1: Indian Telecom Market: When the going gets tough, the tough get going

Details

In 1992, the Indian telecom market was opened for the private operators. There was strong interest from foreign as well as domestic operators. This led to influx of foreign operators wanting to make a pie out of the Indian telecom market, which further led to the entry of foreign telecom companies through joint venture with Indian operators as the foreign investment limit was not 100%.

Thus, we had likes of AT&T, Swisscom, Telstra, Telekom Malaysia, British Telecom, Vodafone, and Hutchison entered in the Indian market. However, by 1997–1999, most of them exited the Indian market due to slow growth, tough market conditions, imminent entry of government entity in the mobile market, unified licensing regime etc.

In this tough scenario, it was only Bharti and Hutchison which went up picking up the stakes being left behind by the battle retreaters.

Hutchison acquired stakes in Sterling Cellular, Usha Martin telecom, and Fascel. Bharti acquired stakes in Telecom, Skycell, and Punjab License of Essar. The nascent state of the regulations allowed them to pick up the key asset in this market *viz.* the telecom license without much regulatory hassle.

Key Learning

- How acquisition done in trough succeeds;
- Having a longer term coherent approach to industry outlook helps in successful M&A

This allowed both Hutchison and Bharti to have larger presence and eventually came to be the leading telecom operators in India, with Hutchison exiting at peak of industry cycle in 2007, while Bharti still continued to be the top telecom operator albeit at reduced valuation.

Thus, the fundamental determinant is the PRICE. This can be further evaluated by the simple matrix given below:

The below combination of the ACQUIRER + TARGET

Acquirer	Target		Acquirer
Revenue	Revenue		Revenue -> Increase
Expenses	Expenses	Should	Expense -< Decrease
PAT/EBIT +	PAT/EBIT	result in	PAT/EBIT -> Increase
Capital	Capital		Return on Capital -> Increases. Price paid should not be so high that balance sheet does not get bloated and impairs the quality of balance sheet.

The above matrix aids in determining the likelihood of success. While the forward looking spreadsheets would give tick on all the four boxes, we will have to evaluate in context with cold probability of that happening given the stage of the business cycle and ground realities such as its peak margin scenario, saturated market, etc.

The below case study highlights how critical it is to follow the above rules, and non-conformity with the same will result in failed acquisition.

Case Study 2.2: Cross-Border and High Value Acquisition: Softbank Acquires Sprint

Details

Sprint is a telecom service provider in the US It was one of the struggling telecom service providers competing with likes of Verizon, AT&T, and regional providers of related telecom services and internet.

Sprint had acquired Nextel in the year 2005 at a value of $35 billion. This acquisition was written down in the year 2008, making a dent of $30 billion for impairment of the goodwill created in acquisition. Since acquisition, the combined company was successful to drive profit in only one year of its operation.

Softbank was a telecom operator from Japan having made successful turnaround of Vodafone, Japan, in 2006 to be the leading player in the Japanese market led by charismatic CEO. Softbank is also known for its jackpot investing into Alibaba converting $20 million to $70 billion.

Sprint was acquired by Soft Bank in 2013 for $22 billion for 78% stake fending-off a competitive bid from Dish TV at a premium of 52% to the unaffected price.

The Enterprise value of Sprint was $33.6 billion having a net debt of $36.3 billion and revenue of $35 billion and accumulated losses at $45 billion.

Origination Elements

Acquirer: Softbank was on a roll having acquired reputation for successful turnaround and investment, and "will be" on lookout. The bigger the target, the more attractive it would be for acquisition. It would catapult Softbank from the third largest in Japan to the third largest in the world. Thus, it was good enough incentive for Softbank to snap Sprint.

Target: Struggling Company with losses, technology, and integration issues with the acquired Nextel.

Valuation Elements

The price paid was one-time revenue or one-time enterprise value. In defence of Softbank, they could have said if, we can turnaround and improve profitability, it will be a win deal for them. The confidence of turning around Vodafone Japan and Japan Telecom as well as launching yahoo broadband and making it the biggest was good enough reasons for Softbank to take the plunge.

a. Whether It Ticks The Four Boxes?

i. **Revenue growth:** The US market was already saturated with entrenched players like Verizon and AT&T to compete against each other. Thus, it would have been difficult to increase the growth rate.

ii. **Improving margins:** This was the only possible scope in the deal but, unlike the Japan success story, a well-known territory to Softbank as well as under investment by Vodafone in the softer issues led to the successful turnaround. This was a cross-border acquisition and there were already big losses of $50 billion underlying the fact that the core operations had serious defects.

iii. **Improving profit after tax (PAT):** While Sprint was heavily indebted, it need not meant that Softbank was going to bring leverage down as its acquisition was also leveraged. Thus, debt reduction or reduction in interest expenses was not expected.

iv. **Putting minimal capital to work:** The acquisition was expensive, with $22 billion being put to play in a company with huge losses accumulated. It will be quete a few years before their payback or return on capital will be realized

The above scenario depicts only one half- hearted TICK($\checkmark$) on the margin front and rest will draw blank. Thus, the acquisition was not heavily discounted for the risk of acquiring loss making company coupled with the fact that telecom is a regulatory intensive industry.

Sell-Side Strategy: During the course of acquisition, there was Dish TV coming around with competing bid. Dish TV which had been built Mr Charlie Ergen a frugal, fiercely competitive entrepreneur made a bid for US $25 billion for entire Sprint. Thus, the bid was placed well to be just notch below that of Soft bank to get it rattled and increase in the offer price by 7.5% and rejection of Dish offer as not pursuable enough.

Key Learning

We see the various origination elements at play that can be used to consummate M&A deals. We also see how the application of M&A acquisition valuation matrix can be used to analyze and figure the realistic valuations for the company.

Last, we see how deal fever and competing bids played by the sell side can coax buyer into making a higher bid for the target.

2.3 M&A Matrix

Now, let us explore the M&A matrix in detail in context with the above case study.

The parameters for acquisition can be laid down as:

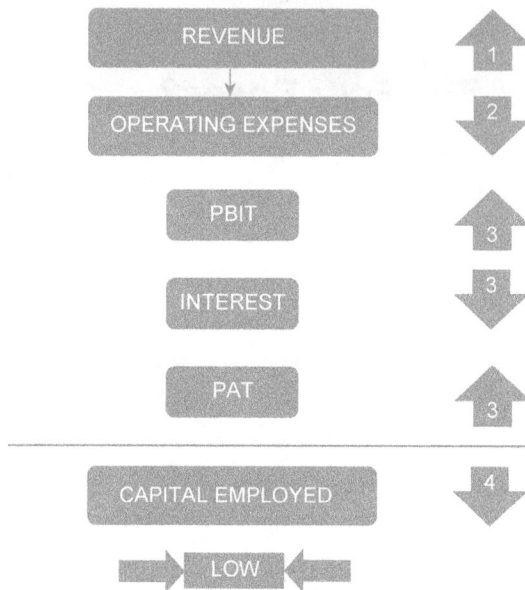

Ideally, for success of M&A, it is essential to tick all the four boxes. The most paramount will be the fourth parameter, which will essentially signify the discounting of the estimated synergies. 4th is mandatory, while 2 out of the remaining 3 can guarantee a better success rate. This would avoid impairing the quality of balance sheet and avoid bloating.

The below matrix assesses the probability of the success of acquisition.

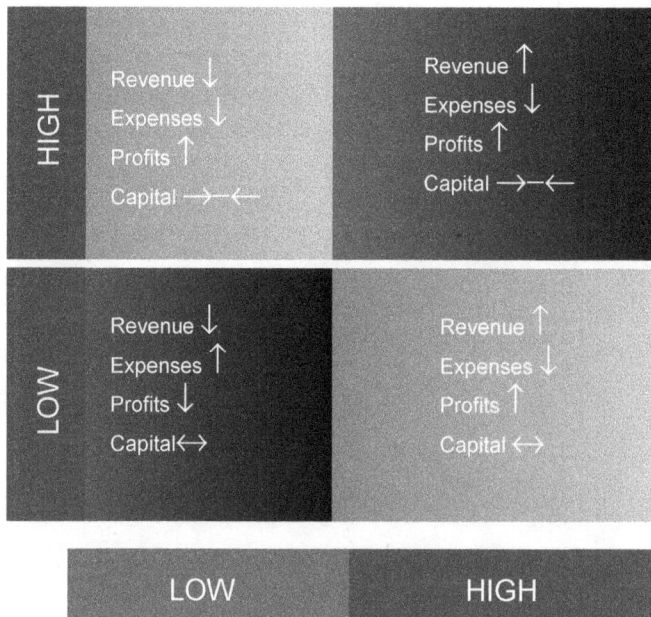

Thus, good business may be acquired, but if they come at the expense of enormous capital, there is no ultimate creation of shareholder value.

Tata-Jaguar would be the case to justify the point. Thus, out of all, point (4) is very important, bad acquisitions can still be stomached because the capital outlay is low; thus, the financial impact is limited.

Therefore, we can conclude that good acquisitions with large outlay are unable to create shareholder value, while the bad acquisitions without capital outlay still will not destroy the value.

This effect provides us a very important dimension for deciding to acquire. How much is the operating risk of buying and financial risk of stomaching the acquisition. Thus, acquisitions which does not marry this risk either would be value creators or at most will have neutral impact.

How the above falls in place is borne out by having a very coherent M&A strategy and not an ad-hoc one.

We can jot down the key lessons for successful acquisition as:

- *Check the above boxes, at least 3 out of 4 should be fulfilled*
- *Price has to discount risk*
- *Do not compound operating risk and financial risk*
- *Acquisitions in business-related geography and small in relation to the balance sheet will have high chance to succeed.*

Case Study 2.3: Tech Mahindra's Acquisition of Satyam: Asymmetric Risk and Return

Details

Tech Mahindra: It is an information technology company focussed on telecommunications services and is a part of Mahindra group.

Satyam: Satyam was the topmost information technology company with strong presence in the banking, financial services, and insurance space. Satyam had also listed its ADRs on NYSE.

Tech Mahindra snapped up Satyam for $580 million following 100 billion rupee accounting fraud by its founders. The gigantic fraud and then the name of Satyam with eminent board being listed in NYSE was a big surprise for all. Thus, when the government seized control and put Satyam on the block, none of the biggies turned up to acquire, fearing the depth of the fraud and class action suits in US of USD 1 billion.

Tech Mahindra's offer of 58 rupees ($1.16) a share trumped 46 rupees (92 cents) a share reportedly offered by the rival bidder Larsen & Toubro. Billionaire Wilbur Ross was the third bidder in the race for Satyam, but his bid of 20 rupees (40 cents) per share was just one-third of the winning bid. The bidding reveals how distressed companies keep large section of buyers out and bring in tentativeness in bidding.

Tech Mahindra observed it as a golden opportunity to acquire company such as Satyam, which will provide business and customer diversification and came at a price which discounted the risk of acquiring it.

Satyam was strong in Banking, Financial services and Insurance (BFSI) space and had contracts with marquee clients and they were annuity contracts; thus not easily cancellable. Discounting the cash and inflated revenues even if one was to travel back down the history lane and take revenue and profits 5 years back before the onset of fraud, it will give you a top-line of Rs. 2000 crores and bottom line of Rs. 300 crores. Therefore, even if there is sizeable attrition of clients still getting to that top-line and bottom line will not be a sweat. Thus, at a price of Rs. 58 per share, the profit/earning (P/E) multiple will work out to 10–11.

For the next 3 years, the senior management of Tech Mahindra was out with their utmost resources to integrate Satyam. This also involved the CEO Mr Anand Mahindra making visits to top 50 clients and assuring delivery from Satyam. Deputing the best personnel to Satyam gave a few hiccups, but they were able to stabilize the ship and improve margins at Satyam. All court cases were fought and settled including the class action suit for ~$100 million.

Thereafter, it announced the merger of Satyam with itself, valuing it for $1.8 billion to become the fifth largest software company.

Key Learning

- Discounting the risk of acquisition is the key to successful acquisition;
- Assessing the risk and taking calculated risk;
- Taking advantage of absence of bidders.

It was fairly evident that although the revenues were inflated, the clients were real. Further, it had good business diversification and manpower. Thus, good enough price that discount the risk of acquiring trouble companies was needed. Soon, it got arms around the target. Anand Mahindra, the CEO of Mahindra, a Harvard Alumini went and met the top clients to assure continuity. Thus, business although shaky came back to some sanity. The legal and court matters were dealt by the efficient legal teams. The settlement of class action suits was 5 cent to a dollar. Thus, USD 1 billion headline potential liability works out to not more than $50 million as long as you have tenacity and competent legal backup.

Here, we see acquisition arbitrage by paying price that discounts the risk to provide asymmetric return to the acquirer.

2.4 Triangulation for Acquisition Price

It is very important to define the quantitative criteria which will help to juxtapose the rationale for acquisition in context with financial metric. The financial metric will need to be achieved for shareholder value creation.

It would be helpful to lay down more than one financial metric so as to be able to triangulate across them and objectively decide whether they are in range or outlier.

Some of the quantitative financial metric can be:

a. Pay-back period
b. Return on investment (ROI)
c. Internal rate of return (IRR) on the expected synergy to be achieved
d. Combined earnings per share (EPS)
e. Asset turnover
f. Gross profit margin

The above metrics if triangulated will help keep the stated rationale for acquisition in line.

For example:

a. If it is stated that ROI is 50%, but the payback period is 7 years. It would mean that the objective is unrealistic;
b. If the IRR on synergistic cash flow produces a 25% IRR, it would mean it is a high return with high risk.

Therefore, it is advisable to use quantitative metrics and triangulate them to justify each other. Based on the aforesaid, a discounted price can be achieved to justify the acquisition price.

Case Study 2.4: Nicholas Piramal Acquires Rhone Poulenc from Aventis Pharma

Details

Rhone Poulenc: It was an Indian subsidiary of Aventis Pharma. Rhone Poulenc was into organic chemicals, synthetic chemicals, and pharmaceuticals. It was acquired by Aventis Pharma as a part of global acquisition of Rhone Poulenc SA. Post-acquisition, it had sold its synthetic chemical division to Solvay and agro-chemical division to Bayer. It meant that Aventis Pharma was in consolidating mode for its portfolio.

Rhone Poulenc, although doing financially well, was a very small business as compared to the size of global business of Aventis. Hence, it was put on block for sale.

Nicholas Piramal India Ltd (NPIL), which was also into pharmaceutical and had an interest in property, acquired 40% stake in competitive bidding in Rhone Poulenc

India Ltd. (RPIL) for Rs. 157.50 crores. The acquisition was made through NPIL's 100% subsidiary NPIL Finvest Ltd. funded by debt.

Within a year of post-acquisition, the five-storey headquarter building of Rhone-Poulenc, Worli, Mumbai, was sold to Birla for a consideration of Rs. 85 crores.

The directors of Nicholas Piramal India (NPIL) also approved the merger of Rhone-Poulenc India (RPIL) with NPIL and the merger was stated to be effective from April 1, 2001.

Pursuant to the merger, 60% paid-up capital of the RPIL was held by NPIL Finvest, a 100% subsidiary of NPIL, along with the debt raised for acquiring the said shares, will get transferred to NPIL, and consequently these shares will get extinguished on merger.

Hence, a leveraged buy-out was done by Piramal. Further, the acquisition cost was reduced by selling the real estate of the target company. The equity value of the acquisition was (2.5 × 157.5) aggregating to ~390 crores and PAT of 36 crores came to PE multiples of 11, which further dropped to 8 after adjusting for the real estate proceeds.

The return on capital employed (ROCE) for Rhone Poulenc was ~40% and return on equity (ROE) of ~30%. Thus, buying came at virtually nothing with undervalued real estate to boot.

Key Learning

The present case highlights how an acquirer makes virtue out of seller focussed on exiting and not necessarily optimizing value. Further, it also states how the buyer optimized the buying price by making optimal use of the undervalued real estate asset of the seller which was not reflected in the market price. Thus, most of the financial metrics were triangulated to arrive at the cheapest price and complete successful acquisition.

2.5 Attributes of Effective Acquisition

Acquisitions are performed as a basic part of coherent M&A strategy, after careful consideration of the requirement of business and selection of targets based on rigorous analysis. Strategic fit is selected due to complementary assets and resources. This would essentially mean the acquisition is done in the same or similar business and preferably in same or similar geography. The acquisitions that are funded largely out of internal financing than external financing and also maintaining balance sheet flexibility to deal with tough times will determine the effective acquisition. Essentially, balance sheet flexibility will mean pursuing acquisitions which have less capital outlay, lower in size relative to buyer, and when the existing business is in good shape, it allows the management to pursue acquisitions.

The acquisitions done in trough of the business cycle would effectively mean the price paid is conservative. This essentially means the risk of acquisition is adequately discounted.

The acquisitions negotiated on bilateral basis result in friendly negotiation rather than in auction or hostile manner would most probably be an effective acquisition. This will effectively avoid winners.

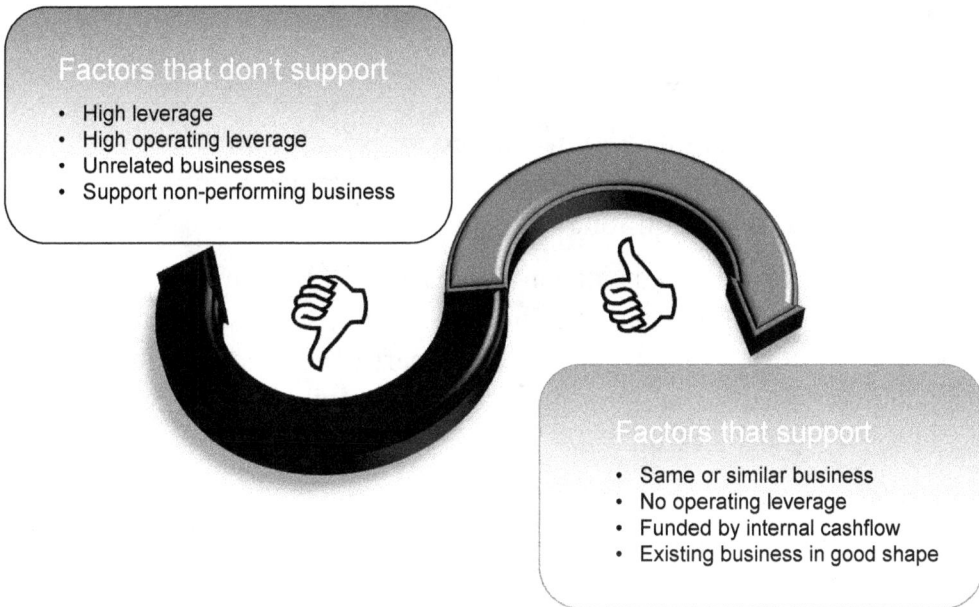

Factors that don't support
- High leverage
- High operating leverage
- Unrelated businesses
- Support non-performing business

Factors that support
- Same or similar business
- No operating leverage
- Funded by internal cashflow
- Existing business in good shape

The below case study drives home the points on attributes of effective acquisition.

Case study 2.5: Motherson Sumi—Managing Growth through Acquisitions (11 in 12 years and still counting)

Details

About Motherson Sumi:

Motherson Sumi belongs to Samvardhana Motherson Group (SMG), which combines the power of innovation and product quality to passionately create world class products that cater to customer needs across diverse industries, especially automotive. Founded in 1975, the Group has a diversified industry-leading portfolio of auto-ancillary products and services that make it a full system solution provider for its customers across the globe. It has a wide spectrum of market leading products ranging from Electrical Distribution Systems, automotive rear view mirrors, polymer processing, lighting systems, and air intake manifolds to Heating, Ventilating, and Air Conditioning (HVAC) systems. SMG's principal focus is the automotive industry globally and in India. SMG acts as a leading supplier to automotive industry across the globe. It also serves a wide number of other industries. The Group recorded a turnover of USD 6.1 billion (approximately) during 2013–2014.

SMG has operations in 25 countries across North America, South America, Europe, South Africa, Middle East, Asia Pacific, and Australia. Its broad range of products are manufactured in more than 170 facilities and 24 design centres across the globe by over 70,000 qualified professionals.

The Acquisition Story

Motherson came into being as a joint venture with Sumitomo Japan as auto-ancillary to Maruti Udyog. Since then, from a modest turnover, it has risen to generate combined revenue of US $6 billion.

The aforesaid has been managed on the back of 11 acquisitions in the last 12 years. The point to be noted is that none of the acquisitions has failed. Thus, it is a success story of stringing the pearls. It is a part of coherent acquisition strategy involving acquisition of smaller companies fitting into their growth strategy and integrating them rapidly as well.

Although the size of the acquisitions had also grown recently such as Visiocorp in 2009 for $39 million and Peguform in 2011 from Euro 140 million, still they have been successfully integrated, and today, they account for 75% of the turnover.

The founder of Motherson Sumi on being asked what has gone right for Motherson in terms of the acquisition has attributed to the following main reasons which are part of the successful acquisition matrix or attributes. They can be stated as:

- Acquiring companies that are known well from operational perspective
- Acquiring companies with good customer base, but are facing trouble and acquiring them at troubled price and using their operational expertise to turn them around.

Therefore, with a discounted price and operational expertise, it has been easy for Motherson to not only acquire companies, but also to drive rapid turnaround successfully.

It has enabled Motherson Sumi to exceed its "five-year plans" always, its blueprint for growth and progression. By 2005, this plan required the group's revenues to grow 10 times to Rs. 1000 crores; it closed that period at Rs. 1029 crores. Its 2010 target was $1 billion in revenues; it achieved $1.5 billion. The 2015 target was $5 billion, which Motherson hit with a year to spare.

Vivek Chaand Sehgal, the founder, is credited with seeking at all times which of his competitors are good or in trouble and worth to buy.

Today, Motherson is one of the best performing stocks in the Indian market growing eight folds in the last 7 years and today boasts of a market cap exceeding US $6 billion.

Key Learning

The integration of the acquisition strategy into the company's growth strategy involves evaluating the target first from the operational perspective then, through financial perspective stringing the pearls followed by rapid integration of the target into the fold. Top management oversight and commitment to integrate the acquired company. The reliance on operational expertise is utilized to identify targets.

Attributes of Effective Acquisition

- Tick all the four boxes of the M&A matrix:
  - Increase in revenue
  - Increase in margin thereby, lowering of expenses
  - Increase in profits
  - While the targets financials are not available in detail, the acquisitions have paid back the price paid within 2 years.

- The acquisition price is adequately discounted by buying in the troubled times of the customer. The operation and strategic fit is well-established and reflected in acquiring companies whose business is well-known to the scquirer and come together with established customer base. Last, the reliance of the company own expertise on its operational expertise rather than the expertise of the adviser and committing top management to integration of target company.

2.6 Problems with Acquisitions

Big isn't beautiful. The resulting firm is too large to be effectively managed. We have seen spate of announcements of mega-mergers fuelled by cheap debt. While the size of the combined firm is a big issue itself somehow, very basic issues such as who will head the combined firm still remain uncertain. The Publicis-Omnicom, an announced M&A between two advertising giants, was called-off as they could not decide the CEO will be from which firm. The Lafarge-Holcim deal also faced the similar issues. If it is the state of affairs at the top then, it is easy to figure out the loose ends all the way down. Thus, bigger the size, bigger the management issues compounded. If the target is multi-country located then, it would present enormous integration challenges.

No strategic or complementary fits. The acquisition is done with a focus on the financial engineering. Financial engineering is done through market players to indicate that earnings per share (EPS) is accretive. The current mass of

M&A driven by tax inversion to manage US taxes are one of the examples of financial engineering. These types of acquisitions are problematic because herein the end justifies the means. There is a pervert incentive to manipulate the items involved in the making of EPS *viz.* EPS (combined co) > EPS (A) + EPS (T). For the aforesaid, either earning ("E") should be high or shares ("S") should be low. Thus, once is set as an objective to be achieved. Either E is manipulated by diverting the expenses from income statement to balance sheet through goodwill or amortization of intangibles or S is manipulated by debt to attain desired outcomes.

More goodwill results in the increase profit as depreciation is not present in income statement. However, tax shield is not present. Amortization of intangibles can provide benefit of tax shield, but it lowers the earning.

The other tell-tale problematic acquisitions include balance sheets that are compromised by taking leverage and buying bigger size companies, resulting in **Operating leverage X Financial leverage = Disaster.** Thus, bigger acquisitions funded through leverage are sure shot recipe for disaster as operating leverage needs to really kick in to pay for the increased debt and the probability of that is on the lower side due to increased risk.

The other problematic acquisition being bought at peak of market cycle, which essentially means the valuation, is based on peak margins, peak profits, and peak business scenario. Therefore, the price does not discount the risk of the target business hitting a trough and will result in loss for the acquirer.

Case Study 2.6: How Not To Acquire

a. Acquiring at Peak of the Cycles

Dr Reddy's Laboratories, India's largest drug maker, which acquired Beta-pharm AG in 2006 for euro 480 million, or over Rs. 3200 crores (Rs. 32 billion), had earned a mere Rs. 800 crores (Rs. 8 billion) in each of the past 2 years. The acquisition failed to yield the desired results and was further hit by a drastic change in the German drug selling system.

While Dr Reddy's total debt climbed to Rs. 2500 crores (Rs. 25 billion) in the fiscal year ended March 2007 and dropped to Rs. 1968 crores (Rs. 19.68 billion) in March 2008, its revenue dropped to Rs. 1500 crores (Rs. 15 billion) in March 2008 from Rs. 5000 crores (Rs. 50 billion). Profit was nearly halved in the period from Rs. 932.7 crores (Rs. 9.33 billion) to Rs. 467.8 crores (Rs. 4.86 billion).

Dr Reddy's was also forced to take a one-time hit of Rs. 236.1 crores (Rs. 2.36 billion) for writing down intangibles at Betapharm.

b. Acquiring in Hostile Situations
Ending up Paying High Price

Arcelor-Mittal was formed by the merger of Mittal steel and Arcelor in 2006. Mittal has a successful track record of turning around sick and bankrupt companies. Mittal Steel paid a huge premium for the deal. As the deal was initially rejected by the Arcelor board, Mittal Steel had to make a revised offer. Mittal Steel had to pay almost double the price that was initially planned. This deal represented the biggest premium ever paid for acquiring a steel company.

Finally, Mittal Steel paid a sum of $33.1 billion for the deal. The current market capitalization of Arcelor-Mittal is around $16 billion, which is 50% less than what it paid 8 years ago to acquire Arcelor while Mittals own market cap being $49 billion. Thus, against combined equity value of $80 billion, the Arcellor-Mittal market cap today is $1/5^{th}$ of the 2006 value.

What went wrong?

- Huge premium
- High financial leverage
- High operating leverage because of the capacity creation which failed to be utilized due to the downturn in steel industry acquiring at peak of the cycle compounded by operating and financial leverage.

2.7 Risks Involved in Acquisitions

The acquisitions carry some major risk and require careful evaluation for committing to acquire the target company. These risks can be classified into either operational or financial risk. While evaluating the risks, the first port of call should have operational risks involved. Only after the operational risks have been carefully evaluated and the boxes are ticked as manageable then, we should proceed for evaluating the financial risk. The reason for the failure of M&A is that most of the time the financial risk is evaluated first proceeded by the operational risk. The foremost being the debt capacity. Once the financing is in place, the operational risk is evaluated merely as a tick the box rather than the thorough consideration for creation of value through acquisition.

Let us now evaluate the various types of risks.

Types of Risks

Operational risk

The first and the foremost risk to be evaluated in this context is whether the business I am acquiring, is it core to my existing business activity, or incidental to my business activity. The aforesaid is important to understand as it will determine whether I have the operational expertise to understand the business that is being acquired and whether there are enough resources available for the purpose of integrating and to eke out synergy from acquisition.

Whether there are sufficient resources available to deal with the acquisition is determined by whether the acquirer business is in fine shape and firing on all cylinders, thereby giving the top management bandwidth to deal with the acquisition. Many a times, companies resort to acquisition to prop-up growth represent a perfect example of the existing business not being in a good condition, but resorting to further managerial problem of dealing with the acquired company.

Once we have evaluated the operational risks from the acquirer's point of view, we now need to take a look at the target business. The key question to be asked is whether it is under-managed or under-invested. If it is under-managed, would there be substantial scope to improve the business. If the acquirer believes it has the managerial resources and bandwidth to focus on the targets business. On the other hand, if it is under-invested, there will be need to commit further financial resources and would need to be taken into account while evaluating financial risk.

What is the reason? Why the seller is cashing out and whether the acquirer has the competitive advantage to manage that reason. What is the competitive landscape of the target business, whether it has a dominant position or brand or extensive distribution that can be relied upon for creating value for the acquirer.

The above is to be further considered in context with cross-border acquisition. Whether there is understanding of the target's geography and market. The level of understanding will determine the risk as that will determine the value at risk and the realism of synergies. The aforesaid will also deal with the integration and cultural risk associated with acquisition.

Last but not the least is operating leverage that will be injected in the business. High operating leverage will mean high risk of failure.

Example: Tata steel–Corus deal

We will now evaluate the second level of risk *viz*. financial risk.

Financial risk

Financial risk evaluation starts with means of financing *viz*. internal accrual or debt or equity. The mix as well as the quantum will be determining the risk being undertaken. This will determine the cost of capital and how much funds can be committed for the acquisition. Debt being cheaper means of finance provides much more quantum of financing, but the cheap rate of finance also hides the risk of acquiring a larger sized company and compounding the operating leverage.

The other issues in the financial risks include the earnings quality, the tangible assets being acquired, evaluating the balance sheet for receivables and inventory, and whether there are any off-balance sheet liabilities and contingent liability.

Case Study 2.7: Acquiring in Auctions/ Cross-Border/Operating Risk/Financial Risk—Suzlon Energy Acquires RE Power

Details

Suzlon Energy Ltd. (Currency: Rs. in Crores)							
	201403	201303	201203	201103	201003	200903	200803
Equity paid up	497	355	355	355	311	299	299
Net-worth	-381	902	5180	6525	6601	8626	8101
Capital employed	17032	16472	19623	19000	19271	23498	18038
Market capitalization	2761	2426	4496	7935	11193	6352	39458
Debt–equity ratio	53	4	2	1	1	1	1
ROCE (%)	0	0	0	0	2	11	14
RONW (%)	0	0	0	0	-12	9	19

RE Power: Suzlon Wins Takeover Battle

In June 2007, German wind turbine manufacturer RE power was acquired by Suzlon, after a 5-month takeover battle with the huge French state-owned nuclear company Areva.

The takeover process was triggered by Areva CEO Anne Lauvergeon with an opening offer of €105 per share, but this was topped further by Suzlon bid of €150. At the time of the takeover in May, RE power's share price stood at €166, 10% above Suzlon's last offer and over four times more than RE power's stock rating of €40 of last summer. **Suzlon valued the German firm at around 1.2 billion euros ($1.6 billion).**

Prior to the €1.22 billion cash offer for RE Power, Suzlon's most important acquisition had been the takeover of Belgian gearbox manufacturer Hansen Transmissions International in 2006. This strategic deal cost the Indian company about €424 million (US $565 million).

Suzlon Energy Ltd. (Currency: Rs. in Crores)

	201403	201303	201203	201103	201003	200903	200803	200703	200603	200503
Gross block	17622	15502	14791	12852	11538	15102	5599	4321	628	359
Net sales	20402	18913	21359	18090	20619	26081	13679	7985	3841	1942
PAT	-3548	-4731	-472	-1316	-989	428	1017	864	760	365
Net current Assets	2335	2773	5949	4854	8030	10728	10255	4517	2452	966
Cash flow From operating activities	567	555	838	1214	2234	-1223	1211	737	-354	118
Cash flow from investing activities	-438	-327	-643	-803	-1676	-6171	-4636	-3719	-380	-270
FCF	128	227	195	411	558	-7395	-3425	-2982	-734	-152

While Areva has the option to sell its stake to Suzlon after 1 year, Martifer the co-acquirer with Suzlon can sell its share within 2 years up to 265 million euros, also to Suzlon.

Key Learning

What went wrong?

- Growing fast too soon.
  - Multiplying sales
  - Multiplying gross block
  - This created pressure on the cash flows creating negative cash flows
- Did not fortify the existing business before launching bid for other acquisitions. Suzlon had just emerged on the scene and had to establish itself as a sizeable company in terms of process, systems, and managerial resources.
- It had recently acquired Hansen for USD 565 million, before it could integrate Hansen it launched 3× the size of acquisition of Hansen.
- Big size acquisition, immediately on completion of another big, that too in hostile bidding in cross-border and backed by leverage.
- The balance sheet had already started showing the strains of growing rapidly even before the acquisition. It was reflected in the working capital as well as efficiency.

Thereby, creating perfect recipe for train wreck from which Suzlon never recovered experiencing a market cap of ~40,000 down to 2000 crores.

With this brief overview of the problems involved in acquisition, let us move ahead to attain a deeper knowledge of risks involved in acquisitions.

2.8 M&A—What Works and What Not?

We have seen the attributes of effective acquisition and acquisitions which probably won't result in shareholder value creation. Based on the above discussion, we can consummate that acquirers which indulge in stringing of pearls through coherent M&A strategy to acquire smaller firms which fit their strategic needs driven by thorough evaluation of operational and financial risk will be able to deliver better value.

Another aspect worth consideration is that the likelihood of success in the below industry is higher.

- Technology (IT services)
- FMCG
- Pharma
- Insurance/banks
- Resources

- Internet
- Retail
- Real estate

The main reason behind this is easy to project revenues and expenses and to determine whether the acquisition is EPS accretive or not, which is driven by stable cash flows and non-cyclical nature of such industries.

The counterview being, the rest of the industries, which is real estate and commodities suffer from the high rate of failure due to cyclical, capital intensive, inability to time the business cycle, and higher operating leverage.

The corollary to the above being that faced with uncertainty, huge capital outlay and cyclicality better discount the risks and determine the value creation by paying the right discounted price. The determination of discounted price is a factor of the peak and trough business scenario as well as the performance of the companies.

The case studies below highlight the fact that while on forefront a very high price is being paid, the deeper analysis will reveal a discounted price.

Case Study 2.8: Shaw Wallace Acquisition by United Breweries: Acquisitions that Worked Despite Paying Premium

Details

Shaw Wallace held a market share of 36% in the Indian spirits market. It had brands like Royal challenge, a premium whisky, which had 65% market share in its segment. Its other brands which include Antiquity, Antiquity Super, Director's special, Haywards Fine, etc., were controlling 16% market share.

Shaw Wallace was controlled by Manu Chabbaria *viz.* the Jumbo Group. After his demise, the rest of the promoter group were not interested in the business. Shaw Wallace was chugging along on the strength of its brand, but the financial performance of Shaw Wallace had been slackening.

Its revenue stood flat at Rs. 100 crores. Since 2002, the profitability had slipped and operating income has also fallen dramatically. Although, it was the time liquor and tobacco companies were making profits worldwide. The corporate governance was also weak. This had resulted in the poor financial performance as well as poor stock performance.

On February 23, 2005, Mr Vijay Mallya announced 25% open offer for Shaw Wallace Rs. 250. This was an 8.2% premium over the last closed price. **This offer valued Shaw Wallace Rs. 1200 crores which is 120% premium over the market capitalization of last 12 months.** On March 31, 2005, Vijay Mallya announced that UB group had closed the deal with Chhabria family-owned Jumbo World Holdings

Ltd. (JHWL) for Rs. 1330 crores ($300 million) for a stake of 54.54% share of SWC. The deal was evaluated to be Rs. 325 per share. UB group also said that open offer price has been revised to Rs. 260 per share. The deal was financed by borrowing $300 million from ICICI bank with win equal proportion of foreign and domestic currency. UB group has paid Rs. 1545 crores including Rs. 312 crores for acquisition of 25% share through open offer.

Key Learning

Paying premium over depressed financial performance may not be a premium, but a good ruse to entice Seller to commit to deal.

The payment of premium is justified due to the consumer branded business with relative stability to predict the cash flows justifying the leverage financing of the acquisition.

Consumer branded business coupled with leadership and under-managed businesses make good recipe for acquisition.

Why did Acquisition at a High Premium Along with Leverage Succeed?

While there appears to be a premium paid for the acquisition on headline basis, given the depressed performance of Shaw Wallace coupled with strong market presence of Shaw Wallace brands the price paid was actually reasonable. Essentially, the valuation done here is trough EPS × higher multiple, which gave normalized value to Shaw Wallace and allowed the acquisition to succeed.

The results include:

	2004	2008
EPS	0.02	6.14
Net	0.09 cr	29.48 cr

Operating profit margin, gross profit margin, and net profit are observed to increase significantly.

Thus, under-managed brands landing in the hands of superior management at a reasonable price resulted in success of the acquisition.

The above acquisition also highlights the important point on price discounting the risk, as the price paid was normalized. Although, it appeared at premium and also as highlighted it in a consumer goods category where it was relatively easy to predict the scenario and discount risk accordingly.

The acquisition allowed rolling the under-managed brands on existing distribution system of United Breweries without any incremental cost, and there was no sizeable CapEx involved post-acquisition.

Case Study 2.9: Jyothy Laboratories' Henkel Acquisition: Large Acquisitions that Worked Despite Paying Premium

Details

Henkel India was a sister concern based in India of German giant Henkel AG, which is a leading company in laundry and home care, beauty care, and adhesive technologies.

Henkel was operating in India for more than 25 years and had leading brands such as Henko, Margo, Chek detergents, Pril dish cleaners, and Fa deodorant. Henkel India's revenues were estimated to be Rs. 400 crores and it was suffering a loss of Rs. 600 crores. Henkel India needed constant support from the parent due to the losses. Jyothy's revenues were at Rs. 600 crores and its PAT was Rs. 74 crores.

Jyothy Laboratories bought Henkel AG stake in Indian subsidiary at an enterprise value of Rs. 617 crores. Jyothy paid Rs. 118.7 crores, or Rs. 20 for each share for the German firm's 50.97% stake in Henkel India. **It will also assume and re-finance Henkel's Rs. 454-crore debt and buy more than 68 million preference shares worth Rs. 43.9 crores.**

Key Learning

- Relative probability of succeeding in branded business.
- How operational fit takes care to some extent of the acquisition and financing risk.
- Simple triangulation of various values can result in appraising the value of the target.

On similar revenue, Jyothy was making an operating margin of 12% while Henkel was suffering losses. With brands and FMCG sector being in the same business making 12% operating margin would mean that even 5% operating margin would result in ROE of 20% on equity investment of Rs. 118 crores.

To that effect, a strong need emerges to cut down the excess manpower and improving the efficiency of distribution as the brands were strong by themselvs. Seven strong brands survived for more than 25 years, but were not managed well.

On sale of 1200 crores with 8% margin, it started earning 100-crore profits with some sweat but, more on brand power. The acquisition worked like a Leveraged buyout (LBO).

The result is also reflected in numbers. In the first 9 months of FY14, Jyothy's sales raise to 24% at Rs. 925 crores, and PAT 139% at Rs. 77 crores, year-on-year.

The company's stock has out-performed the BSE FMCG Index by 30% in the past 6 months.

Why a Large-Sized Acquisition at a High Premium along with Financed through Leverage Succeed?

Was it large-sized acquisition and at high premium?

While the acquisition was of Rs. 600 crores, the equity shares were acquired at only Rs. 20 per share and that was only 1/5th of the consideration. The 4/5th of the consideration was the assumed debt of a hugely loss-making company which can be easily renegotiated by an able bodied management and company in terms of haircut and reduced interest, thereby making the savings go directly to the bottom line. On large base, even a bit reduction in the haircut and cost makes a tremendous impact to the bottom line.

The rest of the acquisition legwork is to leverage the brands and making the 3 out of 4 checkboxes work which was comparatively easy, being the well-known brands in FMCG industry, with predictable industry scenario, thus price discounting the risk adequately to make the acquisition succeed.

2.9 Bootstrapping

The other safer route for acquisition is to indulge in bootstrapping. Bootstrapping refers to High PE co. acquiring a low PE co. especially, when acquiring under-managed business would have high probability of success.

In case of "High PE co. acquiring a low PE co.," all the four checkboxes for successful M&A should be ticked.

Below is the illustration of the bootstrap effect (multiple-company being acquired improves due to acquisition by target having lower PE).

Boot strap Effect

	A (Acquirer)	B (Target)	A+B	Formulae
EPS	4	1	4.3	600,000/140,000
Number of shares	100,000	200,000	140,000	100,000+(20/100)×200,000
Market price	100	20	107.1	Acquirer PE × EPS (A+B)
Earnings	400,000	200,000	600,000	(A+B)
Market value	10,000,000	4,000,000	15,000,000	Market price × number of shares
P/E	25	10	25	Market value/earnings

Case Study 2.10: TCS Acquires CMC: The Bootstrap Effect

Details

TCS:

Tata Consultancy Services (TCS) is a global leader in IT services, digital, and business solutions. At the time of acquisition, it was a part of the Tata Sons and subsequently was spun-off and listed on the Indian stock exchanges.

CMC:

CMC Limited is a leading systems engineering and integration company in India, offering application design, development, testing services, and asset-based solutions in niche segments through turn key projects for mission critical systems. CMC was earlier owned by Government of India and was a part of the divestment done by Government of India in 2002.

TCS acquired a controlling 51% stake in CMC which had established presence in customer support, facilities management and hardware and software maintenance, large turn key projects, strong research and development focus, and the range of services with complementary domain knowledge.

Tata Sons also came out with an open offer to acquire another 16.69% stake in the company at Rs. 281.26 per share. The total value of the open offer was Rs. 72 crores. Tata Sons came to hold 51% share in CMC, while the Government of India hold 32.31% and the public hold the remaining 16.69%.

CMC although focussed on government business had decent financial performance.

CMC had recorded revenues of Rs. 657 crores in the year ending June 30, 2001. Over Rs. 442 crores or 83% of its total revenue during the last fiscal came from the domestic market representing a 4.6% share. They also had a strong hold on the government market, which accounted for 34% of the total domestic IT market last year. It was also a preferred vendor to public sector banks, which together account for 16% of the domestic IT market. In niche areas, such as maintenance and support, CMC was the undisputed king with an overwhelming 70% market share.

Despite the above, being a government owned as well as largely government contracts, the multiple for CMC was not too high.

For TCS, which got majority of its revenues from overseas, notably the US, this acquisition provides an opportunity to consolidate its operations in India. The key areas in which TCS was likely to benefit from the CMC acquisition was through CMC's expertise in customer support, facilities management, and hardware and software maintenance. CMC also had expertise in executing large turnkey projects. It had a strong research and development focus and can offer a wide range of services with complementary domain expertise.

The delivery capabilities of TCS can be used by CMC to mine its international client base for off-shore work.

Key Learning

How the classical acquisition *viz.* high P/E company acquiring low P/E target creates a bootstrap effect? How target's business is evaluated from operational and strategic fit. How the value creation achieved by bootstrap effect by acquiring under-managed business? The illustration of how risk discounting is done by the acquisition of low P/E target.

Attributes of Effective Acquisition

- Ticks all the four boxes of the M& A matrix:
    - Increase in revenue
    - Increase in margin, thereby lowering of expenses
    - Increase in profits
    - The enterprise value of CMC is Rs. 432 crores (72 crores (17% open offer* 6 times = 100%). Assuming, there is no cash on the balance sheet. Thus, the capital employed is also very low. Assuming no debt, the equity value of CMC is Rs. 432 crores. Thus, the P/E is mere 432/32 = ~13×. The industry average will be at least 20× for the IT industry.
    - The market value of TCS, when it went public in 2004, was Rs. 5000 crores. Thus, the target about 10% of its market cap, which was acquired at 13× multiple, which was also market leader in its domain and complementary to its market and products/services. It represented a perfect bootstrap opportunity for the acquirer. CMC share price never looked back except for a brief period of 2008 Lehman times. It touched a lifetime high of INR 2358 before being merged into TCS.

- Strategic fit due to complementary assets and resources. The acquisition filled up the product gap and market gap prevailing in TCS portfolio. The acquisition was done as a part of coherent M&A strategy. The acquisitions done in trough of the business cycle which would effectively mean the price paid is conservative.

2.10 Playing Your Cards Well

We have covered qualitative and quantitative criteria for making effective acquisition. There are few other key considerations that need to be taken care, which includes planning the acquisition, structuring the acquisition, negotiating it, and strategizing it. The below case studies demonstrate all the aforesaid parameters.

Case Study 2.11: Holcim's India Entry Strategy through M&A

Details

a. Strategy/ M&A Strategy and Environmental Scan

Holcim had been unsuccessfully trying to enter Indian market for a very long time. Its rival Lafarge had already set afoot in India by acquiring Tata Steels Cement Unit and few other small manufacturers.

They clearly had market gap and the feasibility of greenfield was not very appealing.

Grasim, the other cement player, had also acquired few smaller capacities, while Gujarat Ambuja had gobbled up ACC, DLF Cement, and Ambuja Eastern Limited. Holicm tried unsuccessfully to bid for L&T Cement capacity, but Grasim ended up scuttling L&T Management plans to demerge and invite strategic/financial investor in the demerged cement entity.

Thus, there was no capacity left to acquire, except looking out for those companies which could be target.

b. Identifying and Prioritizing Target

Why Gujarat Ambuja?

Although Gujarat Ambuja was an efficient operator, it had strained the balance sheet due to the acquisition. At the same time, it controlled two of India's biggest cement capacities *viz.* ACC and Gujarat Ambuja. Further, its promoters held only 22% shares of Gujarat Ambujas and could possibly look at exiting the ventures.

While Gujarat Ambuja had 14.4% stake in ACC, it did not have overt control and also lacked the financial muscle to cross the 15% takeover threshold and make an open offer for 20% of ACC.

The financing of acquisition of ACC and Ambuja Cement Eastern was done through stake sale of investment vehicle to strategic financial investors and the investors had guaranteed to put on their holdings at pre-determined rate of return.

Therefore, it depicts a perfect case of clock ticking, only needed acquirers with the instinct to sniff the deal and the instincts to understand the dynamics. Furthermore, there was RBI Foreign Exchange Management Act (FEMA) provision which legally prohibited Ambuja Cement India Ltd. to repatriate money to financial investors. Thus, only non-resident acquirer could do the honours.

This sets the roadmap for Holcim's entry into India and effectively shutting the door on the rest of Cement biggies to enter India.

Gathering Intelligence

What can make this acquisition possible?

- Acquisition which makes it appear joint effort with sellers, not seen as overt seller (refer chapter on "Negotiation")
- Decent valuation to sellers
- Using indirect acquisition method (refer chapter on "Structural elements")
- Using the local seller's resources to tackle regulatory approvals as ACC was always a sensitive asset from political/competitive and media point of view.

Background of the Sellers Assets

Gujarat Ambuja acquired a 14.4% stake in ACC from the Tata group in 1999 at Rs. 370 per share. It had also acquired Modi Cements (renamed Ambuja Cement Eastern) for Rs. 166 crores.

- Investments in these two companies were vested with Ambuja Cement India. 40% stake in this company was sold to strategic financial investors and rest of the equity is held by Gujarat Ambuja, which also pocketed a profit of Rs. 285 crores for transfer of Ambuja Cement Eastern to the new company.
- The creation of this investment vehicle enabled the company to quickly cut down the debt burden, which helped bankroll the acquisition of the stake in ACC.
- Gujarat Ambuja also bought DLF Cements, renames it to Ambuja Cement Rajasthan, and completes the merger with itself.

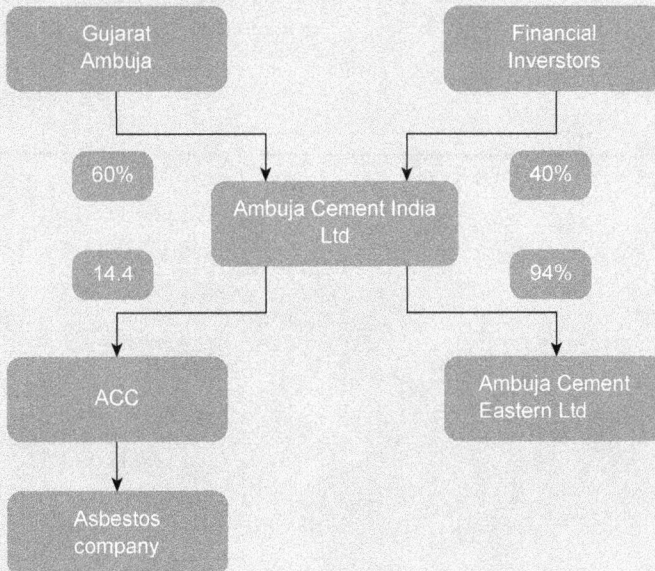

Developing Acquisition Structure

2005 - ACC

In January 2005, Holcim buys a 67% stake in Ambuja Cement India, leaving Gujarat Ambuja with 33% stake. Holcim invests $800 million (about Rs. 3500 crores) in this project.

Gujarat Ambuja was presented an option to sell its stake in Ambuja Cement India to Holcim by the end 2007. Holcim had the call option to buy from 2008.

This is an example of protection of each other's interest. Gujarat Ambuja retains the right to sell at particular value, while Holcim in return seeks call option as it has the sole control of ACC, does not want the gains of value increase to go to Gujarat Ambuja endlessly.

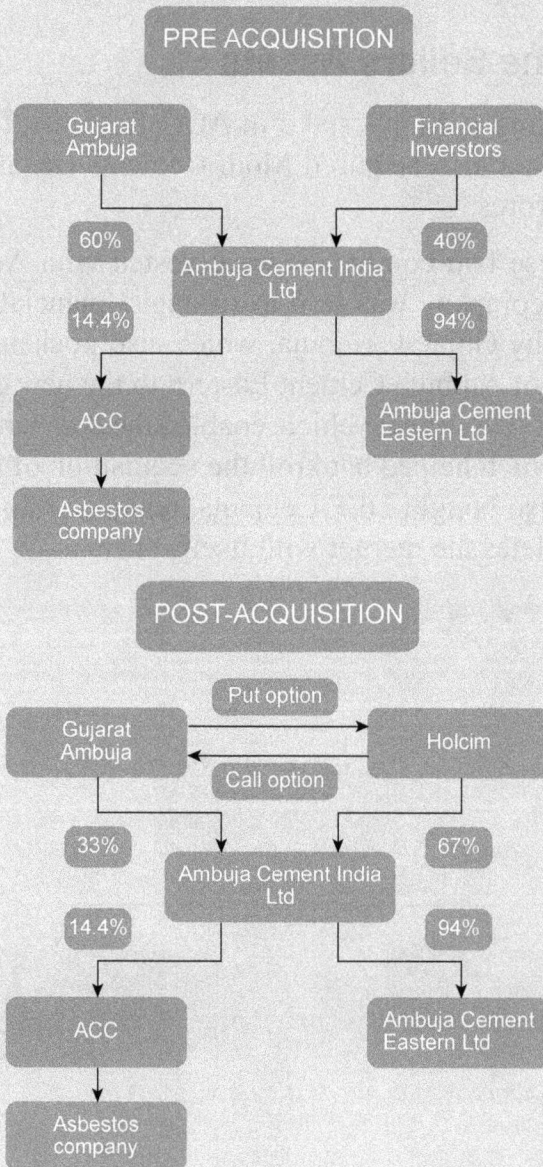

Ambuja Cement India makes an open offer on behalf of Holcim for ACC to raise its stake to a tad over 50%. Investor's response is not up to expectations and it ends up with a stake of 34%.

Holcim makes an open offer on behalf of Holcim for Ambuja Cement Eastern and ends up with a stake of 96.1%.

Holcim ends up selling Asbestos Company, as it was into manufacturing of asbestos sheet being a carcinogenic product.

2006 — Gujarat Ambuja
January 2006

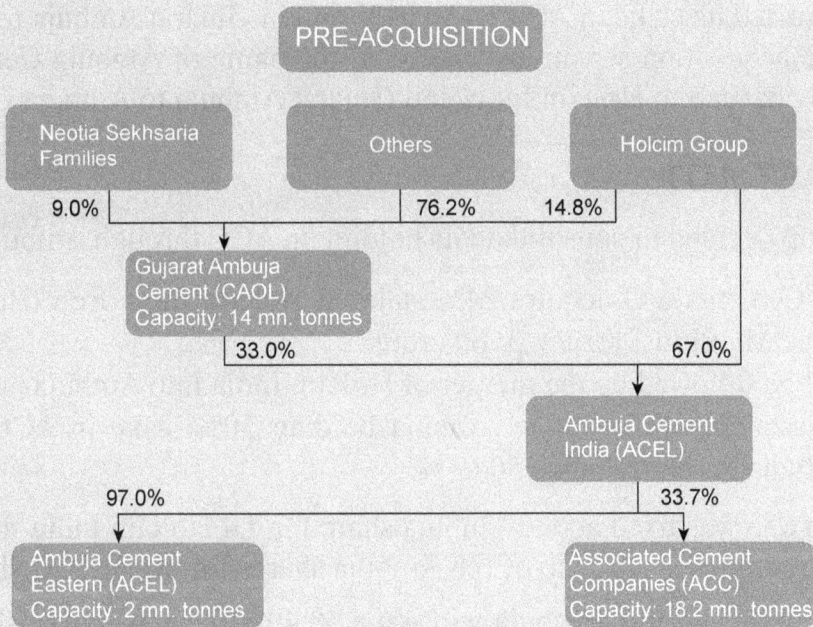

PRE-ACQUISITION

Neotia Sekhsaria Families — 9.0%

Others — 76.2%

Holcim Group — 14.8%

Gujarat Ambuja Cement (CAOL) Capacity: 14 mn. tonnes — 33.0% / 67.0%

Ambuja Cement India (ACEL) — 97.0% / 33.7%

Ambuja Cement Eastern (ACEL) Capacity: 2 mn. tonnes

Associated Cement Companies (ACC) Capacity: 18.2 mn. tonnes

Once the ACC asset was firmly secured with explicit statement that Holcim was in SOLE CONTROL, the next phase:

Holcim buys a 14.8% stake in Gujarat Ambuja Cements and plans to raise it to about 35% through an open offer, price tag: $1.03 billion.

To prevent any competitive bid, the shares were bought just below the takeover trigger threshold of 15% and transferred to the name of Holicm. Post-acquisition, an open offer was announced with a price tag of $1.03 billion, making it the most expensive deal in cement till then. But, the blow was cushioned by offering non-compete to promoters which was not offered to the public shareholders.

After the completion of open offer and gaining control over Gujarat Ambuja, it was proposed to merge Ambuja Cement Eastern Ltd (ACEL) with itself so as to ensure the crossing of 15% takeover threshold without triggering the takeover code.

Acquisition Impact

With ACC and Gujarat Ambuja, Holcim acquired a pan-India presence and a control over capacity of about 35 million tonnes, which accounts for 25% of the industry.

The acquisition bestows Holcim with the status of industry leader in the market with bright growth prospects.

The deal leaves marginal room for its global competitors to grow and match it through the acquisitions route. It also lengthens the gestation period for its competitors should they pursue the route of capacity creation.

After the above offers, the following incidence took place:

a. Holcim raised its stake in ACC to 50.01% and in Gujarat Ambuja to ~20%.
b. Once the acquisition sensitivity was over, the name of Ambuja Cements India Ltd. was changed to Holcim India and Gujarat Ambuja to Ambuja Cement.

2014—LAST ACT

Holcim Group decided to consolidate its holding in ACC through Ambuja Cements.

1. Ambuja Cements will acquire 24% stake in Holcim India from Holderind Investments, Mauritius, for Rs. 3500 crores.
2. This will be followed by the merger of Holcim India into Ambuja.
3. The transaction will result in Ambuja holding 50% stake in ACC, in which Holcim India currently holds 50.01%.

The merger swap was fixed at one Ambuja share for 7.4 Holcim India shares, translating into an implied swap ratio of 6.6 Ambuja shares for every ACC share.

Based on the swap ratio, Ambuja will issue 58.4 crores new equity shares of the company to Holcim as a consideration for the merger.

Post-merger, Holcim will then own 61.39% of Ambuja which, in turn, will own 50.01% in ACC.

Over the next 2 years, Ambuja will invest Rs. 3000 crores to enhance its holding in ACC by 10 percentage points without triggering a mandatory open offer. The scheme of amalgamation did not lead to any open offer for shareholders.

Ambuja Cements intends funding the cash transactions through internal accruals.

Key M&A Learning

- Mapping India entry strategy entirely through M&A. From nowhere to a leading player.
- Hitting multiple birds with one stone.

- How to assess the assets which may be up for sale and making it palatable to sell for the sellers.
- Skillfully negotiating with the seller spanning over 3 years.
- Using the local resources to front the acquisition to keep xenophobia out.
- Utilizing the local resources at non-executive levels and titular positions to consolidate its operations.
- Ensuring custody of assets (sole control over ACC although the offer was made jointly with Gujarat Ambuja) so that Holcim is able to consolidate ACC in its results. Securing hold over 15% stakes in Gujarat Ambuja before announcing the offer.
- Use of effective M&A tool such as:
  - Holding company
  - Using dilution to acquire optics-wise seller is not a seller
  - Put and call options
  - Using takeover exempted route such as merger, creeping to reach desired threshold
  - Ring fencing assets and competition
  - Softer issues of names of entity to keep optics right
  - Consolidating and integrating the assets and returning the cash back to the parent.

Case Study 2.12: Battle for Fraser & Neave

Details

Fraser & Neave, popularly known as F&N, was formed in 1883, but became public company in 1898 formed with interest in aerated water business. In 1931, it entered into Joint Venture with Heineken through Asia Pacific Breweries ("APB") for manufacturing and distribution of beer. The most famous product of the organization is Tiger Beer, which is quite popular in South-East Asia. It also acquired distribution rights for Coke and Pepsi and also developed a range of other drinks which are popular in the South-East Asian market more particularly in Malaysia and Singapore and has a wide range of popular drink brands.

APB's 2012 revenues were SG $2.1 billion. The Profit before Interest, Taxation and exceptional items (PBIT) was SG $515 million in 2012.

F&N had SG $5.5 billion revenue and PBIT of SG $957 million. Thus, both companies had strong financial and operating results.

In July 2012, Thai Breweries controlled by Thai Billionaire, Charoen Sirivadhanabhakdi acquired 22% stake in F&N by purchasing it from OCBC, thereby, increasing its stake to 24%.

Battle for F&N

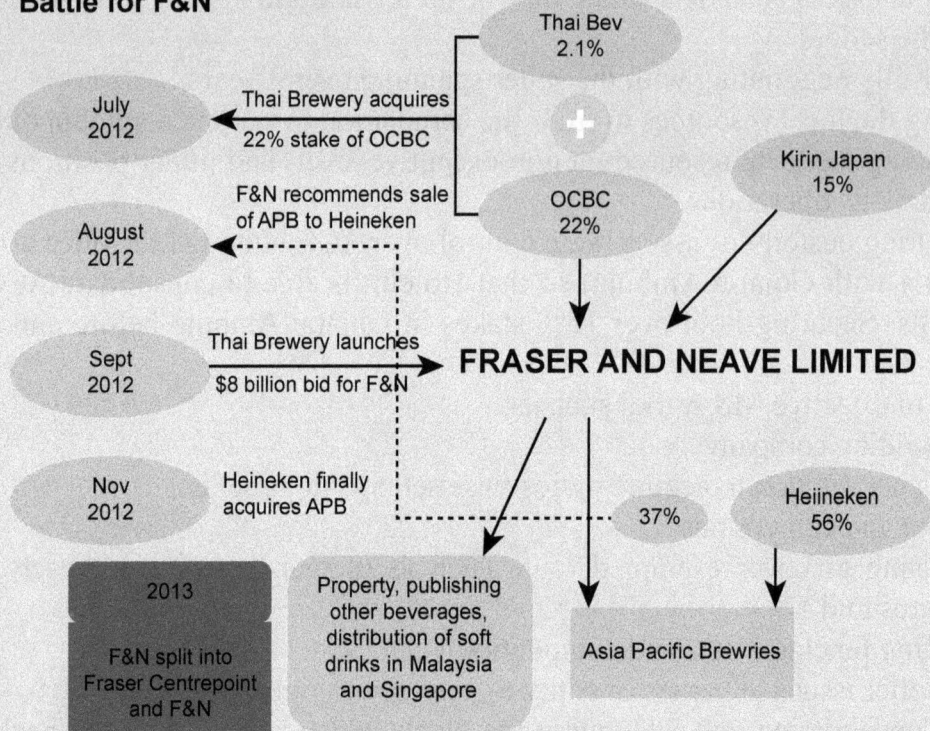

Thai Bev
2.1%

+

July
2012

Thai Brewery acquires
22% stake of OCBC

OCBC
22%

Kirin Japan
15%

August
2012

F&N recommends sale
of APB to Heineken

Sept
2012

Thai Brewery launches
$8 billion bid for F&N

FRASER AND NEAVE LIMITED

Nov
2012

Heineken finally
acquires APB

37%

Heiineken
56%

2013

F&N split into
Fraser Centrepoint
and F&N

Property, publishing
other beverages,
distribution of soft
drinks in Malaysia
and Singapore

Asia Pacific Brewries

Battle for F&N

Shareholders

FRASER CENTREPOINT	FRASER AND NEAVE LIMITED
Mkt cap 54.8 bn	Mkt cap 53.3 bn

In response to this change in shareholding, in August 2012, the management of F&N recommended sale of APB to Heineken at $50 per share valuing it at S$4.8 billion.

In September 2012, to thwart the transfer of APB to Heineken, there was a bid launch by Thai Breweries to control F&N valuing F&N at SG $8 billion.

Heineken after a protracted battle in November 2012 finally managed to secure APB at a value of SG $5.6 billion.

Battle for F&N

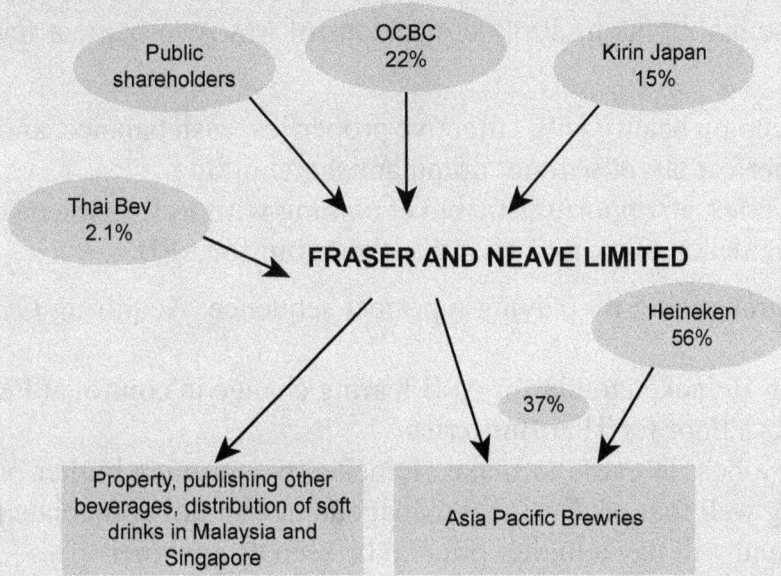

Analysis

Thai Breweries showed a strong acumen for a well-calculated M&A which gave an asymmetric return. They could see the arbitrage value carried by F&N through its 46% shareholding in APB wherein Heineken, despite its 56% shareholding, had grown its business through this venture in which it had built strong local brand like Tiger and distribution of its beer.

A bid at SG $8 billion for F&N was well-covered by the APB value that Heineken will pay in all eventuality and always had a floor of $5 billion. The risk of Heineken walking from the deal was low, but the upside was the brewery stayed with F&N or the rest of the business carried enough value for it not to make a financial loss.

The issue that needs to be considered here is why Heineken never consolidated its stake in the Joint Venture. Rather, why they never considered acquiring control over F&N. Why there wasn't a control change clause in Joint venture which could have given it a stronger ground to negotiate on value. Why the value of Joint Venture continued to increase unbridled; however, it was only a 56% shareholder. Could they have looked the bid of Thai Breweries into eye and not blinked. But, over a period of time the value of joint venture would have withered and built an alternate business at a fraction of cost of $7 billion that was paid to acquire the balance in the joint venture.

Would OCBC have called a competing bid and realized a better value for its shareholding.

Key Learning

The above case highlights multiple dimensions of M&A to name a few in the long list:

- F&N, a sleeping beauty with attractive properties, cash balance, and strong business and perfect target without dominant shareholding.
- Thai Breweries, an opportunistic buyer coming with well-financed offer, enough to make Heineken blink into giving a higher bid for APB.

  - M&A strategizing by playing a perfect sequence: Acquiring OCBC stake in F&N
  - Inducing Heineken to bid for APB fearing change in control at F&N
  - This gets a floor for Thai Breweries
  - Playing a hostile game to make Heineken pay a much higher price for APB knowing well that professional management will not appreciate to be seen as a loser and will pay a higher price to be seen as a winner
  - Return of capital done from the Heineken cash to the shareholders
  - Splitting F&N into Fraser Point, a property company and keeping the drinks business in F&N.
  - Post-demerger, the property company trades at ~5 billion market cap and F&N at ~3 billion market cap.

The above demonstrates how important it is in M&A to think of the target, analyze the shareholders, possible response by the other party, keeping the deal arithmetic intact and keeping a tight control over the deal. Never allowing the price of F&N to run up and upset the applecart.

Case Study 2.13: Activision Blizzard to Acquire King Digital Entertainment for $5.9 Billion

Details:

(*Source: Activision Blizzard Press release November 2, 2015*)

King Background

King is a leading interactive entertainment company that deals with the development of casual online games since 2003. It is based in Ireland. This strategy has allowed King to create a strong, cash generative games portfolio, including its key franchises—Candy Crush®, Farm Heroes®, Bubble Witch®, and Pet Rescue®. Furthermore, in the third quarter 2015 and for the third consecutive quarter, two of the King games were among the top five grossing mobile games in the United States.

King Share Price, since IPO

Additional information

King's daily active players were relatively flat year-over-year from 138 million during Q2 2014 to 142 million during the same period in 2015. Monthly unique players, however, shrunk from 345 million in Q2 2014 to just 340 million in the last quarter.

The company also saw a significant decline in its monthly unique payers — or the people who actually pay money for in-app purchases that dropped from 10,423 million during the 3-month period ending June 30, 2014, to just 7589 million through the same period in 2015.

Activision Blizzard Background

Activision Blizzard, Inc. is the world's most successful standalone interactive entertainment company. It develops and publishes games based on some of the most beloved entertainment franchises including Call of Duty®, Destiny, Skylanders®, Guitar Hero®, World of Warcraft®, StarCraft®, Diablo®, and Hearthstone®: Heroes of Warcraft™.

Activision Blizzard also believes that it is important in its business to have strong intellectual property. They believe that King has a strong portfolio of leading intellectual property, including two of the top five highest grossing mobile games in the US (Candy Crush Saga®, Candy Crush Soda Saga™), and is one of the largest global entertainment networks with approximately half a billion monthly active users, which it believes could lead to the potential benefits for its users and further broaden its audience.

Financing of the Acquisition

The cash consideration payable by Activision Blizzard under the terms of the acquisition will be funded **from approximately US $3.6 billion of offshore cash on the balance sheet of the Activision Blizzard Group** and by an incremental term loan committed by Bank of America Merrill Lynch and Goldman Sachs Bank USA, as incremental lenders, under Activision Blizzard's existing credit agreement to the amount of US $2.3 billion.

Full payment of the Cash Consideration would involve a maximum cash payment of approximately US $5.9 billion.

Additional information

The US $3.6 billion which stands outside of USA is subject to US taxation, if brought onshore.

Transaction Value	
King Equity Value[1] @ $18 per Share	$5.9B
Less: Net Cash	0.9
Transaction Value	$5.0B

Sources	
Cash	$3.4B
New Term Loan	2.3
Rollover Unvested Equity Awards	0.2
Total sources	$5.9B

- Committed Financing
- Accretive Use of Offshore Cash

Capitalization ($ M)			
	9/30/15 ATVI	EBITDA Multiple[2]	9/30/15 Combined[3]
Cash & Investments[2]	$4,519		$2,003
Revolver ($250M)	$0		$0
Existing TLB	1,869		1,869
New Term Loan	0		2,300
Total secured debt	$1,869	1.1x	$4,169
Senior Unsecured Notes	2,250		2,250
Total Debt	$4,119	2.5x	$6,419
Net Debt	($400)	(0.2)x	$4,416
Market Capitalization[4]	$26,616	16.4x	$26,806
Total Capitalization[5]	$30,735	18.9x	$33,225
ATVI TTM Adj. EBITDA[2]	$1,626		$1,626
KING TTM Adj. EBITDA[2]			$875

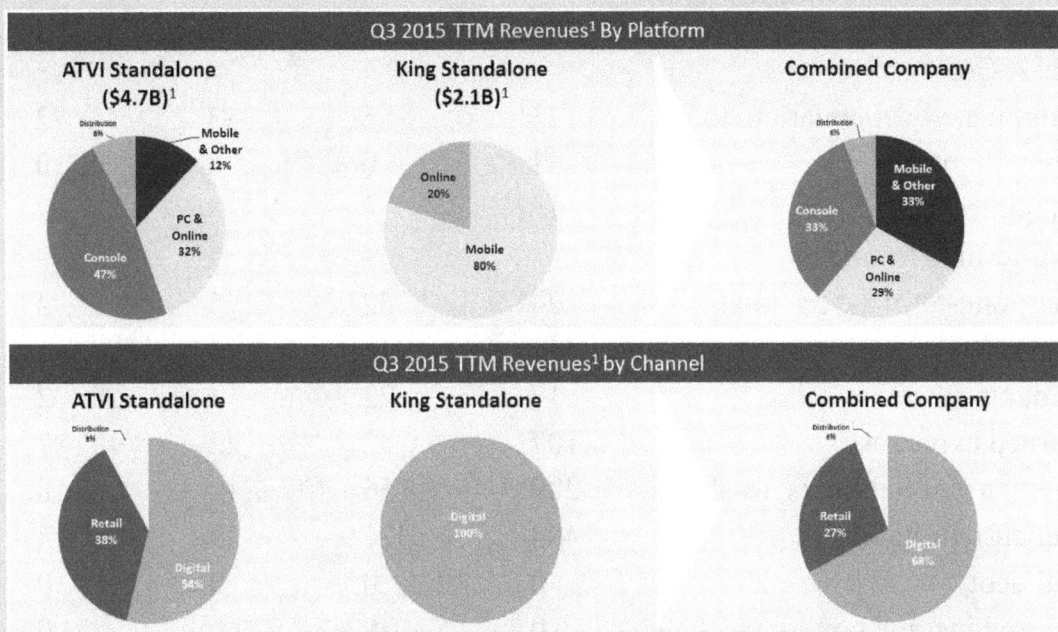

Q3 2015 TTM Revenues[1] By Platform

ATVI Standalone ($4.7B)[1] — King Standalone ($2.1B)[1] — Combined Company

Q3 2015 TTM Revenues[1] by Channel

ATVI Standalone — King Standalone — Combined Company

Kings Financials (Source:-Annual reports and filings)

In Millions of USD (except for per share items)	TTM ending 2015-09-30	12 months ending 2014-12-31	12 months ending 2013-12-31	12 months ending 2012-12-31	12 months ending 2011-12-31
Total revenue	2100	2269	1884	164	63
Operating income		735	716	11	-0
Income after tax	590	574	567	7	-1
Diluted weighted Average shares	321	320	129	128	115
Diluted EPS Excluding Extraordinary items		1	4	0	-0

TTM ended September 30, 2015, Activision Blizzard had GAAP revenues of $4.9 billion net income of $1.1 billion

In Millions of USD (except for per share items)	As of 2014-12-31	As of 2013-12-31	As of 2012-12-31	As of 2011-12-31
Cash and short-term investments	963	408	27	21
Total receivables, net	308	209	26	2
Prepaid expenses	24	13	7	4
Total current assets	1296	631	61	28

Property/plant/equipment, Total—Gross	47	20	6	3
Accumulated depreciation, total	-13	-5	-3	-2
Goodwill, net	31	0	0	0
Intangibles, net	16	9	3	2
Long-term investments	-	-	-	-
Other long-term assets, total	24	52	5	2
Total assets	1,441	811	75	35
Accounts payable	17	22	4	2
Accrued expenses	107	142	22	7
Other current liabilities, total	280	156	12	8
Total current liabilities	404	321	39	18
Total debt	0	0	0	0
Deferred income tax	0	0	0	0
Minority interest	-	-	-	-
Other liabilities, total	67	122	1	0
Total liabilities	472	444	41	18
Common stock, total	0	0	0	0
Retained earnings (accumulated deficit)	512	301	20	12
Other equity, total	456	66	13	4
Total equity	968	367	33	16
Total liabilities and shareholders' Equity	1,441	811	75	35
Total common shares outstanding	321	119	120	120

From the given case study, answer the questions that follow:

a. Discuss the origination elements given here for the buyer and seller.
b. Corporate finance rationale for listing by seller.
c. Discuss the deal quotient.
d. Refer the chapter on "Valuation" to answer the following:

   i. Given the total common shares outstanding being 721.93 (million), calculate whether the deal is accretive for Activison or not.
   ii. Comment on the quality of income statement and balance sheet of King.
   iii. Justify the price paid for acquisition by triangulating various parameters.

Case Study 2.14: GE Agrees to Sell Appliances Business

September 2014 (Press release)

GE Agrees to Sell Appliances Business to Electrolux for $3.3B

- GE's strategic focus was on the infrastructure and technology to reshape the portfolio.
- Deal valued at 8.0× EBITDA (last 12 months), gain of $0.05–$0.07 per share at closing.
- Electrolux continues the use of brand name of the GE Appliances.
- Global reach, quality, and innovation makes Electrolux the right partner for growth of GE Appliances.

GE [NYSE: GE] announced today it has signed a definitive agreement to sell its Appliances business to Electrolux for $3.3 billion. As part of the transaction, GE has entered into a long-term agreement with Electrolux to continue use of the GE Appliances brand. The transaction has been approved by the boards of directors of GE and Electrolux and remains subject to customary closing conditions and regulatory approvals, and is targeted to close in 2015.

Electrolux to Acquire GE Appliances (Press release)

AB Electrolux today announced it has entered into an agreement to acquire the appliances business of General Electric ("GE Appliances"), one of the premier manufacturers of kitchen and laundry products in the United States, for a cash consideration of USD 3.3 billion. The acquisition enhances Electrolux's position as a global player in the home appliances, offering an unparalleled opportunity to invest in innovation and growth, which will eventually lead to benefit the consumers, retailers, employees, and shareholders.

Description of GE Appliances

GE Appliances is headquartered in Louisville, Kentucky, and generates more than 90% of its revenue in North America. The company operates its own distribution and logistics network and has nine well-invested manufacturing facilities with over 12,000 employees.

Proforma financials

The proforma combines the 2013 sales figure for Electrolux and GE Appliances which is USD 22.5 billion (SEK 147 billion) and EBITDA is USD 1.5 billion (SEK 9.7 billion). Electrolux and GE Appliances together have 73,000 employees.

Key financials 2013 (before synergies):

USD billion	Electrolux	GE Appliances incl. 48.4% of Mabe	Combined
Sales	16.8	5.7	22.5
EBITDA	1.1	0.4	1.5
EBITDA margin, %	*6.8*	*6.8*	*6.8*

The above figures are for illustrative purposes and do not include any impact from synergies, implementation costs, and amortization of surplus values resulting from the purchase price allocation.

The effect of the transaction on Electrolux's earnings per share is expected to be accretive from year one. The EBITDA multiple for the full year 2014 is expected to be in the range of 7.0–7.3×.

The transaction is expected to contribute positively to the cash flow. The financial position of Electrolux, after completion of the planned rights issue, is expected to be consistent with a financial policy to retain an investment grade credit rating.

December 2015 (Press release)

GE terminates the deal with Electrolux due to opposition from Department of Justice due to anti-trust issues. GE received $175 million from Electrolux as termination fees.

January 2016 (GE Press release)

GE Agrees to Sell Appliances Business to Haier Co., Ltd. for $5.4 billion.

- Deal valued at 10× EBITDA (last 12 months), gain of approximately $0.20 per share at closing.
- Haier will continue to use the name of the GE Appliances brand

FAIRFIELD, Conn. (BUSINESS WIRE) GE announced today it has signed a definitive agreement to sell its Appliances business to Qingdao Haier Co., Ltd. ("Haier") for an amount of $5.4 billion.

The transaction values GE Appliances at 10 times the earnings before interest, taxes, depreciation, and amortization of the last 12 months. As part of the transaction, GE has entered into a long-term agreement with Haier to continue use of the GE Appliances brand. Louisville will remain the headquarters for GE Appliances.

Haier has a good track record of acquisitions and of managing brands. Haier has a stated focus to grow in the US, to build their manufacturing presence here, and to invest further in the business. Innovation, new product introduction and brand management are fundamental to their overall strategy. GE Appliances provides Haier with great products, state-of-the-art manufacturing facilities, and a talented team. In addition, it was also stated "we see the opportunity to work together to build the GE brand in China."

Additional information

As a part of the acquisition, GE will receive a cash consideration from Qingdao Haier of $5.4 billion. The transaction is structured primarily as an asset purchase. Net of certain expected benefits, the transaction value represents an 8.2× multiple based on GE Appliances' estimated 2015 EBITDA, which was up nearly 50% from levels 2 years ago, according to a news release from Haier.

GE had been trying to sell this business, since 2008. Lately, due to pressure from activist investor, it has been trying hard to sell non-core divisions.

About Haier

Haier is the world's leading home appliance provider with global revenues of $32.6 billion and profits of $2.40 billion in 2014.

In recent years, Haier has bought New Zealand's Fisher & Paykel Appliances ($ 766 million) and Japan's Sanyo Electronics ($130 million).

The purchase of GE appliances business will make it #2 in the US market after Whirlpool.

Questions to be answered:

a. In light of the effective acquisitions discussed in Chapter III, discuss the acquisitions by Electrolux and Haier. How are they similar or different?
b. Looking at the proforma financials put forward by Electrolux, what are the reasons due to which the deal is accretive from Year 1? (refer to chapter on Valuation and Regulatory considerations).
c. Discuss the origination elements for GE, Electrolux, and Haier in light of the origination elements discussed in Chapter I.
d. Could Electrolux have negotiated the termination clause better? Do you agree with the termination fee being payable by Electrolux?
e. Discuss if Haier could have negotiated the deal better (refer to the chapter on Negotiations).
f. Is Haier justified in increasing the acquisition multiple due to 50% jump in profits of GE appliances in last 2 years. Discuss (refer to the chapter on Valuation).

2.11 Executive Summary

The key lessons learnt in the above chapter include that good buyers succeed because they are organized and have institutionalized discipline. They make it an integral part of their strategies and support M&A just as they would in any other core department. Do not treat M&A teams as from outer planet, they should also be staffed with balanced personnel with good mix of strategic, financial, and operational background. These are the people who can best assess the quality of the target and will be responsible for the newly acquired firm.

Thus, the corporates need to build a good experienced deal team which will serve as M&A repository of knowledge acquired in deals, who will evaluate all deals done and not done, to upgrade their knowledge and process. The M&A team should be held responsible for the integration as they are for acquisition, this would ensure ownership of the acquisition.

The financial aspect of deal making that is needed to be ensured is whether the risk has been adequately discounted. Focus on smaller deals <10% of the buyer's size, especially firms which will give bootstrap effect. Avoid multiplying financial risk × operational risk, try to keep the balance sheet flexibility. However, it is hard to predict cycles, but strive to buy low and sell high. Given the difficulty in predicting cycles, the valuation is arrived at after triangulating all the valuation metrics and arrived at price which would minimize risk and enhance return.

Also, avoid "deal fever." Be prepared to walk away from a bad deal and set a walk-away price.

Finally, move away from all melee, take a cold shower, and ask the question.

What If the Deal Fails?

Hand on heart, it should tell you the answer whether to or not to acquire.

3

M&A Strategies and Processes

Contents

3.1 Introduction

Preparation, Preparation

"A victorious army wins its victories, before seeking battle."

Sun Tsu, The Art of War

For a successful M&A strategy, whether buy side or sell side, the key is to be better prepared and have coherent strategy to execute the deal so as to create value. One of the main reasons why the success rate is low in M&A is due to lack of preparation and ad-hoc decision-making.

We can have a look at how few of the companies define their M&A strategy, which is good for understanding of students of the subject to state down as criteria because several M&A strategies defined by the CEO's centers around the deal size or revenue targets.

Defining Acquisition Cornerstones:

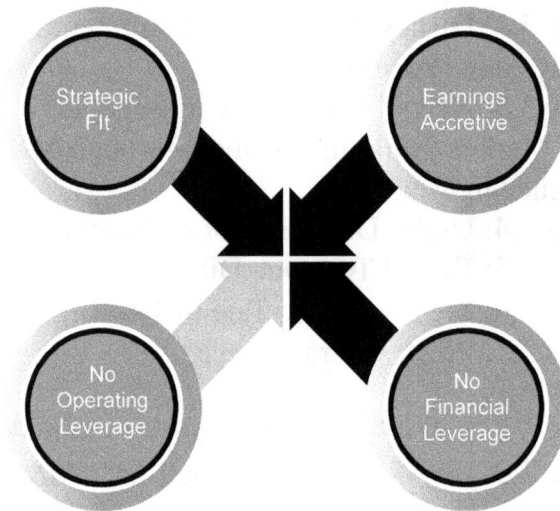

1. They must match company's business strategy.
2. They must be accretive to earnings within a reasonable period of time.
3. They must not jeopardize capital ratios or impair asset quality.
4. They must not present undue operating risk.

CFO Statement on Acquisitions

"It's an incredibly powerful discipline to put in place a rule of thumb (must have) that deals have to be accretive within some (specific) period of time. The rule of thumb states that it has to be accretive within the first twelve months, in terms of Earnings Per Share and it has to reach our capital rate of return, which is over 20 percent return within three to four years."

On analyzing the above statements, we realize the coherence and the strong emphasis on returns and the alignment being maintained with the balance sheet of the company.

It is pertinent to note the criteria which put the matching of company's business strategy as the stepping stone into the financial criteria's for acquisition and not the other way round. Unlike, what we are currently experiencing due to cheap liquidity the financial criteria becomes stepping stone for acquisition. This is making it cheaper for company to borrow bigger size companies and then match business strategy to showing financially engineered accretion to EPS.

3.2 Buy-Side Merger & Acquisition

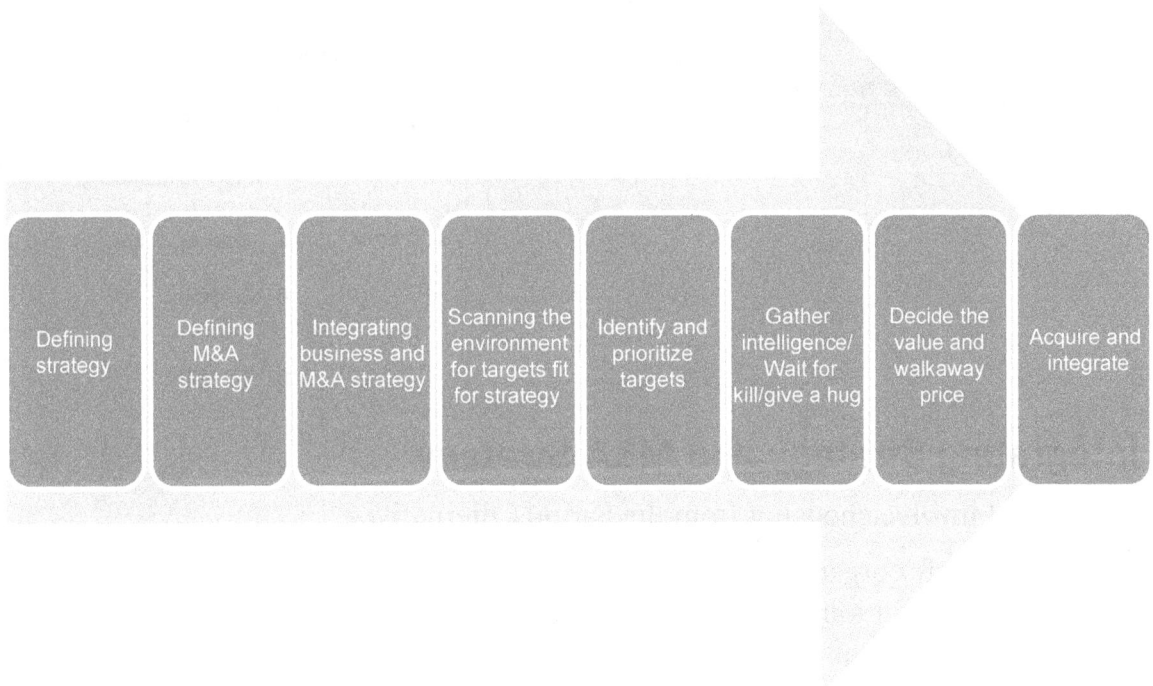

Defining strategy	Defining M&A strategy	Integrating business and M&A strategy	Scanning the environment for targets fit for strategy	Identify and prioritize targets	Gather intelligence/ Wait for kill/give a hug	Decide the value and walkaway price	Acquire and integrate

Let us move to analyze buy-side targets and how the process can be undertaken and use of finance to play around with possible value consideration to acquire the target business.

Defining strategy

This would involve laying down the missions and objective by doing Political, Economic, Social, and Technological (PEST) analysis, which will provide external scanning, Strength, Weakness, Opportunities, and Threat (SWOT) analysis, which will provide internal scanning.

This will lead to the strategic options that will be on the drawing board. Part of these would be organic and part of it would be inorganic.

Defining M&A Strategy

Based on the strategy definition and the laid out objective, one can formulate the M&A strategy. The M&A strategy could involve:

- Which business to grow
- Which skill-sets to be acquired
- Backward or forward integration
- What geographies to target
- What is the size of acquisitions in absolute term and relative to the acquirer

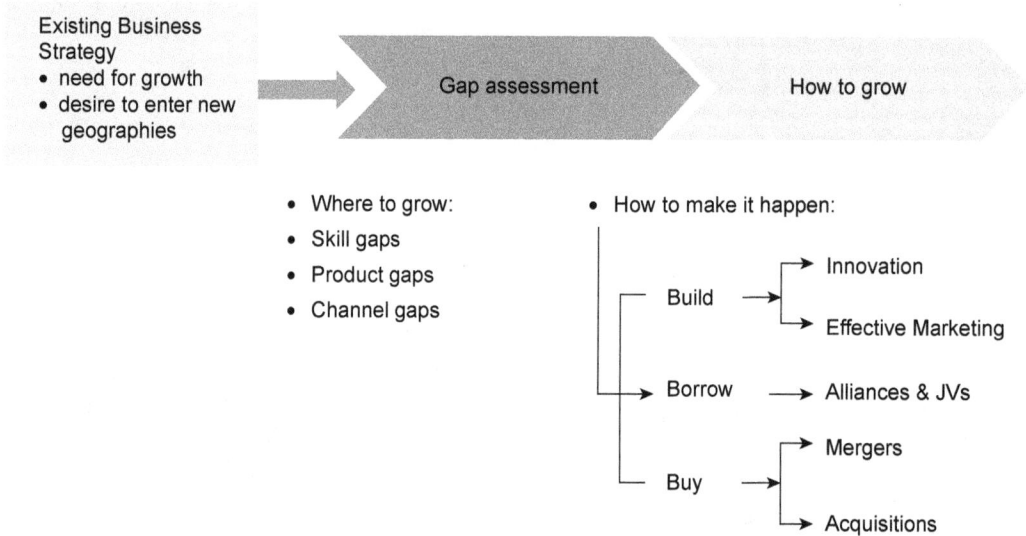

Integrating Strategy and M&A Strategy

This would involve choosing from the various alternatives:

- Build—go for organic growth
- Borrow—go for joint venture or alliances
- Buy—go for acquisition

The M&A strategy is a subset of the overall strategy that needs to be executed with precision due to the high risk involved to suit the strategic objective laid down by the management.

Scanning the Environment to Fit in the Strategy

The merging of company and M&A strategy leads to the scanning of the environment for the opportunities to execute the M&A strategy.

Identify the Possible Targets

Based on the above scanning, identify the possible targets and road map how they would fit into the company's and M&A strategy attributing value based on strategy fit and synergy attribution.

Ranking them with Feasibility and Probability

Based on the value attribution, we arrive at ranking of the targets and the probability of acquiring them.

Start Building up Intelligence

This would involve finding the various stakeholders *viz.*

- Founders
- Significant minority
- Dispersion of shareholding
- Free float
- Directors
- Key Management personnel
- CEO, CFO, CMO
- Board dynamics and thought leaders
- Labor unions
- Distributors
- Monopoly laws
- Government and politics quotient if the acquisition was announced
- Media reaction
- Key rival bidders and their reactions
- Key legal obstacles and open offer obligations

Wait for the Kill

This could be based on timing the acquisition which could be any one (not exhaustive) of the following:

- Fall in market value
- Founders in distress
- Significant minority stake up for sale
- Split in controlling shareholder
- Change in regulatory scenario
- CEO wants to exercise golden parachute rather than work for organic growth

Give a Hug

Always try to do deals on bilateral basis and in congenial atmosphere, if and only if, no longer possible to have a friendly deal then go for a bear hug, armed with full intelligence on the stakeholders.

Decide the Value and Walk-Away Price

It is important to decide the price which discounts the risk involved in the acquisition and put in a walk-away price rather than take the winners, curse by trying to win the auction but lose the war.

Acquire and Integrate

The biggest challenge and least focused aspect of M&A is integration plan. Integration plan needs to be well-defined with clear responsibilities and incentives. The management incentives should be linked to integration and not to just acquisition.

The above can only emanate with solid corporate finance team built up from core finance as well as operational background team. Teams should include personnel who can strategize, identify opportunities, map out synergies, and execute the transaction which makes us win half of the game.

The other half being ability to create enough managerial resources bench strength to take on the integration of the target and move toward quick grasp of the target. The key decisions to be taken post-acquisition should be formalized beforehand including clarity on the operational matters which are crucial for the success of the organization.

Transformational deals are appealing, but they carry high risk and are hard to achieve success. Thus, to improve the probability of success, we need to tick the following boxes:

- Familiar industry or business
- Experience of doing business in that geography or is from similar geography as acquirer
- Achieve best fit in terms of size of the target, skill-sets, and labor. Do not under estimate these elements.

Case study 3.1: Integrating Business Strategy and M&A Strategy

M&A Strategy: Hindustan Lever

Food, Personal care

1998 onward
International best foods, Modern bakery, Rosell tea, Captain cook

1996
Merger of all Lever cos
Buyout of Lakme

1995
JV Kimberly-Clark (baby & woman care)
Lakme (cosmetics)

1994
:Kwality ice cream
:Acquisition of Tata oil mills (Hamam)

1993:
Kisan (jams and ketchup)
Cadbury (gollops ice cream)

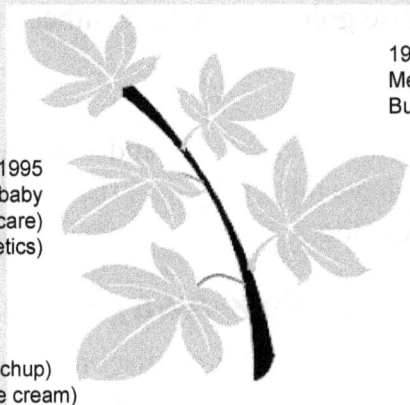

Details

Hindustan Lever was the pioneer in M&A landscape in liberalized India.

Defining strategy

Hindustan lever decided to take advantage of the business opportunities after the 1991 reforms.

It identified that Food and Personal care has the thrust area and relied on both organic and inorganic growth for the said purpose.

Defining M&A strategy

Priority was given to inorganic growth, and series of acquisitions were done to plug the product gap.

Integrating strategy and M&A strategy

Hindustan Lever upon deciding the space of Food and personal care initiated environmental scan to integrate them into the strategy. They picked on the following probable targets, ranked them based on intelligence, and went about acquiring in measured manner with reasonable valuation and frequency between acquisitions.

Target	Brand	Current Status
Tata Oil Mills soap	Hamam	300-crore brand
Kwality and Cadbury ice cream	Kwality walls	Leading ice cream brand
Kissan Jams and Ketchupa	Kissan Annapurna	Leading brand in jam and ketchup
Lakme cosmetics	Lakme	Leading cosmetic brand

Acquire and Integrate

It was one of the first corporate to engage into the exercise of consolidating the entire business under one roof and merged the following entities into Hindustan Lever, which we know today.

- Brooke bond
- Lipton India
- Ponds

The rationale for the inorganic growth was to acquire under-penetrated brands. Thereafter, gain the market share in an arena that was rapidly opening up and turning hyper-competitive and then use the new-found domination to cut supplier costs and hold margins.

It kept the distribution and the marketing might of Hindustan Lever behind the acquisition and made them successful. Most of their acquisitions could be termed as success barring one or two. The key reason could be attributed to putting adequate resources from top to bottom behind each of this acquisitions, so as to make them successful.

Key Learning

The above case highlights the top-down approach to acquisition. Defining the space in which they would like to thrust the inorganic growth in line with their ability to leverage their marketing and distribution capabilities.

The acquisitions have been of size that was within their financial and operational capabilities and incidental to their line of business.

The acquisitions were not parallel, but sequential new acquisition can presume only after integration of the prior acquisition.

The coherence in the business strategy and the acquired businesses is pretty apparent. The timing of acquisitions is critical as observed. Hindustan Lever virtually went absent post-year 2000 in the M&A market. It picked up businesses prior to year 2000 when they were of decent size and at reasonable valuations.

It can be said that Hindustan Lever introduced M&A to the Indian markets. It seized on the shedding-off non-core business pronouncements of Tata group, when Ratan Tata took over the reins of Tata Empire. They acquired the ailing Tata Oil Mills and made it a success as also picked up the cosmetic brand Lakme and took it to new heights, thus giving us the glimpse of the integration capabilities of Hindustan Lever.

Inspired from Hindustan Lever, quite a few companies entered the M&A space which made acquisitions unrealistic at reasonable valuations and we saw HLLs retreat from that market.

They did not have any big bang acquisition or any transformational diversification of its business, despite facing growth issues in the last few years. Although it introduced M&A to Indian, corporates only a few could imbibe the integration capabilities of Hindustan Lever, especially the need for coherence, the quality of acquisitions, reasonable valuations, and having the managerial resources to integrate and turnaround businesses.

3.3 Operational Strategies Post-Acquisition

Let us look into the ticklish operational matters that do not receive much consideration and end up being milestone around the neck.

Key management personnel: CEO, CFO, marketing, human resources needs to be evaluated beforehand, and swift action should be taken as soon as the acquisition is completed with the backup plan.

Many a times, the acquirer feels that they will benefit by keeping the old guard in the target company. While the idea seems sound in theory, the practicality of it is that the old guards fail to realize the new master and continue with building their fiefdoms. The insecurity of new master makes them being more destructive than constructive, obstructing decision-making. This adds to the confusion of the second line and transforms it into a WE v/s THEY battle. Although painful, it is suited best to put a new team in place who are well-briefed about their task and responsibility. This makes it clear to the underlying personnel, the authority, and reporting lines. There may be some loss due to discontinuity but is a swifter resolution than down the line when it becomes a more painful problem.

Dismantling structures which contributed to inefficiencies

- Perks of the executives not linked to performance
- Non-productive assets
- Flattening the organization structures
- Changing the distribution or dealership structure or the incentive structure
- Moving offices and manufacturing locations from high cost to low cost
- Deciding on branding
  - ☒ Whether to use existing brand
  - ☒ Whether to kill the existing brands
  - ☒ Whether to co-brand
  - ☒ Orderly phase out of the brands

Deciding on organization structures

Softer issue but important from psychology point of view is the naming of combined entity or acquired entity—whether you want to keep the existing ones or rename it with the acquiring entity.

When Holcim acquired ACC and Gujarat Ambuja, they did not change the brand name to Holcim, rather preferred to continue with the same names. This could be to quell xenophobia about foreigner acquiring big Indian assets. Only down the line, they were re-branded.

DSP Merrill Lynch Ltd. was also not renamed, so that they do not lose the focus due to softer issue on naming of the organization. It keeps the seller happy if the legacy is continued in the name.

Arcelor-Mittal is also one of the prime examples of quelling opposition of government, public, and media to across the border takeover.

Cleaning up the Books

Getting audits done for stocks, payables, receivables, key accounts. Writing-off assets aggressively to initiate a clean start. A bitter medicine but it does not sweep the problems under the carpet. The focus should not be on the stock price or markets or the reaction to immediate write-off, whether it will create bad press or evaluation but, will it help in later stage to enhance the quality of the acquisition.

Communicating and winning small battles rather than fighting big wars

Resolving conflicts in terms of:

- Reporting lines
- Cultural issues especially, in cross-border
- Merging structures and to eliminate pay inequalities
- Merging offices and manufacturing locations at common sites.

The following case study represents the entire cycle from acquisition to integration resulting in tremendous value creation.

Case Study 3.2: Disney Acquisitions – Integration – Value creation

Details

Disney has acquired a string of strong animation intellectual property in the past 5–6 years. The acquisition has been done of properties which could be leveraged over the Disney network and the ability to successfully monetize and mint those properties beyond the acquisition values.

The below slides give details about the coherence of acquisition and the business strategy of Disney. It also reflects the strong integration achieved by it.

Acquisition thoughts

Igor, CEO of Disney, said the importance of Pixar became clear during opening ceremonies for Hong Kong Disneyland in September 2005

He noticed many characters from Pixar films featured in the kickoff parade. But there was nothing from Disney's recent animated movies, whose latest characters weren't popular.

Acquisition coherence

Pixar	2006: Acquisition for $7.4 billion
Marvel	2009: Acquisition for $4 billion
Star wars	2012: Acquisition for $4 billion

Acquisition Effect

Box office collection > $6 billion (cars, Toy story, Inside out)

Marval has released three films that have topped $2 billion at the box office: "The Avengers ," "Iron Man 3" and "Avengers: Age Ultron."

$2 billion expected sales from latestflick

Rules the box office

Showcasing a picture

- # 2 Movie studio
- Profits of $7.5 billion last fy dwarfs all others in the Industry
- #1 in managing intellectual property (movies & merchandizing)
- Market cap $186 billion
- Stock price has more than quadrupled

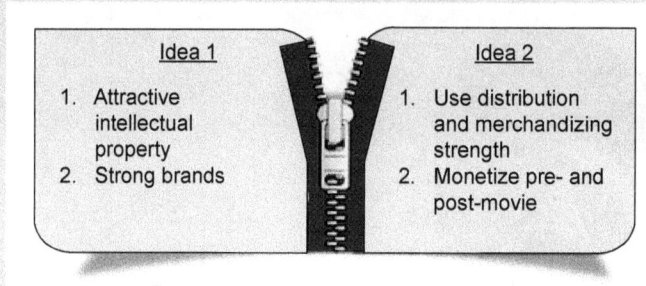

Combining two ideas

Idea 1	Idea 2
1. Attractive intellectual property 2. Strong brands	1. Use distribution and merchandizing strength 2. Monetize pre- and post-movie

Focus on assets, innovate and improve

Ideas fitting into each other

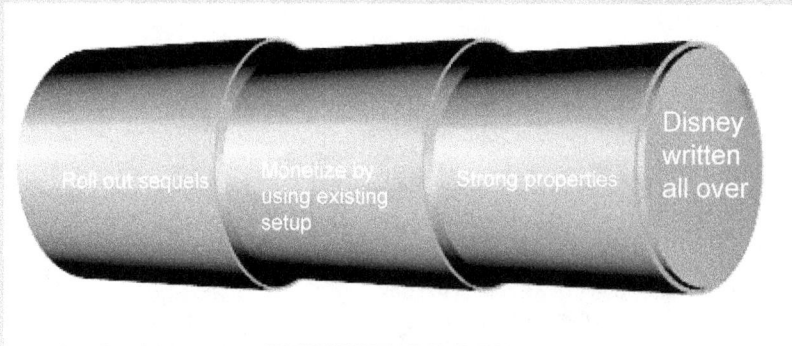

Roll out sequels · Monetize by using existing setup · Strong properties · Disney written all over

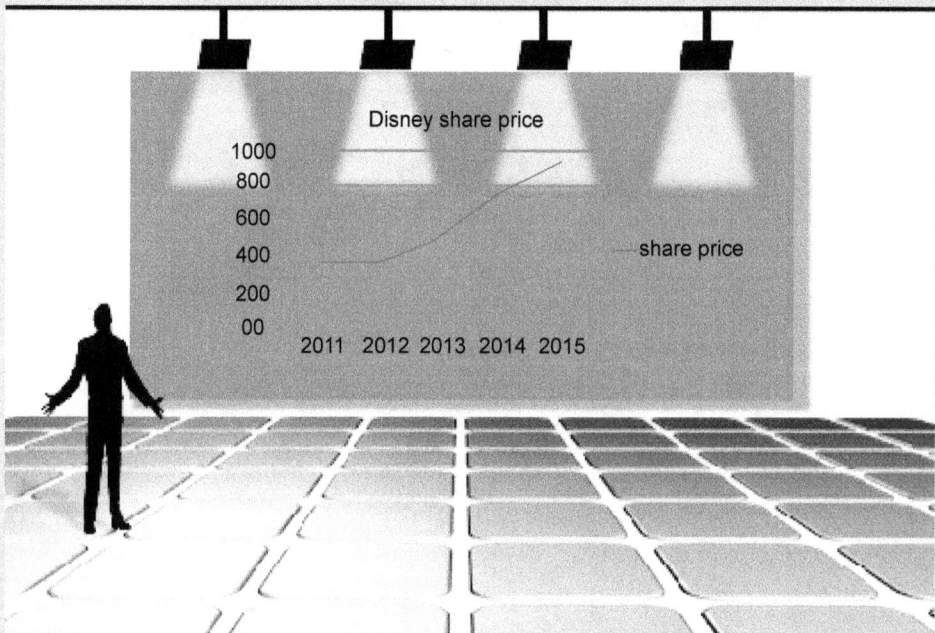

Disney share price

share price

Key Learning

This case teaches the single-minded focus on the type of properties to be acquired. How they will fit into the business strategy alongside acquisition price that will fit into expected return on investment. The different ways in which the acquired assets have been minted and monetized teach us the effective integration achieved.

3.4 Typical Buy-Side Process

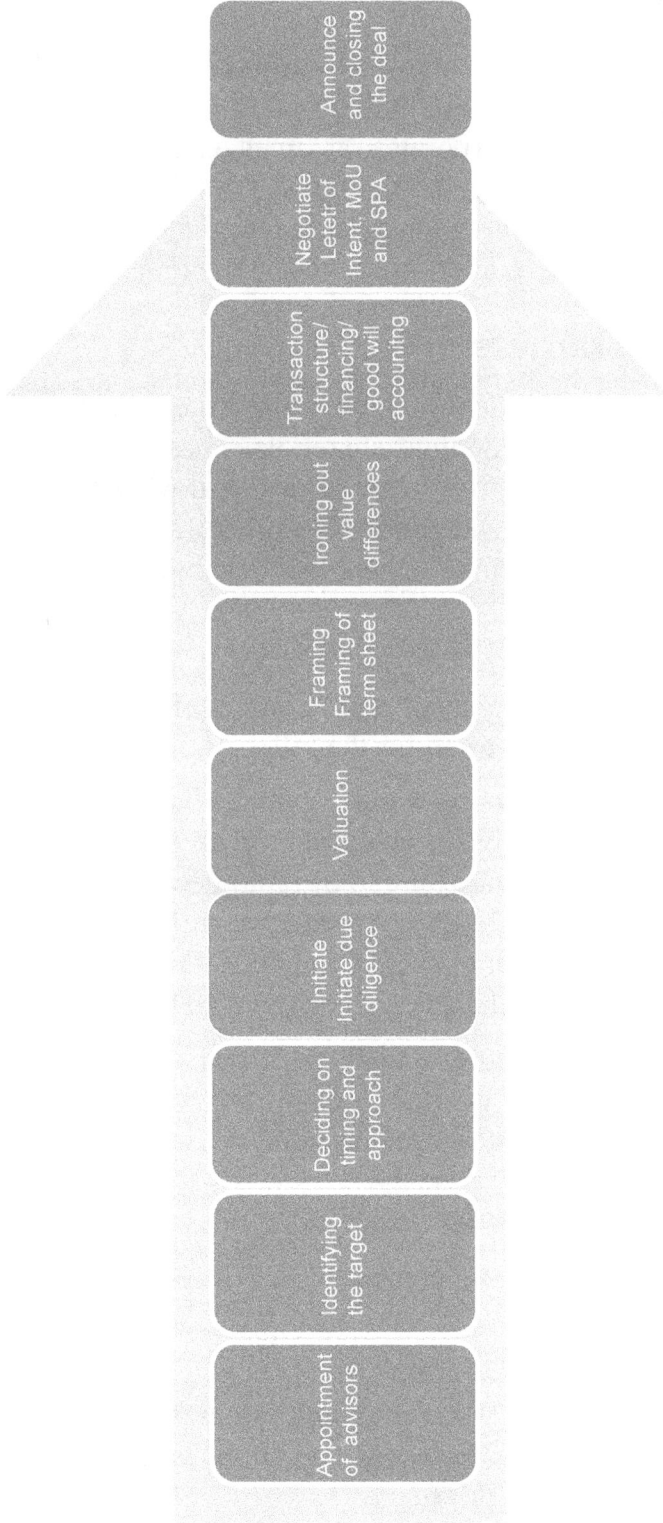

Appointment of advisors → Identifying the target → Deciding on timing and approach → Initiate Initiate due diligence → Valuation → Framing Framing of term sheet → Ironing out value differences → Transaction structure/ financing/ good will accounitng → Negotiate Letetr of Intent, MoU and SPA → Announce and closing the deal

Buy-Side Process

Appointment of advisors

The appointment of right advisors for the process is critical. There is a growing trend that investment bankers are not critical to the process and the corporates can handle it themselves. The corporates, at times, can be conflicted or lack the market expertise to close and execute the transaction. Thus, having the right advisors becomes critical to originate, execute, and close the transaction. The fees should be negotiated carefully to have appropriate incentivization in place.

Identifying the targets

This step involves not only identification of the targets and their business intricacies, but the intelligence to include their shareholder base also, i.e., the composition of the board of directors. The probability of deal and what can make the deal happen should also be taken into consideration. The other issues include regulatory environment and feasibility of clearing the potential deal breakers.

Deciding on timing and approach

There may be times when the hand will be forced. There may be times wherein the timing can be chosen, when to go for the kill.

In terms of approach, friendly overtures are the best. The communication if it can be handled at the decision-maker levels can break the ice much better. Whatsapp–Facebook deal is an excellent example of rapid decision-making. Even in the case of Arcelor-Mittal, the folklore goes that Laxmi Mittal made phone call to the CEO of Arecllor who was in midst of flight catching. While the contact was right but the timing could have been much better which resulted in sustained hostile deal.

Only when friendly overtures fail, Plan B can be activated which can include bringing in market makers, buying blocks in market, proxy war, etc. The aspects which are critical in hostile deal are discussed in the chapter on "hostile offers."

To initiate due diligence

We have discussed the type and content of due diligence in detail in other section .

Valuation

This step includes arriving at the range of values based on the due diligence and using various methodologies, to triangulate all the values to arrive at the sweet spot that could be the walk-away price.

Try to see how to mitigate the risk of higher price by use of structures he nudged to pay higher price than the walk-away price

Letter of intent and term sheet

The legal sanctity of such documents is doubtful, but it lays down the framework to which parties will adhere to and help drive the negotiation as well as forms the basis for drawing up of the formal agreements.

Ironing out the value differences

This would involve negotiation on the valuation as well as would involve seeking representation and warranties to support the valuation from either side.

Getting transaction structure, financing, and goodwill accounting in place

This will involve in practical sense structuring of the transaction depending on the type of accounting allowed for merger and can help engineer the EPS of combined entity that the acquirer wishes to achieve. This is to get the moneybags lined up so that the covenants on escrow can be met as well as be prepared for hostility.

Drafting and finalizing the agreements

These are formal agreements drawn from the term sheet. Special care needs to be taken to make it actual reflection of the intent of the parties.

Announcing the deal

Announcing the deal with press releases carrying the right kind of detail and information is critical. The timing of announcement is also crucial to allow the acquirer to make the announcement as well as move in to acquire shares on the market or outwit the competition.

Closing the deal

It involves the execution of the acquisition including getting various approvals, making open offers, and completing the formalities of share transfer.

Case Study 3.3: News Corp's Entry into Indian Television Market: Building Business through M&A

Details

Rupert Murdoch is one of the leading M&A stalwarts having used M&A as a tool to grow its business.

Let us look at the entire buy-side process in the M&A strategy employed by Rupert Mudroch's News Corp to enter into the Indian television market and acquire leadership position.

Vehicle Acquisition

The entry into the Indian market was through vehicle acquisition by buying Star TV from Li-Ka-Shing in 1990s to gain entry into the Indian market. During this time, Star TV had an agreement with Zee TV, which allowed Zee to use Star's airtime rights to telecast Hindi channels.

Star TV inherited this agreement, but Zee barred Star TV from telecasting Hindi programs. Knowing that the Indian TV audience was largely Hindi, they started bickering and eventually broke the agreement with Zee TV and started looking out for Hindi content.

Content Acquisition

Star TV initially plodded but could not make much advancement with the Hindi content. To acquire superior Hindi content, it decided to invest into Balaji Telefilms and acquire 26% stake to attain negative rights over the Company and first right of refusal over all the content being generated by Balaji. Balaji Telefilms was a leading Hindi content producer in the prime time slot specialized in the Saas-bahu genre serials.

It followed it up with acquisition of Star Vijay and Asianet channel to gain entries in other Indian markets.

Distribution Acquisition

To gain control over the distribution, it again picked up 26% stake of Hathway Cable, a leading provider of content through cable. But, given that it could only be a minority in this setup and cable would be too demanding and challenging.

Star India and M&A

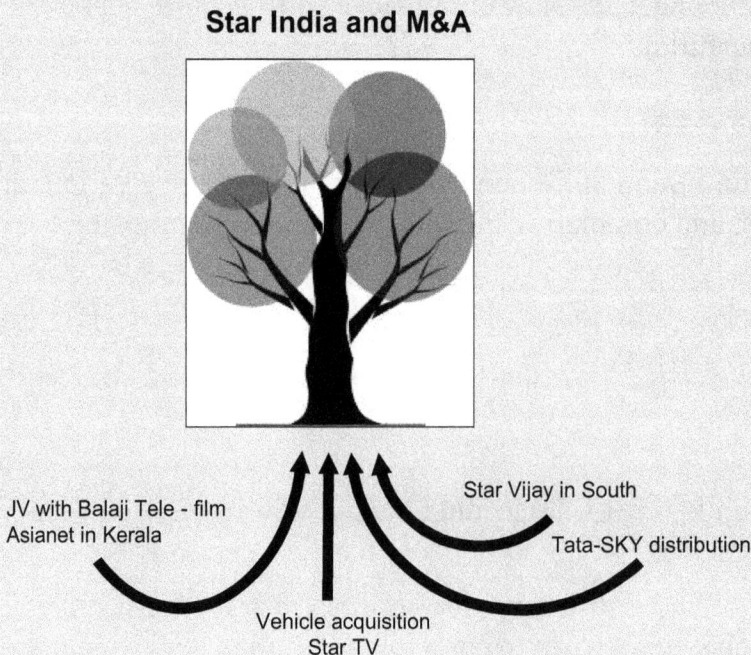

JV with Balaji Tele - film
Asianet in Kerala

Star Vijay in South

Tata-SKY distribution

Vehicle acquisition
Star TV

Further, it went on to have DTH distribution, by getting into joint venture with Tata's, who were there for fulfilling the regulatory requirement and face which would make it easy to get regulatory approval but operationally the control rested with Star. Tata Sky emerged as the leading provider in the DTH mode.

Key Learning

Through these studies, we have made an attempt to elucidate the way to go about integrating strategy and looking for targets that will deliver the strategy. Star India represents a perfect model wherein the entry and setup in India has been M&A driven and then the operations have been fortified after getting strong roots into the Indian television market.

It represents the entire buy-side process starting from identifying targets to discussing and negotiating the right clauses in the agreements that will fit the business strategy and filling in with the right structures to successful acquire and build business.

Let us now dive deep into the framework within which we shall do the due diligence and then evaluate the feasibility of the M&A.

Once this stage is crossed, we can move to basic and advanced due diligence.

3.5 Due Diligence in M&A

The trap awaiting us

Due diligence is central to decision-making

Let us now, move ahead to due diligence aspects and the ways to avoid traps. The case studies highlight the traps and how to side step them.

Basic due diligence

- Why is the owner exiting
- Is it peak valuation exit
- Is this business for me

- Are my assumptions sound enough
- Finally, WHAT IF,,, the acquisition does not work out

Advance due diligence

- What is the state and stage of industry
- What are the drivers for growth and the profitability or the margins? This will help in the identification of drivers merit, close look, and their sustainability for the future.
- What is the X-factor in business?
- What is being bought through the company:

  - Brands
  - Distributorship
  - License
  - Entry through Brownfield expansion in foreign country or new business line
  - Customer contracts
  - Employees
  - Manufacturing facility
  - Balance sheet
  - Co-opting competition
  - Killing competition

The above parameters assist in identifying the efficacy of acquisition, the price, and what's really being bought or are there alternatives to reach the objective.

Boot Camp Due Diligence

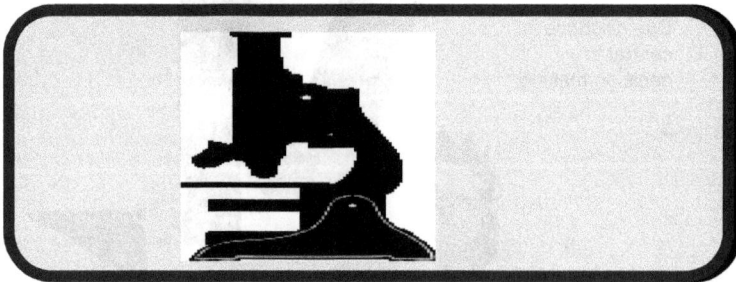

- Talk to existing customers, suppliers, and vendors about their relationships with the business.
- Speak to ex-employees, if possible.
- Put a big emphasis on the past earnings history and its financial statements. The radical departure from the financial statements for future projections should have sound justification.
- Balance sheets, income statements, cash flow statements, footnotes, and tax returns for the past 3 years are all key indicators of a business's health.

- Prepare a co-ordinated plan for going through data room. Employ experts, but only for expert opinion.
- The ground-level digging is performed by the operating team. The operating team should be capable enough to kick the tyre and check inside the hood whether everything is in order.

Peeling Onion

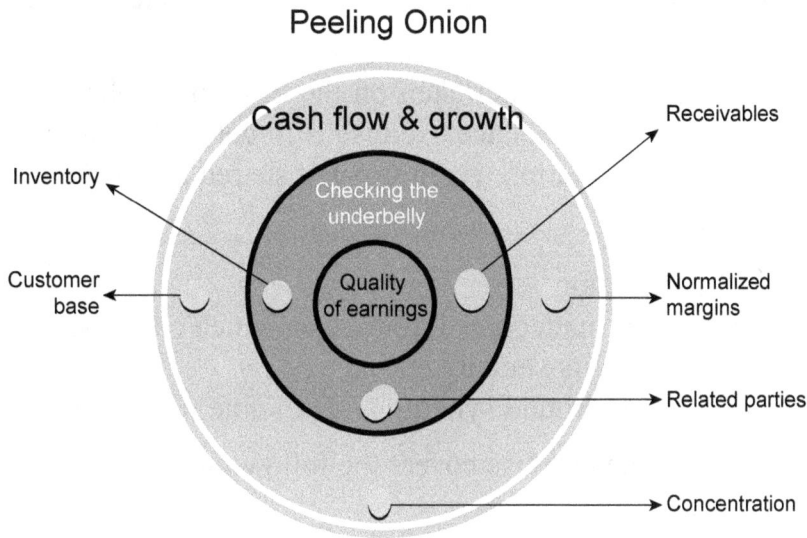

The above diagram depicts the peeling of iron to ascertain the quality of earnings and the assets. The key to earning quality is through the quality of the balance sheet reflected in the assets and liabilities.

When we look at the balance sheet, the key is the working capital. The working capital represents the core of a company. If the core of the Company is good, then the capital structure of the Company will reflect a rosy picture.
Therefore, special attention needs to be paid to:

- Inventory, whether it is in-line with the revenues and the industry
- Receivables, ageing of receivable, and the trend in ageing. Will help identify whether revenues are getting jacked up
- Payables, whether the payables as reflected in the balance sheet is due to bargaining power of the company or whether it is a cash flow problem.

The other aspects that need attention include:

- Transaction of related parties: Is it creating an abstract picture and masking financial issues.
- Customer base and concentration: Whether there is product, customer, or geographic concentration.
- What is the normalized margin: Is it a peak cycle margin or trough cycle margin.

The outcome of the above two areas is the quality of cash flow and the growth being reflected. This reflection allows the buyer to take right decision in terms of buying as well as covering the weak areas in the form of indemnities, representations, and warranties.

Financial Due Diligence

Due diligence is a fact finding exercise to submit a bid or it can be described as an exercise undertaken to validate the bid submitted under "Letter of Intent" or "Memorandum of Exercise."

The preliminary exercise is undertaken on the basis of publicly available information. The subsequent due diligence exercise is to get to the source of that public information as well as information which was not shared or private in nature.

Due diligence establishes:

- Correctness of information
- Gaps in information or inadequate information which could be subject of representation from seller on its veracity
- Validate the hypothesis around synergy and possible valuation

The financial due diligence exercise covers the following areas:

- Corporate records
- Financial and tax information
- Indebtedness
- Employment and labor matters
- Real property
- Personal property
- Trademark and intellectual property
- Agreements
- Supplier and customer information
- Compliance with law and information

Further, it may include other documents which are pertinent to the functioning of the business.

In case of failed deal, it is always asked was not there a due diligence? Rather lot of deals have got blown up very soon, after they have been negotiated or to be negotiated.

This begets the question what is due diligence? Is it a science? Is it an art? Or a combination of both?

Due diligence in M&A cannot be copybook checklist that needs to be ticked-off. In context with each acquisition, the areas of focus and attention need to be carefully circled. A due diligence team consisting of personnel from cross-sectional functional areas, corporate finance team, bankers, and accountants will ensure due diligence else, just relying on external agencies report may lead to deficient due diligence and has potential to blow up the deal.

Due diligence has to be wary of the following pitfall:

- Spike in revenues and profits
- Gap in profit and cash flow
- Outlier from industry

- Take a pause from deal fever
- Don't get over-confident
- Don't fall for tight deadlines

- Crossing the t's and dotting the i
- Use right mix of personnel

An investigative eye should be able to pick up tell-tale signs of danger or weak areas.

Indicators of Earnings Quality

Sr. No.	Indicators	Implication
1.	Conservative revenue recognition methods are implied.	This would mean the revenue is closely tracking the cash flow. Aggressive accounting reflects presence of a big gap between profits and operating cash flow.
2.	Bad debt reserves high relative to receivables and past credit losses.	This means the credit losses can be well-absorbed as well as reflects management quality in terms of business conservatism.
3.	Use of accelerated depreciation methods and short lives.	This would mean the management is choosing cash flow over profits. Thus, acts as an indicator of management quality.
4.	Rapid write-off of acquisition goodwill and other intangibles.	Same as above.
5.	Minimal capitalization of interest and overhead.	It again means that there is no deferment of actual expenses by capitalizing the interest and overhead. Thus, the financial statement reflects the actual state of the affairs of the company.

(*Continued*)

6.	Expensing startup costs of new operations.	Same as above.
7.	Adequate provisions for lawsuits and other loss contingencies.	This means losses can be absorbed from potential liabilities.
8.	Conservative assumptions in employee benefit plans.	This means there is no deferment of actual expenses by conservative assumption. Thus, the financial statement reflects the actual state of the affairs of the company.
9.	Minimal use of off-balance sheet financing techniques.	No hidden liabilities.
10.	Absence of non-recurring one-time gains.	No props to the profits of the company.
11.	Absence of non-cash earnings.	No props to the profits of the company.
12.	Clear and adequate disclosures.	Helps understand the financial and business state of the company and indicates the quality of the management and business.

The conditions opposite to the above represent bad earnings quality like deferral of expenditure, deferral of cost or unrecorded stock compensation costs, or recognition of deferred tax asset which reduces tax expenses and increases profit. Several changes and alternating between accounting policies as well as alternating between write-off and write back indicate the need for deeper plunge into the financial statements. Additionally, the following red flags will also necessitate an in-depth analysis.

Revenues, earnings, and cash flows—when red flag shows up?

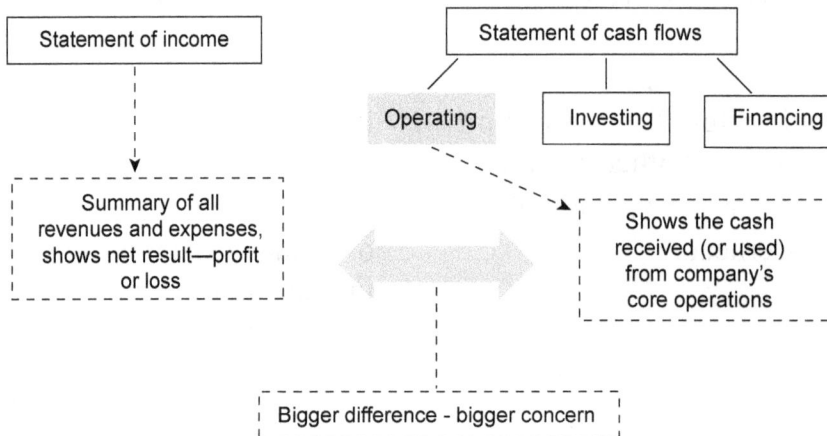

Financial Criteria

- EBIT margins are out of line with the industry unless it is due to operational leverage.
- Effective tax rate is less than the industry.
- Cash conversion cycle is more than 90 days.
- Free cash flow before CapEx for the past 3 years less than 90% of earnings adjusted for depreciation.

Accounting and Audit Criteria

- If the auditor has resigned in the past 12 months.
- Depreciation policy changed in the past 3 years.
- Capitalization of costs other than interests.
- Different auditors for the parent and subsidiaries.
- Listed company and its subsidiaries have different year-ends.
- Company has revalued assets.

Business Practices Criteria

- Loans extended to sister companies and/or shareholders.
- Shares in listed associates and subsidiaries pledged for loans.
- Investment securities portfolio on the balance sheet.
- Investments in sister or related companies greater than 5% of shareholder funds.
- Major acquisitions, equivalent to more than 20% of book value, over the past 3 years.
- Goodwill accounts for more than 10% of share funds.
- Large restructuring provisions or provisions on acquisitions over the past 3 years.

Toothcomb

- Carefully read the footnotes for information about transactions with the related parties, affiliated companies, SPV's, and joint ventures.
- Analyze the cash flow statement (1st part—cash flows from operations) to spot the potential problems with revenues and receivables.
- Whether series of acquisition has been done to depict increased revenues.
- Abnormal increase in accounts receivables or inventories.
- Accounting policy used by the company to recognize revenue (sales). If such policy differs significantly from local or international generally accepted accounting principle (GAAP) or acceptable industry norms, it should immediately raise a red flag.
- Try to identify if a company's accounting policies are unusual or differ from the industry norms.

- Try to identify an unusual non-recurring item (gains or charges) on the income statement.
- Look for indication of debt and undisclosed liabilities in the annual report or footnotes to financial statements, press releases, and other statements made by the Company.
- Look for any unusual or unexplained reserves that either substantially decrease or increase the earnings for the year.

Macro Due Diligence

It covers the macro-environment in which the target operates covering the following areas:

- Management team
- Regulatory environment. Whether lax environment is likely to be tightened or tightened one expected to be relaxed.
- Contingent risk and liability
- Culture of organization
- If cross-border, then greater emphasis on hostility from completion and the government
- Scan and check the entire eco-system—employees, ex-employees, vendors, and distributors. They can provide real insight into the happenings in the company.

Best Practices for Due Diligence

The best due diligence is to go through the financial statements/annual reports of at least last 10 years with fine toothcomb and lots of cobwebs will be cleared.

Specifically, areas such as receivable, inventory, loans and advances, cash balances, Fx transaction, and cash flow can give away a lot about what lies under the veil.

While the above areas can be due diligence by the professional team and should be given appropriate time to do thorough due diligence. A creative eye needs to look out for possible areas that may not be covered by standard checklist.

A perfect example of this is Reliance communication–MTN deal where everything was sealed and only to be delivered that everybody forgot that there is NOC that may be required from Reliance Industries and predictably it scared the seller due to probable litigations.

Thus, basing the due diligence as above will help arrive at sounding board to obtain valuation of the business.

Last, to check whether there is a deal fever or not. Just take a cold shower and re-ask the question what if the deal fails, whether there is a risk that the acquirer will suffer huge loss and you will arrive at conclusion of whether you have a fever or healthy appetite to do M&A.

Case Study 3.4: Under Due Diligence: Daiichi–Ranbaxy Deal

Details

Daiichi–Ranbaxy deal is an excellent example to demonstrate the view. It was one of the deals wherein the existing management was allowed to be continued at the helm of the affairs. However, it did not result in any uptick in the performance of Ranbaxy. Soon, the senior management quit. Ranbaxy started receiving FDA strictures including facility closure letters.

This not only created reputational issues for Daiichi, but possible legal and monetary liabilities as well.

The share price had reacted adversely to the developments and is nowhere paid by the acquirer. The buyers are contesting the reps and warranties provided by the seller and alleging non-disclosure of material issues to the buyer.

Key Learning

Due consideration should be given to due diligence. A bit deep dive and interaction with ex-employees or vendors may also give lead on the matters related to the FDA inspections going on with Ranbaxy.

Due diligence should never be compromised. Deal fever or rush to close the transaction shall never override, unless a trusted operational team of the acquirer certifies good to go signal. While the professional due diligence firms are helpful, the final call by own independent team is the best affirmation.

Last, in terms of closing the transaction if time is really not a luxury, then the legal agreements need to be watertight and very focused covering liabilities on areas that appear weaker.

Case Study 3.5: Tale of Two Due Diligences—Caterpillar and HP-Autonomy

a. Caterpillar acquires Chinese mining manufacturing company Siwei for $886 million and writes-off $580 million 7 months later.
b. HP acquires autonomy for $11.6 billion and writes-off $8.8 billion a year later.

Detail

(a) Caterpillar acquires Siwei

Caterpillar Inc. is the largest mining equipment manufacturer. In the heydays of commodity cycle of 2009–2010, it felt that it was under-exposed to China where they were battling local manufacturers.

To buttress their presence in the Chinese markets, they went on to purchase Siwei for $886 million manufacturer of roof supports for mines.

Siwei was formed out of reverse merger with ERA Holdings, a defunct video-distribution company in September 2010. The valuations around that time are not available.

Precedent to the acquisition of Siwei, there was another Chinese company named International Mining Machinery which was acquired by Joy Global for $1 billion by rival of Bucyrus (acquired in 2010 by Caterpillar). The expansion and aggressiveness of Joy Global rubbed on Caterpillar to announce aggressive foray into China.

Due Diligence Issues

a. Sizeable write-off immediately post-acquisition as a resultant of stocks and cash
b. Accounting frauds by using accounting methods
c. Ignoring the red flags

Siwei had no cash matching the account records. Not only the cash was absent, it had high receivables as well as high payables. It declared a loss of $2 million as well in 2011.

Key Learning

The losses presented an opportunity to acquire and turnaround the business; however it should have been at distressed valuation. Second, loss-making companies with bad balance sheet or bad business model need to be dissected carefully.

Due diligence is not just to check the box, it is an art requiring forensic skills and eye for catching abnormalities.

While accountants are aid to due diligence, they should not be the end. Acquirers need to have an adept operational team of themselves to do the due diligence. There is also need to have due diligence calls with the eco-system of the target. Their eco-system of the target consisting of the target's vendors, ex-employees, and accountants and it will be quite evident to the acquire the level of due diligence that needs to be pursued.

Last, while one should pursue deal with diligence, one should avoid getting wedded to it that obvious tell-tale signs go unnoticed.

(b) HP acquires Autonomy

Details

In 2011, Hewlett-Packard, the leading manufacturer of laptops, printers acquired Autonomy for $12 billion having specialization in information management software.

The acquisition was for the acquisition of Software Company to support the falling revenues from hardware.

A year later, it wrote down $9 billion from the acquisition of which $5 billion was attributed to accounting improprieties, disclosure failures, and misrepresentations. The magnitude of purchase and the write-off was equally shocking.

Issues

Autonomy had all the classical accounting issues which are easy to spot even by amateurs.

a. Aggressive accounting policies creating revenues and profits without matching cash flows
b. Bundling of hardware and software sales and hiding low margin business
c. Revenues and profits built on back of string of acquisition, thus creating impression of rapid growth
d. Ignoring industry reports on the practices at target
e. DCF valuation was used to justify the accretive nature of acquisition

Key Learning

The gap between profit and operating cash flow is the first point to be hammered. Low cash conversion rations need to be justified before discussing any valuation. This will lead to unearthing of the cause of low cash conversion. Whether the gap in profit and operating cash flow it is due to aggressive accounting or whether it is built on inorganic acquisition.

The price paid was 26 times the trailing cash flow. This obviously can be justified on sophisticated DCF model and is garbage in and garbage out phenomena. Such a high valuation will mean that all aspects of the acquisition should be firing on all cylinders. Thus, extra due diligence is needed where the price being paid is very high and to ensure that there are no obvious loose ends.

Case Study 3.6: Mega Mergers
Tale of Two Big Mergers

Lafarge-Holcim—Finally makes to the tape.

Omincom and Publicis: Fail to make it to the tape.

Details

The above M&As present the dynamics involved when merger of equals are announced. They follow the euphoria of announcement of the coming together of the two giants. The euphoria dwarfs several unresolved issues in the acquisition. They are always touted as merger of equals, but in an entity there can never be TWO CEOs, Boards, CFOs, and host of other things. Thus, in substance, it has to be one company acquiring another and most of the time this stark reality is ignored in announcement and realized only on closing and unless there is a blinking of eye by one of the companies, the merger will more or less fail.

Apart from converging into a single structure, one of the most controversial issues is the valuation agreed at announcement and whether it holds true until the acquisition completes. As these days, there are quite a few regulatory approvals that need to be sorted out and acquisition can drag for more than a year.

Similar Drivers for Merger

Lafarge–Holcim: Merger of the two largest cement companies in the world plagued by over-capacity and stagflation in the cement demand. The combined merger will make a revenue of $50 billion. The driver for the merger is to cut the cost through synergies rather than growth synergies. The expected cost synergy to come through is US $1.9 billion per annum.

Omnicom–Publicis: The merger of the two largest advertising companies makes it $35 billion behemoth in an industry fighting technological advances and data-driven snipers like Facebook and Google.

Similar Clash of Egos

Lafarge–Holcim went through management changes with Holcim objecting to the CEO nominee from Lafarge, while Lafarge saw it as an issue of distrust from Holcim. From merger of equals, it became acquisition of Lafarge by Holcim. Lafarge had to change its CEO nominee in deference to Holcims wishes as the share exchange ratio which was 1:1 representing merger of equals had to be tweaked to 0.9:1 in favor of Holcim to represent a better financial performance of Holcim.

Omnicon–Publicis merger of equals had no execution as to who is going to get acquired by whom. Apart from being joint CEO's of both the companies, there was no prior agreement on the positions like CFO. When Omnicon pushed for its own CFO in the combined entity, it was resisted by Publicis as it made it being felt like a target.

Thus, eventually the egos clashed and the deal got called-off. While in case of Lafarge–Holcim deal, there were not only operational drivers for merger but, both had dominant shareholders who could force the board to fall in line and get things done. Softer issues like giving prominence to the target in the name LAFARGE-HOLCIM also took care of larger issues at play.

Key Lessons in Mega-Mergers

Merger is only in style in substance it represents acquisition and who acquires whom in merger of equals is the make or break point of a deal.

While CEO from respective companies can be made as Co-CEOs or one can get bumped to a sinecure position of Chairman, similar luxury cannot be had for the remaining positions and need clear understanding.

Valuation is one of the key issues in equals. Strong rational for merger ratios which can stand passage of time or change in financial performance of respective companies should be taken into consideration.

What's thy in name? Lafarge–Holcim, Arcellor–Mittal signifies the importance of name play.

These Mega-mergers are distraction for management and rivals use it to snap markets or clients. In case of Omnicon–Publicis, the WPP, the leading company, ended up snaring lot of clients from both the companies.

Origination Off-Shoots from Successful As Well As Non-Successful Deals

Lafarge–Holcim deal: In a successful deal, which is sold on benefits of cost synergies, will generate sell-side business for selling assets.

Omnicon-Publicis: Non-successful deals have larger potential to generate M&A business as there is un-satiated appetite to do business. Thus, immediately after the call of the merger, Publicis announces a ~US $4 billion deal to acquire Sapient in the digital marketing space.

Similar, deals are witnessed with Pfizer, which on being spurned by Astra Zeneca went on to acquire Hospira for US $17 billion.

Similar scenario is observed in the case of Valeant Pharmaceuticals which lost out on acquiring Allergan ended up acquiring Salix Pharmaceutical for $14.5 billion including the assumed debt. What also helped is the fact that Valeant was an acquisitive company led by CEO believing in acquiring companies with promising drugs in the pipeline rather than spend on R&D.

Case Study 3.7: Pfizer–AstraZeneca

Details

Pfizer Inc. is the world's largest pharmaceutical companies based in New York City. AstraZeneca was the second largest Company in UK after Glaxo with sizeable employees in UK along with its R&D located in UK.

Pfizer made a public bid for AstraZeneca in April 2014 at significant premium to unaffected price and stated for purpose of tax planning if its non-US earnings will move its domicile to the UK.

Prior to April 2014, in the end of 2013, they discussed the merger proposal with AstraZeneca Chairman and leadership. However, the board of AstraZeneca neither considered the bid nor recommended it to the shareholder.

Pfizer announced the bid at £50 a share along with making noises about commitment to UK and AstraZeneca. AstraZeneca board rejected the offer.

Being one of the largest companies in UK, the magnitude of bid coming from American company led to the politicians jumping into the fight.

AstraZeneca board having rejected the offer did its own communication on why future is rosy for AstraZeneca.

Pfizer increased its offer price to £55 which was eventually rejected by AstraZeneca and they gave up the bid.

Origination Elements

For Pfizer:

- Tax driven
- Peer pressure.
- Deal frenzy in Pharmaceuticals
- Leverage at low interest rates

Valuation

50% premium to the unaffected price of AstraZeneca was offered. AstraZeneca had depressed earnings so premium may not sound excessive given the drug pipeline it had for coming years. However, that would have been already discounted in the stock price. The significant premium was arising mainly due to low interest rates making it a financially engineered deal (refer to the chapter on Valuation).

Elements

The biggest element in this deal was POLITICS followed by the target company CEO and board. But, for these elements, the bid would have been successful.

Analysis of the Case

What Went Wrong for Pfizer?

M&A strategy

It was a half-cooked attempt. First, courting the board and then making an unsolicited bid and not going full hog in an unsolicited bid by getting all the elements within its control.

An unsolicited bid means taking control of all elements in the deal. It includes:

- Regulations/politics especially in high-profile cross-border situation
- Media
- Employees
- Shareholders

- Selling the deal more as tax inversion for Pfizer rather than a strategic fit. These would have got the shareholders of AstraZeneca more exited.
- The tax inversion pursued by Pfizer resulted in lack of support from American politicians to counter UK politicians.
- Given the political element involved pursuing a high-profile deal which may result in job losses at a time when UK elections were round the corner made it a political slugfest, thus denying it any political backing on the either side of the Atlantic.
- It failed to push forth other targets it would pursue if Astra Zeneca did not come through which would have pressured the board in getting on to the deal.

What Went Right for Pfizer

- While it made a half-cooked attempt, it did not make a desperate lunge for the target by going crazy over the price given the reluctance of the AstraZenca board to play ball.
- Although it made sense from financial engineering point of view to acquire AstraZeneca, it was a big relief that they did not eventually acquire it and subsequently got reflected in the uptick on stock price and they acquired a smaller company worth $17 billion.
- It did not make a bid again after the cool-off period for re-bidding was over.

What Went Right for AstraZeneca

Defensive strategy

- Played it right by not saying AYE at first sight allowed the deal to simmer.
- The above resulted in getting a 50% premium to unaffected price.
- It got control of all the elements in the deal
- Regulations/politics, especially in high-profile cross-border situation, were used to hilt

  - Media went all agog with negatives against Pfizer.
  - Employee job losses made it to deal breaking point.
  - Shareholders were kept in control and nobody raised an activist flag against the board.

What went wrong for AstraZeneca

- It failed to get one element of the deal going that is the absence of competitive bid in the deal crazy Pharma industry. The same could have brought pressure on Pfizer to go aggressive.
- Last, having got 50% premium to the unaffected price and in the absence of competitive bid, it should have taken the bid rather than believing it will be able to deliver a share price rise of 50% in near medium term. Thus, it lost the opportunity of delivering to shareholders a better share price.

Key Learning

The case depicts the elements involved in high-pitched M&A deal. The case shows the rights and wrongs for both the acquirer and the target. Thus, we are able to strategize as a buyer and seller in such kind of deals.

3.6 Sell-Side M&A

Selling a business is as difficult decision to make as buying decision. It is not as intuitive as buying. The problem is compounded by the fact that managements are loathe to cut losses as they do not want to admit defeat, while in the case of bull scenario, there is big resistance to sell in peak value scenario as the business scenario looks very rosy.

Selling Agenda Points

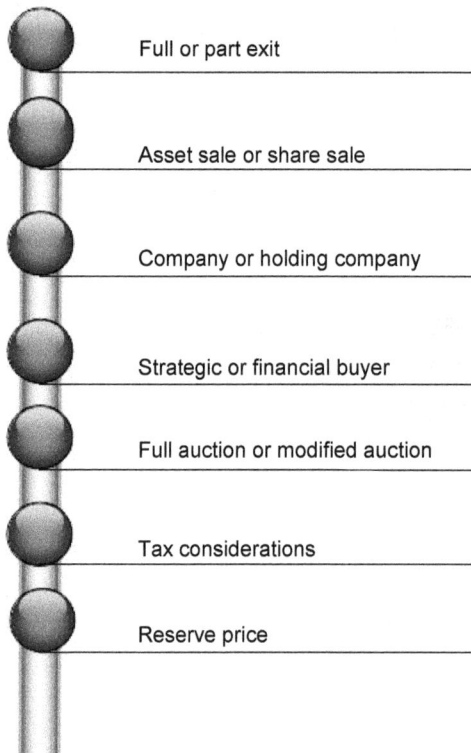

- Full or part exit
- Asset sale or share sale
- Company or holding company
- Strategic or financial buyer
- Full auction or modified auction
- Tax considerations
- Reserve price

Thus, there emerges a strong need to have a clear yardstick to define when to blow the whistle in good business scenario as well as bad business scenario. It helps to determine us how to go about the sell process.

The above means the following decision points:

Full exit or part exit

The full or part exit decisions are affected by the valuations and the buyer. If the valuations are crazy, it would mean better to take cash and scoot home. If the valuations are reasonable, but a better buyer stepping in, then hedge the bets by partially exiting.

Asset sale or share sale

The asset or share sale decisions are generally guided by tax laws, ownership, and liability issues. Asset sale will be guided by partial ownership requirement or the need to avoid liabilities of other businesses.

Company or holding company

These considerations are again guided by taxation, ownership and liability issues as discussed above.

Strategic or financial investor

The considerations for choosing a financial or strategic investor are discussed in detail in later sections of this chapter.

Full auction or modified auction

The consideration for choosing a full or modified auction is discussed in detail in the later section of this chapter.

Tax impact

The tax impact is very critical from optimizing the cash flow back to the shareholders. Since the M&A values are very high, they have significant impact on the net cash flow back.

Reserve Price

The consideration for reserve price is a matter of timing and is discussed in the subsequent paragraph.

Above all, the most critical decision is timing. The approach while selling is to find the greater fool rather than becoming one in the process. These would mean not to get carried away by the crazy industry scenario but to draw a line when the valuations run a lot ahead of fundamentals. It is the time when valuations become a support in the negotiation, business quality takes a backseat and financing is much easier to come by when it should be the other way round. The easy recourse to finance and gung-ho sentiments brings hostility to bidding process, thereby enabling a rich exit.

Therefore, sellers who end up missing the bus have to say bye-bye to those rosy valuations, when the euphoria subsides and maturity takes over.

As long as sanity prevails which allows the chaffing of the valuation and business fundamentals, the seller should be able to take the right timing decision.

Cue arises for Asian sellers when there is M&A frenzy in the developed markets in their respective industry, they should start thinking of selling decision. Thus, once decides to sell the next logical steps are as under:

Getting Ready for Sale on Business

(i) Stage I:

1. Deciding the structure of the transaction listed as decision point above.
2. Getting confidential teaser or information memorandum prepared.
3. Getting the financial statements in order.

(ii) Stage II

1. Appointment of advisors and defining their roles.
2. Deciding on media strategy, as it is crucial to get the right momentum going among the bidder.
3. Deciding on the mode of auction. Whether full or partial.

(iii) Stage III

1. Preparing a shortlist of potential investors that will determine full or partial exit.
2. Decision points with respect to choosing "Strategic" or "Financial Investor."

Strategic Investor

Selection criteria

Follow the same decision points listed in buy-side origination in Chapter 1.

Target bidders loaded with cash or CEO's laying down grand vision for inorganic growth.

(iv) Stage IV:

1. Getting valuation done and deciding the reserve price.
2. Modeling of the strategy.

Strategic buyer

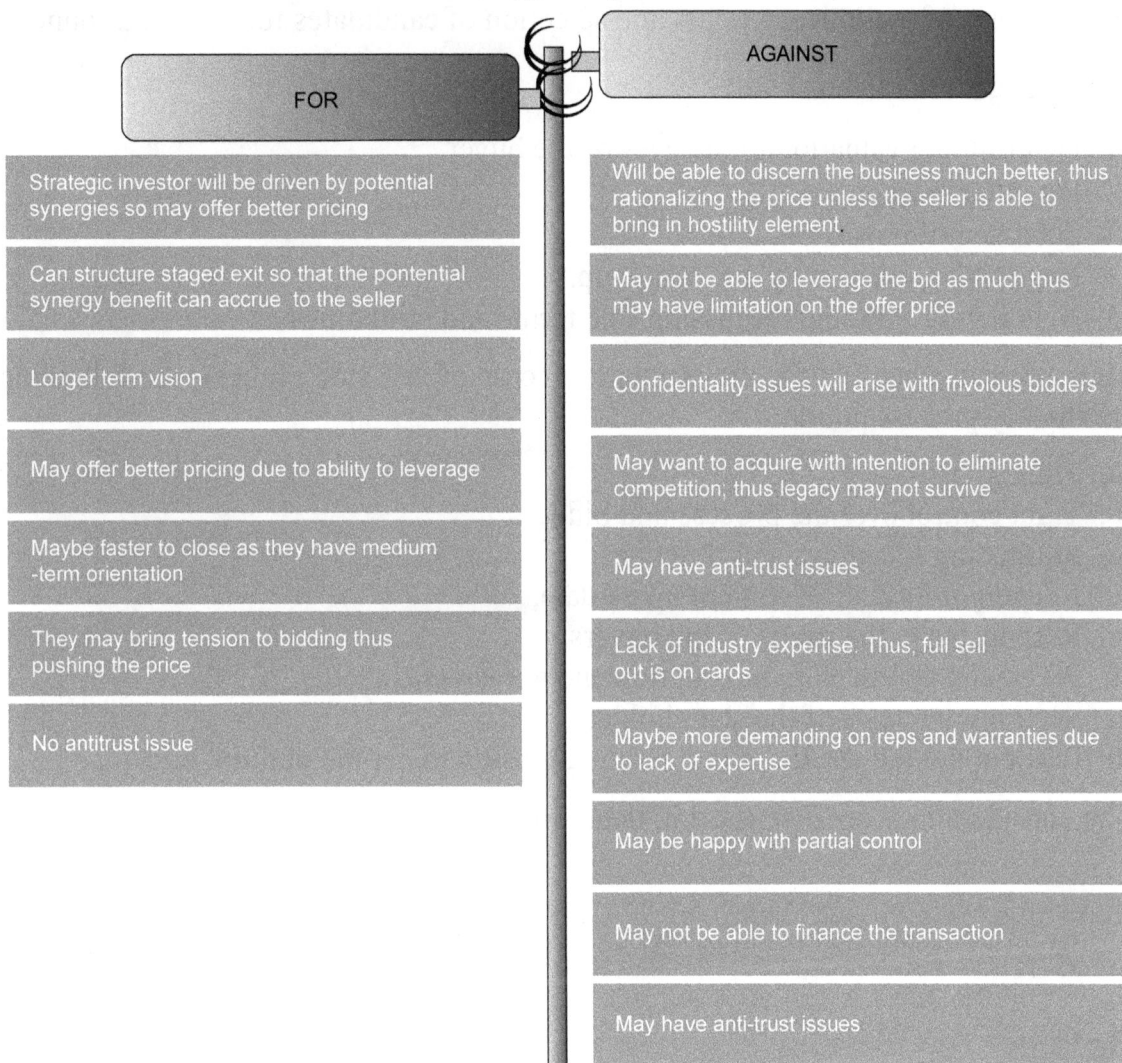

FOR	AGAINST
Strategic investor will be driven by potential synergies so may offer better pricing	Will be able to discern the business much better, thus rationalizing the price unless the seller is able to bring in hostility element
Can structure staged exit so that the pontential synergy benefit can accrue to the seller	May not be able to leverage the bid as much thus may have limitation on the offer price
Longer term vision	Confidentiality issues will arise with frivolous bidders
May offer better pricing due to ability to leverage	May want to acquire with intention to eliminate competition; thus legacy may not survive
Maybe faster to close as they have medium -term orientation	May have anti-trust issues
They may bring tension to bidding thus pushing the price	Lack of industry expertise. Thus, full sell out is on cards
No antitrust issue	Maybe more demanding on reps and warranties due to lack of expertise
	May be happy with partial control
	May not be able to finance the transaction
	May have anti-trust issues

3. Getting ready with Q&A.
4. Prepare data room and access control.

(v) Stage V:

1. Establishing contact with candidates.
2. Forwarding of teaser and/or information memorandum.
3. Preparation of data room.
4. Draft sale and purchase agreement.

(vi) Stage VI:

1. Creating heat and dust.
2. Actively managing media to generate bidding tension.

3. If the company is listed using the stock price as leverage to drive the bidders.
4. Analysis of preliminary offers and sélection of candidates for a second round.

(vii) Stage VII

1. Determining valuation in the eyes of the buyer.
2. Potential synergies.
3. Selection of buyer.
4. Negotiating exclusivity and break-up.
5. Negotiating SPA and discussing sale terms and modalities.

Thus, we can state that for the ultimate success of sell-side process, the following are the key process points:

a. Timing,
b. Tight control over the process and bidders,
c. Marinating schedules and timelines,
d. Keeping information content up-to-date,
e. Responsive to the needs of the buyers,
f. Pragmatic approach to negotiation and agreements,
g. Securing interests of the shareholders,
h. Last but not the least, optimal bidding tension to get the optimal price.

The considerations are discussed in detail in the below case study.

Case Study 3.8: Sell of Indian Telecom Assets by Hutchison:

Details

Hutchison was one of the leading telecom operators in India. It had rolled out its services under the "Hutch" brand name. It had built a leading brand and operations. The sale of Hutchison India represents a classic sell-side execution.

The case study is run on lines of the parameters outlined above for executing sell-side mandate:

(a) Timing:

The sell was initiated at the peak of telecom cycle. Thus, the valuations were riding high. There was strong interest from players who had missed the second largest telecom market and from existing players wanting to consolidate its telecom business. Further, the government has already announced issue of 3g licenses. Thus, the timing checks all the boxes of executing sell-side mandate.

(b) Preparing for Sale:

This included:

a. Hutch built a strong business and customer care numbers. The growth in subscriber base was kept attractive by having aggressive sell of pre-paid customer base putting in place strongly incentivized and competent management team.

b. A good set of advisers were put in place that started getting the sale in perfect order.

c. The sale was structured to sell the holding company in Mauritius to avoid the taxation issue. It also appeared that they did not indemnify or gave a rep on the tax issue that has put the eventual buyer Vodafone in hot waters with Government of India.

d. There was a controlled auction resulting in slow build-up of interest from various buyers. Rumour mills were set into action, providing selective leaks on the sale. Hutch denied the rumours initially, may be they wanted to get the reaction from Essar who had the first right of refusal or they may have wanted to know what could be their reaction to the potential sale by Hutch.

"Hutchison seems to have replaced Apple as grist for the rumour mill... There's been rumours going around for a while about various entities being interested in buying Hutchison's Indian mobile operations although, so far Hutchison has reiterated that it is not interested in selling, or in selling its European operations for that matter".

e. Generating an appropriate mix of strategic and financial bidders to ensure bidding tension.

"Bidders jostle for India's Hutchison Essar..."

However, in the end, it appeared that the active bidders probably were only Vodafone and Reliance Telecommunication. The rumours suggested the virtual list of "Who's" who to have made it to the bidding party.

Name of few of the bidders who appeared in the news media were:

Verizon wireless, NTT DOCOMO, Orascom, Maxis, Blackston, Carlyle, Texas pacific group, Altimo, Hindujas, Qatar telecom

f. Putting yourself in the shoes of the buyer and evaluating from the buyer's eyes.

The Vodafone chief executive had called the acquisition as defining deal of the decade.

When the seller sees the open profess for the asset they wish to sell, we can see the sky-high valuations. The enterprise value of Hutch jumped from US $10 billion to US $20 billion in a matter of months.

g. Structuring the transaction

The natural outcome of being in driver's seat gave the seller the liberty to dictate the terms including structuring the transaction as sale of the holding company rather than the onshore Indian company which could have resulted in the buyer to deduct withholding tax. As also, it allowed Hutchison not to indemnify the buyer against potential tax liability.

Key Learning

Thus, we conclude it as a successful sell-side case study. The above are ingredients of successful execution of sell-side mandate. There is another ingredient named "Negotiation" which will be discussed in detail in the upcoming chapter.

Case Study 3.9: Buy-Side M&A to Sell-Side M&A—The Story of Making and Selling of Centurion Bank

Details

The Centurion Bank was an Indian private sector bank that provided retail and corporate banking services. It was one of the first banks from private sector after the liberalization in 1992. It operated on a strong nationwide franchise of 403 branches and had over 5000 employees. The bank listed its shares on the major Indian stock exchanges and on the Luxembourg Stock Exchange.

Centurion bank had fallen into distress due to lack of management oversight. The attempt to rescue it through capital infusion came to nought. Sensing this is a good opportunity, Rana Talwar, CEO of Standard Chartered, due to his contacts in the government and central bank was well suited to make distress investment in Centurion.

Acquisition of Centurion Bank

Sabre Capital, led by Rana Talwar, acquired control over the Centurion bank by infusing equity and diluting the existing promoters.

The strategy followed was:
Given the eroded net worth of the bank, the equity value was written down from face value of 10 to face value of 2. Thereafter, infused equity into the bank at 4 per share and took loads of long-dated warrant (5 years) with no upfront margin.

Thus, the bank was acquired at distress value and the downside was hedged by taking up long-dated warrants, thus keeping the upside open. The market cap at the time of acquisition was Rs. 150 crores.

Strategy Post-Acquisition

The balance sheet was restructured and cleaned up with infused equity, and all non-performing assets were written-off. The debt on balance sheet was renegotiated for deferment and haircut.

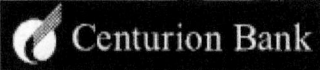

Centurion Bank

BALANCE SHEET AS AT 31ST MARCH, 2004

(Rs. In lacs)

	Schedule	As at 31st March, 2004	As at 31st March, 2003
CAPITAL & LIABILITIES			
Capital	1	5,675	15,247
Reserves & Surplus	2	13,620	2,335
Deposits	3	302,879	283,471
Borrowings	4	4,397	6,048
Other Liabilities & Provisions	5	28,316	31,446
		354,887	338,547
ASSETS			
Cash & Balances with Reserve Bank of India	6	26,095	21,984
Balances with Banks and Money at Call and Short Notice	7	24,866	26,863
Investments	8	100,418	99,925
Advances	9	155,641	131,372
Fixed Assets	10	18,468	23,034
Other Assets	11	29,399	35,369
		354,887	338,547
Contingent Liabilities	12	112,657	140,576
Bills for Collection		24,124	16,325
Significant Accounting Policies	18		
Notes to Accounts	19		

Once the balance sheet was stabilized, the bank optimized the operations to reduce credit losses. Professionals were brought in and given stock options.

Enhancing Value through Acquisition

Given its presence only in the western region, the bank started scouting for acquisition that will increase its pan India presence and make it a bank ripe for acquisition. On June 29, 2005, the board of directors of Centurion Bank and Bank of Punjab agreed for the merger of the two banks, thereby increasing presence in North India. The name of the bank was changed to Centurion Bank of Punjab. The aforesaid depicts the effectiveness of softer tool such as NAME to entice the sellers.

The next year, Centurion Bank of Punjab acquired Kochi-based Lord Krishna Bank, thus marking the presence of bank and its branches in the south as well. The share price expectedly performed and it was able to bring in private equity investors to finance the growth for next 2 years. On reaching a certain stage, it was sold on May 23, 2008, to HDFC bank at a valuation of 1500 crores.

Thus, transforming from 150 crore to 1500 crore value in a span of 5 years and Sabre exited the bank with handsome gains.

Timeline in Brief

Moving Up to Selling Path

2003: Initial Invest of 40 million shares at 1 per/share value

2004: Restructuring the balance sheet

2005: Strategic move to acquire Bank of Punjab (North India)

2006: Strategic move to acquire Lord Krishna Bank (South India)

2007: Private placement to ICICI Ventures

2008: Sold to HDFC at market cap of INR 10,500 million

Key Learning

Thus, we see how an asset was acquired. The acquired assets was cleaned, enhanced, perfumed, and sold out for handsome gains, by following the ingredients of successful sell-side execution.

3.7 Executive Summary

The chapter explains the three broad areas of M&A.

- The buy-side M&A criteria and process.
- The various elements of due diligence and the areas of focus in due diligence to avoid traps.
- The sell-side criteria and process.

The case studies highlight the various elements of each of the above areas.

Chapter IV: Valuations

Contents

4.1 Introduction

A lot has been written about the valuation methodologies and detailed description which is generally part of any valuation discussion.

Here, we will concentrate on those aspects of valuation which are basis of valuation and value attribution. These are critical part of valuations in the real world, especially in the context of acquisitions. There is a big price risk or value risk being taken while acquiring companies which may cause enormous destruction of value.

We will start with looking into financial statements and looking at each item of these and understand how they form the basis for further work in applying valuation methodology.

4.2 Analyzing the Balance Sheet

Balance Sheet: We have often heard about balance sheet quality, but valuation literature as well as most valuation in the market is driven by income statement rather than balance sheet ignoring the fact that balance sheet quality will drive the quality of the income statement.

We would see most practitioners stating that just by a mere look at the balance sheet, we should be able to get a sense of the balance sheet quality. As a student, I always used to struggle with this one look, whether it is debt equity ratio or is it the share premium commanded by the company or the ever confusing statement that current assets should cover current liabilities.

For example: Most textbooks state that the current asset/current ratio should be greater than 1, as one of the indicators of better balance sheet quality.

This is contrast to the real world valuation.

A current ratio of lower than 1 indicates better fitness of the company as compared to greater than 1. Instead of current assets covering current liabilities, it is a better business model to have current liabilities paying for current assets rather than relying on company's cash/financing or external financing to finance the current assets.

Thus, the magic one look formula to assess the quality of balance refers to the "working capital management of the company." It refers to the underbelly of the company. As in human fitness, the emphasis is given to "core"; similarly, in company fitness, the "core" of the company is the "working capital management."

So, if the business model is such that the vendors give credit for their supplies of raw material and the customers pay advance to receive the products. Why not, no capital employed just skimming the returns back to the shareholders.

The industries driven by brand *viz.* consumer goods, FMCG, internet-based or industries like automobile and smartphones, which rely on outsourced manufacturing, will have this characteristic. In case of non-branded, capital-intensive industries, the working capital management of companies will tell you almost everything about the quality of company and its management. In such cases, it is observed that the current ratio is maintained closed to 1. These companies maintain very tight control over the inventories as well as have very good credit policies, thus keeping their receivables manageable. This avoids bloating of incremental capital required to finance these current assets, thereby impairing the shareholder returns.

For example: There are companies that avoid doing government contracts as they are very lax with payments leading to pile up of debtors/receivable. While, there are other companies, which will maintain customer diversification and keep revenue tickets smaller to manage the risk of receivables going bad affecting the cash position of the company.

This is against conventional wisdom, wherein management may want to show higher and higher revenue and may go for big ticket contracts at the expense of balance sheet and adversely affecting the working capital management of the business.

The ill effects will start showing up sooner or later, thereby affecting the financial health of the company and resultant valuations.

Let us have a look at the elements of balance sheet and their impact on valuations.

a. Liability side of the balance sheet

These include:

Share capital

The constituents of the share capital include its par value and premium. The quantum of premium will indicate the quality of share capital. In addition to the constituents, very critical is the dilution history of the share capital. If the company has managed its business without raising capital is an indicator of the inherent strength of the company. It is also indicative of management philosophy on whether or not they rely excessively on external financing. It also indicates whether they are trying to grow at frenetic pace by using external capital. At times, this would also mean that the company is having capital allocation mismatch, wherein capital raised is being used for business expenditure and not entirely for the capital creation. Thus, long-term capital is being used for short-term purposes. This mismatch or fault line will show up later in valuation.

It is also pertinent to note the purpose for which the capital was raised:

Good end use will be for:

- Capital expenditure
- Deleveraging the balance sheet

Not so good uses will be for:

- Acquisition
- Write-offs
- Financing working capital

The other factors to note include the amount of percentage dilution that has been done. If it is greater than 10%, then it requires a closer look as to whether there has been excessive dilution. Whether the management has identified the end use of the funds or the funds have been raised use predatory pricing just to grow at a fast pace or whether it has been raised because markets were good, so it was treated as loose cash rather than the real meaning of Equity, the other name of share capital.

The frequency, percentage, and purpose of dilution is indicative of the philosophy of management in running the business, whether they treat equity as instrument of last resort, whether they use it as a loose cannon for carpet bombing opportunities.

The last point to be considered, while looking at equity, is the split between par and premium. The managements will tend to dilute at the highest premium Thus. it is the subscriber who undertakes the risk associated with the high premium. However, the management equity will suffer, if they are unable to deliver returns to such subscribers. The premium results in managing earnings per share (EPS) as lesser number of shares are issued, but would not help with return on equity (ROE); the equity figure in denominator will stand bloated without commensurate profits in numerator if the cash raised is in excess of the requirement and idle cash will eat in the overall ROE of the company.

Further, twist in the tale is whether the company has undertaken buybacks. What has been the timing of buyback? Has it been taken at near bottom valuations or whether the buyback has been used as a tool for financial engineering where in the low cost leverage has been used to replace equity capital.

Till now, we have only looked at share capital, assuming it is made up entirely of equity share capital. The other aspect to look into is whether to circumvent equity dilution, whether there is preference share capital component, or whether the company is over leveraged; hence, it has resorted to preference share capital.

Convertible or cumulative preference share capital, the dividend rate, redemption period, and terms are other aspects to be looked into while analyzing the capital. It is suited best to avoid the preference share capital due to its hybrid nature as it is difficult to understand and categorize. Further, dividend is not tax deductible, thereby making it a costlier means of financing.

Reserves and Surplus

This indicates the quality of net worth of the company. The reserves and surplus also has to be kept optimum with return of cash to shareholders. These reserves and surplus should be carved out of the internal accruals and not due to revaluation reserves or redemption reserves or provisioning reserves, which are used to ease the earnings for the company.

Non-Current Liabilities

This is obviously the leverage factor in business while the "Capital theory" pushes for optimal capital structure stressing maintaining an optimal balance between equity and debt.

However, in equity markets, the companies with net-debt capital structure (cash in excess of debt) or with no debt at all have commanded better valuations. This may be due to the reason that capital market theory looks at the relative cost of financing between these two components, ignoring the risk element of debt including the inflexibility it brings in when it acts as millstone, thereby disallowing the company to take advantage of market opportunities.

Another important aspect that needs to be discussed is the degree of leverage *viz.* debt equity ratio, how many times EBIDTA, etc.

Minimum the amount of leverage, the better it is for balance sheet. Another important factor is the terms of the debt *viz.* term, currency, rate, and convertibility.

Further, whether there is a natural hedge between debt and operations of the company. It can be described as whether the company cash flow is predictable enough to repay the debt or, if the company is having foreign currency bonds, whether the company has enough income stream in that foreign currency to repay the interest and principal.

The above illustrates the quality of the debt that sits on the balance sheet of the company. Thus, debt taken for buying out companies may not have the above natural hedge because of the strain that the acquisition may create on exiting cash flow as well as the risk inherent in the acquisition, which may not result in the targets cash flow coming in as per expectation to service the debit.

There is need to be more particular with foreign currency denominated debt due to the X-factor of currency and what is the hedge effectiveness of such currency and the risk arising out of it. Different currency bonds may present different currency risk and other macro-economic risks. Next aspect that comes in the line is the convertibility option that comes with such debt.

The convertible debt is again a hybrid instrument. Usually, the convertible instrument comes with a lower interest cost in effect subsidized by the convertibility option, which is pegged at a certain premium to current price with tenure of 3–5 years. Thus, the companies see it as easy way of raising money because they are getting lower interest rates plus the bond is getting converted into equity at premium to current market price.

However, convertible bonds are not at all beneficial for company that assumes to do well. It only benefits hedge funds as a trading instrument, splitting the option and the bond. Companies are confused as to how to treat the convertible bond. Is it bond or is it equity? When company is sure to achieve more than promised % growth in stock prices, then they would end up diluting cheap. If not, the poor performance of the company may result in huge debts residing on their balance sheet.

Current Liabilities:

• Payables

Payables should be generally high, unless it is an insolvency issue. High payables indicate that the company is using its supplier's money to fund its operations and therefore has no need for short-term financing for its own requirements. Inventory and receivables can be financed using the money saved through higher payables.

Example: In case of Apple pre-orders and orders from Foxcon, they ask for advance from the customers, essentially giving itself a negative cash conversion cycle for some of its products.

Thus, negative current ratio or low net current asset is beneficial.

For example: Automobile industry, Apple, etc.

• Deferred Revenue

Higher the deferred revenue better is the situation. Pre-orders are a typical example of deferred revenue that facilitates negative working capital, thus providing high return on the capital employed.

• Provisions

It is used for doubtful debts and inventory. Written back during bad times, increased during good times may represent accounting malice directed at smoothened earnings. Thus, it warrants a close look at the actual requirement and the provisioning. This can be tested against the growth in revenues and growth in provisioning. Is it a consistent percent that is provided or is there a spike in the provisioning?

b. Asset side of balance sheet

Gross block assets (GFA) Or net fixed assets (NFA)

It is generally considered to be better to have a lower GFA as compared to the revenue which represents higher asset turnover. In addition, another factor that requires a close look is the rate of addition of GFA. Whether it has been at a frenetic pace or at a measured pace, sudden addition of GFA may cause imbalance in the company's operation. NFA accounts for depreciation and hence acts as a measure to check the depreciation policy. Higher depreciation is better for company since it reduces the tax and increases the cash flow, and since depreciation is a non-cash expense it will produce higher return on assets (ROA) and higher profits later (deferred profits).

Goodwill and Intangibles

A higher value may indicate that the company is constantly paying more than fair value for its acquisitions. Goodwill faces the problem of not being amortized and directly impaired. Once impaired, it represents a direct loss. Hence, it can be concluded that the lesser the better it is the goodwill for the company.

Investments

It should be noted whether the investments are of strategic nature or financial. Strategic investments are required to be valued individually, while the financial investments are defined as the investments that are well-diversified in money market instruments. If it is too high, it may raise concerns because it questions whether the company should invest in its core business or return dividend or hoard cash for the sake of notional safety.

Inventory

The lower the inventory, the better as it contributes to improved turnover of the asset. Further, the analysis of inventory is conducted to inspect whether it is finished goods or raw materials.

Receivables

Receivables along with inventory are the key components of working capital that contribute majorly toward the operating capital employed in the business. The lower the better as well as its one step away from cash and bloated receivables which mean less free cash flow and reflect the mindset of the management in terms of balance sheet and profit/loss account.

Ageing analysis of receivable is a must to figure out the quality of receivables and whether the company has under-provided for bad debts.

Cash marketable securities

Whether it is optimal or bloated is the question to be answered in this context. Many a times, it is the tendency of management to pile on cash instead of putting it back in the business or declaring dividends. Usually, it is regarded as a safety buffer. However, the managements do not realize that such buffer signals that the business is inherently risky and hence, the market gyrates toward lower multiple than companies which keep optimal cash on the balance sheet. Further, the cash accumulated on the balance sheet is prone to abuse and management whims.

Loans and Advances

Too much loan and advances along with related party transaction does not present a good picture of quality of the balance sheet.

c. What Makes A Good Balance Sheet

1. Companies who grow their balance sheet in a measured way and by not taking undue risks.
2. Growing the gross block/fixed assets in a measured manner in line with operating cash flow, which can support asset financing.
3. Prioritizing balance sheet over profit and loss account. It means not booking undue revenues and bloating the receivables without concurrent cash flow.
4. Sensible capital allocation in capital expenditure and using equity as last resort in financing.
5. Efficient in using all types of capital not necessarily trying to be optimal in capital structure by taking undue leverage to take advantage of tax shield offered by leverage.
6. Efficient in working capital management. Current liabilities covering the current assets *viz.* current ratio lesser than 1.
7. Focusing on internal accruals to finance the growth of the company.
8. Achieving balance between growth in sales and profits, capital, and returns.

4.3 Analysing Income Statement

Let us now focus on the quality of income statement. Lot of analysis is required to focus toward the growth in top line. However, the premium valuations are approached by looking through the quality of revenue as described below:

Revenue

We will separately look into the revenue growth rates and how to analyze them. Let us first start by understanding the quality of revenue and what we mean by it.

The questions to be asked in this regard include:

How diversified is the revenue base?

It refers to whether there is:

- Customer concentration
- Product concentration
- Geography concentration
- Segmental concentration
- Domestic or export concentration

- Whether the company has fixed or variable type contracts or whether there is appropriate mix of the same to attain stable revenue growth. It should also be noted if the contracts are short term or long term with escalation clause and how predictable is the revenue pattern.
- Whether the company is operating in B2B or B2C markets, whether it has government type contracts, or whether it is operating in business segment which has L1 *viz.* lowest bid criteria for business awards.
- The ability of the company to pass on costs to its customers is also an important factor in the analysis.
- What is the Intellectual Property ("IP") *viz.* brand, design etc., that is driving the revenue and whether the IP lies with the company or is it fixed tenure licensed or franchised.
- The kind of distribution channels used by the company and what is the degree of control of the company on such distribution channel so that the distributor channel would not swing revenue.
- Whether the company has cluster of brands or focused brand strategy.
- Is it operating in a protected industry, which is allowing it to show revenue growth rate.
- Is it able to compete in a competitive environment or there is a threat of import tariffs changing it or taxation rules likely to change or is it in industry where foreign investment is not allowed.
- How has the revenue performed in lean times? Was it able to hold itself in difficult market conditions? This is especially true for cyclical companies.
- How big is the conversion factor arising out of change in currency or change in commodity price. For example, Jewelry company would have a big conversion factor if the gold prices are on upward trend.

At times, there may be acquisition-related growth in revenue. We need to check for the growth rate in the organic revenue to see whether the organic growth rate is getting camouflaged by inorganic growth rate.

The above can be customized for retail kind of companies by checking on same store sales growth.

It is very important to note that the revenue recognition policies are followed by the company. Of the aforesaid, the cash is taken by the companies which have deferred revenue by the virtue of advances. The next best would be receiving the cash on delivery followed by the dispatch of goods/services with minimum credit period.

In case of manufacturing companies, we need to monitor whether service fees is a decent component of revenue as after sales revenue has least capital involved and good margins.

Product life cycle and threat of substitutes are other aspects that require special consideration.

Another component to be looked into is the mix of value and volume in the revenue growth to question whether it is coming through increase in the value or the volume. A balance between two is desirable.

Having looked into the above factor, we move ahead into the trend of revenue and tools to analyze the same.

Whether the revenue has secular stable growth rates

Check on the following quantitative tools in analysis (examples later in the chapter)

- Year on year growth rates
- Compounded annual growth rates
- Rolling compounded growth rates as simple compound annual growth rate (CAGR) may be fallacious if the starting base is low.

Rolling CAGR provides a better growth profile through years. Use 3-year rolling or 5-year rolling or both to have a better framework.

- Use data over long period of time to cover the entire trough and peak cycles and avoid data of recent years as they may represent peak or trough resulting in variable outcomes.
- Calculate constant currency growth rates
- Calculate organic growth rates
- Calculate indexed growth rates to account for inflation or these USD figures to find real growth

The above tools can be used in conjunction with the qualitative analysis of the revenue to be achieved at the quality of revenue.

Expense

It refers to the cost at which the goods are sold. The following questions should be taken into consideration while analyzing the expense of the company.

- Which cost is dominant and whether it is substantial or not? If it is substantial, then what is the company's control over the cost and procurement? Whether it has the ability to pass increase in that cost to its customers?
- Whether it has multiple sources of raw material?
- Whether it is dealing with dominant supplier or a source such as oil or rare earths?
- Does it have fixed type contracts or variable?
- Is it able to take in substitute?
- Is it procured from related party?
- Is there a natural hedge arrived between revenue and expenses of the company?

Salaries

- Structure of salaries
- Fixed or variable. Whether appropriately incentivized

- Whether being paid to relatives not in business
- Whether underpaid relative to market. Especially, if its domestic vis-à-vis MNC
- Is there any labor arbitrage involved

Selling, General, & Administrative Expense (SG&A)

- Whether the company is spending appropriately in SG&A
- Whether it is being spread appropriately
- Whether it is spending more on the dealer incentivization rather than at marquee events or sponsorship with very ethereal impact or on celebrity endorsement without commensurate benefit
- Represents CapEx for FMCG companies
- Structure of dealer incentive or sale people incentives

Earnings before Interest, Depreciation and Tax ("EBITDA") AND Earnings before interest and Tax ("EBIT")

What is the trend? Whether they are at peak or at trough? What is the long-term average margins? Find out whether they are sustainable. How they performed through business cycle? Whether depreciation policy is making any impact or not? Lower depreciation will mean higher profits, higher taxes, and lesser cash flow, while higher depreciation will mean lower profits but higher cash flow. That is why we analyze the trend between EBIDTA and EBIT, where the difference between the two numbers is the depreciation.

Profit before Tax ("PBT") AND Profit after Tax ("PAT")

What is the trend? Whether they are at peak or at trough? What is the long-term average margins? Find out whether they are sustainable. How they performed through business cycle?

Take net interest (aggregate interest expense and interest income) to calculate PBT or PAT. Check out tax rates. If tax rate is too low make suitable adjustments.

What Makes A Good Income Statement

1. Secular trend in all the line items. Not too much volatility
2. Easy to analyze. The profits and operating cash flow converge.
3. Income driven by core operations and not due to other income or one-time gains or losses.
4. Movements into reserves, bad debts, and provisions. Whether in conformity with trend in revenue or losses.

5. Accounting for stock compensation, depreciation, pension provisions are prudent and conservative.

4.4 Concentration and Valuations

a. Geography concentration

Prada, the luxury goods manufacturer has 36% revenue coming from Chinese markets. After years of soaring growth, the concentration of Chinese market started hitting its financial statements.

Prada owns and operates the largest number of stores in China among all the luxury goods manufacturers. However, the Chinese market concentration and the weakness in Chinese economy has led to precipitous fall in the stock price from $58 to $22 million in 52 weeks.

Below are Prada's numbers:

52 week	20.20 - 52.00
Mkt cap	HKD 58.60B
P/E	18.80

The Group at a glance—Full year

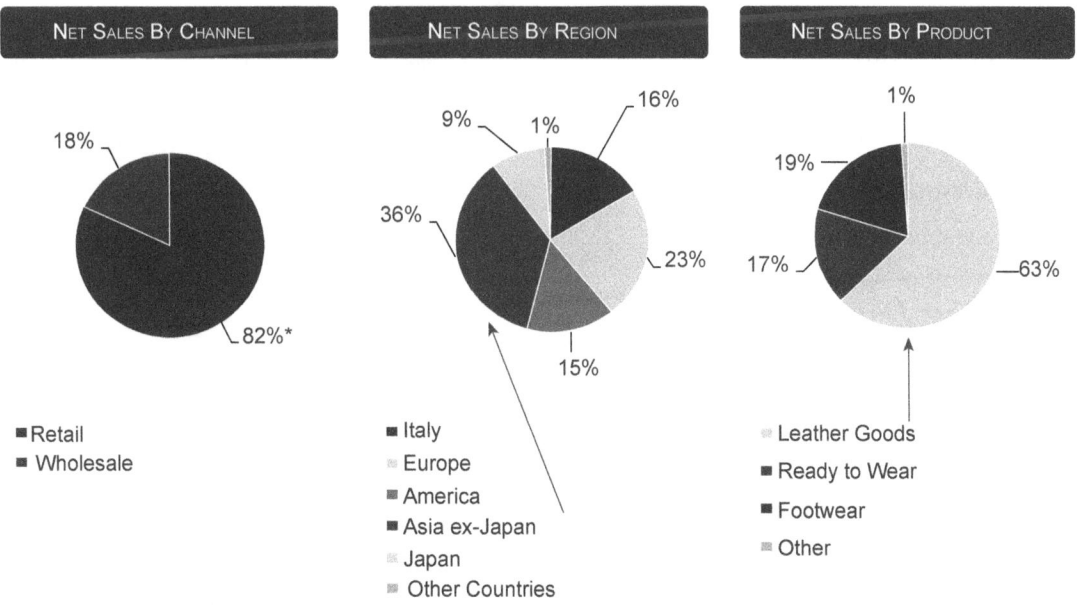

NET SALES BY CHANNEL

18%
82%*

- Retail
- Wholesale

NET SALES BY REGION

9% 1%
16%
36%
23%
15%

- Italy
- Europe
- America
- Asia ex-Japan
- Japan
- Other Countries

NET SALES BY PRODUCT

1%
19%
17%
63%

- Leather Goods
- Ready to Wear
- Footwear
- Other

b. Customer concentration

Hon Hai Precision Ltd., popularly known as Foxconn, is the supplier of screens and other parts to global phone and related manufacturers. Foxconn has ~40% customer concentration with Apple. The growth in Apple through Iphone, Ipod, and Tablet has fuelled the growth of Foxconn as well with top-line and bottom-line compounded the growth rate of 15%. Despite the growth rates and ROE of ~15%, the stock trades at 0.27 sales, 1.2 times book, and had high P/E of 15 and low of 8.

These numbers are completely contradictory to that of Apple Inc. Apple has delivered revenue and profits to Foxcon, it has taken away the valuation multiples due to the concentration effect.

Foxconn

VALUATION RATIOS

P/E ratio (TTM)	7.9
P/E high—Last 5 years	15.1
P/E Low—Last 5 years	9.5
Price to sales (TTM)	0.2
Price to book (MRQ)	1.2
Sales—5-year growth rate	16.5
Return on assets (TTM)	6.7
Return on assets—5-year average	5.3
Return on investment (TTM)	14.1
Return on investment—5-year average	12.9
Return on equity (TTM)	16.4
Return on equity—5-year average	15.5

4.5 Clinical Examination of Company's Health

We have looked at quality of balance sheet and income statement as well as the valuation drivers and attributes. Let us now focus on dissecting the balance sheet and income statement.

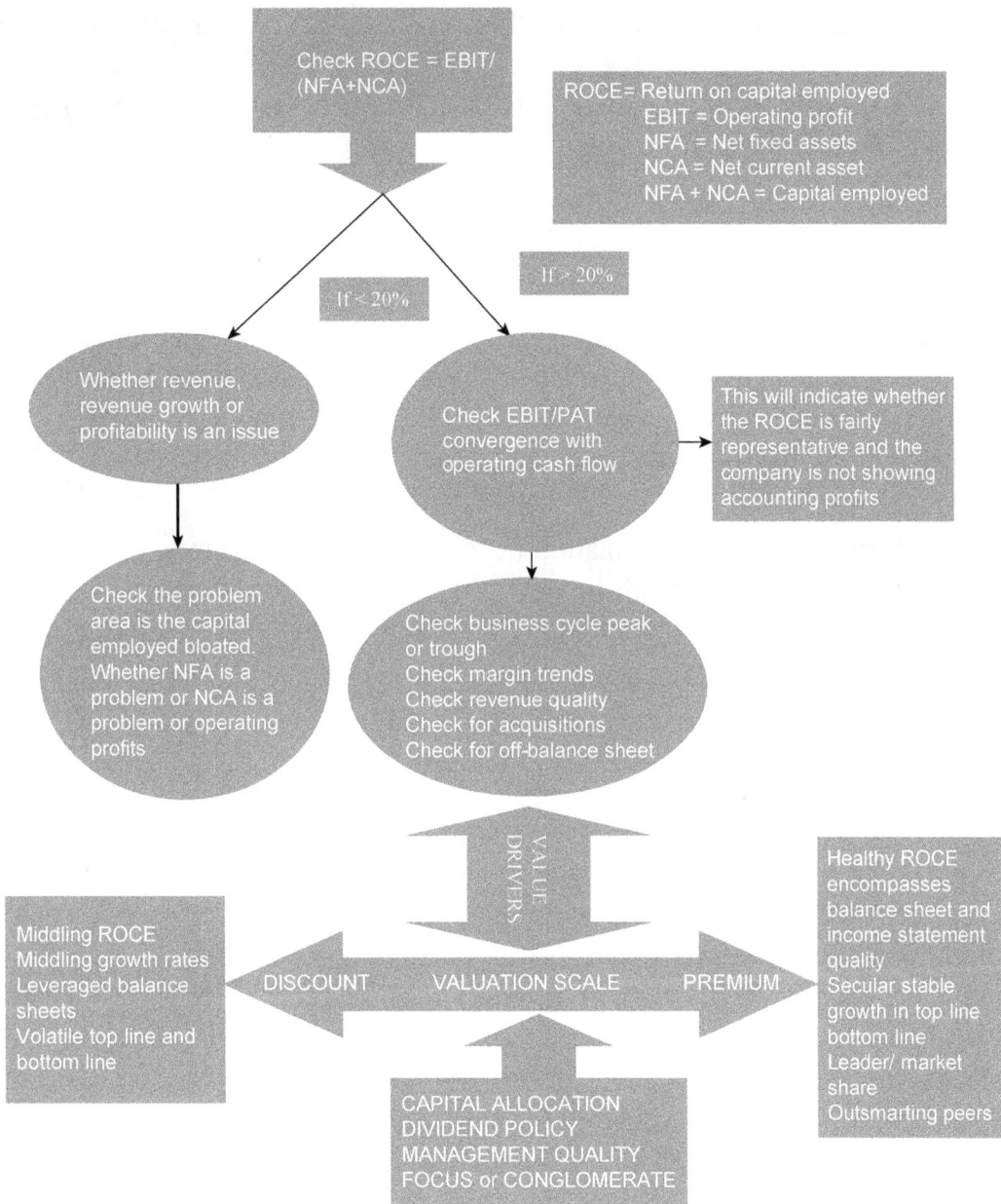

4.6 Cornerstones to Perform an Effective Discounted Cash Flow (DCF)

1. Revenue growth rates after computing year on year, CAGR, 3- to 5-year rolling, constant currency, and organic growth. Then decide on appropriate growth rates. Do not just take future growth rates. Justify it against available data.

2. EBITDA/EBIT margin trends and sustainability—What has changed in the business to understand how the margins have changed in the business and to see

how they will perform in the future. Take average that cuts through the business cycle.

3. Build in sensitivity of various inputs based on peak and trough business scenarios.

4.7 Normalization

Normalization is a concept wherein any abnormality in the trend or numbers are smoothened out or adjusted to present a factual picture of a situation. For example, if there is excess cash on the balance sheet, the excess cash is adjusted for the amount. That is required for the working capital of the company. Thus, if $100 is the excess cash on the balance sheet and the cash requirement for purpose of working capital is $20. Then, $80 is treated as excess cash.

We will deep dive into normalization beyond the above concepts, with the objective of getting the true picture of the operating company in a normalized state after weeding out abnormality or smoothening out the outliers.

In short, shorn of externalities, whether the normalized balance sheet and income statement does it gives better picture of intrinsic value drivers of companies.

a. Principles of Normalization

1. **Symmetric principle:** Dual accounting slightly similar to double entry book keeping system. Every adjustment made in the balance sheet will have impact on the P&L account and vice versa. For example, if we adjust for excess cash in the net current assets, we will have to adjust the other income on such excess cash in the income statement; thus, symmetry is maintained.

2. **Recurring or non-recurring principle:** There will be certain income or expenses which may be recurring or non-recurring. This may be specific for an industry or a company and depending on its recurrence frequency it needs to be taken into account whether to normalize or not.

   For example, export-oriented company may have recurring forex gain or losses, which would be taken as part of core income, due to its recurring nature. While for other type of companies, they may have forex gain or losses as one-off, making it a non-core income and requiring non-recurring normalization.

3. **Core or non-core principle:** There will be certain income or expenses which as per accounting norms may get classified into different categories. This may be specific for an industry or a company which would then be taken as core income, while if it is not specific and one-off, it will be non-core and depending on its nature they may need to be normalized.

For example, scrap income gets classified as other income. While scrap income is of recurring nature for a manufacturing company; hence, in this case, it may need to be added back to the core income.

b. Normalizing rules

- Pick any data be it in a horizontal or vertical analysis that is an outlier and try to normalize them.
- Which parts of the financial statements are recurring or non-recurring; adjust for whatever is not recurring. Following are some examples of normalizing non-recurring and extraordinary losses/profits.

Example 1: A company gets hit by a $920 million fine and for instance their profit for the year was $50 million; this makes their total profit equal to $970 million (920+50). Assuming tax rate is zero.

Example 2: Gain from sale of building = $1000 million, profit = $1050 million. Therefore, after normalizing, the net profit will be $50 million (1050–1000)

One time uptick or dip is considered as an outlier. Examples include sale of assets, legal settlements, and asset impairments,

c. What to normalize?

1. Non-core asset (knock-off)

Core assets are those which are needed to be used directly to produce goods or provide service. The remaining assets are considered as the non-core assets and stated below are the examples.

> Ex:Real estate
>> Aeroplanes
>> Investments
>> Loans and advances
>> Deposits

2. Non-core income (knock-off)

Core and non-core income is explained in the preceding section. Income on the above non-core asset should be knocked-off from the income statement following the symmetrical principle. The other examples of the aforesaid can be Fx gain, compensation, and tax subsidies.

3. Capital Work in Progress (CWIP)

Capital work in progress should not be accounted for in the capital employed, as the income is missing because the asset is yet to be capitalized *viz.* not yet put to use in operations to generate revenues. However, if the capital expansion needs to be taken on a regular basis, you CAN consider including your CWIP in the B/S meaning that CWIP are normal part of the business.

4. Goodwill—if the company is having regular merger and acquisition

Generally, the texts treat goodwill as non-core asset. However, if the company is indulging in frequent M&A, then it will be in order to include the goodwill as a part of capital employed in denominator because the earnings of the would be a part of the core income of the company.

5. Recurring (taken into account)/non-recurring (not taken into account)

a. Provisions made in the income statements: Provisions are made in the income statement or written back to income statement to maintain normal profits and smoothen their earning. The recurring and non-recurring frequency of provisions needs to be normalized.
b. Non-recurring expense (like expense due to calamities) eliminate it from expenses during normalization.

6. Other examples of normalization

c. **Constant currency:** It includes especially those into export companies that need to assess the real performance–constant currency on base year to check the currency benefit.
d. **Organic growth rates:** Any spike due to acquisition must be checked to know how the existing and acquired company has performed.
e. **Real estate:** Real estate is recorded on book value, but during valuation the market value will be taken. For example: BV = $50 million, MV = $400 million
f. **Operating leases:** It is an off-balance sheet asset. Hence, there is a need to bring it back on to the balance sheet.
g. **Goodwill and intangible:** If goodwill has not been impaired, then auditors will verify. On the other hand, if it needs to impaired, it will hit the balance sheet of the company and consequently the net worth.
h. **Inventory:** Whether "first in, first out" (FIFO), "Last in First out" (LIFO) or weighted average is used. LIFO is discarded, most companies follow weighted average or FIFO. Normalization is done to check and confirm if the inventory is obsolete.
i. **Debtors:** Most critical because this is where the revenue lies that has not been realized. Bogus receivables and the realizable time need to be checked and to see whether there is any need to be written-off. Aging profile of the debtors needs to be considered.

j. **Revenue recognition policy:** There are different revenue recognition policies in different industries. For example: The mercantile policy says that whatever is received will be declared as revenue irrespective of the time period over which that revenue is being generated. Let us assume, if a company receives a high advance payment of $100,000 and expense for that year is $1000 and revenue applicable for that year is only $10,000, then PAT should be $9000 and not $99,000.

k. **Standalone and consolidated:** For instance, if you are looking to acquire a consolidated company in which the holding company A is very big with PAT of $100 million and has a subsidiary company B with PAT of $5 million. In this case, we will not look at company B at the time of acquisition. For example: A subsidiary company B needs a loan of $100 million, but the bank refuses to give a loan. Hence, the holding company A takes the loan for B and pays 10%. Interest per annum is $10 million. If B generates a profit of $5 million, the actual net profit for B is negative $5 million (5–10) because of the interest recognized by the holding company.

l. **Other examples of normalizing will be:**

a. Averaging out the growth rates for the company by taking cyclical averages or rolling CAGR or simply CAGR.

b. Taking normalized margin for a cyclical company. For example: If at the peak of cycle the margin is 18% and at trough 12%, then the normalized margin may be 15%.

c. Net interest expense for the company = Interest expense – interest income. Thus, if the company has $5 million as interest expense, the interest income is $1 million. In this case, the net interest expenses will be $4 million.

d. Net debt would mean debtless cash or marketable security. A company has a debt of $150 million, equity is $100 million, cash and marketable security is $75 million.
The normalized debt will be = 150–75= 75.
Normalized debt /equity = 75/100= 0.75

m. Numerical example of normalization:

1. A company has profit after tax (PAT) of $100 million. It has interest cost of $15 million and interest income of $10 million. Given the tax rate is 20%, calculate the normalized or adjusted PAT. Further, assuming P/E multiple of 20, also calculate the market cap.
Adjusted PAT = $100 (profit) – $10 (deduct interest income) + $2 (add back tax on interest income) + $15 (add interest expense) – $3(less tax shield on interest expense) = $104
Net interest expense = $15 – $10 = $5. Tax shield = $1 (20% × $5).

Adjusted PAT = $104.
Market cap = 20 × $104 = $2080.

n. Normalizing unrelated business cost

2. A company is in debt of $100 million. The debt has been taken to acquire unrelated business having negligible profit. The interest expense on the debt is $5 million. Given the tax rate is 20% and company has PAT of $50 million, calculate the adjusted PAT.

Adjusted PAT = $50 + $4 (non-tax shield interest expense of unrelated business) = $54.

o. Normalizing market cap and P/E multiple

3. A company has a market cap of $1000 million. The company has cash and marketable securities worth $200 million. It has PAT of $50 million of which $10 million comes from cash and marketable securities. Calculate the adjusted P/E multiple.

P/E multiple = (market cap – cash)/(gross PAT – other income earned on cash)

P/E multiple = ($1000 – $200)/($50 – $10) = 800/40=20

p. Normalizing profit across cycle

4. A company has a market cap of $300 million. The profit earned by the company for five successive years is $10 million, $30 million, $15 million, $5 million, and 25 million, respectively. Calculate appropriate P/E multiple for the company.

P/E multiple = 300/17 (average 85/5) = ~18X.

q. Normalizing growth rates

Growth rates	2011(a)	2010(b)	2009(c)	2008(d)	2007(e)	2006(f)
Net operating income	1403.8	1237.4	1122.2	670.6	332.4	81.1
Year over year (YoY) $\left(\frac{a}{b}-1\right)\times100$	13.5%	10.3%	67.3%	101.7%	309.8%	
3 Year CAGR (1/3 YRS) $\left(\frac{a}{d}\right)^{\frac{1}{3}}-1$	28%					
5 Year CAGR (1/5 YRS) $\left(\frac{a}{f}\right)^{\frac{1}{5}}-1$	77%					
Rolling 3-year CAGR	28%	54%	138%			

The above example depicts the base effect if we take initial and last of period numbers. As also if we take the recent numbers or simple CAGR, it could present an incorrect growth rates. Thus, rolling the CAGR over third- or fifth-year will give a clear picture of the growth rates achieved which can be further used to calculate DCF.

Income Statement Normalization

The below table highlights an income statement under normalization. Please refer the column on normalization adjustments for explanations.

	Normalization adjustments	2015	2014	2013	2012	2011	2010	2009	2008	2007	2006
INCOME											
Net sales		3816.8	3771.9	3393.9	3016.6	2132.2	1527.5	1366.6	1120.3	865.0	584.1
Other income		277.4	14.1	4.5	4.0	92.4	66.3	41.4	33.8	22.8	42.5
Export incentives	Company seems to be in export so need to be added back to operating income or net sales	0.0	0.0	0.0	0.0	0.0	36.3	33.5	13.4	12.4	36.1
Dividend income	Not core income	7.6	11.5	0.3	0.3	3.1	0.5	0.0	0.0	0.0	0.0
Interest income	To be netted off against interest expense	2.7	1.9	1.5	2.6	7.6	1.5	1.6	1.0	0.5	0.5
Profit on sale of fixed assets	Not core business. No adjustment	0.1	0.0	0.6	0.3	0.0	0.0	0.0	0.0	0.4	0.0
Profit on sale of investments	Not core business. No adjustment	0.4	0.2	0.0	0.6	0.1	0.0	0.0	0.1	0.0	0.0
Provision for diminution in value of investment	Not core business. No adjustment	0.0	0.0	0.0	0.0	0.0	0.0	1.7	0.0	0.0	0.0
Gain on Cancell. of Forward Contr/forex trans	Company seems to be in export so it need to be added to regular income	266.1	0.0	0.0	0.0	81.2	18.4	0.0	11.1	0.0	0.0
Sale of scrap	Being in manufacturing, it can be added toward regular income	11.1	0.0	23.5	15.6	0.0	21.7	17.7	0.0	9.8	0.0
Refunds / claims received	No adjustment needed	0.0	0.0	0.0	0.0	0.0	1.9	0.0	2.8	0.0	0.0
Provision written back	Depends on treatment of provision when it was made	0.0	0.0	0.0	0.0	0.0	0.0	0.6	0.0	0.0	0.1
Miscellaneous income	No adjustment needed	0.7	0.5	2.1	0.2	0.4	7.6	5.7	5.5	8.8	5.7

EXPENDITURE

											Comment
Raw materials	1962.9	1834.8	1930.6	1869.5	1334.6	775.5	800.9	652.4	479.5	330.2	
Power and fuel cost	175.5	168.7	167.6	141.5	116.6	89.8	82.9	76.8	56.9	44.7	
Employee cost	227.3	168.6	133.8	93.8	71.8	48.6	40.2	33.0	23.9	18.3	
Other manufacturing expenses	292.3	267.9	233.4	205.8	134.1	113.4	91.2	55.5	39.8	29.6	
Selling and administration expenses	388.5	338.8	261.8	210.9	169.9	132.0	125.1	100.3	82.4	66.1	
Miscellaneous expenses	27.4	116.1	33.7	35.3	13.9	13.0	59.9	10.3	14.4	7.1	
Loss on sale of assets	0.0	0.2	0.0	0.0	0.1	0.1	0.0	0.6	0.8	0.4	Not core business. Add lock
Loss on sale of investments	0.0	0.0	0.0	0.0	0.0	0.0	0.0	0.0	0.0	0.0	Not core business. Add lock
Loss on revaluation of investments	0.0	0.0	0.0	0.0	0.0	0.0	0.0	0.0	0.0	0.0	Not core business. Add lock
Loss on Forex transactions	0.0	91.8	14.5	18.0	0.0	0.0	38.7	0.0	0.0	0.0	Fx. gain is taken as operating income so FX loss will also be operating expense
Bad debts written-off	0.0	0.0	0.0	0.0	0.0	0.0	0.0	0.0	0.0	0.0	If one-time expense and not regular can be reduced from operating expense
Expenses amortized	0.0	0.0	0.0	0.0	0.0	0.0	0.0	0.0	0.0	0.0	The entire amortization can be aggregated and expensed
Provision for doubtful loan/deposit/ advances	0.0	0.0	0.0	0.0	0.0	0.0	0.0	0.0	0.5	0.0	Depending on the nature of provision to decide whether to adjust the operating expense
Provision for contingency	0.0	0.0	0.0	0.0	0.0	0.0	0.0	0.0	0.0	0.0	Depending on the nature of provision to decide whether to adjust the operating expense
Other provisions and write-offs	0.0	0.0	0.0	0.0	-0.2	0.2	0.3	1.3	0.1	0.0	Depending on the nature of provision to decide whether to adjust the operating expense
Provision/impairment of assets	1.4	0.1	0.0	1.2	0.9	1.0	0.1	0.0	0.1	0.0	Depending on the nature of provision to decide whether to adjust the operating expense
Other miscellaneous expenses	26.0	24.0	19.2	16.1	13.1	11.7	19.2	8.4	13.0	6.7	No adjustment
Provision for diminution in value of investment	0.0	0.0	0.0	0.0	0.0	0.0	1.7	0.0	0.0	0.0	Similar treatment as in income

BALANCE SHEET NORMALIZATION & CALCULATING OPERATING CAPITAL EMPLOYED

Gross block	3322.3	3082.5	1858.3	1283.6	1055.2	909.3	772.2	600.1	564.5	390.4
Less: Impairment of assets	0.0	0.0	0.0	0.0	0.0	0.0	0.0	0.0	0.0	0.0
Net block [A]	2415.4	2389.0	1335.3	873.1	724.9	646.5	564.1	450.8	399.5	259.8
Capital work in progress (ignored) [D]	634.0	564.9	1012.6	476.7	56.4	68.7	81.5	131.9	75.8	68.9
Investments (ignored)	444.1	370.2	3.3	2.5	13.8	61.7	3.9	3.9	2.1	5.1
Current assets, loans and advances										
Inventories	411.4	568.4	456.7	498.5	423.0	217.7	133.3	200.6	122.4	106.9
Sundry debtors	579.7	613.8	519.7	490.0	335.8	253.1	220.8	207.9	168.7	79.6
Cash	434.2	14.9	278.0	369.8	12.3	5.4	11.7	10.3	5.6	76.9
Less: Excess cash (80% of cash)	347.4	11.9	222.4	295.9	9.8	4.3	9.4	8.2	4.5	61.5
Adjusted cash [C]	86.8	3.0	55.6	73.9	2.5	1.1	2.3	2.1	1.1	15.4
Loans and advances	231.7	279.6	257.3	221.6	129.1	382.3	287.5	301.0	195.3	149.4
Total current assets	1657.0	1476.7	1511.7	1580.0	900.2	858.6	653.2	719.7	492.0	412.8
Less : Current liabilities and provisions										
Current liabilities	459.1	479.4	317.2	270.4	234.5	133.0	88.3	121.2	75.1	53.2
Provisions	35.4	29.0	22.4	20.6	18.7	285.8	199.2	178.4	100.9	71.6
Total current liabilities	494.4	508.4	339.7	291.0	253.2	418.8	287.5	299.6	176.0	124.8
Net current assets [B]	1162.5	968.3	1172.0	1289.0	647.0	439.8	365.7	420.1	316.0	288.1
Operating capital employed (A+B−C)	905.5	1408.7	-59.1	-711.9	68.0	202.4	189.1	22.4	79.0	-89.8
Operating capital employed including capital work in progress (A+B+D−C)	1539.5	1973.6	953.5	-235.2	124.4	271.1	270.6	154.3	158.8	-20.9

Normalizing and Analyzing

Presented below is the financial statement that needs to be normalized and analyzed.

Sales	1238.72	1123.53	670.69	332.48	81.14	21.5	6.03
PBIT	232.9	260.41	182.67	81.34	20.04	4.87	0.44
PAT	121.85	152.86	108.95	58.51	15.08	3.73	0.38
Market capitalization	602.6	412.69	1740.86	731.65	362.19	94.31	4.06
Cash flow From operating activities	-117.57	-133.09	-143.12	-47.63	-19.53	0.95	-0.11
Cash flow from investing activities	-33.55	-92.38	-79.79	-5.86	-3.46	-3.29	-0.06
Cash flow from financing activities	154.78	227.59	194.19	140.48	23.21	2.37	0.18
Key ratios							
Debt–equity ratio	0.77	0.61	0.72	1.04	0.1	0.07	0.08
Current ratio	2.16	2.26	2.29	2.17	1.67	2.17	4.11
ROCE (%)	20.85	35.03	46.71	59.71	94.89	58.6	8.26
RONW (%)	18.62	31.47	44.85	81.04	68.7	44.17	7.8

Do you agree with the ROCE number? Why and Why not?

No. For the following reasons:
The company is showing operating profit but negative cash flow from operating activity.

Thus, the profits are locked in receivables. Therefore, it can be concluded that the ROCE numbers are not actual and will need to be normalized for the profits not realized.

The locking up of profits in receivables is explained below:

In the example given below, the company has rising sales and profits. It is also evident that the company is engaged in a business which allows revenues to be based on the contract completion method. The company's sales as we see shows rising trend along with profits, ROCE, and ROE.

However, a careful analysis of balance sheet and cash flow reveals the increase in debtors, debtors greater than 6 months, and the recognition of debtors based on

HEADLINE PE MULTIPLE AND ADJUSTED PE MULTIPLE

	2015	2014	2013	2012	2011	2010	2009	2008	2007	2006	2005	2004	2003	2002	2001
INCOME :															
Net sales	1243.8	1039.4	998.9	932.2	996.9	964.6	851.6	794.5	714.3	725.3	801.4	842.5	796.5	662.9	618.8
Other Income	119.2	104.7	301.5	39.7	513.4	36.7	37.0	124.8	123.0	103.5	94.0	115.5	90.6	49.3	67.3
Total income	1363.0	1144.1	1300.4	972.0	1510.3	1001.3	888.6	919.2	837.3	828.8	895.4	958.0	887.1	712.2	686.1
Total expenditure	1119.9	921.8	897.5	856.1	898.7	890.1	808.9	758.5	676.0	692.0	777.9	853.4	758.8	603.0	580.4
Operating profit	243.1	222.3	402.9	115.9	611.7	111.2	79.6	160.7	161.4	136.9	117.5	104.6	128.3	109.2	105.7
Profit before tax	219.9	200.0	378.7	90.4	586.2	85.5	55.7	131.5	133.2	107.2	86.9	64.2	75.9	70.5	69.6
Tax	41.3	44.4	84.0	26.6	140.0	29.9	2.4	31.0	32.9	13.4	17.8	0.0	14.5	20.0	27.5
Reported net profit	176.6	159.3	294.6	60.2	448.4	50.2	47.2	109.1	107.7	80.5	69.1	64.2	61.4	50.5	42.1
Market cap	2500														
Reported net profit	176.6														
PE multiple	14.2														
Other income	119.2														
Normalized profits (net of other income)	57.4														
Excess cash refelcted as investments in liquid instruments on balance sheet	985														
Normalized market cap (market cap less investments)	1515														
Normalized PE Multiple (normalized market cap/normalized profits)	26.4														

Thus, we see that on the headline PE basis, it appears cheaper. However, after normalizing we see that its fairly valued.

NORMALIZATION EXAMPLE

PROFIT AND LOSS

		2015	2014	2013	2012
INCOME :					
Net sales		15998.1	11508.5	8436.9	8660.4
Other income		1803.4	556.8	495.6	507.2
Other operating Income		**443.5**	**302.1**	**259.3**	**165.3**
Export incentives	Added back to operating income	443.5	302.1	259.3	165.3
Interest income	Not considered as operating income	333.9	97.6	104.6	127.8
Profit on sale of fixed assets	Not considered as operating income	9.4	5.7	3.5	7.2
Profit on sale of investments	Not considered as operating income	54.2	43.4	45.4	20.9
Total operating income		**16441.7**	**11810.6**	**8696.2**	**8825.8**
EXPENDITURE :					
VRS compensation	One time expense. Hence reduced from expense	0.0	183.3	183.3	102.4
Loss on sale of assets	Not considered as operating income on income side. Hence reduced from expense	20.1	3.4	3.9	6.3
Provision for dimunition in value of investment	Not considered as operating income on income side. Hence reduced from expense	102.3	0.0	2.5	0.0
Total expenditure		13410.8	9564.7	7806.7	7922.6
Total operating expenditure		**13288.4**	**9378.0**	**7617.0**	**7813.9**
Total operating profit		**3153.3**	**2432.6**	**1079.2**	**1011.9**
Interest		1.7	6.0	21.0	5.2
Depreciation		122.8	136.5	129.8	174.0
Reported net profit		3339.7	1702.7	654.5	755.8
Gross profit (total operating profit - interest)		**3151.6**	**2426.7**	**1058.2**	**1006.8**
Profit before tax (gross profit-depreciation)		**3028.7**	**2290.2**	**928.4**	**832.8**
Tax rate		20%	20%	20%	20%
Tax		605.7	458.0	185.7	166.6
Profit after tax		**2423.0**	**1832.2**	**742.7**	**666.2**

contract completion method. Thus, normalizing will involve reduction in sales and profits to certain percentage of these outstanding debtors to get the true picture of the profitability of the company. We can either write off 100% of these debtors or lesser depending on the facts of the situation.

The increase in debtors also has to be seen with the provisioning done by the company for bad debts. Absence of provisioning indicates a strong need to be more aggressive in normalizing.

Analyzing Company's Financial Statements

Below are the financial highlights of the company to understand the financial health of the company.

We have highlighted some important observations that require consideration.

	2012	2011	2010	2009	2008	2007	2006	2005	2004	2003
Equity paid up	48	48	48	48	19	19	19	19	19	19
Net worth	443	381	339	301	261	231	205	184	174	158
Capital employed	615	530	397	360	326	314	254	234	213	237
Gross block	317	290	232	193	185	174	142	136	129	119
Net working capital	357	298	236	261	223	222	178	163	136	141
Net sales	803	620	546	522	505	400	327	294	275	253
Other income	3	9	8	7	1	5	2	2	1	9
PBIT	176	129	122	106	95	78	66	52	49	54
PAT	111	80	78	68	59	54	43	36	31	35
Market capitalization	1384	1380	1314	1217	474	920	514	574	461	295
Payout (%)	41	45	46	37	45	46	48	48	49	43
Cash flow from operating activities	12	43	55	77	51	22	40	22	47	36
Cash flow from investing activities	-8	-95	-32	-8	-21	-28	-12	-7	11	-22
Cash flow from financing activities	-5	46	-23	-64	-28	6	-25	-16	-59	-12
Key ratios										
Debt–equity ratio	0	0	0	0	0	0	0	0	0	1
Current ratio	2	2	3	4	4	4	4	3	3	3
Turnover ratios										
Fixed assets ratio	3	2	3	3	3	3	2	2	2	2
PBITM (%)	22	21	22	20	19	19	20	18	18	21
ROCE (%)	31	28	32	31	30	27	27	23	22	24
RONW (%)	27	22	24	24	24	25	22	20	19	24

Observations

- The paid up equity has stayed constant. There is increase in the paid up capital most likely due to bonus issue.

- There is jump in the capital employed. The reason for the same need to be checked.
- The gross block increase has been secular and moderate. No sudden spike.
- The net working capital has also increased but, observed to be a bit moderate.
- Sales and profits have never declined and have CAGR of ~15%.
- The margins have been in a steady range.
- The operating cash flow has always been positive as also free cash flow.
- No leverage.
- The ROCE and ROE are observed to be in a healthy range of 20–30%.

4.8 Key industry metrics to be observed for the purpose of valuations

FMCG

- Growth rates in the top and bottom line.
- Working capital management
- Return on capital employed.
- The advertising expenditure compared to the revenue.

Construction

- Revenue recognition policy
- Operating cash flow convergence with profits
- Working capital management especially receivable and outstanding for greater than 90 days

Infrastructure

- Debt/equity and other leverage parameters
- Debt coverage through annuity income
- Working capital management
- Government receivables

Information technology

- Growth rates
- Employee strength and turnover
- Constant currency and organic growth rates
- Stickiness in the contracts
- Client concentration
- Geography concentration

Retail

- Growth rates
- Same store growth
- Working capital management and efficiency in merchandising
- Real estate
- Debt/equity
- Asset turnover
- Land bank and cost
- Advance sales and cash management across projects given the cyclicality of the industry
- Capital intensive business
- NAV NET ASSET VALUE
- P/B
- EV OR EBITDA
- EBIDTA/TURN = EFFICIENCY USAGE OF THE CAPITAL

4.9 Triangulating parameters for valuation

Valuation is regarded as an inter-play of the following parameters:

a. **Growth rates:** The higher the compounded growth rates, the better. It is best, if they are being higher and consistent with those growth rates. The same being reflected in top line and bottom line makes it an icing on the top of cake. Thus, lower growth rates or flattish or volatile growth rates will give a lower valuation and higher top-line growth while bottom line will lead to a lower valuation. However, the contradictory situation may generally lead to higher valuation.

b. **Profit margins:** Steady margins meaning neither too high nor too low or oscillating margins will lead to lower valuations. Low margins indicate that the company is struggling, while too high margins reflect higher profits. It would mean that the company is not raking in sales growth by keeping margins high unless it is able to keep higher growth rates with higher margin as well. It is a very unlikely case for long, as sales growth will suffer or competition will play a pricing game to take market shares.

c. **Return on capital employed:** Above average ROCE and sacrificing it for higher growth rates will lead to higher valuation than higher ROCE but lower growth rates.

This would also mean optimizing the following:

- Growth rates
- Capital expansion
- Dividend rates

Case Study 4.1: Triangulating the Valuation Parameters across the Troika of A, B, and C Operating in the Same Industry.

Company A

	201503	201403	201303	201203	201103	201003	200903	200803	200703	200603	200503	200403	200303	200203
Equity paid up	11.2	11.2	11.2	11.2	11.2	11.2	11.2	11.2	11.2	2.4	2.4	2.4	2.4	2.4
Net worth	386.8	289.0	213.5	165.8	123.8	99.0	86.8	77.4	67.7	12.5	6.7	5.2	5.4	3.7
Net sales	1543.0	1187.7	876.3	696.6	491.6	346.7	254.7	192.4	135.9	101.2	74.7	62.5	49.6	37.6
PAT	196.0	153.8	112.5	90.0	58.6	39.6	31.6	23.8	17.0	11.4	4.2	5.3	3.1	1.8
Market capitalization	15311.7	7228.2	3704.5	3011.6	1811.4	889.8	401.5	465.9	330.2	0.0	0.0	0.0	0.0	0.0
Payout (%)	44.0	47.0	54.0	50.0	54.0	66.0	67.0	51.0	30.0	45.0	62.0	105.0	41.0	59.0
Cash flow from operating Activities	167.0	74.8	87.1	122.6	-0.2	29.8	33.2	11.2	9.1	10.8	3.7	6.7	2.1	3.1
Cash flow from investing Activities	-53.1	-48.9	-41.9	-25.3	-27.3	-20.9	-2.8	-36.5	-26.0	-3.7	-2.2	-2.2	-3.3	-1.0
Free cash flow	113.9	25.9	45.2	97.3	-27.4	8.8	30.4	-25.3	-16.9	7.1	1.5	4.5	-1.3	2.1
Key ratios														
Debt–equity ratio	0.5	0.5	0.5	0.7	0.8	0.5	0.5	0.4	0.5	1.4	2.0	1.8	1.5	1.4
PBITM (%)	20.2	20.9	19.1	19.1	19.1	18.1	19.6	19.1	20.0	17.9	9.9	13.2	12.0	9.5
ROCE (%)	54.5	57.3	57.2	54.2	45.7	44.3	41.9	36.4	47.6	83.0	41.2	55.4	53.0	41.2
RONW (%)	58.0	61.2	59.3	62.2	52.6	42.6	38.5	32.8	42.4	118.6	71.4	99.3	68.6	47.8
Equity base		Constant since 2007												
Rolling 3-year sales CAGR	39%	27%	40%	32%	51%	8%	64%	61%	92%	19%	27%			
Rolling 3-year PAT CAGR	30%	34%	36%	40%	37%	37%	36%	37%	30%	27%	26%			
Rolling 5-year sales CAGR	39%	39%	35%	19%	62%	48%	49%	40%	63%					
Rolling 5-year PAT CAGR	35%	36%	35%	39%	37%	36%	32%	31%	29%					
5-year average PBITM %	19.7													
5-year average ROCE	53.8													
5-year average RONW	58.7													

Company B

	201503	201403	201303	201203	201103	201003
Equity paid up	12.3	12.3	12.3	12.3	12.3	12.3
Net worth	319.8	290.6	253.9	225.6	197.8	175.2
Net sales	416.8	373.8	304.6	301.9	236.6	175.2
PAT	66.2	67.0	53.4	52.1	46.2	32.5
Market capitalization	2614.0	1396.4	893.4	819.9	673.1	302.1
Payout (%)	51.0	41.0	43.0	43.0	47.0	24.0
Cash flow from operating activities	75.3	42.2	66.2	36.9	38.9	30.2
Cash flow from investing activities	-24.3	-37.4	-78.7	-13.7	-12.3	8.0
Free cash flow	51.0	4.9	-12.5	23.3	26.6	38.2
Key ratios						
Debt–equity ratio	0.0	0.1	0.1	0.1	0.1	0.1
PBITM (%)	24.2	26.7	24.8	24.2	30.1	29.2
ROCE (%)	30.9	34.3	30.8	34.9	35.8	27.9
RONW (%)	21.7	24.6	22.3	24.6	24.8	19.9
Equity base		Constant since 2007				
Net sales	114%	15%				
PAT	121%	17%				
Book value (Unit Curr.)	30%	12%				
Market capitalization		12%				
EPS (annualized) (Unit Curr.)	22%	36%				
Rolling 3-year sales CAGR	11%	16%	20%	28%	14%	9%
Rolling 3-year PAT CAGR	8%	13%	18%	53%	30%	20%
Rolling 5-year sales CAGR	19%	21%	14%	18%	22%	46%
Rolling 5-year PAT CAGR	15%	36%	20%	23%	32%	54%
5-year average PBIT%	26.0					
5-year average ROCE	33.3					
5-year average RONW	23.6					

Company B

Adjusted operating ROCE (due to huge cash balance)

1. Net block	53.96	42.64	43.54	43.43	40.57	40.03
2. Investments	178.1	166.69	121.62	31.58	18.3	32.9
3. Cash and bank	43.17	34.17	60.77	101.55	103.89	80.18
4. Net current assets	95.69	90.28	95.4	156.24	132.63	113.36
5. Operating capital employed (1-2-3+4)	-71.62	-67.94	-43.45	66.54	51.01	40.31
6. PBIT	100.75	100.08	79.89	78.91	71.31	51.08
7. Other income	7.98	11.82	12.17	11.78	8.34	11.03
8. Adjusted PBIT (6-7)	92.77	88.26	67.72	67.13	62.97	40.05
9. ROCE (8/5)	Infinite	Infinite	Infinite	101%	123%	99%

Company C

C

	201503	201403	201303	201203	201103	201003	200903	200803	200703	200603	200403	200303
Equity paid up	16.8	16.8	16.8	16.8	16.8	7.5	1.5	1.5	0.5	0.5	0.5	0.5
Net worth	185.1	190.2	173.95	158.97	141.23	24.36	14.68	11.99	7.06	5.96	3.06	2.52
Net sales	172.49	159.52	151.09	132.99	101.48	86.95	69.24	60.06	41.54	30.66	15.27	14.53
PAT	19.72	21.16	18.89	21.65	14.09	10.8	2.87	4.16	3.18	2.89	1.16	1.2
Payout (%)	130	21	18	16	18	7	5	4	62	0	49	23
Cash flow from operating activities	3.04	2.65	13.1	4.16	0.2	9.7	12.16	3.42	0.41	2.97	0	0
Cash flow from investing activities	30.95	3.6	-14.41	-15.42	-92.54	-1.61	-10.19	-1.72	-0.63	-0.75	0	0
Free cash flow	-35.01	-6.36	2.79	-0.09	103.98	-7.17	-2.22	-1.27	1.23	-2.14	0	0
Key ratios												
Debt–equity ratio	0.05	0.06	0.04	0.01	0	0.17	0.5	0.68	0.77	0.7	1.21	1.14
PBITM (%)	13.04	15.03	13.6	16.57	19	17.47	11.01	12.32	12.59	16.28	14.36	16.66
ROCE (%)	11.33	12.35	12.32	15.28	23.13	66.39	38	45.03	42.14	45.45	32.32	37.69
RONW (%)	8.32	9.01	9.39	11.85	17.02	55.33	34.8	43.15	47.62	47.99	39.43	45.63
Equity base												
Net sales	-1%	13%										
PAT	37%	13%										
Rolling 3-year sales CAGR	9%	16%	20%	24%	19%	28%	31%	57%	41%			
Rolling 3-year PAT CAGR	0%	16%	19%	76%	37%	42%	1%	46%	29%			
Rolling 5-year sales CAGR	15%	18%	20%	26%	27%	42%	37%					
Rolling 5-year PAT CAGR	13%	43%	28%	40%	31%	45%	16%					
5-year average PBITM %	15.448											
5-year average ROCE	14.882											
5-year average RONW	11.118											

- Returning cash to shareholders
- Optimizing cash on balance sheet
- Working capital management
- Efficient asset turnover
- Keeping capital tight by minimal dilution and conservative leverage
- Optimal play between all elements of ROE formula

d. **Free cash flow:** Last but not least, the quality of operating cash flow and its convergence with the profits is taken into account. The free cash flow at times is a function of growth rates and capital expansion, but keeping the expansion and growth rates in tandem to operate cash flow will lead to higher valuations.

The aforementioned parameters indicate that valuation is an interplay between all the above four elements and in some ways will reflect the qualitative aspect of its operations and financial statements.

Summary and learning

	A	B	C
Equity base	Constant	Constant	Constant
8-year sales CAGR	35%	15%	13%
8-year PAT CAGR	36%	17%	13%
3-year average rolling 3-year sales CAGR	36%	16%	15%
3-year average rolling 3-year PAT CAGR	34%	13%	12%
5-year average rolling 5-year sales CAGR	39%	19%	21%
5-year average rolling 5-year PAT CAGR	36%	25%	31%
5-year average PBIT%	20%	26%	15%
5-year average operating ROCE	54%	Infinite	15%
5-year average RONW	59%	24%	11%
Long-term dividend payout %	55%	37%	16%
Market cap	15312	2614	525

Thus, we see the triangulation of valuation parameters including

- Sale growth
- Profit growth
- Operating profit margins
- Return on capital

- Dividend payout
- Balance sheet quality (leverage, idle cash)

Why C lags behind A and B is self-evident.

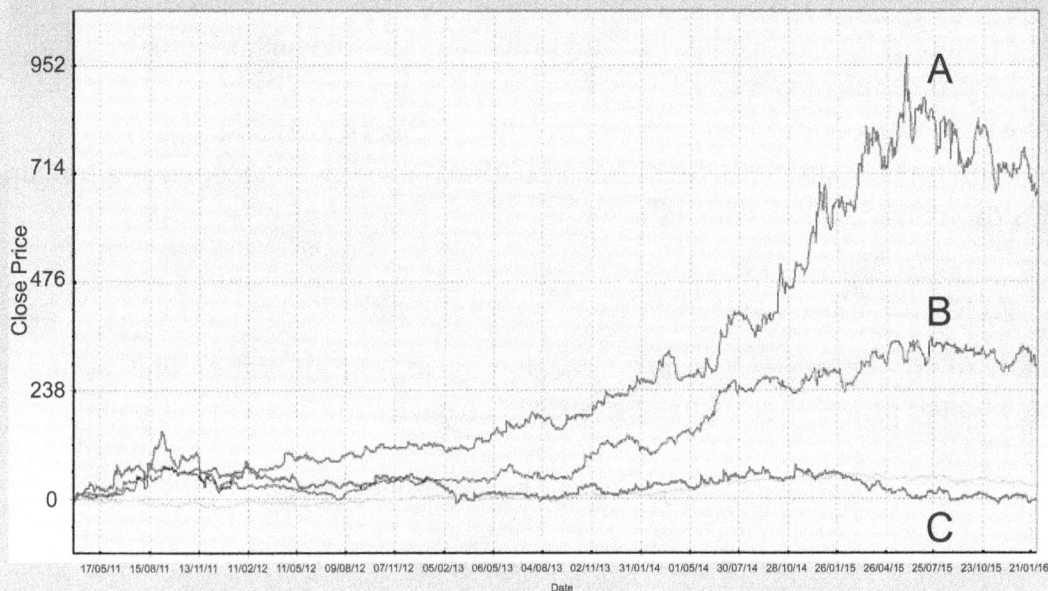

The operating ROCE for B is actually infinite due to negative capital employed and earns higher profit margin as compared to A.

But A has been able to balance lower margins with higher sales and profit growth along with higher dividend payout.

While it has earned lower operating ROCE, it has also generated higher profit and higher return; hence, the market cap of A is 6× that of B.

Further, the growth has been managed out of the free cash flow.

4.10 Common Valuation Mistakes in M&A

1. Not accounting for ongoing capital expenditure or maintenance CapEx.
2. Misplaced growth rates: Relying on either peak period growth rates or trough period growth rates.
3. Overestimating synergies: This can be checked by working out the IRR of the synergies and checking whether it is realistic or not.

Several times, the press releases of acquisition state the synergy value. Doing back of the hand discounting of the value indicates the discounting rate achieved. If the rate is similar to the return ratio achieved by the acquirer, then, they would look realistic else, it will be case of over-payment for the target.

4. Using due diligence as end and not the means to arrive at the value.
5. Not providing for dislocation or integration lag after the acquisition and building the projections from day 1.
6. Not normalizing appropriately over-income or under-expenses.
7. Capitalizing PAT and not EBIDTA in situations, thereby not accounting for capital structure or depreciation effects.

4.11 Margin Cycle and Multiple Matrix

The below matrix describes the various scenarios with profit margin and valuation multiple and the probability of success with each scenario.

Case Study 4.2: Glencore: Peak Market Perils

Details

Xstrata was one of the largest and most diversified miners in the world established just over a decade ago with a collection of zinc and ferroalloy assets and coal mines bought from Glencore.

Glencore is the globe's largest commodities trader, where it also has operations comprising of over 150 mining and metallurgical sites, off-shore oil production assets, farms, and agricultural facilities.

The merger was supposed to bring in the combined sales at the time of $209 billion and an equity value of $65 billion.

Xstrata purchase was valued at $44.6 billion based on the two companies closing share prices following the deal completion.

This was at the peak of the commodity cycle of 2012–2013. To quote the CEO, he spotlighted coal as key: "To really screw this up, the coal price has got to really tank."

Not only coal prices but most commodity prices have tanked in 2015. The following share price graph depicts the fortune of Glencore–Xstrata as of February 2016, the combined company at $12 billion from a peak of $70 billion.

Glencore share price
Mcap: $12 bn

Key Learning

- Do not base deals on factors which are not within one's control.
- Do not buy a volatile business with leverage.
- Discounting the risk by paying a price which will hold the acquisition in bad times also.
- Assumptions have to be conservative.
- Analyze peak and trough market conditions in context with conservativeness.

Understanding the market for your acquired products and services is indeed crucial. Firms foray into market or products or services of which they do not have any expertise and in most cases pay price which reflects optimistic assumptions regarding the potential of the target's and least to their lack of expertise.

4.12 Triangulating Valuation Methodologies

Valuation Methodologies

a. Liquidation approach

The above methodologies come into play depending on whether the business is viable or non-viable. Non-viable situation leads us to liquidation approach and has variant of Forced or Orderly sale.

Forced sale obviously means beating down value while orderly sale depending on the industry can generate a better value especially if done through auction.

b. Going Concern approach

Asset based: In case of cyclical earnings using cyclical averages

Earnings based: In case of stable earning

This will have further variants of:

Capitalized earning: If the ROI is better than cost of capital and have stable earnings

Capitalized cash flow: If there is difference between earnings and cash flow

Discounted cash flow: If there is variation on the future cash flows

c. Comparable multiples of similar companies

- **Identify a universe of public companies which are fundamentally comparable to the target.**
- Judgment and business sense are the key here.
- Similarity of industry/products/markets, business model, financial profile.
- **Analyze key ratios and operating data for each comparable to determine key metrics used by public markets for valuation.**
- Understand how comparable companies are valued relative to profitability, growth, etc.
- Based on data acquired in this analysis, determine a range of values for the target.
- **The valuation range must be adjusted to reflect the differences of the target from the universe of comparables.**
- Private company, size premium, control premium, IPO discount, etc.

Case Study 4.4: CMA CGM Acquires Neptune Orient Lines

Neptune Orient Lines Ltd/Singapore (NOL SP)—Highlights

In millions of USD	FY 1999	FY 2000	FY 2001	FY 2002	FY 2003	FY 2004	FY 2005	FY 2006
Market capitalization	1572.0411	922.4405	618.3143	623.728	1814.3746	2666.8635	2935.352	1981.6419
Enterprise value	3593.3421	2565.8475	2945.0974	3126.1379	2535.3615	2792.4185	2502.579	1992.8019
Revenue, comparable	4279.4902	4671.2202	4736.98	4641.8198	5268.6001	6544.7598	7271.0601	7263.5
Gross profit	762.645	986.9873	746.0703	543.7568	861.4282	1538.405	1592.875	1128.196
EBITDA	409.811	617.139	373.069	197.922	717.535	1267.953	1047.824	620.276
Net Inc,	93.91	178.498	-56.59	-330.156	229.76	942.707	803.872	363.743
EPS, comparable	0.093	0.1373	-0.0433	-0.2538	0.1716	0.5912	0.4998	0.2258
Free cash flow	298.924	161.594	-230.271	-125.088	375.516	728.17	949.248	389.666

Source: Annual report

(continued...)

In millions of USD	FY 2007	FY 2008	FY 2009	FY 2010	FY 2011	FY 2012	FY 2013	FY 2014	Current/LTM	FY 2015 Est
Market capitalization	**4,027.4**	**1,156.9**	**2,912.9**	**4,384.9**	**2,241.9**	**2,420.9**	**2,247.4**	**1,576.1**	**2,259.9**	
Enterprise value	**4,159.8**	**2,016.4**	**3,563.2**	**4,810.3**	**4,419.4**	**5,553.5**	**6,162.5**	**5,675.0**	**4,901.9**	
Revenue	8,160.0	9,285.1	6,515.6	9,422.1	9,210.7	9,511.6	8,831.2	8,616.8	6,333.2	6,042.6
EBITDA	807.1	401.3	-365.3	865.5	-93.7	13.7	333.0	303.7	313.4	296.5
Margin %	9.9	4.3	-5.6	9.2	-1.0	0.1	3.8	3.5	4.9	4.9
Net Inc, comparable	522.8	83.1	-740.8	460.9	-478.2	-419.4	-76.3	-259.8	697.6	679.9
Margin %	6.4	0.9	-11.4	4.9	-5.2	-4.4	-0.9	-3.0	11.0	11.3
Free cash flow	**-82.3**	**-377.5**	**-639.0**	**222.3**	**-1,625.3**	**-1,012.6**	**-1,271.5**	**-278.8**	**199.2**	**1,013.5**

Source: Annual report

Neptune Orient Lines Ltd/Singapore (NOL SP) - Profitability

Returns	FY 2007	FY 2008	FY 2009	FY 2010	FY 2011	FY 2012	FY 2013	FY 2014	Current/LTM	FY 2015 Est
Return on common Equity	33.6	15.4	21.9	3.2	-28.1	15.3	-16.4	-17.4	-3.6	-13.5
Return on assets	17.5	8.0	11.2	1.5	-13.7	7.8	-7.1	-5.4	-0.8	-2.8
Return on capital	27.1	–	18.7	3.0	-18.6	11.8	-9.0	-6.2	0.0	-1.7
Return on invested capital	22.4	–	16.3	2.9	-17.5	12.2	-8.6	-5.9	-0.3	-1.5

Details

CMA CGM, the world's third-biggest French group container shipper, agreed to buy Singapore's ailing Neptune Orient Lines for $2.4 billion plus debt.

- CMA paid a 49% premium to unaffected price at S $1.3 per share
- Valuation of 0.95 times of the book value
- Premium paid equals to $800 million.
- Deal costs ~$125 million being 5% of the equity value.

Thus, the breakeven synergy will have to be at least $900–1000 million.

The analyst comment:

"Annual synergies of $111 million a year, taxed at 17% and capitalised at 10 times, would cover the outlay. This equates to just 1.6% of Neptune's liner revenues last year.

This looks a lot like the trough in the cycle: Shipping rates, industry sentiment, and valuations all were crashed.

Analysis

While, the cost synergy looks only mere 1.6% of revenues, the facts is the business have made profit in only in only ¾ years out of 15–16 years of track record hugely leveraged with no cash flow. These would require either off-loading assets and booking losses or keep supporting through external capital. Thus, the outlay will be much higher than the current acquisition capital while it is in trough times. The Price is 1 time book for negative returns. Even if return to peak profitability of 2006, it would not still mean even high single digit return. If the acquisition had happened at current P/B or by paying some premium to it than it could have been concluded that the risk is discounted. The price looks peak cycle multiple. We will wait to see how the acquisition pans out.

Case Study 4.5: JAB Holding Co. Said It is Buying Keurig Green Mountain Inc. for $13.9 billion

Detail

JAB Holding Co. said it is buying Keurig Green Mountain Inc. for $13.9 billion in the biggest coffee deal on record, adding the US pioneer of single-serve pods to the European investment firm's global coffee empire.

The price is 78% premium for Keurig's shares. Keurig was struggling with decline in sales. JAB Holding is wishing to compete with Nestle SA in coffee dispensing market. Keurig has roughly 20% share of the packaged-coffee market in the US.

The acquisition follows a string of other coffee-related deals for JAB. It bought US-based chains Caribou Coffee Co. and Peet's Coffee & Tea in 2012 and last year, they acquired the parent company of Einstein Bros. Bagels. This year JAB acquired two upscale, niche players in the US, Stump town Coffee Roasters and Intelligentsia Coffee Inc.

Other aspects of JAB's strategy are less clear such as how it plans to leverage its added scale to gain better purchasing price or any other synergies.

The deal values Keurig at $92 a share, compared to that week close of $51.70. Keurig's stock had fallen 67% from its all-time closing high of $157.10 in November 2014.

Net income

in millions

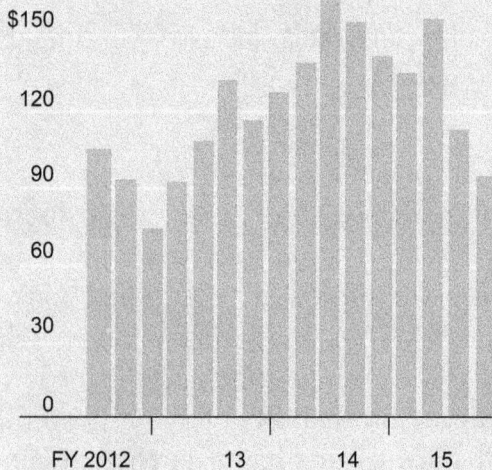

Sales changes from previous year

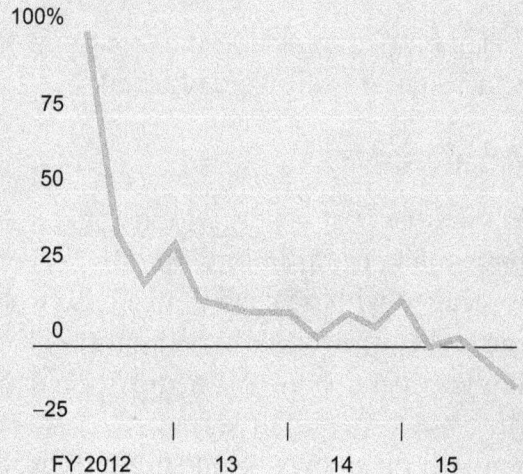

Analysis

The price represents a significant premium to the current performance. We can say that the earnings are down from previous years. However, the sales have also fallen drastically and may not represent trough earnings. If we take 5-year average, the earnings will still be high and being acquired with higher multiple. So, depressed earnings but inflated multiple.

JAB Holdings strategy to expand sales and margins is not clear. Neither are they involved in this business, the competition being Nestle and Starbucks. Thus, the price does not discount the risk of acquisition.

d. Comparable transaction valuation

Value a company or an asset by comparing reported comparable acquisitions and precedent transactions

- Comparability of the target on the basis of similar characteristics (business mix, customer base, distribution channels, industry dynamics, etc.)
- Typical benchmarks include multiples of net income (equity value multiples) and multiples of revenue, EBITDA and EBIT (firm value multiples)

Key is also to understand the key traits of the transaction, besides the comparability of the target

- Friendly *vs.* hostile
- Auction *vs.* negotiated deal
- Majority stake (control) *vs.* minority position
- Merger of equals *vs.* outright acquisition
- Consideration paid: Cash, shares, cash and shares

Outright acquisitions potentially involves a "control premium" above comparable trading company multiples.

e. Other Metrics

Public company multiples

Application of trading multiples (P/E, P/B, P/S, P/CF, etc…)

Transaction multiples

Application of multiples achieved from reported transactions

Rules of thumb:

Industry specific metrics ($X per truck, $X per employee)

Discount factors in applying public company multiples to private companies.

- Size
- Less diversified
- Strength of balance sheet
- Personal goodwill
- Marketability and liquidity
- Cost concentration

Synergy potential to acquirer is the key determinant of value. The above methodologies in conjunction with whether it involves a strategic buyer, private equity, management buy-out, liquidation, control, non-control as well as route taken for acquisitions or divestments and skillful negotiations will determine the level of valuations.

It is important to do the valuation from the eyes of the buyer that will provide a better indication of the value that buyer will be willing to pay.

4.13 EPS Accretion, Acquisition Financing and Valuations

EPS accretion: It is generally stated in the press release of the acquisition that the acquisition will be EPS accretive. The EPS accretion could be for the reason of sound and fundamental buy that are bought at discounted price or it could be financially engineered buy that gives EPS accretion. The example given below depicts the particular point as to how EPS accretion is affected by means of financing.

Thus, given the debt financing on mathematical terms is cheaper than the equity financing. Lower the interest rate, higher is the implied PE (1/interest rate (net of tax) thereby giving higher purchasing power and break even at point of implied PE. Thus, interest rate is essentially the yield expected on 100% debt funded acquisition.

Contrary to that is equity financed. Given the higher PE of the acquirer, lower is the yield required from acquisition (1/P/E) creating the bootstrap effect for the acquirer. Thus, at same PE as the acquirer, the acquisition will be EPS neutral but, for acquisition at PE higher than the acquirer it will turn out to be decretion.

Thus, don't be flummoxed by the accretion statement that need to look holistically at deal valuation and financing to figure out accretion or decretion effect due to acquisition.

TARGET

Equity value	Assumed debt	Enterprise value	EBIDTA	EBIT	PAT	# shares	P/E
100	50	150	50	45	40	2	20

PROJECTED

		(1)	(2)	(3)
EBIDTA	EBIT	PAT	# shares	EPS
80	75	70	2	35

	(4)	(5)	(6)	(7)	(8)
Indicative PE	P/E	P/E	P/E	P/E	P/E
	15	20	17.9	35	40
	(4) × (1)	(5) × (1)	(6) × (1)	(7) × (1)	(8) × (1)
Indicative equity value	1050	1400	1250	2450	2800

Debt financing

Debt financing				Acquirer				
(9)	(10)	(11)	(12)	(13)	(14)	(15)	(16)	(17)
		[(9)×(1–(10))]	1/(11)					
Cost of debt financing	Tax rate (given)	Cost of debt financing net of tax	Implied PE	PAT of acquirer	Number of shares	Share price	EPS	P/E
6%	30%	4%	23.8	50	10	100	5	20

Projected PAT	Equity value of target ((12)×(18))	Combined PAT (13)+(14)	Tax credit on net debt financed PAT (11)×(19)	Combined PAT	Combined number of shares (14)	Combined EPS (22)/(23)	EPS accretion
(18)	(19)	(20)	(21)	(22)	(23)	(24)	(24)–(16)
70	1667	120	-70	50	10	5	0

	Sensitivity analysis for debt financing			
	3%	6%	8%	
Implied PE	47.62	23.81	17.86	Thus, we see that if the implied PE is higher than the debt financing interest
	3333	1667	1250	We will have accretion, if lesser there will be negative effect.

Equity financing

EPS ACCRETION ANALYSIS

(25)	(26)	(27)	(28)	(29)	(30)	
Indicative equity value of target (25)	Number of new shares to be issued (25)/(15)	Total number of shares (26)+(15)	Combined PAT (13)+(14)	Revised EPS (28)/(27)	EPS accretion (29)-(16)	
1050	10.5	20.5	120	5.9	0.9	
1400	**14.0**	**24.0**	**120**	**5.0**	**0.0**	**Neutral at Acquirer PE**
1667	16.7	26.7	120	4.5	–0.5	
2450	24.5	34.5	120	3.5	–1.5	

Case Study 4: Marico Buys Personal Care Brands

Marico buys Paras personal care brands from Reckitt Benckiser and has paidworth Rs. 600–650 crores for the privately held Paras Pharma's personal care brands such as Zatak deodorant, Set Wet hair gel, and Livon hair serum. With the new deal, it will get six brands—Set Wet, Livon, Zatak, Eclipse, Recova, and Dr Lips—that are expected to have a turnover of more than Rs. 150 crores in FY12. Paras brands are among the top three in the hair gel, male deodorant, and hair serum categories. Marico intended to sell 4.8% stake to raise Rs. 500 crores at Rs. 170 per share on a preferential allotment basis.

TARGET

Equity value (purchase price)	Turnover	PAT margin	PAT	Acquired P/E
600	150	10%	15	40

		PROJECTED					
		(1)					
		PAT					
		30					
		(2)					
Indicative PE		P/E					
		20					
		(1) × (2)					
Indicative equity value		600					

				Acquirer					

Debt financing

(3)	(4)	(5) [(3)×(1–(4)]	(6) 1/(5)	(7)	(8)	(9)	(10)	(11)
Cost of debt financing	Tax rate (given)	Cost of debt financing net of tax	Implied PE	PAT of acquirer	Number of shares	Share price	EPS	P/E
10%	30%	7%	14.3	85	10	170	8.5	20

Projected PAT	Equity value of target ((12)×(18)	Combined PAT (13)+(18)	Tax credit on debt financed (11)×(19)	Net PAT	Combined number of shares (14)	Combined EPS (22)/(23)	EPS accretion
(12)	**(13)**	**(14)**	**(15)**	**(16)**	**(17)**	**(18)**	**(18)–(10)**
30	429	115	-30	85	10	8.5	0

Equity financing

If the projected PAT stays at 15

EPS ACCRETION ANALYSIS

(19)	(20)	(21)	(22)	(23)	(24)
Indicative equity value of target (2)	Number of new shares to be issued (19)/(9)	Total number of shares (20)+(8)	Combined PAT (12)+(7)	Revised EPS (22)/(21)	EPS accretion (23)–(10)
600	3.5	13.5	100	7.4	-1.1	Decretive

If the projected PAT ramps upto 30

EPS ACCRETION ANALYSIS

(19)	(20)	(21)	(22)	(23)	(24)
Indicative equity value of target (2)	Number of new shares to be issued (19)/(9)	Total number of shares (20)+(8)	Combined PAT (12)+(7)	Revised EPS (22)/(21)	EPS accretion (23)-(10)
600	3.5	13.5	115	8.5	0.0	Neutral at acquirer PE

4.14 Segmental Analysis

Segmental analysis means analyzing the profitability of the various segments that the company is engaged with. The below example explains the C, E, and M segments and their analysis.

	Profit/loss before interest and tax	
1	C	69.1
2	E	59.0
3	M	80.3

	OTHER INFORMATION	
	Segment assets	
4	C	264.1
5	E	530.8
6	M	589.4

	Segment liabilities	
7	C	164.2
8	E	146.3
9	M	171.7

	Return on capital employed	
10= (1)/(4–7)	C	69%
11=(2)/(5–8)	E	15%
12=(3)/(6–9)	M	19%

Segmental analysis is important to find how the various business lines are performing.

4.15 Sum of Parts Valuation

Sum of parts valuation implies valuing a company in parts and doing summation of all the parts to arrive at the value of company. The sum of part valuation may also value the holdings of the company to arrive at the value of the company. Usually, the market value is lower than the sum of parts arrived by valuer community, sometimes referred to as conglomerate discount and harbinger of demerger.

The reason for such discount can be attributed to following factors, but cannot be quantified as to derive an actual causal effect.

The factors are:

a. Management competence, fiduciary credibility, track record, and demonstrated performance to align with interest of all shareholders. Especially, the public shareholders.

b. Minimal conflicts in businesses and decision-making.

c. Capital allocation and capital management driven purely with considered business and strategic needs.

d. Transparency in operations and financial information.

e. Nature of business and holdings.

f. Timing and uncertainty of realization of this value. The longer the time and greater the uncertainty, higher will be the discount akin to option valuation.

g. Last but not the least, there is always transaction cost (including taxes) associated with realizing this value, which is discounted

Case Study 4.7: Holding Companies and Discounts – Rocket Internet and HDFC Ltd.

Details

Rocket Internet is a Frankfurt listed German Company whose stated mission is to become the world's largest Internet platform outside the United States and China. Rocket identifies and builds proven Internet business models and transfers them to new, underserved, or untapped markets where it seeks to scale them into market leading online companies. Rocket started in 2007 and now has more than 30,000 employees across its network of companies, which are active in more than 110 countries across the six continents.

Rocket has investments in Internet companies operating in:

- Fashion
- General merchandizing
- Food delivery
- E-commerce
- Financial technology
- Travel

It invests, builds, and scales them across the globe. Rocket states that "Our markets are complex, and we embrace that transferring proven business models to new, underserved or untapped markets brings its challenges. We adapt to local habits, developing proprietary solutions that meet customers' needs and circumstances".

The prominent names that it has invested in include the following:

- Jabong
- Lazada
- Food panda
- Hell Fresh

Rocket Internet has been listed since October 2014. The lifetime high, low, and current price is stated below.

	Date	Price (Eur)	Eur (million)
Listed	2/10/2014	37.5	6,192.8
High	28/11/2014	56.6	9,346.9
Current	24/2/2016	18.89	3,119.5
Low	24/2/2016	20.49	3,383.7

Rocket also publishes Last Portfolio Values of its portfolio available on its website. Last portfolio values ("LPV") are usually calculated based on the amount invested and/or price per share paid by a third party, i.e., an investor other than Rocket Internet, divided by the stakes acquired and/or multiplied by the number of shares outstanding. This means that the valuations shown represent the post-money valuations. The LPV concept is independent of the accounting treatment of our network of companies under German GAAP or IFRS.

The LPV as on November 30, 2015 is ~ Eur 6 billion plus cash/commitment of Eur 3 billion, making it a total of Eur 9 billion.

The market price would be 0.7–0.8 times of the reported book value in the audited statements.

Thus, we have a discount of 20–30% over the book value and nearly 60% discount on LPV. The reason for such a heavy discount can be attributed to the reasons stated above from (a) to (g) in varying degree as also in its own stated words the business is complex inviting heavy discounting by public markets.

Let us now consider the case of HDFC Ltd. and analyze the valuations.

HDFC Ltd.

HDFC Ltd is a leading provider of Housing Finance in India. "With our customised solutions, we have fulfilled over 5.1 million dreams since, it's inception," Pioneered Housing Finance, in 1977.

It has gross loans of Rs. 2.6 trillion. It is the largest mobilizer of public deposits outside the banking system having million Deposits Accounts. A model private Housing Finance Company for developing countries with nascent Housing Finance markets.

HDFC Ltd. is a financial institution run by professional management with long history and track record of delivering superior performance and governance. Apart from the housing finance business, it has spawned a number of subsidiaries listed below who are leaders in their field with profit track records. The biggest of them all being HDFC Bank Ltd. wherein it holds 22% and is India's most valuable bank with market cap of US $40 billion.

We see below the details of major investments and the valuation. From the given data, it is evident that the price to book (P/B) is 3.6 and if we adjust the gains on the listed investments, P/B to 1.8. Even if we adjust for the values of unlisted ventures, the P/B will not go below 1.3. The above ratios are again on the gross market price of HDFC Ltd. which has not been adjusted for the profits of subsidiaries and associates. If we do the adjustment and do apples to apples P/B, the numbers will again trend higher.

Rs. crore	SUBSIDIARIES							Associate	Total
	HDFC ERGO General Insurance Company Ltd	HDFC Standard Life Insurance Company Ltd	HDFC Holdings Ltd	HDFC Venture Capital Ltd	HDFC Asset Management Company Ltd	HDFC Investments Ltd	GRUH Finance Ltd	HDFC bank	
Investment cost	645	1509	102	0	236	66			
holding %	74	71	100	81	60	100	59	22	
Sales turnover	1991	27,292	23	90	1064	109	1060		
Profit after tax	104	786	17	55	416	106	204		
Market value							5070.2	37,335.4	42,406
									42,406
Number of shares	157.93								
Price (Rs.)	1022.95								
Mkt. Cap. (Rs. crore)	161,558.16								
2015 book value (Rs.) (BV)	285.25								
Adjusted book value (Rs.) for market value of listed investments	(42,406/157.93) =269+285=554								
P/BV		3.6							
P/Adjusted BV		1.8							

	2015	2014	2013	2012	2011	2010	2009	2008	2007	2006	2005	2004	2003	2002
RONW (%)	17	18	20	19	18	15	13	24	29	28	23	23	21	19

Thus, the market seems to have the superior financial performance of HDFC Ltd. as along with the superlative management and governance track record. Despite being a holding company, it does not seem to suffer holding company discount.

Key Learning

The above two cases highlight the status of two companies in kind of asset management or investment business where Rocket suffered a big discount on its LPV while HDFC commands a premium to its LPV.

The reason for the same can be analyzed by the factors (a) to (g) as described in the section describing the sum of parts valuation.

May be as Rocket gains traction with time and delivers a track record, it will also revert to premium valuation. However, there is complexity of the businesses that they need to manage and sustain performance which will be challenging and the markets are playing wait and watch.

4.16 Merger Exchange Ratios

Generally, in mergers, the exchange ratio represents a swap ratio achieved based on the market price. The theory assumes that market price is supreme and reflects the right value. The variant of that is to use a range of time for the market prices and determine based on the negotiation and the appropriate swap ratio.

The variant of the above is to arrive at a preliminary swap ratio and then negotiate based on the range of financial ratios of individual companies, taking into consideration the future prospects and qualitative inputs on the basis of normalization and quality of financial statements that we read above.

The swap ratio is then fine tuned for various aspects as explained by the case study given below.

Case study 4.8: Dow Chemicals and DuPont Combine in Merger of Equals

Details

In case of Dow Chemical and Du Pont merger of equals combining for $130 bn company. Dow Chemicals will receive 1 share of Dow–Dupont for 1 share held in Dow Chemicals. While, the shareholders of Dupont will get 1.28 shares of Dow–Dupont for 1 share held in Du Pont.

The financial details are as under:

Valuation measures		Valuation measures	
Market cap	54.30B	Market cap	53.06B
Enterprise value	63.10B	Enterprise value	55.90B
Price/sales (ttm):	1.12	Price/sales (ttm):	2.13

Price/book (mrq):	2.55	Price/book (mrq):	5.49
Profitability		**Profitability**	
Profit margin (ttm):	15.76%	Profit margin (ttm):	7.77%
Operating margin (ttm):	12.64%	Operating margin (ttm):	11.01%
Return ratios		**Return ratios**	
Return on assets (ttm):	5.64%	Return on assets (ttm):	3.77%
Return on equity (ttm):	31.30%	Return on equity (ttm):	16.07%
Income statement		**Income statement**	
Revenue (ttm):	48.78B	Revenue (ttm):	25.13B
Gross profit (ttm):	10.94B	Gross profit (ttm):	10.02B
EBITDA (ttm):	8.61B	EBITDA (ttm):	4.10B

Thus, we see from the above while the financial parameters are more or less equal. In fact, could be said to be in favour of Dow Chemicals. However, the growth and profitability of Agrochemical division of Du Pont (Revenue: $11 billion) contributes 1/3rd of the Du Pont revenue and half of profits of Du Pont. The growth rates of the Agrochem division and the profitability as well as the better prospects of Agro Chem industry had edged the share swap ratio little bit more in favor of Du Pont in the combine company.

The merger ratios are generally fixed or floating. The fixed swap ratio determines the share percentage that the transferee will have in the merged entity. The fixed swap ratio works well if the merger consummation is expeditious so that the ratio reflection is appropriate for that time. A floating ratio determines the value of target and swap ratio will be a function of the market price of the respective companies at consummation. This fixes the value but not the share percentage. This works in situations having time element, although the threat of valuation movement for the target remains till the time it goes for shareholder vote approving the swap ratio.

Thus, the merger agreement that appropriately determines swap ratio and put in place the mechanism to get them honoured, are key to successful acquisition. The risk of providing adjustment elements is that market will force ratios to swing around the adjustments. Thus, the key is to have robust agreements that will get the mergers executed as agreed.

Example: A is buying B in a stock transaction with an exchange ratio **0.8**. A has 110 million shares outstanding and B has 155 million shares. Ownership following the acquisition will be:

	Shares out	**Exchange ratio**	**Shares in new company**	**%**
B	155	0.8	124	52.99%
A	110	1	110	47.01%
			234	

- **Acquisition premium**: the percentage premium paid to the target shareholders above the pre-announcement closing price.
- The formula is:

(Acquirer stock price × exchange ratio − stock price of target)/ stock price of target

Acquirer stock price: $43

Target stock price: $25

- The acquisition premium would be:

(43 × 0.8 − 25)/25 = 38%

- **Minimum required economic gains** that are required to be reaped through acquisition can be calculated as under:

(Acquirer stock price × exchange ratio − stock price of target)× number of shares in target

(43 × 0.8 − 25)×155= $1450 million

From the data given below, conclude whether the acquisition is accretive or dilutive for the acquirer.

	A	B
Net income (million)	$110.00	$53.50
Shares outstanding (million)	48	23
EPS	$1.90	$2.15
Merger ratio	1.5 share of A for 1 share held in B	

From the above data, calculate the accretion (dilution) percentage on the EPS of the combined company.

For this, we calculate the number of new shares to be issued and expansion in the equity base of the target. Then, we work out the proforma and the resultant EPS. We see a 4% accretion in EPS assuming zero synergy. With $15 million synergy, an accretion of 14% is achieved.

	Shares out	Exchange ratio	Shares in new company	%
B	23	1.5	34.5	41.82%
A	48	1	48	58.18%
			82.5	

	A	B	100% equity financing Proforma	Synergy	Proforma
Net income (million)	$110.00	$53.50	$163.50	$15.00	$178.50
Shares outstanding (million)	48	23	**82.5**		82.5
EPS	$1.90	$2.15	$1.98		$2.16
		Accretion	4.3%		13.9%

4.17 Thinking Life in USD

USD is global currency and common denominator across resources. The exchange rate subsumes in itself the inflation, interest rates, and growth rates of economies. Thus, measuring the financial statements in USD actually helps in getting the real growth rates without worrying too much for indexing for inflation or accounting for constant currency growth rates. Real life would not be as simple to be reflective of constant currency growth rate and whatever reflected in USD should be taken as real growth rates. We have heard of constant currency growth and growth rates, but, we have not heard of constant currency market caps. If we judge or benchmark companies by USD market cap so be it the final word on all aspects.

The following case study of Titan Industries will illustrate the point. Titan Industries is manufacturer of designer jewelleries and watches having shown robust growth over past 5–7 years and having market cap of $5bn.

Case Study 4.9: Life in USD and Global Real Rates

Titan Industries Ltd	5-year CAGR	201503	201403	201303	201203	201103	201003
INR							
Net sales	20%	11,903	10,916	10,113	8,838	6,521	4,776
PAT	27%	823	741	725	600	430	250
Market capitalization (cr)	34%	34,802	23,300	22,772	20,295	16,916	8,172
ROCE (%)		34.0	40.6	59.7	66.6	65.5	45.5
RONW (%)		29.3	33.0	42.5	48.5	49.2	39.3
Average USD–INR rate		66.768	63.469	60.936	55.911	49.124	47.774
USD							
Net sales	12%	178	172	166	158	133	100
PAT	19%	12	12	12	11	9	5
Market capitalization(mn)	25%	5210	3670	3740	3630	3440	1710

The above table depicts the moderation in growth rates in USD as compared to INR. Thus, in cross-border acquisitions more particularly as well as for evaluating real profitability shorn of inflation, the conversion to USD will present a better picture than use of local currency.

This probably will provide a much deeper and realistic picture than adjusting the cost of equity in DCF calculations, which has stayed at ~15% from the time of establishment of the industry and during the same period; the Indian currency had depreciated more than 50% from 2007 itself. While we have country premium they have also stayed constant more or less. No effect has been given to the depreciation of currency which should be factored in cost of equity.

We will now turn attention to the return ratios. The return ratios will be the same in the terms of percentage adjusting it for 10 year, the G-sec yield will give a clearer return picture than the gross rates.

As depicted below:

OCBC Bank, Singapore							
ROE	14.8	11.6	17.9	11.3	12.1	12.2	11.8
Singapore Govt 10-year bond yield	1.9	2.4	1.4	1.5	2.6	2.5	2.1
Real return	12.9	9.2	16.5	9.8	9.5	9.7	9.7
Differential	0.8	-3.6	3.7	-0.4	0.7	1.3	-0.9
HDFC Bank, India							
ROE	19.9	21.6	20.5	18.8	17.0	16.5	16.9
Indian Govt 10-year bond yield	7.9	8.8	7.7	8.7	8.1	8.1	6.2
Real return	12.1	12.8	12.8	10.1	8.8	8.4	10.6

Despite the superior differential returns but and because of the growth potential of Indian banking industry, the market cap of HDFC will be ~SGD 55 billion against SGD 33 billion of OCBC bank, despite positive differential return, thus bringing out the interplay of growth, margins, returns, etc., for valuing entities.

Case Study 4.12: Samsonite acquires Tumi Holdings

Press release:

HONG KONG & SOUTH PLAINFIELD, N.J.--(BUSINESS WIRE)--Samsonite International S.A. ("Samsonite") (SEHK:1910) and Tumi Holdings, Inc. ("Tumi") (NYSE:TUMI) today announced that they have entered into a definitive agreement whereby Samsonite will acquire Tumi for US $26.75 per share in an all cash transaction, valuing Tumi at an equity value of US $1.8 billion.

"This is a transformational acquisition for Samsonite. It will meaningfully expand our presence in the highly attractive premium segment of the global business bags, travel luggage and accessories market," said Ramesh Tainwala, Chief Executive Officer of Samsonite. "Tumi is a perfect strategic fit for our business. The brand is beloved by millions of loyal customers for its high quality and durable premium business and luggage products. We are excited about the tremendous opportunities this combination provides us to further diversify our product and customer portfolios. In particular, we will expand Tumi's presence in Asia and Europe, while strengthening its business in North America, by leveraging our expertise in global distribution, sourcing, product design and technical innovation, especially in the area of lightweight hardside luggage."

Compelling Strategic and Financial Rationale

Creates a leading global travel lifestyle company. The combination brings together Tumi, an iconic North American purveyor of premium business bags, travel luggage, and accessories, with Samsonite, the world's best known and largest lifestyle bag and travel luggage company, to create a leading global travel lifestyle company.

Ideal and complementary fit with Samsonite. With approximately 2000 points of distribution across 75 countries, Tumi's leading market position in the premium business and luggage segment is a perfect complement to Samsonite's strong and diverse portfolio of brands and products, with limited overlap in market positioning, price point, and distribution. The addition of Tumi builds on Samsonite's proven track record of successful acquisitions across multiple product categories and price points to broaden its portfolio.

Enables Samsonite to strategically expand into the highly attractive premium segment of the global business bags, travel luggage, and accessories market with a business and travel brand that is recognized worldwide as being "best-in-class" in the premium segment.

Presents tremendous opportunities to leverage Samsonite's extensive global retail and wholesale network and its strengths in distribution, sourcing, technical innovation, and localization of products to introduce the Tumi brand to millions of new customers in additional markets worldwide. This includes expansion of Tumi in Asia and Europe, strengthening its platform in North America, and leveraging Samsonite's clear strength in hardside innovation to expand Tumi's hardside luggage offering.

Reinforces Samsonite's strong platform for long-term growth and profitability. Tumi is a highly profitable business and the combined company is expected to generate significant free cash flow to meet interest payments while continuing to make cash distributions to shareholders.

Creates potential for significant operational and top-line synergies. This includes cost savings in such key areas as sourcing, logistics, sales and marketing, distribution, retail and general and administrative costs, as well as potential top-line synergies, resulting from the combined company's enhanced and complementary product development and global reach.

Founded in 1975, Tumi is a leading global premium lifestyle brand offering a comprehensive line of business bags, travel luggage, and accessories. The brand is consistently recognized as "best-in-class" for the high quality, durability, functionality, and innovative design of its products, which range from its iconic black ballistic business cases and travel luggage synonymous with the modern business professional to travel accessories, women's bags, and outdoor apparel.

For the year ended December 31, 2015, Tumi's net sales were US $548 million, representing a year on year increase of 4%. North America accounted for 68% of Tumi's 2015 net sales, with Asia Pacific accounting for 17%, Europe, Middle East, and Africa accounting for 14%, and Latin America accounting for the remaining 1%. Tumi has historically achieved strong growth in net sales, with a CAGR of 17% from 2010 to 2015 and highly attractive EBITDA margins of over 20% during the same period.

Transaction Details

Under the terms of the transaction, Tumi shareholders will receive US $26.75 in cash for each share they own. The transaction values Tumi at an equity valuation of approximately US $1.8 billion. This represents a 13.6× multiple of enterprise value to Tumi's adjusted EBITDA for the last 12 months ended December 31, 2015, and a premium of approximately 38% to Tumi's volume weighted average price of US $19.34 for 5 days up to and including March 2, 2016, the last trading day prior to market rumors.

Samsonite intends to fund the transaction through committed bank financing. In connection with the transaction, Morgan Stanley, HSBC, SunTrust, and MUFJ have arranged the committed financing.

About Samsonite

Samsonite International S.A. (together with its consolidated subsidiaries, the "Group") is the world's best known and largest lifestyle bag and travel luggage company, with a heritage dating back more than 100 years. The group is principally engaged in the design, manufacture, sourcing and distribution of luggage, business and computer bags, outdoor and casual bags, travel accessories, and slim protective cases for personal electronic devices throughout the world, primarily under the Samsonite®, American Tourister ®, Hartmann®, High Sierra ®, Gregory®, Speck®, and Lipault® brand names and other owned and licensed brand names. The Group's core brand, Samsonite, is one of the most well-known travel luggage brands in the world.

About Tumi

Founded in 1975, Tumi is the leading global brand of premium business, travel and lifestyle products, and accessories. The brand is sold in approximately 2000 points of distribution from New York to Paris to London and Tokyo, as well as in the world's top department, specialty, and travel retail stores in over 75 countries.

Tumi Holdings Inc.

In millions of USD	FY 2015	FY 2014	FY 2013	FY 2012	FY 2011	FY 2010	FY 2009	FY 2008	FY 2007	FY 2006
Revenue	547.7	527.2	467.4	398.6	330.0	252.8	196.6	232.6	231.4	197.9
Operating income (loss)	101.5	93.4	88.8	78.2	60.4	40.8	16.7	18.3	31.2	30.1
Net income	63.0	58.0	54.6	36.8	16.6	0.1	-16.0	-12.1	-3.0	-4.7
Free cash flow	50.6	50.6	24.0	37.8	27.2	25.5	13.8	17.9	11.2	—

In millions of USD	FY 2015	FY 2014	FY 2013	FY 2012	FY 2011	FY 2010	FY 2009
Total assets							
+ Cash, cash equivalents and STI	94.6	52.8	37.6	36.7	32.7	19.2	27.3
Total current assets	243.4	185.2	161.7	138.1	125.0	92.4	79.1
Total noncurrent assets	368.6	366.1	344.8	331.1	321.3	316.5	320.7
Total assets	611.9	551.3	506.5	469.2	446.3	409.0	399.8
Liabilities and shareholders' equity							
Total current liabilities	75.6	71.0	70.7	56.9	70.3	60.5	60.5
Total noncurrent liabilities	55.5	53.4	67.8	101.3	357.3	346.8	338.1
Total liabilities	131.1	124.4	138.5	158.2	427.6	407.3	398.7
Total equity	480.8	426.9	368.0	311.1	18.7	1.7	1.1
Total liabilities and equity	611.9	551.3	506.5	469.2	446.3	409.0	399.8

Samsonite International

In millions of USD	FY 2014	FY 2013	FY 2012	FY 2011	FY 2010	FY 2009	FY 2008
Assets							
+ Cash and near cash items	138.9	195.2	110.6	121.2	285.8	290.5	76.9
+ Short-term investments	1.5	30.2	40.8	20.1	0.0	0.0	0.0
Total current assets	835.3	835.4	713.4	611.4	722.5	567.8	474.6
Total long-term assets	1296.0	1099.5	1099.8	933.1	942.5	571.6	556.9
Total assets	2131.3	1934.9	1813.2	1544.5	1665.0	1139.4	1031.4
Liabilities and shareholders' equity							
Total current liabilities	603.6	501.7	493.5	383.5	416.8	335.4	2,207.9
Total long-term liabilities	220.3	202.6	233.5	215.9	485.4	395.3	255.6
Total liabilities	823.9	704.3	727.1	599.3	902.1	730.7	2463.6
+ Minority interest	37.8	37.8	34.5	27.1	22.6	17.1	15.7
+ Share capital and APIC	979.1	976.3	976.3	976.3	836.7	836.1	221.3
+ Retained earnings and other equity	290.6	216.5	75.3	−58.1	−96.5	−444.6	−1669.1
Total equity	1307.4	1230.6	1086.1	945.2	762.9	408.7	−1432.1
Total liabilities and equity	2131.3	1934.9	1813.2	1544.5	1665.0	1139.4	1031.4

Quantitative analysis

All figures in $mn

TUMI

Price per share	$26.8
Transaction equity value	$1800.0
Cash	$94.6
Debt	$-
Enterprise value	$1705.4
(Equity+Debt–Cash)	
TTM profit after tax	$63.00
TTM P/E	28.6
Comparable compnies	
Coach	30X
Financing rate (100% debt)	2.0%	Assumed
Tax rate	27%
After tax financing cost	1.5%
Implied PE (reciprocal of after tax financing rate)	68.5
Break even cost (interest cost on $1800 mn)	$26.28
Operating income (EBIT)	$101.20
Delta over operating income	$74.92
Operating capital employed	$565.00	$50 mn cash is surplus is an assumption
(total assets less $50 mn cash)	

Samsonite

Operating income (EBIT) estimated 2015	$310.00	
Pre transaction operating capital employed (estimated 2015)	$2,300.00	
Pre transaction return on capital employed	13.5%	
Combined EBIT (assuming no synergies)	$411.20	
Combined operating capital employed	$4100.00	$2300 +$1800 (purchase value)
Pretransaction return on capital employed	10.0%	
To reach pretransaction ROCE extra EBIT required	$143.50	
3.5% of capital employed		
Growth in EBIT in % terms	35%	
EPS pre transaction	0.13	
Number of equitry shares	1412.07	
Combined profit assuming no synergies	264	Samsonite (201), Tumi (63)
EPS post-transaction	0.19	
EPS accretion	44%	

Qualitative analysis

- Samsonite moves from net cash position to debt equity coming to 1.2×.
- The acquisition is financed by debt; hence with no dilution of equity we see EPS accretion of 44% even without assuming synergy and based on last 12 months profit figures. The risk is Tumi sales falling off the clip during the integration.
- While, EPS accretive the return ratios are coming off drastically and will need 35% growth in EBIT terms, which would mean increased growth and cost cutting. The 3-year CAGR in EBIT is 9%. This is a tall order to pull off as this would mean increased expenditure/capital on opening more stores and advertising and promotion as Samsonite brand and Tumi brand will need different channels and stores due to brand positioning.
- Thus, leverage which is 4× EBIDTA will be further affected and free cash flow will be negative due to increased expenditure.
- Against a market cap of US $4.5 bn, a takeover of $1.8 bn constituting 40% of its market cap is a big risk with Tumi's limited range of products.
- Further, Samsonite has done two small acquisitions of backpack maker High Sierra and Luxury luggae brand Hartman. The Tumi acquisition represents addition to luggage.

4.18 Valuations of Banking Companies

Banking valuations can be classified into three categories:

a. Profitability
b. Liquidity
c. Capital adequacy

In addition, there are other criteria such as level of non-performing loans and provisions, but they are more emasculated in the "Profitability ratio" namely:

Net interest margin (NIM)	Interest income - Interest expense	
Non-net interest income (NNII)	Majorly fees and commission from core banking business rather than capital gains or investment income.	
Return on total assets	Net income/total assets	Factor of NIM spread and proportion of NNII
Return on equity	Net income/total equity	Factor of ROA and leverage used. Lower ROA can be compensated through higher leverage and vice versa. As stated below, the relationship of ROA into equity multiplier.
Return on equity	$\dfrac{\text{Net income}}{\text{Total assets}} \cdot \dfrac{\text{Total assets}}{\text{Total equity}}$	

Return on equity	Return on total assets	Equity multiplier
		Control of overheads
Cost to income ratio	$\dfrac{\text{Non - interest expense}}{\text{Net interest income} + \text{fees / comm.}}$	

The above in summation will explain whether the bank is profitable enough or not. The above quantitative metrics can be juxtaposed with the below-mentioned qualitative factors:

a. Loan growth rates.
b. Product, customer, sector, industry, geography concentration.
c. Extent of branch network or distribution.
d. Level of non-performing loans and the loan loss provisioning policies.

The above can be seen in context with industry trend or peer comparison. Banks report card is like a human body health report that needs to have a right balance. It can neither have high growth rates nor sluggish growth rates. It cannot have high yield on loans or low yield or have high or low leverage. It needs to have a fine balance of return on assets and equity multiplier to generate the expected return on Equity.

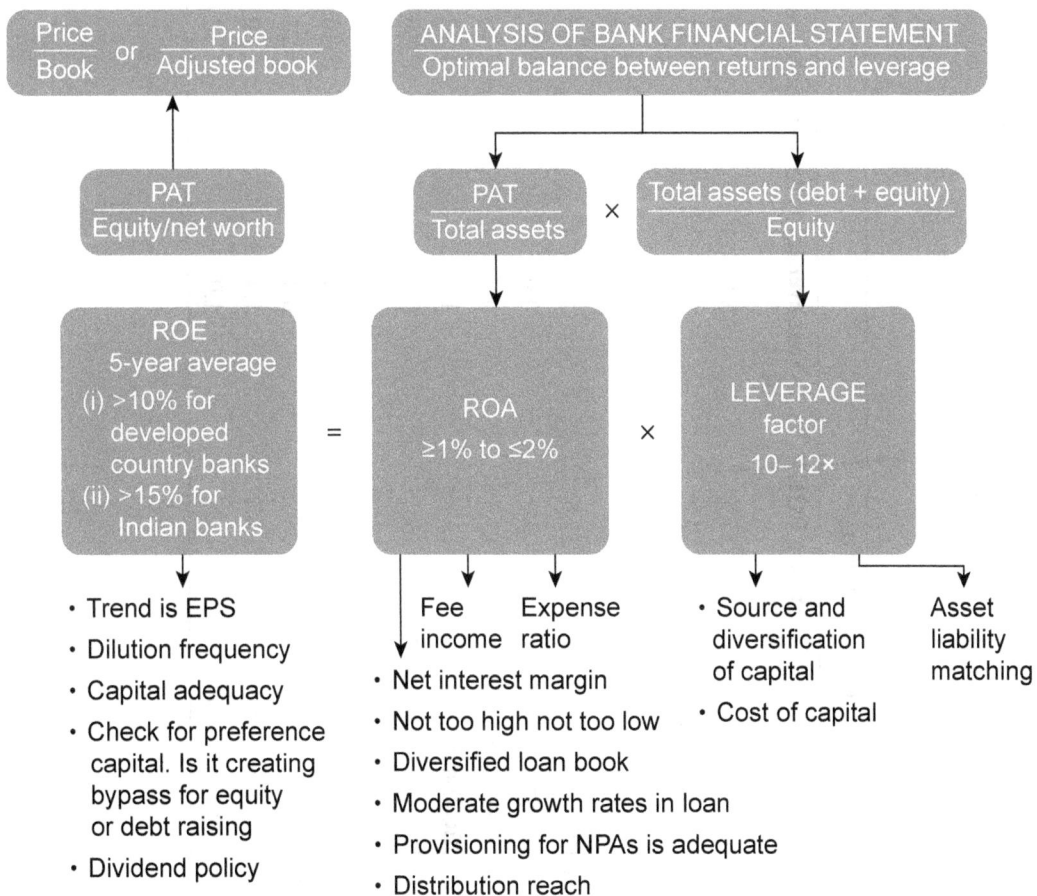

ANALYSIS OF BANK RETURNS

Name of Bank	5Y Avg ROE in %	5-Year average ROA in %	5-Year average factor	Comments
BCA Bank, Indonesia	24.7	3.0	8.1	ROA is higher than usual. While leverage is on lower side
Commonwealth Bank	17.9	1.0	17.1	Decent ROA, but higher leverage
DBS Bank, Singapore	11.5	1.0	11.5	Optimal balance in ROA and leverage
HDFC Bank	19.9	1.9	10.7	Optimal balance in ROA and leverage
ICBC	21.0	1.4	15.0	Good ROA, but leverage on higher side
JP Morgan	9.9	0.9	11.2	Slightly lower ROA, but optimal leverage
National AUS Bank	12.3	0.7	18.9	Low ROA, but very high leverage
OCBC Bank	13.4	1.0	12.9	Optimal balance in ROA and leverage
RBC	18.7	0.9	19.9	Decent ROA, but higher leverage
Scotiabank	17.3	0.9	18.9	Decent ROA, but higher leverage
U.S. Bancorp	15.5	1.5	10.0	Optimal balance in ROA and leverage
UBS	5.8	0.3	21.3	Low ROA, but very high leverage
Wells Fargo	13.2	1.4	9.6	Optimal balance in ROA and leverage
Westpac	15.6	1.0	15.6	Decent ROA, but higher leverage

How to interpret the above from acquiring point of view:

First, look into if the target bank profitability is low due to the below listed factors and whether the acquiring bank has the wherewithal to set right any of the following factors. Thereafter, go about ascribing a multiple to it book value from acquisition point of view leaving enough scope to make virtue out of the acquisition.

	Poor factors	Rectifying opportunities
1.	Low asset yield	• Increase highest yielding loans • Reduce funding cost • Reduce asset liability mismatch • Shed non-core assets
2.	High cost of funds	• Reduce funding cost • Reduce asset liability mismatch
3.	Inadequate non-interest income	• Introduce new products and services to generate fees and income
4.	High loan charge off	• Improve credit process • Reduce product, client, geography concentration
5.	High loan loss provisions	• Improve credit process • Reduce product, client, geography concentration
6.	Mismanaging taxes	• Tax planning
7.	High overhead costs	• Reduce expenses • Rationalize compensation structure • Close unproductive branches • Bring in technology • Induce loan growth to have operating leverage
8.	Lower loan to deposit ratio	• Increase the conversion of deposits to loans at a higher rate
9.	Low leverage	• Improve leverage in tandem with an adequate equity base

Apart from the above framework, the other factors that need to be considered are capital adequacy and liquidity profile of its assets and liability.

Last but not the least is the equity base and the dilution history of the bank. Bank which has calibrated equity dilution rather than reckless dilutions will tend to be able to generate higher return on equity.

The extraneous factor will be the economic growth rate of that particular region and how much loan growth or banking services can be expanded.

Bank Multiple

Unlike the normal corporates, the banking valuations do not require as much normalization. The key to understand is the above framework and the economic cycles in which it operates.

The key metric being "return on equity," and how it emerges from marriage of "return on asset" and "equity multiplier" will determine the book value multiple for that particular bank rather than P/E multiple.

Thus, ROE of 15% indicates 1 time book value meaning investment of $100 in that bank will generate 15% return.

The only normalization that needs to be effected is adjusting the book value for net non-performing loans. Meaning, if non-performing loan is $500 and provision for losses is $100, the net non-performing loans will be $400. Thus, if the book value is $2500, the adjusted book value will be $2500 less than $400 equal to $2100.

Given the above context, the right book value is the adjusted book value and the acquiring bank needs to able to determine the increase in the net income of target it will be able to achieve to maintain the particular return.

Thus, if we look at the above example, at one-time adjusted book value for ROE of 15%, an investment yield of 15% will be achieved. Thus, paying a 2-time book value will bring the investment yield down to 7.5%, reflecting that the acquiring bank needs to work doubly higher to generate pre-acquisition yield and improve it beyond the benchmark.

This brings into focus the acquisition timing. Thus, buying at peak of the economic cycle at peak multiple will illustrate how much harder the acquirer is required to pace with the sustainable ROE.

Ratios to be analyzed in a Bank

Growth-YoY	
Net worth	Need to check, whether it is due to growth in profits or share capital.
Balance sheet size	How fast is the bank growing? Is it too fast or slow?
Advances	How the advances are growing?
Investments	Whether the liability is making way into investments instead of loans
NII	The spread between interest income and expense. Whether the spread is reasonable. Not too high or low.
Total Income	Growth in profitability
Preprovision operating profitability ("PPOP")	Growth in profits without the impact of provisions
PPOP excl. one-offs	Normalizing the profits for extraordinary gains or losses
Provisions	How much is the provisions? Whether it is adequate with respect to the assets and in-line with the industry.
PBT	Growth in profitability
PAT	Growth in profitability
EPS	To measure profitability per share
Dividend per share	To measure dividend per share
Fee income growth	Growth in non-advance income

Asset–liability profile

Financial leverage	The risks in capital structure and how much it is contributing to Return on Equity
Adv–deposit ratio	What is the conversion ratio of deposit into advances?
Investments–deposit ratio	Proportion of investment to deposit
CASA as a % of deposits	Proportion of retail deposits
CASA as a % of balance sheet size	Proportion of retail deposits to balance sheet
Term deposits as a % of balance sheet size	Proportion of wholesale deposits
Borrowings as a % of balance sheet size	Proportion of wholesale deposits
Short-term advances as a % of advances	Asset profile
Short-term advances as a % of bal size	Asset profile
Term loans as a % of advances	Asset profile
Term loans as a % of bal size	Asset profile
Secured advances to total advances	Asset profile
Unsecured advances to total advances	Asset profile
Unsecured advances to net worth	Asset profile
Capital market exp. to total advances	Asset profile
Capital market exp. to net worth	Asset profile
Real estate exp. to total advances	Asset profile
Real estate exp to net worth	Asset profile
Priority sector to total advances	Asset profile
Contingent liabilities to total assets	
Contingent liabilities to net worth	

Exposure of advances	**Industry or sector concentration**
Capital market	Asset profile
Real estate	Asset profile
Residential mortgage	Asset profile
Commercial real estate	Asset profile

Investments in MBS	Asset profile
Indirect exposure	Asset profile
Commodities	Asset profile
Priority sector	Asset profile
SMEs	Asset profile

Profitability

Interest earnings assets

Interest income/ (investments + advances)	Quality of income
Yield on advances	Whether too high or low. Benchmarking against industry. Too high means riskier loans or too low means too safe lending
Yield on investments	Risk profile of investments

Interest bearing liabilities

Interest exp/(depo + borr + subord debt + bp)	Cost of borrowing. Whether too high or low.
Cost of deposits	
Cost of borrowings	
Cost of other liabilities	

Spread	**Profitability profile**
Net interest margin (NII/average IEA)	
RoE	
RoA	
PAT/(NII + Other income)	
Interest expended/interest earned	
Other income/(interest earned + other income)	
Fee income to NII	
PPOP	
Loan loss provisions/PPOP	
NII/GII	
Tax rate	

Efficiency	**For benchmarking against peers**
Number of employees	
Branches	
ATMs	
Op ex/ PAT	

Empl. cost/ Op ex	
Advances/ branch	
Deposits/ branch	
NII/ branch	
Advance/employee	
Deposits/employee	
Business/employee	
Business/branch	
PAT/employee	
PAT/branch	
Employees/branch	
Average employee cost	
Opex/(NII + other income)–CIR	
Opex/assets	

RoA and RoE decomposition	**Discussing the source of ROE generator**
Net interest income to average total assets	
Other income to average total assets	
Total revenues to average total assets	
Operational expenses to average total assets	
Provisions to average total assets	
Total costs to average total assets	
Return on assets	
Average equity to average total assets	
Return on equity	

Asset liability mismatch

This is to figure out the risk profile and whether the bank will skid if there is sudden turn in the economic conditions.

Particulars	Annual					
	FY1	FY2	FY3	FY4	FY5	FY6
Liabilities						
<= 1 year	37.3%	34.9%	37.9%	27.0%	30.5%	30.6%
> 1 year	62.7%	65.1%	62.1%	73.0%	69.5%	69.4%
Assets						
<= 1 year	39.7%	37.4%	47.2%	45.5%	37.6%	40.5%
> 1 year	60.3%	62.6%	52.8%	54.5%	62.4%	59.5%
Mismatch	**-2.4%**	**-2.5%**	**-9.3%**	**-18.5%**	**-7.0%**	**-9.9%**

Asset Quality

We need to know about the level of non-performing assets and provisions against it. This data is very important because the profitability of the bank is very contingent on level of non-performing assets and provisions made against the loans. The naked exposure is used to adjust the book value and valuations are done using adjusted book value.

Asset quality	
Gross NPAs	
Provisions	
Net NPAs	
Gross NPA (%)	
Net NPA (%)	
Loan loss coverage	
Slippage	
Growth in gross NPAs	
Growth in net NPAs	
Provisions to assets	
Standard assets proven	
Income bearing assets to TA	
Interest bearing liabilities to TA	

Valuation	
EPS	Earnings per share
Number of shares	
Book value per share	Important to value the bank as costly or cheap
Adjusted book value per share	Valued based on loan losses accounted
Share price	
Market cap	
P/E	Earning multiple
Price to book	Book multiple
Price to adjusted book	Adjusted book multiple
Dividend yield	Valuation justification
P/PPOP	Price to operating profit
P/PPOP excl one-offs	Price to normalized operating profit

Example: Analyzing bank financial statements

Profit and loss

		Year 1	Year 2	Year 3	Year 4	Year 5	Year 6
	BANK						
	Profit and loss						
1	Total interest income	10,115	16,332	16,173	19,929	27,099	32,655
2	Total interest paid	4887	8911	7786	9384	15,096	18,563
3	Net interest income	5228	7421	8387	10,545	12,003	14,092
4	Total other income	2283	3319	3808	4283	4893	5680
5	Total operating expenditure	3746	5533	5765	7102	8263	10,011
6	Operating profit before provisions & contingencies	3765	5207	6430	7726	8633	9761
7	Total provisions and contingencies	1485	1908	2141	1907	1577	1398
8	Profit before tax	2281	3299	4289	5819	7057	8363
9	Tax	690	1054	1340	1892	2251	2634
10	Profit after tax	1590	2245	2949	3927	4805	5729

Balance sheet

		Year 1	Year 2	Year 3	Year 4	Year 5	Year 6
	Balance Sheet						
11	**Equity share capital**	354	425	458	465	468	468
	gross reserve	11,143	14,221	21,062	24,914	29,043	33,678
12	**Tangible net worth**	11,497	14,646	21,520	25,379	29,511	34,146
13	**Total borrowings**	4479	2686	12,916	14,394	24,634	29,943
14	**Total deposits**	100,769	142,812	167,404	208,586	248,160	313,140
15	**Total other liabilities**	16,432	22,721	20,616	28,993	36,747	36,805
16	**Total liabilities**	133,177	182,864	222,456	277,353	339,052	414,033
	ASSETS						
17	**Total loans and advances**	63,427	98,883	125,831	159,983	200,925	247,350
18	**Total investments**	49,393	58,818	58,608	70,929	80,232	96,465
19	**Total current assets**	14,778	17,507	29,942	29,669	30,270	36,625
20	**Net fixed assets**	1175	1707	2123	2171	2654	3240
21	**Total other assets**	4403	6357	5955	14,601	24,972	30,353
22	**Total assets**	133,176	183,271	222,459	277,353	339,052	414,033

Ratios

Total operating income (TOI) (1+4)	12,398	19,651	19,981	24,212	31,992	38,335
Profit after tax (PAT) (10)	1590	2245	2949	3927	4805	5729
Net profit margin = PAT/TOI	12.83%	11.42%	14.76%	16.22%	15.02%	14.94%
Equity (11)	11,497	14,646	21,520	25,379	29,511	34,146
Average equity (AVE) (Year 1+ Year 2)/2	11,497	13,072	18,083	23,449	27,445	31,828
Return on equity (ROE) = PAT/average equity	14%	17%	16%	17%	18%	18%
Total assets (22)	**133,176**	**183,271**	**222,459**	**277,353**	**339,052**	**414,033**
Average total assets (AVTA) (Year 1+Year 2/2)	133,176	158,224	202,865	249,906	308,203	376,543
AVTA/AVGE	11.5	12.1	11.2	10.6	11.2	11.8
TOI/average total assets	9.3%	12.4%	9.8%	9.6%	10.3%	10.1%
Return on assets (ROA)	1.19%	1.4%	1.4%	1.5%	1.5%	1.5%
ROE	13.8%	17.1%	16.3%	16.7%	17.5%	18.0%
OVERHEAD EFFICIENCY	60.9%	59.9%	66.0%	60.3%	59.2%	56.7%

Example 2:

	2012	2011	2010	2009	2008	2007
Total interest income	1242	2152	9368	8894	9410	13,785
Total interest paid	838	1559	7944	7015	6571	9597
Total other income	220	575	1968	3065	3416	4983
Total operating expenditure	298	558	1506	2032	2709	3856
Operating profit before provisions and contingencies	327	609	1886	2912	3546	5314
Total provisions and contingencies	64	255	1791	470	429	1594
PBDT	263	354	95	2442	3118	3720
Depreciation on fixed assets	36	64	506	539	590	624
Profit before tax	227	290	(411)	1902	2527	3097
Profit after tax	161	258	15	1637	2005	2540
Tangible net worth	1302	6403	6445	7402	12,306	21,870
Total borrowings	18,424	97,357	99,529	116,868	154,759	28,833
Total liabilities	19,726	104,110	106,324	124,621	167,415	251,054
Total assets	19,726	104,110	106,324	124,621	167,415	251,053

Question: From the above financial statement, calculate the below-mentioned ratios.

TOI
PAT
NPM
Equity
Average equity

ROE

Total assets

Average total assets

AVTA/AVGE

TOI/average total assets

ROA

Non-Int. income/Non-Int. Exp.

NIM

Case Study 4: Analyzing Two Banks

Compare and contrast the below data of JP Morgan and Wells Fargo (the financial performance, the share price, how will you assess the loss in JP Morgan and the write back in Wells Fargo).

JP Morgan

Profitability	
Profit margin	26.89%
Operating margin	36.35%

Management effectiveness	
Return on assets	0.97%
Return on equity	10.04%
Valuation measures	
Market cap	243.29B

JP Morgan has litigation charge of $9.2 billion. This has to be added lock to profit being a one-time loss.

Wells Fargo

Profitability	
Profit margin	27.47%
Operating margin	42.97%

Management effectiveness	
Return on assets	1.38%
Return on equity	12.44%
Valuation measures	
Market cap	280.47B

Wells Fargo releases loan loss provision to the tune of $900 million. Uses the loan loss provisions to keep the profitability going.

Analysis

We see the outperformance of Wells Fargo against that of JP Morgan. The reason for that can be seen apart from the profitability margins.

The ROA for Wells Fargo is markedly superior to JP Morgan. The outperformance is nearly 40% while the outperformance on ROE is 20%.

Thus, it means that Wells Fargo has produced a much better performance by employing lesser leverage than JP Morgan.

Therefore, a much better return with lesser risk has been achieved by Wells Fargo.

To conclude banking valuation, the Bank parameters have to be the same as human body parameters. Everything has to be mid-range normal, not high–not low that effectively means a vigrous balancing act and better risk management.

Thus, banks which are able to manage the tight rope walk are the banks which command a much higher premium.

The below case studies will assist you to gain a better knowledge of bank valuation in context with M&A.

Case Study 4.10: Royal Bank of Scotland – ABN Amro 2007

ABN Amro was acquired by a consortium led by Royal Bank of Scotland at A hefty price tag of $99.9 billion.

This was pursuant to a competitive bid from rival Barclays which was paying $90 billion.

At peak of the economic cycle and out of competitive bid, the acquisition multiple was three times the book value of ABN Amro.

	2007	2006	2005
Return on average total assets	1.04	0.58	0.61
Return on average ordinary shareholder equity	38.4	20.7	23.5
Leverage	36.92	35.69	38.52

Thus, three times book multiple is justified for ROE of ~36%. However, as discussed, we need to see the ROE as a combination of ROA and equity multiplier. Thus, it is evident that ROA is pretty pedestrian and very high leverage has been used to skew the ROE.

Apart from the big size acquisition, the single biggest factor being price paid at the peak of cycle without discounting the pedestrian ROA and the cyclical banking business being run on such a high leverage, it would lead to failure of not only the acquisition but also the acquirer.

Eventually, RBS sank under this weight and was nationalized by the UK Government in the year 2008.

Summary

What Went Wrong

a. Buying in auction
b. At peak of the cycle
c. Peak multiple at peak earnings
d. Ignoring the pedestrian ROA

This case highlights bank valuations and key metrics of ROE, ROA, leverage, and book value.

Case Study 4.11: Banking Valuations Tale of two Singaporean Acquirers

a. OCBC Acquires Wing Hang Bank

Details

Oversea-Chinese Banking Corp. ("OCBC") on April 1, 2014, made a formal offer to buy Hong Kong's Wing Hang bank for HK$38.4 billion ($4.99 billion).

OCBC values Wing Hang at ~1.77 times the book value. Post some adjustments to the asset values, it will be at ~2 times the book value representing a premium of 49% to the trading price.

The offer is a premium of 49% to Wing Hang's closing price on September 16, the last day before reports of takeover talks were released.

Wing Hang, founded in the year 1937, has 42 branches in Hong Kong, 15 branches and sub-branches in mainland China, and 13 branches in Macau.

OCBC

	Ratios (%)									
Cost-to-income ratio	39.1	42.0	33.9	42.9	42.3	37.3	41.9	39.2	34.7	39.6
Cost-to-income Ratio excluding non-core gains	41.0	42.0	40.6	43.2	42.3	37.3	43.7	40.1	41.1	39.6
Loans-to-deposit ratio	84.5	85.7	86.2	86.4	85.1	80.4	84.8	80.3	79.0	86.0
NPL ratio	0.6	0.7	0.8	0.9	0.9	1.7	1.5	1.7	3.0	4.1

ROE	14.8	11.6	17.9	11.3	12.1	12.2	11.8	14.8	16.6	11.4
Core ROE	13.2	11.6	12.5	11.1	12.1	12.2	9.9	13.4	11.8	11.4
Core ROA	1.11	1.05	1.19	1.09	1.32	1.35	1.23	1.66	1.92	1.30

Wing Hang

Ratio:

Loan to deposit ratio	63.2	71.0	68.5	67.3	73.0
Average liquidity ratio	38.6	53.6	45.6	39.9	38.6
Total capital ratio	17.8	16.6	15.9	15.7	15.9
Cost to income ratio	55.1	48.8	45.8	47.6	52.0
NPL	0.4	0.55	0.5	0.45	0.6
Return on average assets	0.86	1.09	1.20	1.07	0.95
Return on average shareholders funds	10.6	10.6	12.2	13.7	9.8

Analyzing the financials of Wing Hang: Bank looks to be a very conservatively run bank with:

- Small branch network
- Lower loan to deposit ratio
- Cost to income ratio on lower side
- Non-performing loans also on lower side
- Return on average assets being decent with lower ROE, a function of lower leverage as well.

Acquisition Attractiveness

Valuation metrics.

Increase in top line	Possible as under-banked and under-branched.
Increase in margins	Possible as the current NIMs could be increased by expanding products.
Increase in profits	Possible as under-banked and under-branched alongside raising fee or non-interest income.
Lower capital	While price paid is two times book, halving the returns. It has come in trough of the cycle plus although, the outlay is on higher side at 15%, its market cap was quickly supported by rights issue.

Given the precedent transaction at 2 times book and auction process conducted by the sell-side bankers, probably this was the best outcome for the acquirer. This highlights a bit aggressive move but with enough upside potential.

b. DBS to acquire Bank Danamon, Indonesia

In April, 2012, DBS announced acquisition of Bank Danamon valuing it at $7.25 billion. The deal price is a premium of 56.3% to the average price of Danamon's shares and values Danamon at 2.6 times of the book value of its assets.

After the acquisition, DBS will be in the "top five players" in Indonesia, according to the company. "Indonesia's banking sector is highly attractive for DBS given its demographics, strong macroeconomics and fast-growing economy," DBS said in a statement.

The financial details of Danamon are not available but they had high single-digit ROE and ROA of around 1%.

Conclusion

Bank Danamon did not look like under-banked or under-branched bank. It had middling returns and the scope to tick all the four boxes did not look plausible. The valuation was stiff at 2.6 times of the book and coming at the peak of the economic cycle. Thus, it can be regarded as the blessing in disguise for DBS in a way that the acquisition did not go went through.

4.19 Executive Summary

In this chapter, we have focused on the empirical valuations that need to be relied on for the purpose of M&A. We have not touched upon DCF as other books cover it in detail. We have focused on the elements that go in forming the valuation's beyond excel sheets.

We have looked at interplay between growth, profitability, and capital ratios as also the triangulation involved between various valuation methodologies.

The intricacies of various metrics of various industries to quantitatively judge the peers are a required necessity. However, the key to understand valuation is to understand what is a good balance sheet and good income statement which is an outcome of financial discipline and measured growth. This seems to be the key to valuation that all the practitioners of corporate finance need to imbibe.

5

Structural Elements in M&A

Contents

5.1 Introduction to Deal Structure

Deal structure is the most important part of the entire deal. A well-designed deal structure can assist in lowering the cost of acquisition, even though the deal may have been committed at a high premium. On contrary, an ill-designed structure can raise cost of acquisition and convert a good deal into bad deal. A watertight deal structure is required to ensure that the deal closes expeditiously so that there the rights and liabilities are well-protected.

In euphoria of deal making, several times the critical structural elements are overlooked causing financial as well as reputational loss. Also, in a hostile situation, it becomes critical to ensure that the acquisition stays on course.

Incidental structural elements such as regulations, media, employees, politics, etc., become critical in sensitive or high-profile or competitive acquisitions where counterparties or competition may wish to scuttle the deal by raising the pitch through the above-mentioned elements.

A careful consideration is required of what elements are involved and the objective to be achieved, to carefully sew up the right kind of structure. Given the resource sapping discussion on the valuations and efforts put on reaching agreement on the price, the fatigue factors may sometimes lead to lesser time and attention given to the structure, which at times is left to the lawyers and the B-team which can result in upsetting the entire applecart.

Thus, incorporating a good team of lawyers, bankers, and internal M&A team to brainstorm and add finality to the deal structure is essential sine qua non to a successful deal.

To be a good M&A practitioner, a good grasp of technicality of structural elements is very essential. A good grasp of technicality also allows better negotiating position as well as gloss over the stiffer points of the counterparty.

A well-versed M&A practitioner would be required to have grip on finance, law, and accounts to navigate the maze of deal making. A lot of emphasis in M&A books or literature is placed on valuation techniques and methodology, but very less or nothing at all is placed on encapsulating the deal and successful execution of the deal. Thus, deal making elements are learned more by practise rather than academics. The current chapter focuses on teaching the basic and advanced structural elements to the students of M&A.

Structural Elements

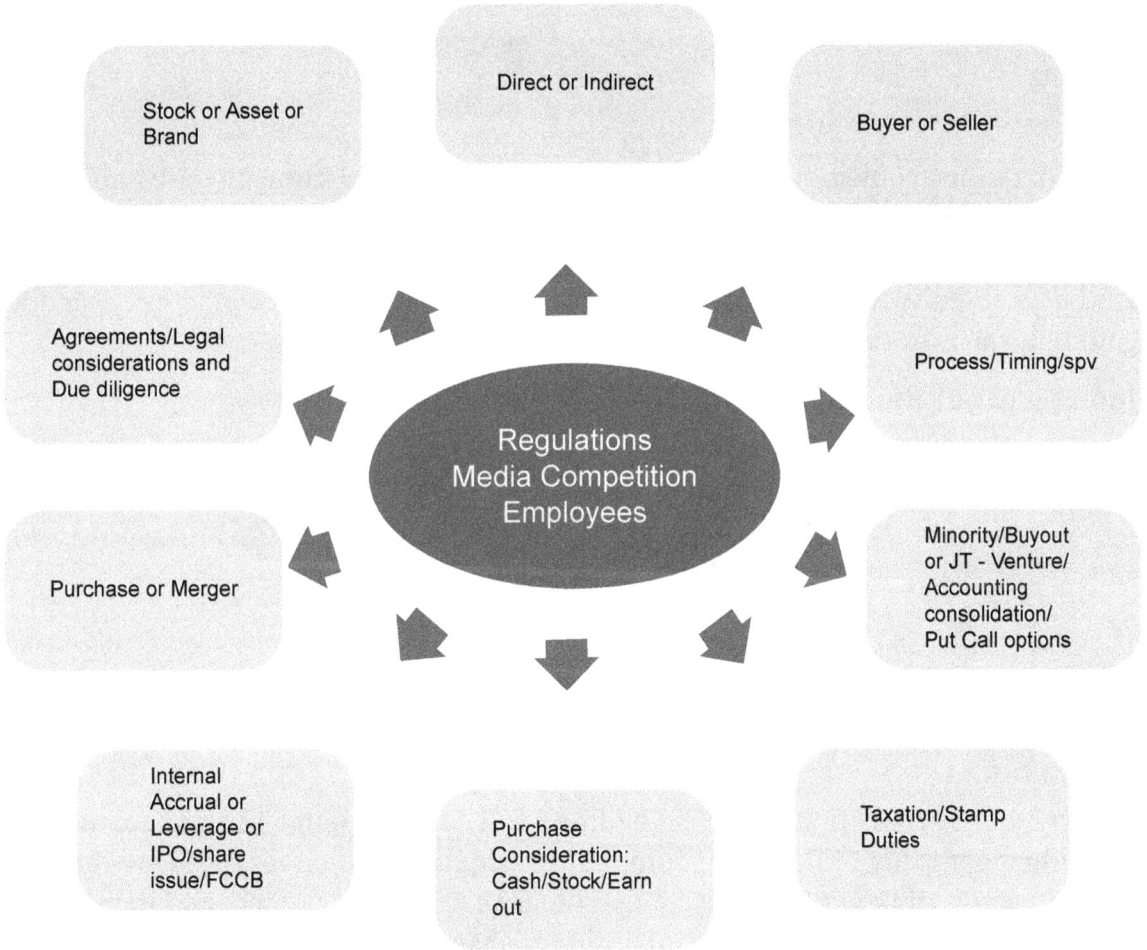

Stock or Asset or Brand	Direct or Indirect	Buyer or Seller
Agreements/Legal considerations and Due diligence	Regulations Media Competition Employees	Process/Timing/spv
Purchase or Merger		Minority/Buyout or JT - Venture/ Accounting consolidation/ Put Call options
Internal Accrual or Leverage or IPO/share issue/FCCB	Purchase Consideration: Cash/Stock/Earn out	Taxation/Stamp Duties

5.2 Structural Elements

The elements which make up the structure for effecting acquisition can be described as structural elements. These elements are important in structure design so as to take care of optimal execution of the deal, regulatory matters, taxation, and tax effectiveness. The various elements involved are described below:

Direct or Indirect acquisition

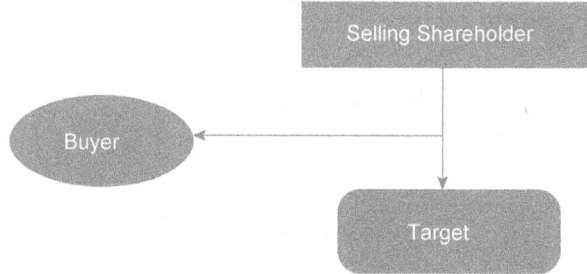

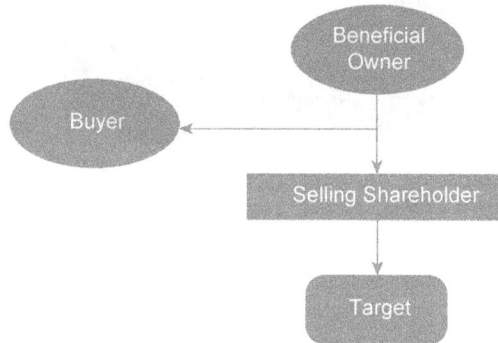

Direct acquisition:

It refers to the acquisition wherein the shares of the target company are subject of transfer between the buyer and the seller. Direct acquisition is preferred when speed and transparency are the essence of the transaction. Direct transactions avoid any kind of ambiguity and are easily assessable. The buyer, in this case, is interested in getting its arm around the target as soon as possible without hiccups.

Indirect acquisition:

It refers to the acquisition which is not direct and could be in the form of acquisition of holding company of the target company or acquiring the target company through issue of shares of target company so that other shareholders are reduced in minority and the buyer ends up owning the majority of shares.

It represents arbitrage over the direct acquisitions. The objective of indirect acquisition is to exploit arbitrage which could be in the form of:

- Avoiding open offer for the target company by acquiring economic interest through holding company but not control over the target company.
- Avoiding taxation by selling-off the unlisted holding company or holding company located in tax haven.
- Generally, the disclosure rules, securities law, or tax laws are more oriented toward direct transaction or listed target companies; thus, the acquisition done at one level up provides opaqueness to the transacting parties. Instead of put and

call option in the target company which can be subject matter of disclosure, they may be structured at holding company level.

- At times, indirect acquisition may keep the public shareholders or other stakeholders guessing, thereby avoiding run up in the target price which in turn avoid scaling up of offer price from public shareholders, especially if the acquirer is interested in buying further shares in an open offer.
- Indirect acquisition by way of dilution can provide optics, wherein the seller does not want to be seen as seller or there is need for bringing in money in the company. Seller can also end up as seller through dilution without being seen as seller in the eyes of the taxman.

Examples of indirect acquisition

Singapore Telecommunications Ltd. ("Singtel") has shareholding in Bharti Telecom Ltd. Bharti Telecom holds approximately 43.57% shares of Bharti Airtel. The effective interest of Singtel in Bharti Airtel Ltd. stands for 32.34%. This aids Singtel and Bharti having shareholder arrangement at the Bharti Telecom Ltd., the holding company of Bharti Airtel.

Other examples include:

- Hutch acquisition by Vodafone
- ACC and Gujarat Ambuja acquisition by Holcim

Case Study 5.1: Indirect Acquisition Structures — Hero Motor Corp.

Details

In December 2010, Hero decided to buy Honda's 26% stake in Hero Motor Corp. for ~Rs. 3600 crores. The promoters of Hero needed the financing to buy the 26% stake. The structure was designed as follows:

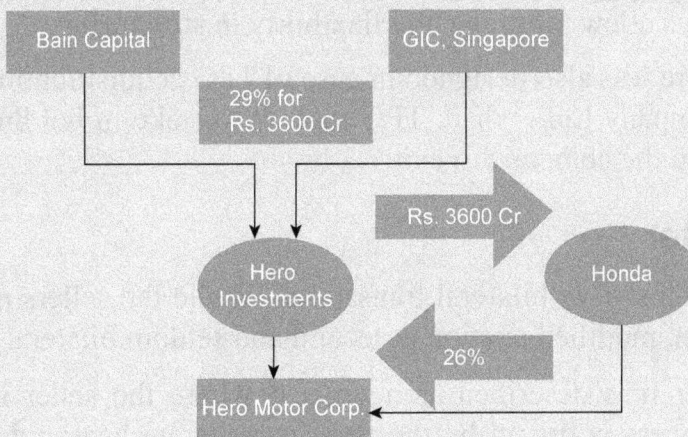

In March 2011, the private equity investors Bain and GIC picked up 26% stake in Hero investments for Rs. 3600 crores which was used to buy the 26% stake of Honda.

Hero Investments, being a promoter entity, the stake acquisition of 26% did not trigger takeover code due to inter-se transfer of shares amongst promoters. Although, it was financed by private equity who took 29% stake in Hero Investment, without any control rights probably with the only assurance that the entity will be merged subsequently into Hero Motor Corp. Ltd, so that they will get the direct stake in Hero Motor Corp.

In 2013, Hero Investments was merged into Hero Motor Corp. Bain as well as GIC became direct shareholders in Hero Motor Corp. Both GIC and Bain exited Hero Motor Corp. in 2014 and 2015.

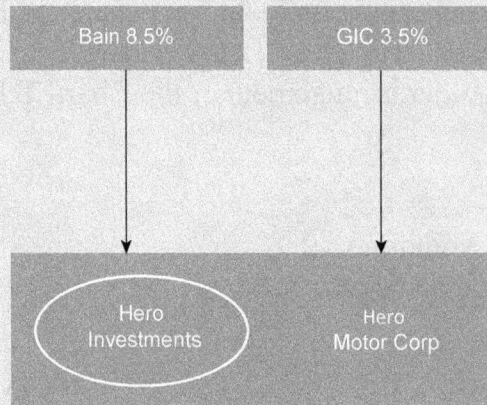

Key Learning

The above case study reflects the advantage of indirect acquisition through the financing achieved by the Hero promoters through structuring without raising their cash. The successful exit to investors by eventually merging the investment company into Hero Motor Corp. is also evident in the study. This case illustrates how holding companies allow arbitrage and flexibility in structuring.

Similar structure was also designed in case of TPG acquisition in Shriram Transport Finance Company Ltd., where TPG took 49% stake in holding company and eventually merged the company to exit.

Buyer or Seller

Buyers prefer exclusive or bilateral transaction. While the sellers most of the time prefer full auction, modified auction is second and seldom bilateral transaction.

- **Full auction:** It is described as a process where the seller invites bid publicly. The process is driven by the need to generate heat and dust and create enough bidding tension among bidders to extract the best possible price from the acquirers playing on the egos of the competing bidders. It is a preferred process where the target is seated at the cusp of peak valuation and bidders are enthused by future valuations. Media leaks the competing bids or reserve price or bid prices that act as tools to drive up bidding price or competition intensity to extract best price for the seller. The sell-off of Hutchison India is an excellent example to represent full auction process.

– **Modified auction:** It is a process where bilateral process is turned into a modified auction with limited number of bids. This process is preferred where the target company board is fulfilling its fiduciary duty by seeking better bids, while granting first right of refusal to the first bidder. The first bidder can seek to protect its interest by seeking stiff breakup prices in case the target company turns to another buyer.

The attempt to sell-off of Blackberry can be presented as an example of modified auction.

– **Bilateral negotiation:** It is a process where exclusive talks between the buyer and the seller are conducted. The seller or the target company is in a precarious position and wish to conclude the sale confidentially. Bilateral negotiation is a buyer-driven process and works to its advantage.

Jet-Etihad is an example of bilateral negotiation.

Stock/Assets/Brands

Takeover of a target company can be done either through acquisition of stock/shares, assets, or brands,

– **Stocks/shares:** Acquisition of stocks and shares is generally the most favored way of acquisition as it is comparatively direct and transparent with an established market price if it is a listed company. In case of unlisted company also, it is easy to value the shares based on the comparable companies. The other advantage to selling shareholder is that they receive the consideration from the buyer. The acquisition of shares leads to the acquisition of interest to participate in the assets and liabilities of the company. The acquirer becomes the owner to the extent of the shareholding percentage in the company. The acquisition of shares can be through cash, swap, or by merger. The consideration for acquisition will be dealt separately below.

The acquisition rules generally govern acquisition of shares. Thus, any other mode of acquisition by way of assets or brands will provide arbitrage in case the acquirer desires to avoid the acquisition/takeover rules. However, if the seller holds the power to bargain, they would sell through shares as a preferred mode of selling rather than through any other means.

Assets

Asset Purchase Structure

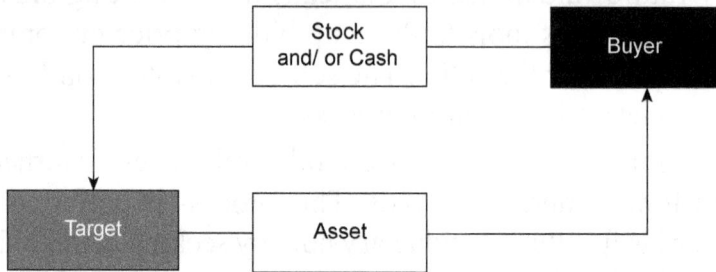

- Enables specific buying of assets, especially brands/ intellectual property
- Enables buying assets less the liabilities,especially when uncertain
- May be possible to upsize the assets post acquisition
- Disadvantage is business tax on value realized over WDV

The acquisition of assets is done under following situations:

- The balance of bargaining power lies with the buyer and wishes to avoid the takeover rules by simply purchasing the assets. The acquisition of Piramal's enterprise pharmaceutical business was done through assets.
- The acquirer is interested in only buying a certain portion of the business of the company, which is having multiple business lines.
- The acquirer/buyer is not sure of the liabilities of the company and wishes to avoid the liabilities and is purely interested only in takeover of assets. Purchase of Lehman's Asia business was by way of shares by Nomura, while the purchase by Barclays of Lehman's North America business was by way of assets as there was no backstop provided by the Fed on the liabilities of Lehman.

The acquisition of assets is comparatively complicated than the acquisition by way of shares for the following reasons:

- Absence of directly identifiable market price as in case of shares.
- Identification of correct profits attributable to that business line given the complexity of spreading overheads and common facilities enjoyed by that business line.
- Freezing of assets and liabilities of that business lines on a particular day.
- Asset sale is subjected to taxation, while the sale of shares of listed company is tax free.
- The purchase consideration is paid out to the company; thus the flow through to the shareholders is after the transfer to the reserves and dividend distribution tax. Therefore, there is substantial leakage before the consideration reaches the shareholders.

- Further, in the event the company decides not to distribute dividend, the cash remains trapped in the company, without giving consequential effect to the market price of the shares and the shareholders do not get any uptick in the value of the shares.
- There is additional charge of stamp duties and getting the receivables transferred to the buyer company is tough as the bank accounts lie in the name of the seller company and requires complicated assignment of receivables and re-invoicing of the billing.

The biggest advantage to the buyer is the avoidance of takeover offer to the minority shareholder and in case of distressed companies, there is ring fencing of liabilities that the buyer wishes to undertake.

The summarized advantages and disadvantages of shares vis-à-vis assets is stated as under:

Shares:

Advantages	Disadvantages
• Direct and fast.	• Inherit both assets and liabilities.
• Easy to value compared to asset purchases.	• It cannot cherry pick assets.
• Tax advantages to the shareholders.	• Generally, unable to mark-up the underlying assets and would result in the goodwill or intangibles.
• Sale consideration is received by shareholders.	• Sale consideration does not come to the company.

Assets:

Advantages	Disadvantages
• It can cherry pick assets.	• Tedious and cumbersome. Requires board and shareholder resolutions.
• Liabilities are ring-fenced.	• Difficult to value.
• Can mark-up assets.	• No particular tax benefits for the shareholders.
• Sale consideration is received by the company.	• Sale consideration not received by the shareholders and may suffer taxes and transaction expenses before money reaches them.

Case Study 5.2: Pharma Industry Thrives in Asset Swap

Details

Pharma Industry had witnessed a spate of asset swaps wherein they have exchanged each other's non-core businesses. The below highlights the transactions that have been effected.

Asset swap

Glaxo	Novartis
Oncology business	Vaccines and OTC business

Value Exchange

- Allows focus on certain pharma segment
- Develop leadership in the segment
- Avoid cumbersome acquisition of companies and resorting to demerger

Key Learning

The above case study highlights the structures that have been designed to suit requirements of buyer and seller, namely the targeted acquisition of business of their interest rather than the entire company. This gives a faster control over the assets rather than the cumbersome acquisition of the entire company and later demerging businesses in which the acquirer does not have any interest.

Handing over

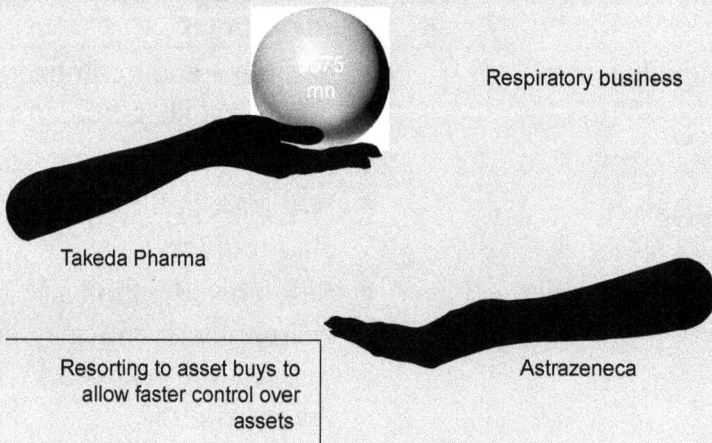

Respiratory business

Takeda Pharma

Astrazeneca

Resorting to asset buys to allow faster control over assets

Case Study 5.3: Mahindra Acquires Scooter Business of Kinetic Motors

Why asset and not the stock?

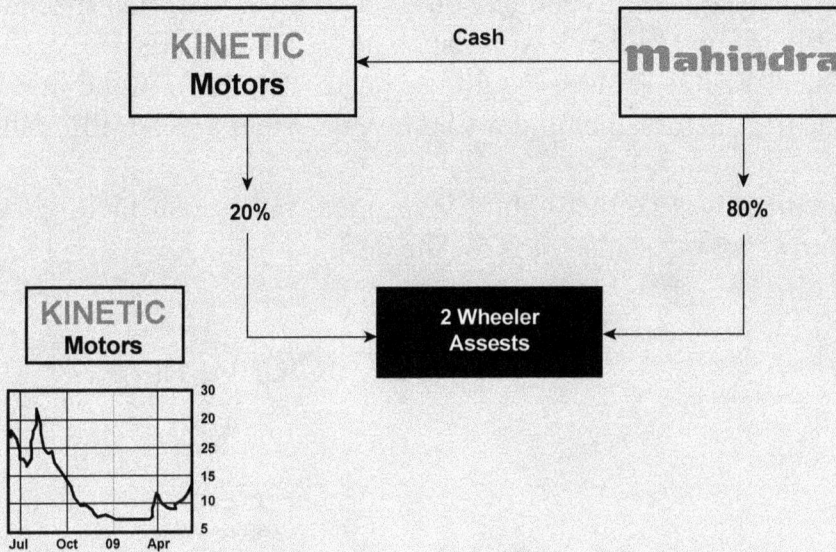

Details

Kinetic Motors had put their scooter business for sale. It had leveraged balance sheet and defaulted on loans. In anticipation of the sale, the shares of Kinetic Motors had zoomed. There were already news reports of acquisition by Mahindra.

Thus, the purchase of shares from the controlling shareholders of Kinetic Motors would have resulted in an open offer for the minority shareholders under the takeover code.

However, the bargaining power was with the buyer and they resorted to asset purchase as it allowed them to settle the loans because the payment consideration went to the company and not the shareholders. Further, the need to make an open offer for public shareholders was also avoided.

Key Learning

The use of asset purchase structure to settle the liabilities of the company and avoiding the liability to make an open offer to the public shareholders is demonstrated in this case study.

Case Study 5.4: Dr. Reddy's—ICICI Ventures

Details

- In March 2005, Dr. Reddy's and ICICI Ventures announced a $56 million partnership for the commercialization of Abbreviated New Drug Applications (ANDAs) by Dr. Reddy's Labs Ltd.
- As a part of the deal, ICICI Venture would set up a 100% owned special purpose vehicle (SPV) to fund research work taken up by Dr. Reddy's.
- Under the deal, ICICI Venture would invest $22.5 million in the first year and based on the risk factors, the fund would invest further $33.5 million in the next year.
- The arrangement was neither equity investment nor a loan facility, but an arrangement to share risks and gains for the development.

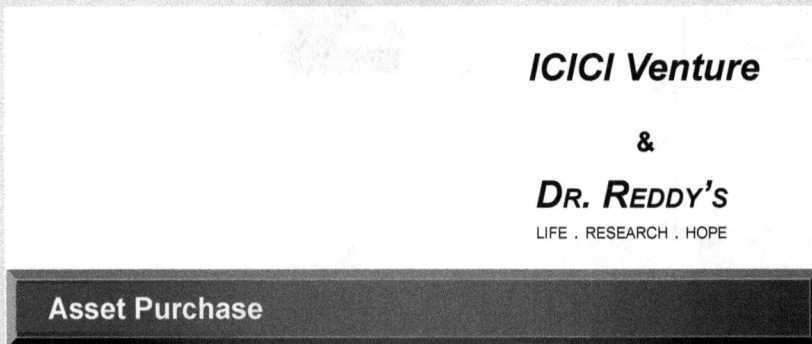

ICICI Venture

&

Dr. Reddy's

LIFE . RESEARCH . HOPE

Asset Purchase

The Rationale

- Dr. Reddy's unique initiative to partner with India's largest private equity investor for pipeline expansion for the U.S. Generics market.
- Dr. Reddy's to leverage global scale and infrastructure for pipeline expansion.
- ICICI Venture to share product development costs and make windfall gains if any of the ANDAs go into commercial production.
- DRL had chosen a high-risk–high-gain strategy to grow by going into direct competition with the existing patent holders. This was one of the methods through which it tried to de-risk its overall strategy.

The Deal Structure

- ICICI Venture will fund the development, registration, and legal costs related to the commercialization of ANDAs on pre-determined basis.

- This agreement was to cover most of the ANDAs to be filed by Dr. Reddy's during the years 2004–2005 and 2005–2006.
- On commercialization of these products, Dr. Reddy's will pay ICICI Venture royalty on net sales for a period of 5 years.
- The specific financial terms of the agreement were not been disclosed.
- In case ICICI Venture was unable to take additional exposure in the years ahead, Dr. Reddy's was free to approach other financers to balance funding.

Uniqueness of the Deal

- It was marked as the first-of-its kind business development in the Indian drug industry.
- It was an exciting and new concept of R&D risk capital funding model presented in India. It helped share the product development costs while leveraging on global scale and infrastructure.
- It not only strengthened Dr. Reddy's war chest to support research, but it also mitigates the risks in patent-related litigation.
- The deal came around the time that the WTO came into effect prohibiting Indian drug companies from violating the patents of multi-national drug companies and creating copy-cat drugs (TRIPS Agreement).

3. Brands

The acquisition of brands is done when the value of the business is driven by the brands as in the FMCG business. The acquirer would generally have the manufacturing lines or the distribution lines needed for rolling out the acquired brands. Thus, for them, the acquisition of brands is the only relevant asset that they are interested in acquiring.

The advantage and disadvantage of acquiring the brands is the same as acquisition of assets. Compared to the assets of a particular business line, the valuation of brands is easy given, the earning power of the brands is required to be valued, and balance sheet of the business line carrying those brands is not required.

Further, by structuring the sale of brands through licensing, assignment or franchising few of the taxation/stamp duty niggles associated with asset purchase can be avoided.

The purchase of Henkel umbrella of brands by Jyoti Labs and purchase of Louis Phillipe, Van Heusen, and Peter England from Coats Viyella by Aditya Birla Nuvo are the examples of brand acquisitions.

Case Study 5.5: Acquisition of German Remedies and its Brands

Details

This case study highlights very succinctly the advantage of acquisition through shares and brands.

The controlling shareholder of German remedies had put it on the block for sale. The controlling shareholder also had few brands licensed to German Remedies. A public auction was held for German Remedies, a listed company. Hence, any acquisition of it would result in an open offer for the minority shareholders.

The controlling shareholders requested for bids for its shareholding and brands licensed to German Remedies.

All bidders put in a composite bid for shares plus brands considering that value of equity will encompass the brands as well.

However, there was one smart bidder viz. ZydusCadilla who categorized the bid into "Shares" and "Brands." This allowed the bid for the shares to be lower as the consideration for brand was going to controlling shareholders and not the public shareholders as well.

This was advantageous to the selling shareholder as a part of the brand consideration was situated overseas thus not taxable. Second, it allowed the bidder to bid higher for the shares as they were not required to account for the brand consideration in an open offer to the public shareholders.

This case highlights the distinctions between acquiring shares and assets.

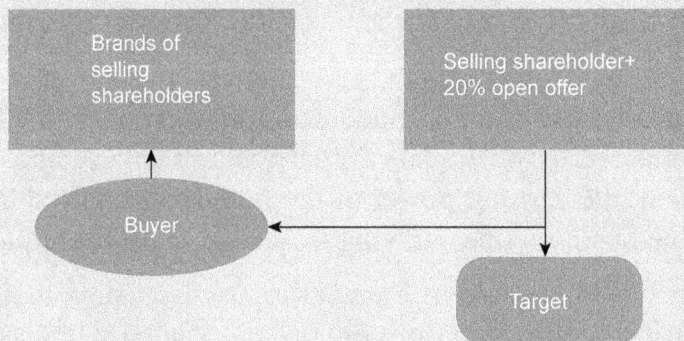

Another case that highlights the distinction between "Share" and "Asset" is the sale of Lehman Brothers. While Nomura acquires Lehman lock stock and barrel through share purchase of its unit other than North America. Barclays ended up picking the assets minus the liabilities as they were refused backstop on the liabilities by the Fed.

5.3 Mergers

In common parlance, merger refers to a process in which two or more commercial organizations combine into one. The difference between merger and acquisition is that in merger only one organization subsists as a combined one. While, in acquisition there will be more than one entity with control being the determinant of the accounting treatment whether as a consolidated entity or an associated one.

Pros	<ul><li>It holds regulatory arbitrage, under the Companies Act as per majority vote while the acquisitions done under the takeover regulations are driven by minority shareholders.</li><li>Valuation more discretionary.</li><li>Manageable, interested party can vote in some situations.</li><li>Disclosure is still minimal as compared to acquisition subjected to Security and Exchange Board of India (SEBI) regulations.</li><li>Favorable tax treatment and stamp duty.</li><li>Carry forward of losses and depreciation.</li><li>Benefit of pooling accounting under Indian GAAP.</li></ul>
Cons	<ul><li>Time consuming.</li><li>Carried out more in Intra-Group then, as a purchase acquisition.</li><li>Purchase accounting may result in goodwill creation</li></ul>

Types of Mergers

- **Forward:** Merger of target into the acquirer.
- **Reverse:** Merger of the acquirer into the target.
- **Triangular:** Use of a special purpose vehicle (SPV) to undertake forward or reverse merger.
- **Demerger:** Hive-off of an undertaking into a separate company (will be dealt separately in the next chapter).
- **Dual Head Merger**

Reverse merger:

It is the process in which the acquiring company folds into the target. The reason for this is to take advantage of some benefit carried by the target such as the target being a listed entity or target carrying tax benefit.

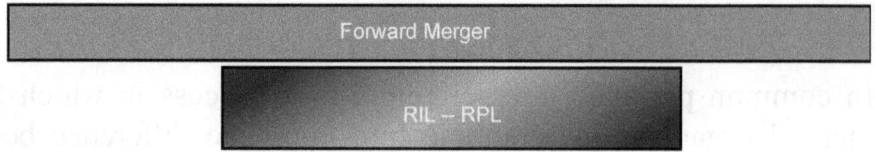

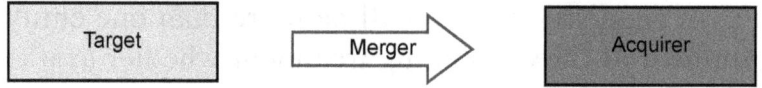

- Straight Forward and Simple
- Tax Advantage
- Minimize Leakage

- Target advantage
- Keep target happy

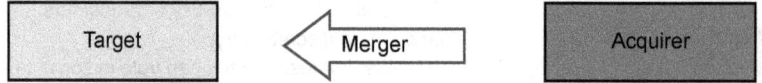

An example of reverse merger is the Merck-Schering, where Merck folded into Schering to maintain the contract that Schering had which would have been lost if it had undertaken forward merger. Generally, the acquiring entity is larger. The demerger of TCS from Tata Sons and merger into a loss making entity to take advantage of the losses of the target is also an example of reverse merger.

Reverse Back End Merger

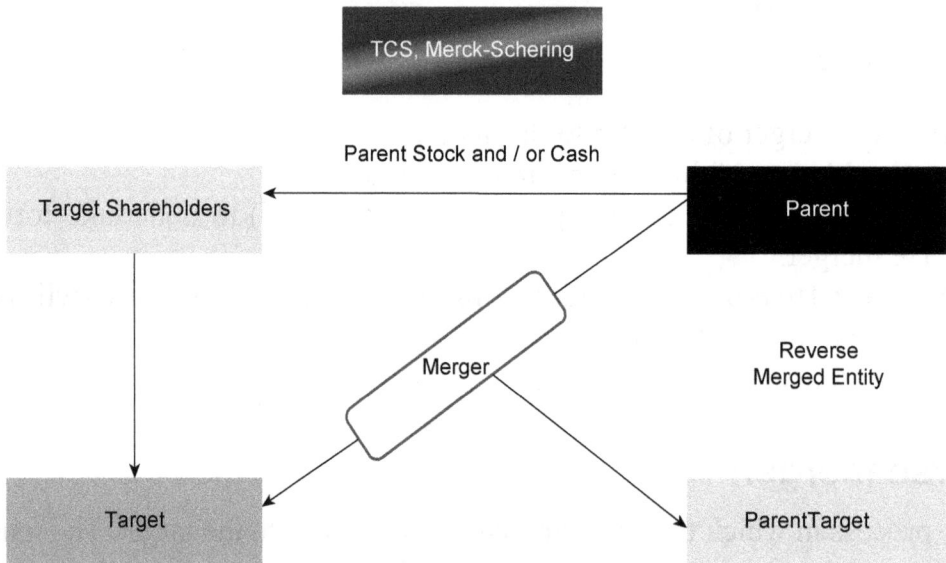

Triangular mergers:

It involves acquisition followed by the merger. The acquisition is generally done through SPV to maintain speed and at times for leverage purpose. Once the acquisition is complete, the merger is undertaken with the parent company.

In case of acquisition of Spice telecom by Idea, Idea first gained control through acquisition followed by merger of Spice into Idea.

The acquisition of Rhone-Poulenc by Piramal also fulfils the above criteria.

Tender Offer and Merger

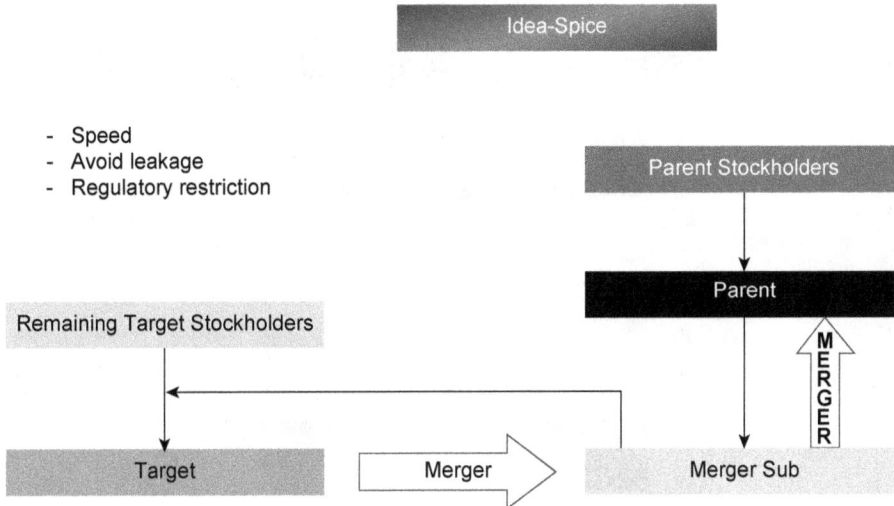

Idea-Spice

- Speed
- Avoid leakage
- Regulatory restriction

Parent Stockholders

Parent

Remaining Target Stockholders

MERGER

Target → Merger → Merger Sub

Merger of Foreign Company into Indian Company or vice versa

There have been few instances of foreign companies being merged into the Indian company, but it never happened vice versa. While the Companies Act allows both types of mergers now, the introduction of rules of capital convertibility has made them infeasible.

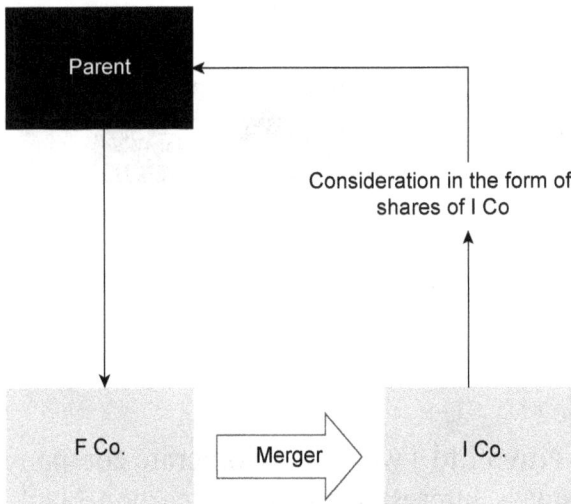

Parent

Consideration in the form of shares of I Co

F Co. → Merger → I Co.

- Rarely used Structure.
- Can be used for Leveraged Buyout Structure.
- However, clarity on treatment of debt of the Foreign SPV given the ECB rules is not yet present.
- Will encourage Leverage Buyouts for Tax Shield purposes if the above stands clarified.

5.4 Structuring Strategies in M&A

Structuring strategies in M&A would mean building deal structure in a manner that makes it a best fit within the framework permissible which could be regulatory and/ or valuation or market framework, thereby making it cost and time effective. The below case studies will elucidate the aforesaid point.

Case Study 5.6: Making of Aditya Birla Nuvo

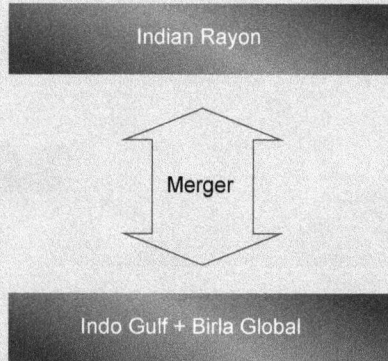

Merger- of Indo Gulf, Birla Global and Indian Rayon

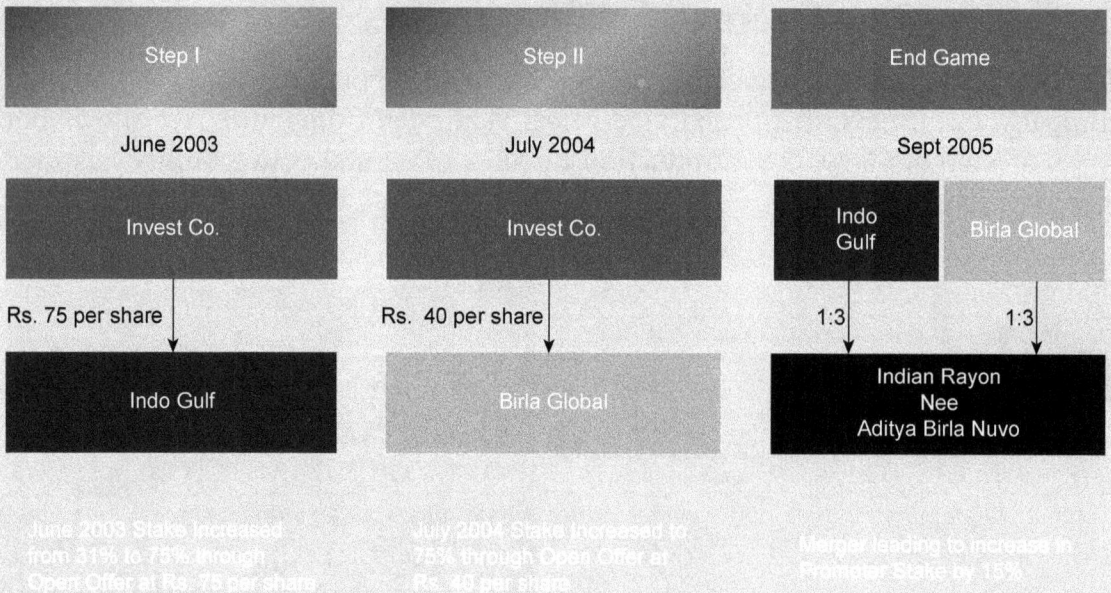

Step I	Step II	End Game
June 2003	July 2004	Sept 2005
Invest Co.	Invest Co.	Indo Gulf / Birla Global
Rs. 75 per share	Rs. 40 per share	1:3 / 1:3
Indo Gulf	Birla Global	Indian Rayon Nee Aditya Birla Nuvo
June 2003 Stake increased from 31% to 75% through Open Offer at Rs. 75 per share	July 2004 Stake increased to 75% through Open Offer at Rs. 40 per share	Merger leading to increase in Promoter Stake by 15%

Details

Indian Rayon (now known as Aditya Birla Nuvo Ltd.) was a conglomerate company of Aditya Birla Group having varied business interest from rayon, carbon black, telecom, insurance to branded garments.

The Aditya Birla group had a shareholding of ~26% that was comparatively lower given the strategic interests it held for the group.

However, given the share price and the fact that there is creeping acquisition limit of only 5% per year will make it years before substantial stake is acquried. Further, disclosure requirement makes it a herculean task to increase the stake directly in face of market having knowledge of stake consolidation.

Indo-Gulf Fertilizer Ltd. on the other hand was operating in copper and fertilizers business. It had recently demerged its copper business into Hindalco, another group company and left with only fertilizer business with huge cash concentrated on the balance sheet. The share price was just about the cash book value of the company.

Birla Global Finance was engaged in financing and had subsidiaries in insurance and asset management. It was a lean time for finance companies on the stock market.

The promoter holding in both the companies was ~30%.

Strategizing

Year 2003: The promoters made an open offer to consolidate their stake in Indo-Gulf at trough valuations by offering a decent premium over the market price. Since, the markets were unable to perform well and Indo-Gulf having been left with fertilizer business which was government regulated, the offer received good response and the stake increased to 75%, being the maximum permissible promoter holding under the regulations.

Year 2004: The promoters made an open offer to consolidate their stake in Birla Global at trough valuations by offering a decent premium over the market price. Since the markets were not doing well and Birla Global share price not reflecting the valuations of insurance and asset management, the offer price from the perspective of promoters was very attractive. Given the lacklustre markets and increasing the offer price mid-way through the offer gave the promoters a 75% stake, the maximum permissible promoter holding under the regulations.

Year 2005: The SEBI takeover code exempts stake increase through mergers done under the Companies Act. Under the prevailing Companies Act, the valuation rules were opaque and relied on the expert opinion being the final word as per the ruling of Supreme Court in Hindustan Lever case. The rules placed more emphasis on the book valuation rather than the market values, the focal point of SEBI regulations.

The merger ratios were more in favor of companies which had a higher promoter shareholding and consequently the merger of Indian Rayon, Indo-Gulf, and Birla Global resulted in the increase of promoters shareholding and the resultant company was renamed as Aditya Birla De Nuvo by ~10% providing saving of $100–200 million in the process.

Key Learning

a. How to perceive valuations in trough of market and the company valuations.

b. How to view under-valued companies in portfolio and seize opportunity to increase stakes when chips are down.

c. How to increase stake in companies by utilizing market valuations and various options available under the framework by planning and strategizing the moves to save on cost and achieving the objective.

d. Structuring the transactions by using the best available routes. To use takeover code, when the need was to move fast and acquire at the prevailing valuations.

e. Using valuation premium in trough market to garner response in takeover offers.

f. Then, using the arbitrage of merger route to finally merge at the desired valuations.

Case Study 5.7: Making of Tata Consultancy Services

Details

This case study demonstrates the use of asset sale and converting it into share purchase which avoids the impact of taxation on Tata Sons, the 100% owner of TCS pre-IPO.

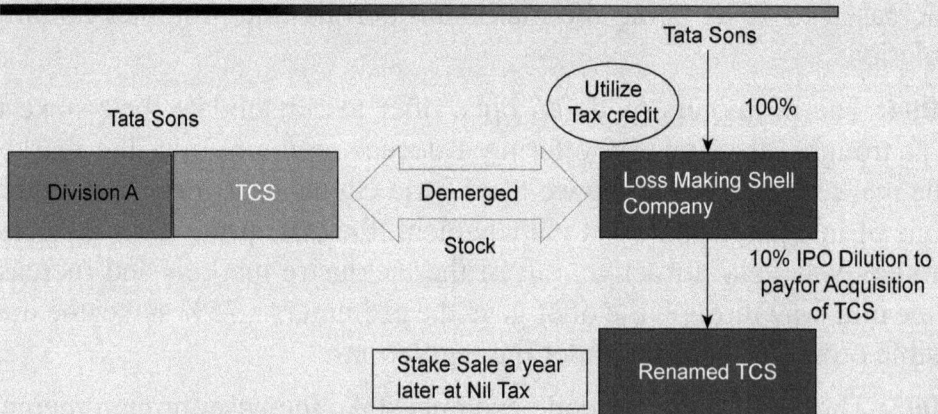

De merge and Slump Sale rolled into one

- Huge saving in capital gain tax
- Demerger effective on IPO
- Stamp duty benefits
- Undertaking enjoying tax benefit

TCS was a very profitable division of Tata Sons. Thus, any transfer of this division to any other form or entity would have resulted in huge tax for Tata Sons.

Thus, a scheme of arrangement was devised which had the following sequencing from asset sale to share sale resulting in "nil" taxation for Tata Sons.

First, TCS was transferred as a part of demerger to loss making company owned by Tata Sons. Thus, the losses were absorbed by TCS.

Thereafter, the company was rechristened as Tata Consultancy Services and the payment for the demerger was structured as share proceeds to be received from IPO of TCS and only upon the IPO being declared successful by signing an underwriting agreement.

Thus, the IPO proceeds were made tax neutral by putting it through court-approved scheme of arrangement. Subsequently, the company became a listed company and after expiry of one year lock-in, the shareholders were free to sell their shares on the stock exchange paying only Securities Transaction Tax (STT) and no capital gain tax.

This deal represents the beauty of structuring, taking advantage of both share sale and asset sale, thereby saving huge amount of tax.

Tax Considerations

Shares	Asset/ Brand
No long-term capital gain tax for sale on exchange.	Subjected to long-term capital gain tax.
No stamp duty.	Subjected to stamp duty as well.

5.5 Buying Elements

How much percentage stake to buy in the target company

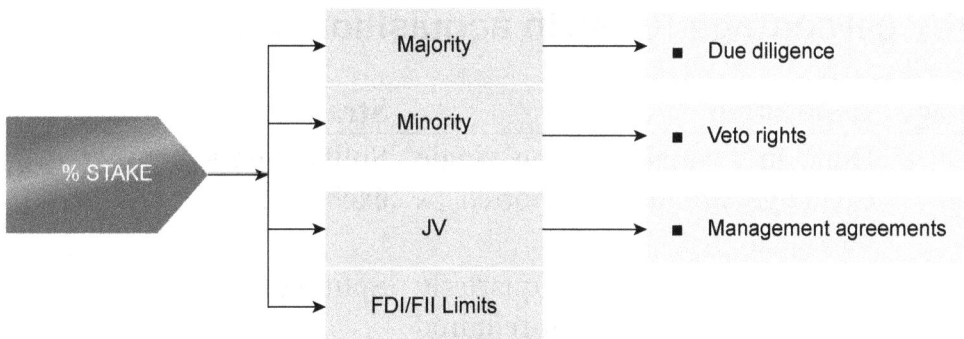

Buyer's Perspective

The buyer's perspective in deciding to buy the exact percentage is driven by the objective. Generally, the foreign buyers wish to buy 100% and take private as they would like to keep only single listed entity viz. the parent company. They also wish to bring in proprietary intellectual property only if they own 100% or near 100% stake. However, achieving 100% acquisition is tough at least in case of listed companies. In such cases, the aim is to achieve 75% stake. This is easier said than done unless the selling shareholder holds substantial shares in the company. The recent acquisition of United Spirits by Diageo is the perfect example to justify the case being discussed in which the target percentage was achieved by resolving United Spirits to issue shares to Diageo, so that purchase from promoters plus issue of shares by United Spirits will help the buyer to reach the desired threshold rather than depending on the minority shareholders to tender in an open offer.

The structuring of acquisition of ACC/Gujarat Ambuja by Holcim or Cairn India are the other examples to represent the scenario.

The key consideration for most buyers is to be able to consolidate the results of the acquired entity.

While, the Indian acquirers given the evolution of control in India are more than happy to acquire a certain percentage which will give them control over the target company rather than specified percentage such as 51% or 75% or 100%. They would tend to keep the acquisition outlay at minimum.

The other consideration for buyer at times is to park surplus funds to acquire certain percentage generally, starting with greater than 5% and lesser than 25%, to preclude other buyers or ward them off given the head start they have in the event, the battle turns hostile. The acquisition of 17% stake by Reliance in EIH falls in the aforesaid category.

Serious buyers with strategic intent would wish to achieve at least 26% to have the ability to block special resolutions.

The key percentage levels in acquisition are:

Percentage	Implication	Strategy
>0.5%	Done in a single day on single exchange would get reported as bulk deal.	Split the trade between two exchanges.
1%	Will get reported in quarterly shareholder information required to be filed as per listing agreement	Split the buying entities.
5%	It is required to be disclosed by the acquirer as per takeover and insider regulations.	Try to acquire as much before the holding gets disclosed and create price rise in the market.
24.9%	Just short of % which will trigger takeover regulations.	Wait for the price to cool down before the next acquisition.

(*Continued*)

>25%	Triggers takeover regulation as well as provides ability to block special resolutions.	Depends on objective.
>50%	Defined, as majority control is achieved. It provides the ability to pass ordinary resolution on its own. Also, the argument to be able consolidate is quantitatively demonstrated.	49.9% plus managing the International Financial Reporting Standards (IFRS) consolidation rules may permit the acquirer to hoodwink consolidation. At the same time, it is practically a 50% stake. However, if the consolidation is not an issue and the acquirer aims to have as much so that the benefit of proprietary IP will flow back to the parent.
>75%	Defined as super majority control giving the ability to pass special resolutions. It is also the max acquiring limit in case of listed companies so as to maintain 25% public shareholding.	To aggregate the benefit of proprietary IP to flow back to the parent.

Arbitrage options through holding company and depository receipt

Holding company: Acquisition of 49.9% at the holding company level with no controlling right over the target company can help achieve certain percentage acquisition as well as economic percentage without making an open offer.

Such a holding company can then be merged into the target company to cross 49.9% threshold as the mergers are exempted from the purview of the takeover code OR there can be call option on the remaining shares held by the other shareholders that can be exercised at opportune time and complete acquisition is accomplished.

Example: TPG's acquisition of stake in Shriram Finance and Blackstone acquisition in Jagraan Prakashan

Another instrument that is outside the purview of takeover code is the depository receipts until converted into shares carrying voting rights as long as there is no control established through the depository receipts. The conversion of depository receipts can be timed to be opportunistic with the market price that will have to be offered to the minority shareholders.

Example: The acquisition of IL&FS Investmart by E*Trade is an excellent example of structuring by taking advantage of the loophole in the regulations.

5.6 Sellers' Perspective

The sellers' perspective is driven by the following two considerations:

a. Price being offered
b. The profile of buyer

   a. **Price:** In case the price being offered is very stiff, it makes sense to walk away by selling lock stock and barrel. In such an instance, the buyer should insist to buy the entire stake if he is offering a stiff premium. The price will be driven by control premium given the intense competition for that asset.
   b. **Buyer's profile:** If the buyer profile is of higher pedigree and likely to cause value creation in the target company, then the seller may wish to hold back 10–20% for sell at a later date with the put option to sell at least at the previous acquisition price with carrying cost or simpliciter acquisition price. In such an event, the buyer should insist on the call option with cap on the price at which put option can be exercised. The buyer should also insist on the right of first refusal (ROFR) in such case. The mechanics of ROFR, however, need to be very precisely detailed.

Examples: Merrill Lynch-DSPML and Vedanta-Cairn Plc explains the above scenario.

5.7 Purchase Consideration

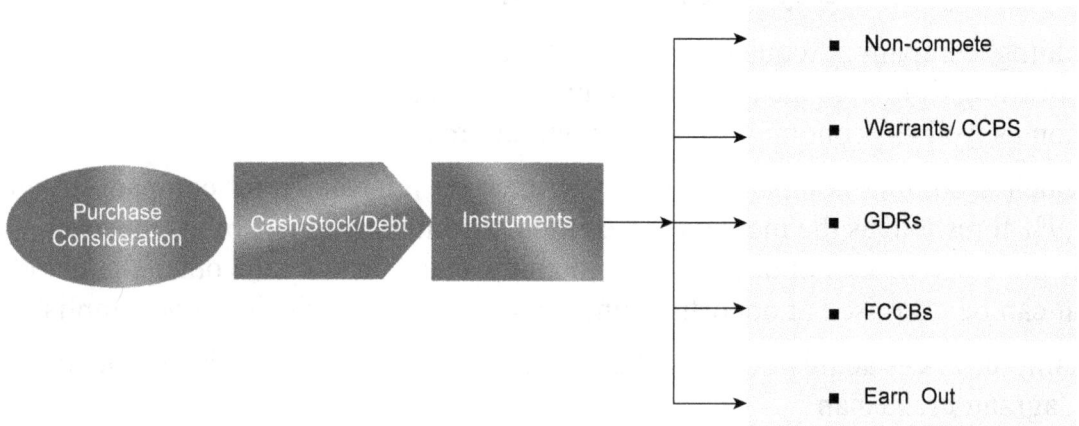

a. **Cash:** It is the most preferred consideration in India. The reason for its preference is that the buyer does not want the (majority) selling shareholder to continue to own substantial stake in the merged entity. While the seller especially, if the acquisition premium is high, would generally like to take cash and go home rather than invest back in the stock of the acquiring company making a high priced acquisition.

b. **Stock**: When the buyers use stock as a currency, it needs to make a careful evaluation of the following:

- Is there a lot of cash idle on the balance sheet which could be used better than the issue of stock:
- The multiple at which stock is being issued and the dilution effect of the stock. Lower trading multiple will lead to higher dilution and vice-versa, but the dilution at higher multiple also represents the challenge of compounding the return to the incoming shareholder;
- However, in big ticket acquisition or where the cash is essential to be maintained in the banking/insurance business, there is no choice but to go through stock issue;
- Further, the securities laws in India with respect to issue of shares in takeover are not clear with respect to the applicability of prospectus regulation and have not taken-off to that extent as in the west.

- Acquisition of Enam by Axis bank is an example of acquisition through issue of shares.
- Acquisition of mid-day by issue of shares by Jagran Prakashan is another example of acquisition through issue of shares.

c. **Earn-out**

It is a mechanism where the purchase consideration is linked to the future EBIDTA or EBIT achieved by the sellers of the target company. This is to ensure that the potential as stated by the seller is achieved as well and the purchase consideration is neatly tied into the earnings delivered by the target company. For structural reasons, the earn-outs can only be issued in the takeover of small-to-medium private companies. It is ticklish issue for the seller to justify the valuation as well as link it to earn-out as demanded by the buyer. Thus, it is dependent on the bargaining power of the seller.

Earn-out as a mechanism has not been successful, as the sole aim of the seller is to achieve the revenue or the EBIDTA and bends the seller to achieve it by hook or crook. Although well-intended, in Indian context it has not been successful to carve out a win–win situation for the buyer and the seller.

d. **Non-compete fee**

It is the amount paid to the seller to restrict him for a certain period from operating in that line of business and/or geography.

Earlier, it was carved out for non-compete fee paid to the seller from the price being offered to the public shareholders. However, the abuse of the same in being paid to the sellers who hadn't demonstrated any competency also led to the deletion of the clause. Also, the taxation of it as normal business income led to the demise of non-compete fee as a part of consideration.

e. Parallel consideration

This could be a possible example of parallel consideration. Vendor loans or backing the loans of the target company previously guaranteed by the selling shareholder can also be used to mask the real consideration paid to the seller.

Summarization of Pros and Cons

	Pros	Cons
Cash	• Freezes the valuation. Hence, no further downside. • Best option if the sale is being made at peak valuation.	• Limits further upside as the valuation stands frozen. • Difficult to deploy cash in alternate avenues.
Stock	• Valuation upside is observed by participation in future economic gains. • Facilitates the transaction for the buyer as they don't need to raise cash.	• Valuation downside is present, but it can be protected by Put option. • It may create stock overhang, with selling shareholder in perpetual selling mode. • It represents expensive means of financing due to dilution as well as the yield due to inverse PE. Thus, the key is to use it in high price multiple-scenario limiting dilution.

Case Study 5.8: Financing in Sun-Pharma Acquisition of Ranbaxy Laboratories from Daiichi Sankyo

Details

Sun Pharma acquired Ranbaxy Laboratories in the merger acquisition. The financing consideration used was shares by Sun Pharma.

The various reasons for the same can be ascribed as follows:

1. Sun Pharma was trading at high headline PE multiple of ~40×. Thus, the use of stock is justified for acquisition.
2. The deal size of $2.5 billion meant that cash was ruled out.
3. Given the lower multiple of Ranbaxy and superior management of Sun Pharma and track record of turning around companies meant bootstrap effect will come into play.
4. Daiichi Sankyo will benefit from the bootstrap effect through the rise in valuations of combined entity.

5. Also, Daiichi Sankyo will be able to exit on the stock exchange giving it the benefit of securities transaction tax and exemption from capital gains.

Eventually, Daiichi Sankyo exited Sun Pharma stock on the completion of merger, benefitting from the rise in the stock price of Sun Pharma.

Incase of Mid-Day Publication, the acquirer Jagran Prakashan also used stock as currency to acquire. However, the acquisition size was relatively small. Further, the multiple of Jagran itself were high but not excessively high to warrant the dilution for the small-sized acquisition.

5.8 Financing Consideration

a. **Stock/Rights Issue to finance acquisition:**

This type of financing is very ticklish corporate financing decision to be taken by the buyer. For the following reason:

– If issuance is done in the anticipation of takeover, then the sellers would sense the cash pile and play on the price. Further, more the delay in making acquisition after raising the capital, more is the pressure to deploy the cash raised;

Example: In Indian scenario, it is hardly observed that the funds are raised in anticipation of acquisition, as the disclosure rules prohibit no names fund raising.

Case Study 5.9: Financing by Raising Cash through Share Issuance or Rights Issue—Suntory Acquisitions and Acquisition of Smithfield Foods.

Details: Suntor acquisitions

July 2013

Suntory Beverage and Food raised US $4 billion in July 2013 marking one of the biggest IPO's in the year 2013 exclusively stated for the purpose of overseas acquisition.

September 2013

Suntory Beverage & Food Ltd. agreed to buy Lucozade and Ribena drink brands from GlaxoSmithKline Plc. for 1.35 billion pounds ($2.1 billion). Lucozade is an energy drink that competes with PepsiCo Inc.'s Gatorade and Coca-Cola Co.'s Powerade. While Ribena, a liquid concentrate marketed toward children, had combined sales of about 500 million pounds in 2012.

Thus, the deal was estimated to be three times the sales and off-loaded by able distributor like Glaxo.

Key Learning

The above deal highlights how having cash in briefcase of the acquirer incentivizes both the buyer and the seller. Buyer thrives on cash luxury while the seller preys on the cash in the briefcase.

Details: Acquisition of Smithfield Foods

Shuanghui International acquired Smithfield Foods in USA for approximately US $5 billion to create the world largest pork manufacturing and marketing company. The acquisition was financed by a debt of approximately US $4 billion in expectation of eventual listing of combined company and paying-off the debt.

However, the company's plan to eventually list the company after 6 months of the takeover fell flat as the concerns of the combined company and the debt got the investors, cold feet. The Initial Public Offering (IPO) was shelved, leaving huge debt on the balance sheet of Shuanghui.

Similar case was observed in the acquisition of Corus by Tata Steel, wherein Tata Steel had to do rights issue to keep the Corus financing going.

Key Learning

If issuance is done after the acquisition, there is a bigger problem of managing the value as it would arise in big ticket acquisition. This means emergence of high risk leading to fall in share price; thus, it would challenge to raise proceeds in the falling price scenario. If the price performs after the acquisition, the positive equity created would lead to the deferment of issuance unless the management is risk averse and will take risk-off the table by going ahead with acquisition.

Internal Accrual The internal accrual is represented by the cash and profit generated by the company should be the most preferred mode of financing for the following reasons.

- It limits the acquisition to the earning power of the buyer.
- Absence of financial risk taken beyond the exiting balance sheet.
- Lack of operating risk, as the acquisition ticket is conservative relative to the size of the buyer.
- Even debt can be used in small proportion or keeping the company's net debt position (debtless cash) to near even position. Thus, allowing the buyer some tax shield as well.

Leverage The debt taken to acquire companies would mean leveraging for the purpose of acquisition. If the acquisition is funded nearly by 70–100% debt is termed as leveraged buyout.

Although this mode of financing should be least preferred, it is the most commonly used means of financing. However, it the most preferred mode during economic boom and due to abundant liquidity it allows buyers to acquire companies beyond their capabilities. This financial risk multeplied with the operating risk is a sure shot recipe to disaster as adequately evident in the below cases. If the operations don't crank, EBIDTA goes for toss and financial distress takes over creating more operational pressure, thereby creating vicious cycle and whirlpool in which the buyer gets sucked, destroying the value for shareholders.

The litany of overseas acquisition done by the Indian corporates represents use of leverage and its devastating effect on shareholder wealth.

Maybe proving a point, the leveraged buyouts are probably more suited for LBO funds than the corporates.

However, use of moderate leverage not exceeding 1:1 debt /equity and not more than two times EBIDTA can provide tax shield as well as cheaper means of financing with low financial risk.

Leverage Companies and Leveraged Buyouts (LBO's)

Leveraged companies trading below book value also provide leveraged financing opportunities minus the risk of pure levered buyouts as the equity value paid for acquisition is lower. While in the pure levelled buyouts, the equity value is replaced by essential huge debt taken for financing that equity value.

Foreign Currency Convertible Bonds (FCCB's)

Foreign currency convertible bonds are generally US $ denominated bonds issued in the International markets having a tenure of 3–5 years with an option to convert it into equity shares of the company at pre-determined price. Due to the conversion feature, the cost of borrowing is minimal. However, it means that the equity conversion is happening at a lower value, thus proving to be high cost of financing. Apart from the risk of leverage, the added complications of FCCBs are:

- Foreign currency risk and cost of hedging the risk.
- Equity dilution risk at low value if the share price of the company performs.
- Distress risk if price doesn't perform. This means that if the share price does not perform, the convertible instrument becomes pure debt and serving of the redemption can make it a distress risk.
- Matching of Fx stream of income earnings and Fx liability on interest to make a natural hedge.

Pros and Cons of various means of financing:

	Pros	Cons
Shares/Rights issue	• Use of stock as currency. • Facilitating to raise if controlling shareholder is @ 75%. • Better than leverage.	• Results in dilution of existing shareholders. • Dependent on reaction of market to the deal. • External financing.
Internal accrual	• Relying on the free cash flow to support the acquisition. • Valuation is reasonable as there is no external financing involved. • Deployment of excess cash generated by the business distribution rather than as dividend.	• Limits ability to bid in a competitive situation. • May create additional risk by deployment of surplus cash in risky business over dividend distribution.
Leverage	• Cheap leverage allows ability to bid higher but still keeps the deal EPS accretive. • Easy to raise in a low interest liquidity scenario.	• Can create high leverage restricting business flexibility. • Difficult to refinance in tight liquidity scenario.
Foreign currency leverage	• Foreign currency loans will come at lower rates. • Allows natural hedge against the underlying business earnings in foreign currency.	• Risk of Fx fluctuation is present unless there is natural hedge.

The Valuation chapter will deal with the accretion and decretion analysis, emphasizing on the ability to pay changes through financial consideration.

5.9 Legal Structural Devices

Letter of Intent (LOI) or Memorandum of Understanding (MOU)

LOI and MOU represent the partnership between parties involved in the deal. The broader terms are agreed upon in writing including the price range and contingency events based on which the deal will be approved. These contingency events could be due diligence, financing arrangements, regulatory approval, divesture of non-core assets, etc.

Advantages of Letter of Intent:

- Creates a roadmap.
- Helps to expose any "deal breakers."
- May enhance parties' commitment/moral obligation to the deal.
- Solidifies understanding—helps to avoid "selective memory."
- May be useful to buyer in seeking financing.
- Can help facilitate compliance with the regulatory requirements.

It may also include:

a. Exclusivity.
b. Break-up fees.
c. Terminating conditions including the date by which deal is to be agreed upon.
d. Adjustment mechanisms to price.
e. Conditions precedent before concluding the deal.

The letter of intent is generally used to ring-fence the deal from rival bidders as well as to allow both the parties to comply with their regulatory obligations to inform the exchanges about materially price sensitive event.

The exclusivity and break-up fees negotiation is reflective of the balance of bargaining power between the two parties. The buyer will have to pay higher price for exclusivity, while the seller has to pay higher break-up fee for going shopping for the better deal.

Other protective clauses

Earn-outs: The clause looks protective in nature but gives an appearance of half hearted attempt toward the asset. It creates pervert incentives to archive targets hence, putting the best foot forward, asses the asset, determine the value, pay the price, take control, and make virtue of the asset.

Hold-backs: Unlike earn-outs, the hold-backs work well and protect the buyer from downside. However, it is very rare to get holdbacks unless the seller is desperate to strike a deal.

Escrow mechanisms for both purchase consideration and shares so that there is absolute protection over both the parties and no lender, bankruptcy, rival claimants can seize them.

Case Study 5.10: Legal Implications and Considerations—Cooper Tyre and Apollo Deal

Details

Apollo Tyres, India, announced acquisition of $2.5 billion Cooper Tyres in USA. Being a cross-border transaction, the size and nature of transaction meant it will take some time to consummate the transaction.

Soon after the announcement, the employee Union of Cooper Tyres opposed the acquisition and petitioned the Courts against the acquisition citing their interests being harmed by the new acquirer.

At the same time, there was this Chinese joint venture partner of Cooper Tyres in China, which held 35% of the venture who opposed the acquisition and even refused records and entry to Cooper or the Acquirer into factory premises.

Further, the Chinese venture was part of the deal, but it was not featured in the consolidated financials of the Cooper Tyres.

The above two events threw spanner in the works for both the parties.

This led to Apollo Tyres relying on "Material Adverse Change" clause for renegotiating and lowering the offer price by $9 per share. Cooper, in turn, accused Apollo for buyer's remorse and trying to wriggle out of the deal.

This tug of war led to finally Apollo stating it that financing was no longer available as closing conditions of the deal were not met due to unavailability of Chinese venture and absence of the employee issues when the deal was signed.

Cooper terminated the deal and approached the court for break-up fee of US $122 million. The claim was rejected by the Delaware Court.

Key Learning

- Both the buyer and the seller failed to recognize the issues around employees and Chinese venture.
- Especially, the seller did not cover the two critical issues in the legal agreements.
- How well-drafted agreements allowed the buyer to rely on Material Adverse Change clause to wriggle out of the deal.
- The successful defence of buyer of the break-up fees clause provides an idea of how adept one had to be in drawing up the agreements to minimize the liabilities.

5.10 Regulations, Media, Employees, Politics

The other challenging aspects of deal completion are discussed below. For a successful negotiation, it requires:

a. Enormous attention to detail

- Requirement of NOC by Reliance Industries in Reliance communication-MTN deal led to the eventual cancellation of the deal.

b. Understanding regulatory landscape

- Bharti-MTN deal was regulatory minefield to achieve dual listing, keeping in mind the third-world politics that was needed to be managed and government assurances.

c. Managing media

- Jet-Etihad is an example of how media can rake up issues to get the law makers involved raising issues in shades of gray.

d. Managing employee and other stakeholders expectations;

- In case of Diageo-United Spirits Ltd., the creditors of United Spirits raised objections to the takeover due to their outstanding dues.

e. Speed in getting the deal executed,

- In case of Spice Telecom, the acquisition was done first to take control and after that effect, it put forward the merger with Idea Telecom.

f. Lying low and keeping low media profile

- Both these deals suffered from undue media and competition attention leading to delay and eventually the cancellation of deals.
  - Cairn-Vedanta deal
  - Bharti-MTN

g. Not declaring victory before it is done

- Please refer the case study on Fortis-Parkway-Khazana Deal in the Chapter on Negotiation.

h. Managing optics:

- In Holcim-Ambuja deal, the name of the entities retained at ACC Ltd. and Gujarat Ambuja just to keep the xenophobic elements low as well as the acquisition was affected through infusion of capital into the company, thereby acquiring control through dilution of existing shareholder.

Thus, a very thorough analysis of the below elements is essential to analyze the risk.

5.11 Tax/ Duties: Structuring M&A

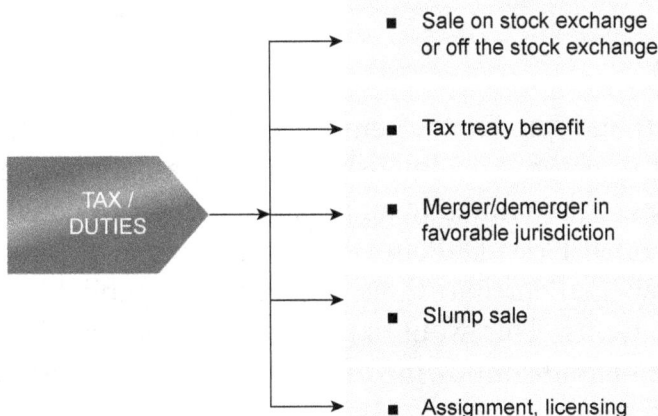

TAX / DUTIES

- Sale on stock exchange or off the stock exchange
- Tax treaty benefit
- Merger/demerger in favorable jurisdiction
- Slump sale
- Assignment, licensing

Tax is a very important part of the structuring that requires careful consideration. The key taxing questions that need to be answered are:

a. What should be the mode of acquisition?

There are certain tax benefits for buying on exchange essentially, if sold on the stock exchange, the securities transaction tax is applicable and no capital gain tax is required. While, selling-off the exchange would mean certain taxation.

There are certain benefits for acquisitions achieved through court-driven merger transaction against a purchase transaction effected through direct shares acquisition.

b. What should you acquire (assets or shares)

Difference in tax treatment exists between acquiring the shares and assets. The tax treatment of shares has been already discussed above, while the assets can either be acquired through slump sale or through demerger of the assets. The slump sale attracts taxation, while the demerger is tax neutral as long as few conditions are met.

c. How should you acquire it?

We have already discussed the modes of acquisition whether purchase or merger. The other issues include use of treaty benefits in cross-border acquisition and make it a well-planned acquisition to neutralize tax.

To observe the importance of the above point, refer to the German Remedies case study to see how the acquisition is planned.

d. How will you pay for it?

The financing aspect of acquisition is also determined by the financing tax impact. The use of debt will mean the interest becomes tax deductible. The use of cash reserves would not give any tax benefit, while the use of shares creates a mode which could be tax neutral.

Case Study 5.11: Dow Chemicals and DuPont Merger and Eventual Split

Press Release

DuPont (NYSE:DD) and The Dow Chemical Company (NYSE:DOW) announced that their boards of directors unanimously approved a definitive agreement under which the companies will combine in an all-stock merger of equals. The combined company will be named Dow–DuPont. The parties intend to subsequently pursue a separation of Dow–DuPont into three independent, publicly traded companies through tax-free spin-offs. This would take place as soon as feasible, which was expected to be 18–24 months following the closing of the merger, subject to regulatory and board approval.

The companies will include a leading global pure-play Agriculture company, a leading global pure-play Material Science company, and a leading technology and innovation-driven Specialty Products company. Each of the businesses will have clear focus, an appropriate capital structure, a distinct and compelling investment thesis, scale advantages, and focused investments in innovation to deliver better superior solutions and choices for customers.

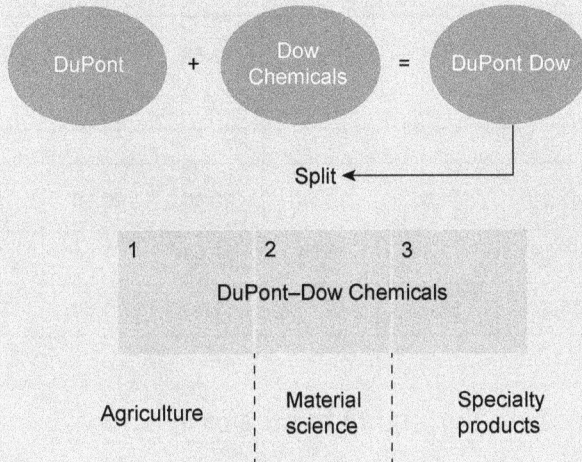

Key Learning

Why merge and then split?

To obtain tax-free spin-offs the companies initially merged and then split. A direct merger of each of the three divisions between DuPont and Dow Chemical would have resulted in huge tax pay-off.

The process of merger followed by split results in neutralization of tax, making it the preferred mode of merger.

5.12 Structuring M&A—Guiding Principles

- Think Arbitrage
- Think Indirect
- Think Options
- Think Upside Down
- Focus on Exemptions and Provisions

Strategizing in M&A

	E*Trade Acquisition of IL&FS Invest mart						
Category	30-Sep-05	30-Dec-05	30-Mar-06	30-Jun-06	30-Sep-06	30-Dec-06	30-Mar-07
	% Holding	% Holding	% Holding	% Holding	% Holding	% Holding	% Holding
Indian Promoters	46.31	31.63	29.58	29.58	29.58	29.58	29.58
Foreign Promoters	0						43.85
Sub Total	46.31	31.63	29.58	29.58	29.58	29.58	
E:Trade	11.14	7.53	7.04	7.04	7.04	7.04	0.00%
GDR	35.32	58.62	19	17.53	31.52	31.52	0

All the above principles are highlighted in the case below.

Case Study 5.12: E*Trade Acquisition of IL&FS Investsmart

Details

E*Trade, US-based stock broker specialized in electronic trading platform especially for retail investors. They did not have any presence in India. Around 2004, the listing of IndiaBulls who were engaged in electronic trading and quite a few private equity deals in electronic brokers had put spotlight on these businesses. IL&FS Investsmart, an arm of IL&FS, had also entered the business and had made a sizeable presence in this segment. Subsequently, it got itself listed on the Indian Stock Exchanges followed with listing of GDRs in overseas market.

Strategizing

At this time, the SEBI Takeover code had exemption for acquisition of Global Depositary Receipts (GDRs) as long as they weren't converted into shares carrying voting rights. Further, it allowed change in control without triggering the takeover code as long as it was ratified by special resolution of the shareholder.

Given the lofty valuations, the retail e-trading companies were trading, it was bit difficult to complete acquisition by acquiring shares and make an open offer at high ruling market price.

As a precursor to the takeover of IL&FS, Investsmart got its GDR program listed. The GDRs were silently acquired by E*Trade. It can be observed in the above chart how the nibbling happened. Since GDRs were outside the purview of the SEBI takeover code, they could acquire greater than 15% GDRs and also avoid any kind of reporting.

Thereafter in 2007, they announced the conversion of GDRs into shares and announced an open offer at the time and price of their choice.

Key Learning

The above case study highlights the use of exemptions and provisions to affect a cost-effective takeover.

5.13 Structural Checklist

Deal structure	We have already dwelt into the various structures used to advantage by the buyer or seller. We have also seen how deal structure can enhance or protect value. The key elements being- – Direct or indirect – Stock or asset or brand
Deal consideration	We have seen how critical cash or equity is used for selling consideration as well as financing the transaction. The impact of deal consideration is studied in Chapter on Valuation.
Deal financing	We have seen the pros and cons of various methods of financing. The pre-acquisition financing and post-acquisition financing and the likely impact of the same.
Deal strategizing	The synchronization of the moves in such a manner that it creates an effective acquisition with least impact.
Due diligence, representations and warranties, indemnities, non-compete	The importance of this cannot be understated as it is used to make the structuring airtight.
arbitraging, thinking options, and upside down	It is important to optimize the deal rather than thinking conventionally.
Regulations, employees, politics, and media	It is important to understand the sensitivity of each one of them to have better control over the transaction.
Competition	Whether competition can improve the structure and lure the seller to their side.

5.14 Executive Summary

The chapter highlighted the various structural elements and the role they play in deal structuring. A careful study of these elements is critical as also deep thought to each one of them is critical to sew a deal structure that can withstand the acquisition and execution.

The chapter has given pros and cons of various elements to enable choosing the right elements to meet on the requirements of the deal.

The case studies highlight the importance of them and will hopefully help in future structuring.

6

Leverage Buyout

Contents

6.1 Introduction

The leverage buyout (LBO) methodology is a much talked about topic covered widely in academic books. In the current chapter, we have made an attempt to discuss briefly about the methodology, the process, and the valuation approach involved in leveraged buyout.

LBO was brought to fore by buyout funds like Kohlberg Kravis Roberts (KKR) and made popular by case of RJR Nabisco Inc. LBO's came to fore around the late 1970s due to couple of reasons. The foremost being the fact that the world had already seen two world wars and the cold war spectre was always looming on the business and economy. Due to the aforesaid, the corporates had got habitual to uncertain business scenario and hence relying on low leverage capital structure to run their business.

While the business scenario looked uncertain, it also created an environment in which nuclear deterrent on the either side made the war unlikely. As a consequence, we had on platter low leveraged companies with good cash flow and abundant liquidity in the credit market.

Thus, reversing the capital structure from low leverage to high leverage was enough to deliver alpha for the buyout funds. Over the years, due to intensified competition among the buyout funds as well as cycle of low and high liquidity in credit market has been the bugbear of buyout funds, but LBOs have come here to stay relying on leverage plus value addition and frothy capital markets to make a return for its investors.

6.2 Process involved in LBO

The process of LBO involves the incorporation of LBO fund that contains 90% debt and 10% equity as its capital structure. It then look out for target listed companies which have fallen out of favor with the public market.

The listed companies have the following characteristics:

- Mature industry
- Mature company
- Strong management team
- Low leverage
- Low CapEx requirements
- Strong cash FLOWS
- Good exit options
- Discretionary expenses very high
- Overheads very high
- Excess of non-core assets

The above criteria give comfort while plunging into high leverage–high risk strategy. Ensuring stable cash flow to pay-off the debt and thereby increase the equity value is the basis of LBO.

Stage I

The LBO fund buys out 100% of the public shareholding of such listed companies. The financing of the buyout has evolved from plain financing to hybrid financing. It has evolved from plain simple vanilla bonds to the junk bonds. The earliest wave involved plain simple financing, only till the time the buyouts went turtle. Instead of equity holders, the debt holders ended up bearing the brunt of the losses. Since then, plain financing has shifted to mezzanine financing, so that the lenders also participate in the profit sharing, if the buyout succeeds. Thus, the lenders would aim to make 15% return while the LBOs will target around 30% return.

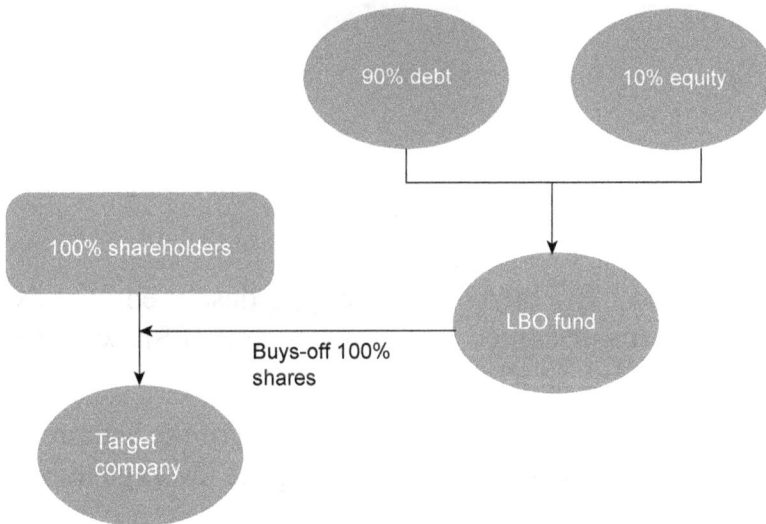

Stage II

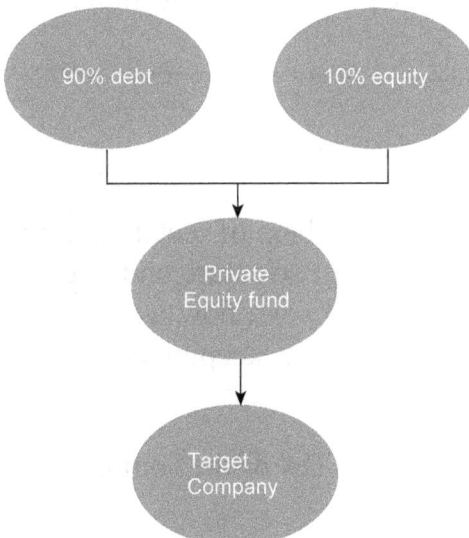

The Stage II involves completing the process of buyout and achieving control over the target company.

Stage III

The last leg of the transaction involves merging the LBO fund and the underlying target company to change the capital structure of the target company to the leveraged capital structure of the LBO fund, thereby utilizing the tax shield of the leverage and accumulated losses, if any, to maximize the cash flow and pay-off the debt.

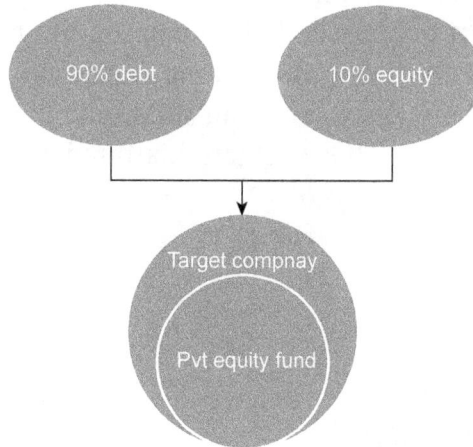

India has not witnessed LBO buyouts of the type described here except for Tata–Tetley deal or Tata–Corus or United Breweries buyout of Shaw Wallace or Radico–Khaitan or Piramal's buyout of Rhone–Poulenc.

None of the above involved LBO funds or merging of the acquirer and target; to a maximum extent they were involved in just taking the leverage to buy out the target companies.

The reason for the incapability lies in the banks in India that are not allowed to extend loans for takeover.

6.3 Methodology and Valuing an LBO

LBO valuation can be explained with the help of rectangle given below. Initially in the buyout, the debt is 90% of the capital structure and equity is 10%. During the progression of the buyout, the enhanced cash flow as described below is used to reduce the debt and increase the equity value, keeping the enterprise value constant.

It can be achieved through:

- Eliminate expenses that reduce EBITDA of the company.
- Selling off redundant assets.

- Use the cash flow to pay for the debt and improve the equity value in the enterprise value.
- Operational improvements.
- Increase gross margins.
- Evolve business toward higher margin design areas.
- Relocate production from higher cost to lower cost locations.
- Improve operating leverage.
- Utilize excess capacity by increasing the unit volume.
- Rationalize other capacity.
- Improve working capital management.
- Extend payables to suppliers.
- Improve receivables collections.
- Reduce inventory

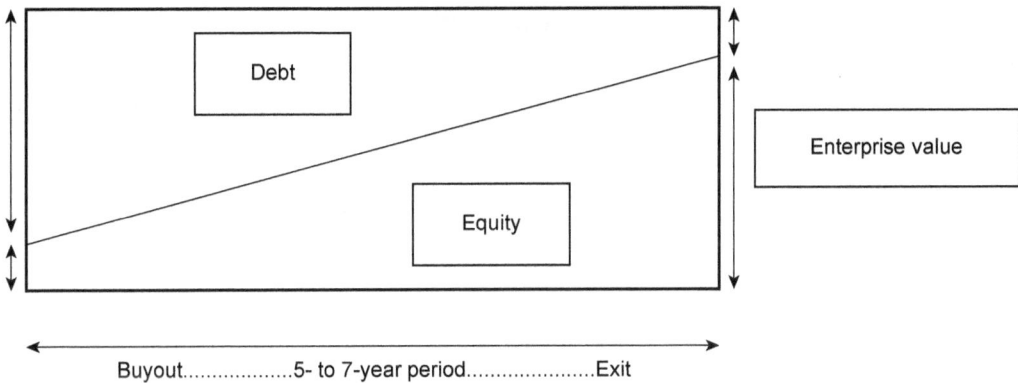

However, in practice, with the decrease in leverage, the figure below should be trapezoid instead of rectangle as the reduced risk will increase the equity value of the buyout.

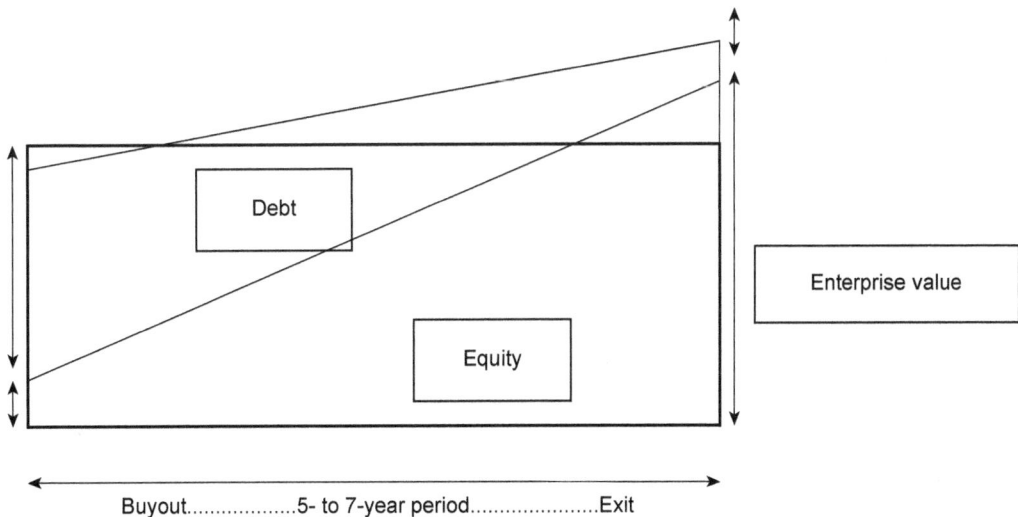

There are pitfalls in assuming a trapezoid instead of rectangle enterprise value as it leads to the optimistic assumption in LBO. A high risk–high leverage strategy would mean the high risk involved in servicing leverage from cash flow of a company, which is not exactly in pink of the health. These may result in the over-payment for buyout funded by huge debt. It creates possible trap of EBIDTA not cranking up to repay the debt. The aforesaid methodology would fall in the bucket of variable risk method, which adjusts the discount rate as the cost of capital keeps trending lower due to debt pay down. This is essentially predicting the buyout to go as per the plan over a period of 5–7 years.

Thus, the key to LBO modeling is to keep the entry and exit EBIDTA multiple in range to avoid overvaluation.

LBO modeling is relatively easy as compared to others. It can be demonstrated by the simple examples given below.

1. The key is to predict the entry and exit EBIDTA of the buyout firm.
2. The enterprise value (EV)/EBIDTA multiples are available from market for the industry.
3. Let us assume the Exit EBIDTA to be 200. The Exit EV/EBIDTA multiple is 6. Therefore, the enterprise value of the firm will be 1200 (6 × 200).
4. The buyout fund expects 35% IRR.
5. If the outstanding debt is 255, the equity value will be 945 (1200 × 255).
6. Discount equity value of 945 back by 35%, being IRR expectation and assume it for a period of 5 years.
7. The discounting will provide the entry equity value of 211.
8. The LBO can now be financed by mix of debt, mezzanine financing, and equity. The relative component of the same will be driven by the return expectations of the each of these components.

Steps involved in the LBO process

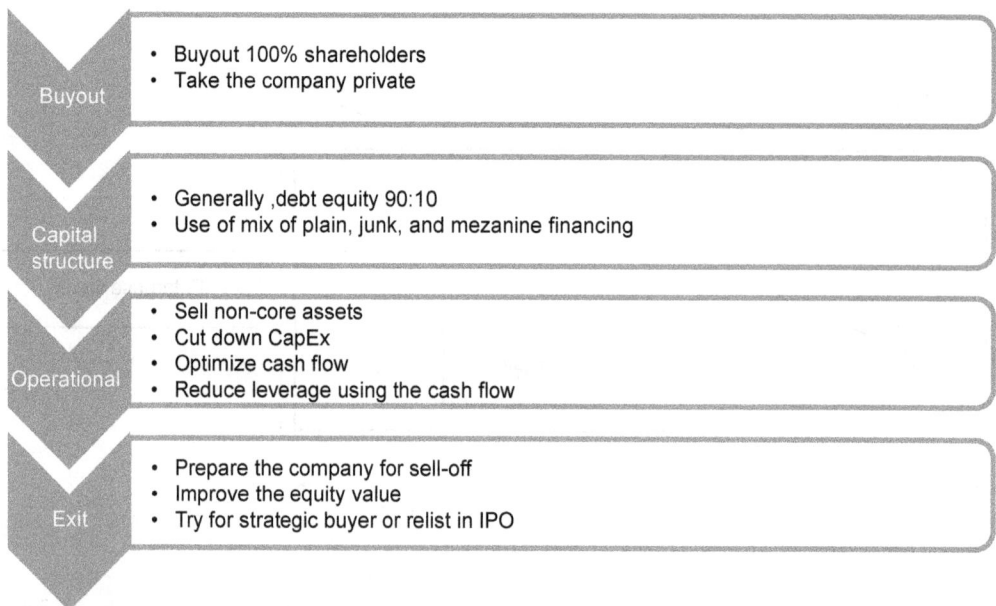

Buyout
- Buyout 100% shareholders
- Take the company private

Capital structure
- Generally ,debt equity 90:10
- Use of mix of plain, junk, and mezanine financing

Operational
- Sell non-core assets
- Cut down CapEx
- Optimize cash flow
- Reduce leverage using the cash flow

Exit
- Prepare the company for sell-off
- Improve the equity value
- Try for strategic buyer or relist in IPO

6.4 Problem 1

Calculate the following from the data given the table below.

 a. Calculate the equity value at the end of 5 years.
 b. Calculate the equity component, assuming 30% IRR expectation.
 c. If the fees and expenses are 0.15% EBIDTA, what will the entry multiple?

(Given: LBO transaction is 0.15 times EBIDTA)

1 First year EBIDTA	$150		
2 Initial cash balance	$5		
3 Secured debt	550	90% of the secured debt to be amortized in 5 years	
4 Debt capacity	5	Times EBIDTA	
5 Exit multiple	6		
6 Exit EBIDTA	$200		
7 Total debt	$750		
8 Secured debt	550		
9 Subordinated debt	200	Outstanding at end of LBO	
10 Amortized	495	90% of the secured debt ($550) amortized in 5 years	

			Formulae
11 Enterprise value at exit		$1200	$(5) \times (6)$
12 Secured debt outstanding at end of LBO		$55	$(8) - (10)$
13 Subordinate debt outstanding at end of LBO		$200	(9)
14 Future equity value		$945	$(11) - (12) - (13)$
15 Entry equity component at 30% IRR		$211	$(13)/(1+30/100)^5$
16 Net debt at entry		$745	$(7) - (2)$
17 Equity at entry		$211	(15)
18 Enterprise value at entry		$956	$(16) + (17)$
19 LBO transaction expenses		$23	$0.15 \times (1)$
20 Affordable price		$978	$(18) + (19)$
21 EBIDTA at entry		$150	(1)
22 Affordable multiple		6.5	$(20)/(1)$

6.5 Problem-2

From the given data, calculate:

 a. What will be the enterprise value and equity value at the end of fifth year?
 b. Find the return to sub-ordinate debt holder at the end of fifth year.
 c. What will be the return to fund at the end of fifth year?

1	LBO purchase/entry price	$300		
2	Secured debt	$80		Paid-off during the 5 years
3	Subordinate debt	$120	Coupon of 6% p.a.	Redeemable at end of fifth year and additionally get 20% of equity
4	Fund equity	$75		At the end of fifth year has 80% of equity.
5	Free cash flow (FCF)			Totally utilized toward amortization of secureddebt and interest.
6	Fifth year EBIDTA	$60		
7	Exit multiple	8	Times EBIDTA	
8	Enterprise value fifth year	$480	(6) × (7)	
9	Less: Debt outstanding in fifth year	$(120)	(3)	
10	Equity value in fifth year	$360	(8)–(9)	
11	of which			
12	Subordinate holder	$72	20% of (10)	
13	To fund	$288	80% of (10)	

YEARS	0	1	2	3	4	5
IRR						
Subordinate holder	$(120.00)					
Coupon		$6.00	$6.00	$6.00	$6.00	$6.00
Principal						$120.00
Equity kicker						$72.00
	$(120.00)	$6.00	$6.00	$6.00	$ 6.00	$198.00
IRR	14%					

YEARS	0	1	2	3	4	5
Funds initial investment	$(75.00)					
Exit proceeds						$288.00
	$(75.00)	$ -	$ -	$ -	$ -	$288.00
IRR	31%					

Adjustments in LBO Modeling

It can be done through:

- Adjusting EBIDTA: EBIDTA less maintenance CAPEX
- Debt coverage: Adjusted EBIDTA to cash interest expense and other fixed charges

Let us move ahead to observe the relative ease of calculation in LBO modeling.

Case Study 6.1: Lixil to Buy Grohe in $4 billion Landmark Deal

Details

(*Source Press release*)-Germany's biggest bathroom fittings company, Grohe has been snapped up by the Japanese building products group Lixil (5938.T) for a $4 billion deal including debt, the largest ever investment done by a Japanese company in the Europe's biggest economy.

Lixil leveraged buyout of Grohe from the financial investor TPG Capital TPG.UL and Credit Suisse's (CSGN.VX) private equity arm highlights the renewed appetite among Japanese companies for foreign acquisitions following a slowdown in the pace of deal blaming the decreased value of Yen.

Lixil Group Corp. has formed a 50–50 joint venture with the state-backed Development Bank of Japan (DBJ) to buy 87.5% of Grohe GROH.UL, creating a global group with more than 4 billion Euros in the annual sales. The deal was expected to close in the first quarter of 2014.

According to the deal, Grohe will give Lixil the footprint in Europe that it was seeking and help it expand in China through Joyou (JY8G.DE), a Grohe bathroom fittings unit that sells through 4000 distributors in the Asia's largest economy.

Lixil Chief Executive, Yoshiaki Fujimori, said that the acquisition would fill out a global network built on its 575-million-euro deal for Italian curtain walling maker Permasteelisa in 2011 and its $542 million purchase of US toilet and fixtures maker American Standard earlier this year.

"With this deal, we have secured a global platform," said Fujimori, a former General Electric (GE.N) executive who has put Lixil on a path to growth through acquisitions since, taking the helm 2 years ago.

Grohe's private equity owners, who had purchased the German maker of high-end bathroom and kitchen fixtures for 1.5 billion in the year 2004, had also been considering a stock market listing alongside efforts to sell the company.

Lixil, formed by mergers of several Japanese building product makers with a product line-up ranging from high-tech toilets to window frames, said that the deal valued all of Grohe at 4.06 billion dollars or 10.3 times its 2013 earnings before interest, taxes, depreciation, and amortization.

2004	TPG buy price	Enterprise value	1,500,000,000
	Assumption funded by:		
	debt	90%	1,350,000,000
	Equity	10%	150,000,000
2013	Sold at enterprise value		4,000,000,000
	Debt assumed of crore		500,000,000
	Equity value		3,500,000,000
	Equity IRR		41.9%

Case Study 6.2: Leveraged Buyout of Bausch & Lomb

Details

In the year 2007, Bausch & Lomb which deals with ophthalmology products and maker of famous Ray-ban sunglasses was acquired by Warburg Pincus, a large private equity firm at a total consideration of $ 4.5 billion.

The acquisition financing can be broken down into the following:

Mode	Value ($) million	%
Equity	1900	42
Assumed debt	800	18
Leverage	1800	40
Total	4500	100

Initially, Warburg Pincus tried to sell the company but, given the financials as stated below, it proved to be hardsell. Further, it filed for IPO reportedly looking for an enterprise value of $10 billion.

However, it was not successful. The key financials of the company are stated as under:

Dollar amounts in millions, except share and per share data	December 27, 2008	December 26, 2009	December 25, 2010	December 31, 2011	December 29, 2012
Net sales:(1)	2,601.1	2,518.3	2,576.9	2,845.4	3,037.6
Operating (loss) income	117.8	125.2	36.9	156.4	237.5

Other expense (income):					
Interest expense and other financing costs	228.1	220.9	180.9	169.3	246
Interest and investment income	6.6	5.4	3.8	3.1	4
Foreign currency, net	2.8	14.4	1.6	9.1	9.8
Loss before income taxes and equity in losses of equity method investee	336.5w	104.7	141.8	18.9	14.3
(Benefit from) Provision for income taxes	15.9	4.6	33.4	76.5	27
Equity in losses of equity method investee	—		17.8	20.8	24.1
Net loss	320.6		193	116.2	65.4

(Source: Prospectus)

From the above data, it is palpable that the financial data is quite weak. The top line has shown modest growth and losses are observed at profit level. The operating profit is positive, but the interest expenses have pulled the company in red. Free cash flow is near to zero.

However, it turned out to be lucky with the acquisitive Valeant, the Canadian drugmaker, who bought it for $8.7 billion cash deal. About $4.5 billion will go towards the equity value and the rest toward assumed debt. Warburg, with 87% of Bausch ownership, was likely to receive about $3.9 billion. The $8.7 billion comprised of debt to tune of $4.2 billion of Bausch and Lomb itself. Thus, we can say that the enterprise value remained static.

Just before the sale, it had also got dividend to the extent of $671 million. The dividend was paid out of debt by Bausch & Lomb.

The returns for Warburg can be stated as below. If we knock-off the dividend, it will be in range of 15%. However, due to dividend was estimated to be ~18%.

	June 2007	July 2012	July 2013	IRR
Buyout price	(4,500,000,000)		8,700,000,000	12%
		Dividends	Exit price	
Equity	(1,700,000,000)	671,000,000	3,915,000,000	18%
Debt assumed of Bausch	830,000,000			
Leverage	(1,970,000,000)		4,785,000,000	

If we analyze the IRR above, the increase in the equity value is due to the leverage. This IRR is coming at leverage ratio of 60:40.

Let us visit scenarios which will demonstrate the impact of leverage on the returns.

Scenario 1: 90:10

The capital structure for the buyout is debt 90% and equity 10% which delivers IRR of 49%.

	June 2007	July 2012	July 2013	IRR
Buyout price	(4,500,000,000)		8,700,000,000	12%
		Dividends	Exit price	
Equity	(450,000,000)	671,000,000	3,915,000,000	49%
Assumed debt	830,000,000			
Leverage	(3,220,000,000)		4,785,000,000	

Scenario 2: 80:20

The capital structure for the buyout is debt 80% and equity 20% which delivers IRR of 32%.

	June 2007	July 2012	July 2013	IRR
Buyout price	(4,500,000,000)		8,700,000,000	12%
		Dividends	Exit price	
Equity	(900,000,000)	671,000,000	3,915,000,000	32%
Assumed debt	830,000,000			
Leverage	(2,770,000,000)		4,785,000,000	10%

Scenario 3: 75:25

The capital structure for the buyout is debt 75% and equity 25%, which delivers IRR of 27%.

	June 2007	July 2012	July 2013	IRR
Buyout price	(4,500,000,000)		8,700,000,000	12%
		Dividends	Exit price	
Equity	(1,125,000,000)	671,000,000	3,915,000,000	27%
Assumed debt	830,000,000			
Leverage	(2,545,000,000)		4,785,000,000	11%

The above scenarios highlight the proportionate effect of various level of leverage on the equity IRRs. The higher the leverage, the higher will be the return keeping in tune with the risk–return profile.

Key Learning

The current case study depicts leverage as the prime driver of the IRR. The case also highlights that despite a marginal increase in the financials, the buyout investor could make a decent return. It could have made an egregious return if the leverage component was higher.

Case Study 6.3: Leveraged Buyout of ADT Inc. by Apollo Global Management

Details

Press Release

The ADT Corporation agrees to be acquired by an affiliate of certain funds managed by affiliates of Apollo Global Management, LLC for $42.00 per share in an all cash transaction.

Transaction delivers significant value to the ADT Corporation stockholders and provides path for future growth of the businesses through a combination of ADT and Protection 1.

Acquisition represents premium of 56% over closing stock price.

CHICAGO, NEW YORK, and BOCA RATON, Fla., February 16, 2016 (GLOBE NEWSWIRE) -- The ADT Corporation (NYSE:ADT) ("ADT"), a leading provider of monitored security, interactive home, and business automation and related monitoring services in the United States and Canada, today announced that it has entered into a definitive agreement to be acquired by an affiliate of certain funds (the "Apollo Funds") managed by affiliates of Apollo Global Management, LLC (NYSE:APO) (together with its consolidated subsidiaries, "Apollo") and co-investors and merged with a subsidiary of Prime Security Services Borrower, LLC (with its subsidiaries, "Protection 1"), a leading full-service business and home security company in the United States also owned by the Apollo Funds, for $42.00 per share in cash. The purchase price represents a premium of approximately 56% over ADT's closing share price on February 12, 2016 and when combined with Protection 1, represents an aggregate transaction value of approximately $15 billion. The headquarters of the combined company will remain in Boca Raton, FL, and the combined company will operate primarily under the ADT brand.

Pro-forma for the transaction, the newly created company will generate a combined $318 million in recurring monthly revenue and total annual revenue in excess of $4.2 billion, placing the businesses in a strong position to drive innovation and to capitalize on growth opportunities in the future.

The transaction, which has fully committed financing in place, will be financed primarily through the incurrence of $1.555 billion in new first lien term loans, $3.140 billion in new second lien financing, the issuance of $750 million of preferred securities to an affiliate of Koch Equity Development LLC, the investment and acquisition subsidiary of Koch Industries, Inc., and an equity contribution of approximately $4.5 billion from funds managed by Apollo and co-investors. Protection 1 will also enter into a new $255 million first lien revolving facility concurrently with the closing of the merger, bringing the total combined senior secured revolving facility to $350 million. Protection 1 further expects that its existing $1095 million first lien term loan and $260 million second lien term loan will remain outstanding. In addition, concurrently with the closing of the merger, Protection 1 intends to redeem all of ADT's outstanding senior unsecured 2.250% notes due July 2017 and senior unsecured 4.125% notes due April 2019, which will be redeemed in accordance with the applicable indenture, and to repay all outstanding borrowings under ADT's revolving credit facility. Finally, ADT's remaining $3.750 billion of the total senior unsecured notes will be guaranteed by Protection 1 and all wholly owned domestic subsidiaries of the combined company and will be secured by first priority security interests in substantially all of the assets of the issuer and the guarantors.

About ADT

The ADT Corporation (NYSE:ADT) is a leading provider of security and automation solutions for homes and businesses in the United States and Canada. More information is available at www.adt.com.
Financials of ADT

Period ending	September 25, 2015	September 26, 2014	September 27, 2013
Total revenue	3,574,000	3,408,000	3309,000
Gross profit	1,999,000	1,951,000	1,931,000
Operating income or loss	639,000	659,000	735,000

Questions:

a. Calculate the historical operating profit margin for ADT.
b. Based on the projected first-year revenue, work out the operating profits for the combined company viz. ADT + Protection 1.
c. Break up the enterprise value into equity and debt.
d. Calculate entry EV/EBIT multiple.

e. Based on the return expectations, calculate the exit equity value at 5 years and 7 years.
f. Based on the exit value, calculate the ending enterprise value. Assuming, EBIDTA being used to pay-off outstanding loans.
g. Whether the premium of 56% to buyout ADT is justified?
h. Is the first-year revenue expectation of US $4.2 billion realistic?

6.6 Executive Summary

In this chapter, we have described LBO as a method of M&A that is purely dependent on the financial engineering. The phenomenon has been dependent on the liquidity of cheap leverage and inverting the capital structure of the companies.

Thereafter, using the cash flow to pare down the leverage and increase the equity value as explained through use of rectangle and trapezoid enterprise value.

The financial modeling and the valuation as we have exemplified is also relatively easy to understand.

If the EV/EBIDTA is kept at a conservative level at entry and exited at the same level with paring down of leverage, it may provide good equity kicker.

The case study related to Bausch & Lomb elucidates that equity value kicker can be achieved through leverage despite not so good financial performance.

7

Spin-off and Demergers

Contents

7.1 Introduction

Spin-off and demergers have been bit of late entrant to the Indian corporate scenario. To be a conglomerate was a bit vogue and divesting was not the culture. In late 1990s, the laws were transformed to make it tax efficient to effect demergers.

The earlier practises in demerger were in the form of subsidization, spin-offs. The demerger of cement business by Indian Rayon to Grasim became a trend-setter. Thereafter, there have been few instances of demergers and Birla group has been one of the active proponents of the demerger. For example, Hindalco–Indo Gulf deal. Although, the fancy for demergers got lift only after the massive value creation in the L&T demerger. Since then, we have had quite a bit of demergers and variants of the same that we will deal with shortly in this chapter.

Spin-off and demergers are the situations in which divisions of parent companies are spun-off into separate companies.

The above can be achieved through various methods:

- Full spin-off
- Partial spin-off
- Vertical demerger
- Partial demerger

7.2 Types of Demerger

(a) Full Spin-Off

Spin-off structure

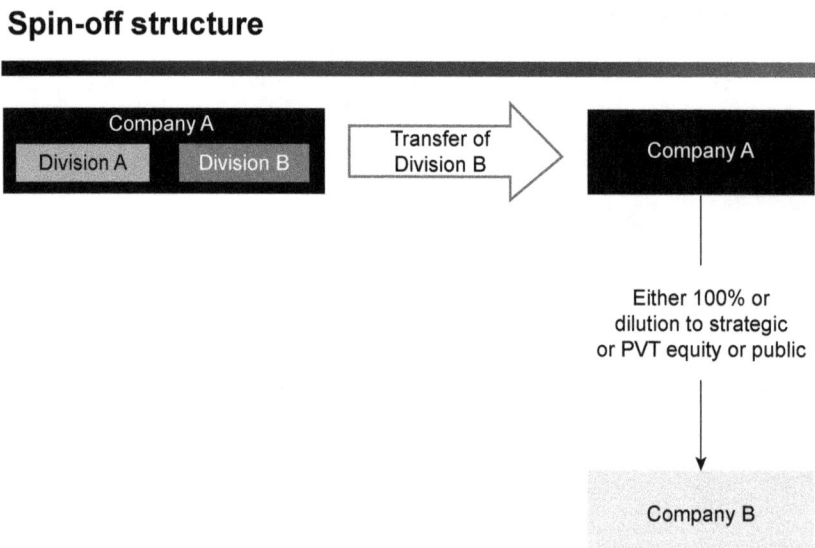

Objective

In this type, an existing division is taken-off and is put under the parent company as 100% subsidiary. The reason for such spin-off is to give wings to that particular division to provide an independent identity and is considered an interim step toward full or partial sell-off.

Process

The process involves slump sale of the business to a newly incorporated entity or an existing entity which has tax losses or carry/forward and shares are issued to the parent company as consideration. The differentiation from demerger in this form is that the parent comes to own 100% of the spun-off division. While the slump sale is the preferred mode due to speed of execution, but for tax consideration there might be need to go through the scheme of arrangement under the Companies Act and it may be time intensive.

Shareholder value

In full spin-off process, not much is emphasized on the shareholder value as there is no immediate impact of value creation even though it now has separate financial statements. However, having owned 100% will end up being consolidated in terms of the profits. Further, there would be holding company discount suffered equivalent to the transaction cost of distributing dividends to the shareholders of parent. Assuming 17% is the dividend distribution tax, the dividend will have 17% × 17% impact on the cash flow, thus suffering value impact of minimum ~30%. Thus, any benefit of spin-off in creating the shareholder value is lost. Furthermore, there is implicit signaling that the parent company wants to lean on the cash flow of the spun-off division, thereby signaling that the parent company business is inherently risky and needs to be more risk discounted, creating more value loss for the shareholder.

Slump Sale

Slump Sale Structure

- Fast track demerger
- Certain tax advantage in income tax over itemized sale
- But not over demerger
- Sales tax and stamp duty benefits
- Beneficial in case of undertaking enjoying tax benefit
- Simple and straight-forward
- Needs only simple majority through postal ballot
- May be possible to upsize the assets post-acquisition

Objective

In slump sale, the company wishes to sell a division and the buyer is interested in picking up the division. The division is sold as an undertaking comprising its asset and liabilities.

As compared to demerger, it is a faster way to spin-off, although it is not tax neutral and other set of shareholder may end up owning that division unlike the demerger.

Process

The process is pretty simple. On an appointed date, the division is transferred as per the agreement. The consideration is received by the company and not the shareholders. The company can dividend out the consideration received, subject to the profit rules.

Shareholder value

Since this is a division and not listed in the form of shares, it is difficult to ascertain the market value. Hence, there is not much shareholder value creation due to slump sale because the money is received by the company and not the shareholders. Even if the shareholders were to receive it in form of dividend, it will have to suffer taxation. Thus, multiple-taxation inhibits value creation.

Example

US-based Abbott Laboratories acquisition of the pharmaceuticals solution business of Piramal Healthcare for $3.72 billion (Rs 17,500 Crore) is an example of slump sale acquisition.

(b) Partial Spin-Off

Objective

The objective of partial spin-off is to take-off an existing division and keep it under the parent company for a minimum of 51% subsidiary. The reason for such spin-off is to escalate division to attain independent identity as well as seek outside shareholders. The outside shareholders can be brought in by seeking strategic/private equity investors or by doing an initial public offering (IPO).

This method enables us to achieve twin objectives of:

a. Giving separate identity to the spun-off division.
b. Bring in outside shareholder at a premium to create value for the shareholders of the parent company.

Process

The process involves the slump sale of the business to a newly incorporated entity or an existing entity which has tax losses or carry/forward and shares are issued to the parent company as consideration. It differs from other methods of demergers as in this method, the parent comes to own a minimum of 51% of the spun-off division. The slump sale is the preferred mode due to speed of execution, but for tax consideration they might need to go through the scheme of arrangement under the Companies Act and the process may result to be time intensive.

Spin-off structure

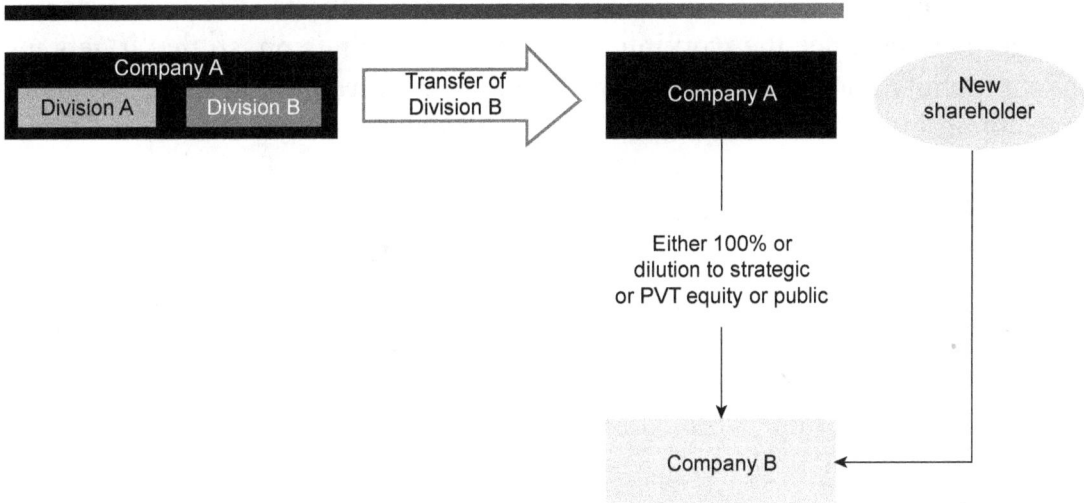

Shareholder value

Partial spin-off structure although sounds to be a better structure than the 100% spin-off due to the establishment of market pricing due to dilution in the spun-off entity to the outside shareholder. The benefit of the same is not experienced by the shareholder as more or less the cash is either trapped into the spun-off company or it goes back to the parent company who may use it to retire debt, which could be positive for the shareholders or the dividend distribution suffers from transaction cost leakages. However, the presence of bigger parent dwarfing the spun-off division does not create much value to the shareholders of the parent company. The situation is analogous to the overbearing parent and off-spring, resulting in lesser independence. Furthermore, there is inherent indication that the parent company wants to transfer the cash flow of the spun-off division, thereby indicating the inherent need of the parent company to be more risk discounted, resulting in more value loss for the shareholder.

Demerger is an efficient alternative to spin-off procedures. The technical difference between spin-off and demerger is that the ultimate shareholders will come to own the shares of the spun-off division directly in vertical/identical demerger or both directly and indirectly through the partial demerger.

It has been observed that vertical demergers result in comparatively more value than any other type of spin-off. Let us now analyze the reasons for the same and why partial demergers or demergers of investments have not created the same value impact as other demergers.

(c) Partial Demerger

Objective

In partial demergers, an existing division is taken-off and shares are issued to the parent company as well as the shareholders of the parent company. The extent of holding between the two is driven by various considerations. The reason for such demerger is to enhance the working of that particular division, so that it gets independent identity and creates value for shareholder as well as give the parent company support by its cash flows.

Process

The process of partial demerger involves slump sale of the business to a newly incorporated entity or an existing entity that is experiencing tax losses or carry/forward and in which shares are issued to the parent company and its shareholder as consideration. The differentiation from spin-off in this form is that the parent as well as the shareholders of the parent company will own the division.

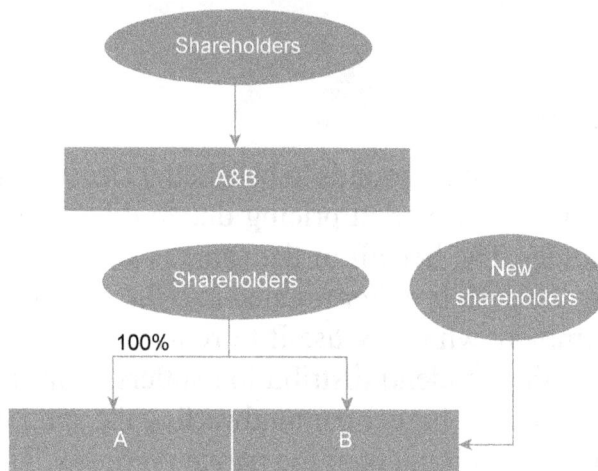

Examples

The spin-off of Infratel assets from Bharti Airtel into separate company and soliciting the external investors followed with eventual IPO is a perfect example to illustrate the above structure.

Shareholder value

Although the partial demerger is an improvement over spin-off, it is unable to develop much value as compared to vertical demergers due to value loss to the extent of parent's shareholding in the demerged entity. Further, partial demerger lacks clarity or clear corporate structure to the investors as the parent's ownership in the demerged entity, whether the majority is owned or minority is owned, presents the same dilemma to the shareholders. Here, majority owned means the effect of demerger is lost while minority owned refers to the mere representation of an investment with no possible liquidation in future for the shareholder of parent company to realize value for themselves. It can be concluded that although partial demerger appears to be the best of both worlds, in practise, it is driven by non-shareholder value consideration and hence does not create much shareholder value.

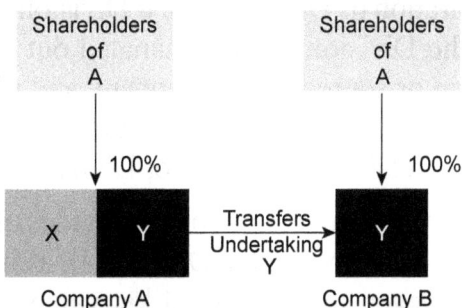

(d) Vertical Demergers

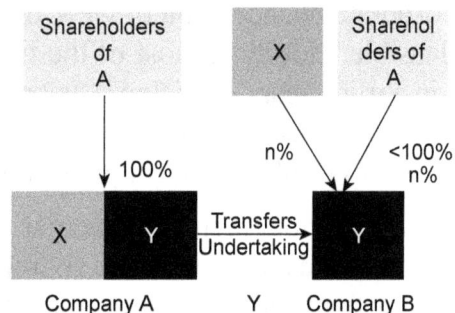

Objective

In vertical demergers, the company aspires to take-out an existing division of the company and shares are issued to the shareholders of the parent company. The reason to do such type of demerger remains the same, being to increase the productivity of that particular division, also to provide an independent identity, thereby creating value for shareholders.

Process

Similar to partial demerger, vertical demerger also follows slump sale of the business to a newly incorporated entity or an existing entity which has tax losses or carry/forward and shares are issued to the shareholder as consideration. It differs from other methods in the fact that the shareholders of the parent company become the owner of the division.

Demerger Structure

- Demergers are one type of spin-offs
- Unlocking shareholder value
- Tax advantage
- Stamp duty benefit

Shareholder Value

The vertical demerger has provided to be ultimate value creator for the shareholders if carried out in appropriate manner in terms of the splitting it between the two non-congruous division and providing absolute clarity or clear corporate structure to the investors.

We will spend major part of this chapter on why vertical demerger succeeds and what is the formula, rationale, and the importance of right structure that will create shareholder value.

Vertical demergers bestow the power in the hands of the ultimate shareholders. They are given the opportunity to decide whether they wish to stay invested in both the companies or one or none of the companies.

Vertical demergers, separating various businesses without any cross holding, have proven to be the best value creator for the shareholders of the previous entity.

Vertical demergers succeed best, when there are two divisions of the company. The characteristics of them are as stated below:

Division A

- Loss making/low profitability business at times relying on the cash flow from Division B.
- Guzzling capital due to huge asset requirement or working capital needs.
- Poor return on capital.
- Generally highly leveraged.
- Provides top line to the company but very less to the bottom line
- Can be termed as Dog business.

Division B

- Highly profitable.
- Negative capital employed or very low capital requirement.
- High return on capital.
- Cash surplus balance sheet/zero leverage.
- Provides the bottom line to the company but very less to the top line.
- Can be termed as cash cow business.

From corporate finance point of view, the separation of Division A and Division B looks very plausible. However, most of the times the Division B had emanated out of Division A in earlier years. Division A is the origin or source of the company and provides sentimental reasons for management not to be given up for the benefit of cash flow of Division B or be sold at control premium while retaining control over Division B.

In such a situation, vertical demerger of Division A and Division B provides ultimate shareholder value creation for the shareholders as compared to Division B, as it would be enjoying fantastic multiple in market. However, the fall in market value of Division A will temper the gains made in Division B. Lesser the fall in the market value of Division A, higher will be the net gain to the shareholders of the parent company.

Given the patronage to Division A by the management of the parent company, either the vertical demerger is avoided or instead of vertical split, a partial demerger is proposed which limits the value creation. The ultimate value creator would be created by vertical demerger and Division A is sell-off at control premium, thereby achieving value creation in both Division A and Division B.

On the basis of ROCE (PBIT/Capital employed) formula, it will be stated as under:

$$[(-) \text{ Division A} + (+) \text{ Division B}] / [(+) \text{ Division A} + (-) \text{ Division B}]$$

PBIT   PBIT   Capital employed   Capital employed

Thus, negative PBIT of Division A and positive capital employed of Division A will end up canibalizing the positive PBIT of Division B and negative capital of Division B. Thus, on aggregated basis (A+B), we will have negative PBIT or low PBIT in numerator and huge capital employed in denominator resulting in low return on the capital employed.

Thus, vertical split through Division A and Division B will create the best value creation with sell-off of Division A. Of course, the timing of demergers also plays a crucial role as the valuation in case of demerger is entirely a function of the market multiple for Division A and Division B.

Vertical demerger

ROCE (EBIT/Capital employed) formula:

$$\frac{(-) \text{ Division A} + (+) \text{ Division B} = \text{EBIT}}{(+) \text{ Division A} + (-) \text{ Division B Capital employed}}$$

Company A   **Company B**

- Loss making/low profitability business at times relying on the cash flow from Division B.
- Guzzling capital due to huge asset requirement or working capital needs.
- Poor return on capital.
- Generally, highly leveraged.
- Provides top line to the company but very less to the bottom line.
- Can be termed as DOG business.

- Highly profitable.
- Negative capital employed or very low capital requirement.
- High return on capital.
- Cash surplus balance sheet/zero leverage.
- Provides the bottom line to the company but very less to the top line.
- Can be termed as CASH-COW business.

Few examples of the successful vertical demergers are as under:

Case Study 7.1: L&T's demerger

We will delve into the case study of Demerger of L&T's Cement Business and EPC business.

L&T had rapidly expanded its cement division during 1994–2001 from 2.9 mtpa to 14 mtpa. This rapid expansion in asset base consumed the free cash generated by EPC, which was non-asset intensive, engineering expertise-based business of L&T and was financed by debt. Cement is a low return on capital or loss making due to cyclicality of business and usually suffers due to high interest cost. Thus, the cement division is regarded as Division A and EPC as Division B makes it a perfect fit for demerging Division A from Division B.

The demerger brought the following effects for L&T:

- Asset base down by 64%.
- Debt was knocked-off the balance sheet.
- The return ratios jumped by five times due to shrinking of denominator and the expansion of the numerator, thus, creating a compounding effect.

This resulted in 765% return from Jan 2004 to June 2007 against sensex return of 169%.

The shareholder return was further enhanced by selling Division A to Grasim for which they received control premium, given the size of the capacity.

Thus, ticking all the boxes required for a successful demerger.

Below are few other examples of demerger of Division A and Division B, creating enormous value for shareholders

Case Study 7.2: Unsuccessful Vertical Demergers –Grasim Jindal

There have been vertical demergers of operating business and investment. The anticipation was to initiate trading of the investment book at its market value which was not being recognized in the parent company. The demerger of Grasim and Jindal fall under this category.

However, we need to assess whether the vertical demerger satisfies the formula outlined above.

On the basis of ROCE (PBIT/Capital employed) formula, it will be as under:

(-) Division A + (+) Division B/ (+) Division A+ (-) Division B

Thus, there is absence of characteristics of classical vertical demerger associated with Division A and Division B. The above also highlights that the parent company was itself trading on virtual demerger given that the markets were only valuing the operating business and giving very low value to the investments, given the lack of clarity on the liquidation of investment book and dividend out of the same.

Thus, no value was created in the demerger for the operating division. At the same time, the investment division lost more value as the shareholders had no interest in the minority shareholder in the investment company.

However, the loss of minority shareholders results in gain for the majority shareholders as it provides ability for them to consolidate its stake in the underlying investments at substantial discount to their market value and still retain economic right over dividends.

Case Study 7.3: Unsuccessful Partial Demergers—Bajaj Auto

Bajaj Auto Ltd. at the time of demerger was not a success, which involved the separation of:

a. Investments
b. Two wheeler auto division
c. Insurance arm

This demerger cannot be stated as the classic vertical demerger of the separation of bad Division A and good Division B due to the confusion with respect to the structure of demerger which did not represent a pure vertical split. The demerger provides rise to the Bajaj Investment and holding company, which was holding 30% into each of the operating companies. Given the nature of the investment company, it traded at discount, giving the ability to enhance control over the subsidiaries at lower than book value.

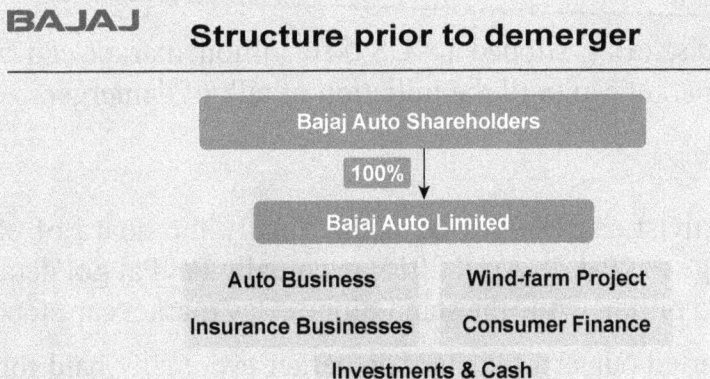

BAJAJ **Structure prior to demerger**

Bajaj Auto Shareholders

100%

Bajaj Auto Limited

Auto Business   Wind-farm Project

Insurance Businesses   Consumer Finance

Investments & Cash

Partial Demerger

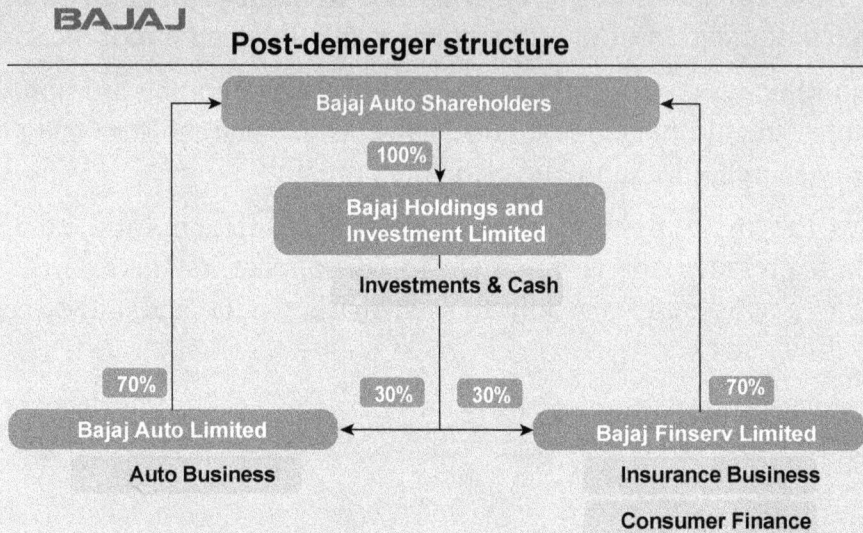

BAJAJ

Post-demerger structure

Bajaj Auto Shareholders

100%

Bajaj Holdings and Investment Limited

Investments & Cash

70%   30%   30%   70%

Bajaj Auto Limited ←→ Bajaj Finserv Limited

Auto Business   Insurance Business

                                  Consumer Finance

Case Study 7.4: Tale of Two demergers (eBay and Motorola)

a. e-Bay and PayPal

Introduction

eBay was one of the earliest internet marvel and darling of the markets. It started-off as a marketplace for used and new goods. It had reached a peak market value of US $60 billion in 2005 and then stuttered to grow after that period.

It acquired PayPal, a payment site in the year 2001 for $1.5 billion and since then, it became one of the safest, omnipresent, and easiest ways to pay for the internet purchases. The arrival of Apple pay and Google has heightened the interest in payment sites. PayPal is regarded as the market leader with 152 million users in 200 countries.

Post-2009 crisis, eBay slipped to US $16 billion market cap and was within $30–40 billion market cap until the initiation of talk of demerger.

Demerger

Based on the activist shareholder demands, finally the board of eBay reluctantly agreed to demerge PayPal. In April 2015, eventually PayPal got demerged at a market cap of US $45 billion while the stand-alone eBay market cap stood at $30 billion.

Thus, what started out as a reluctant demerger eventually paid for the shareholders with a combined market value of $75 billion, raising the market values from the languishing $30–40 billion market cap of eBay.

eBay can take a leaf out of Motorola and sell itself to the likes of Alibaba or Yahoo to realize premium value for its residual business.

b. Motorala

Introduction

Motorola Inc. was engaged in the business of mobile handsets and mobile network enterprise. In the year 2006, it was ranked the #1 handset producer holding a market share of 22%. During its peak market share, it had a peak market cap of US $54 billion. Thereafter, it started losing ground with plethora of smart phone handsets based on android hitting the market due to which it slumped to a market cap of US $1.5 billion by 2009. The enterprise business was profitable but had comparatively slow growth.

Demerger

The slow growth in the enterprise business and the loss in the handset business led to the activist investors taking stake in the company.

The activist shareholder called for break-up of the company into "mobile" and "enterprise" business. Thus, Motorola Inc. was eventually demerged into "Motorola mobility" and "Motorola solutions."

The demerger was done with the intention to eventually sale each of this business and realize premium valuations.

The market expected Motorola Solutions to fetch a better price due to its profitability, but it was the Motorola Mobility which got a handsome price of $12.5 billion from Google by launching a slew of products and marketing blitz to create market share.

Motorola Solutions sold most of its business to Zebra Inc. for ~$4 billion and retained just a smaller government business. Thus, from down in the dump market cap of US $1.5 billion by 2012, crafting demergers and selling them out created a combined market cap of $16.5 billion.

Key Learning

Demergers are a great way to split non-congruent business housed in a single company which depresses the market value as in many cases the "dog" business ends up dwarfing the "cash-cow" business, thereby dwarfing the market value which can be unlocked by demerging this disparate business.

While the above is the primary learning about demergers, the more important learning is that the most optimal market value creation can be done by selling the "dog" business at modest to great premium and realizing the market value of "cash-cow" business through demerger.

Case Study 7.5: Tyco International —A Demerger Saga

Details

Tyco International

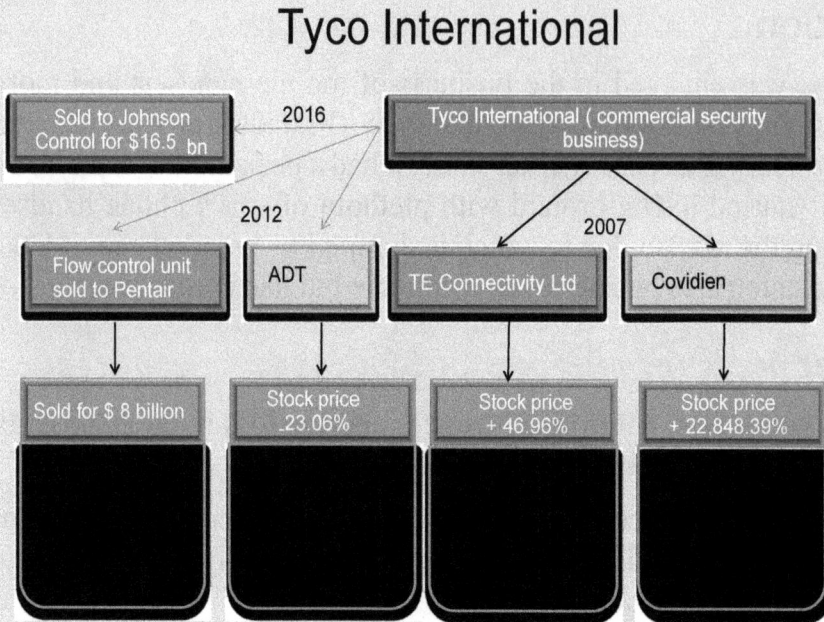

| | | 2016 | Tyco International (commercial security business) | | |
| Sold to Johnson Control for $16.5 bn | | | | | |

| Flow control unit sold to Pentair | ADT | TE Connectivity Ltd | Covidien |
| Sold for $ 8 billion | Stock price -23.06% | Stock price + 46.96% | Stock price + 22,848.39% |

Founded in 1960, Tyco International was one of the largest manufacturing conglomerates in the United States with four key business units, namely Fire & Security, Electronics, Engineered Products and Healthcare.

In the year 2007, it demerged its business into three core businesses Covidien Ltd. (medical business), TE Connectivity (formerly Tyco Electronics engaged in auto comp) and Tyco International.

In 2007, a further spin-off was done into ADT, a residential security business that sold flow-control systems division to Pentair for $8 billion and retained commercial security business in Tyco International.

Subsequently, Tyco International relocated its tax domicile to Ireland and in January 2016 sold its business to Johnson Controls for $16.5 billion against a market cap of $14 billion.

Key Learning

Of all the spin-offs based on the principles highlighted in the chapter, the performance of Covidien stands out. It was eventually acquired by medical-device maker Medtronic Inc. for $42.9 billion in cash and stock.

Connectivity's stock languished following the move being cyclical in nature; it was the post-credit crisis period owing partly to the auto industry's collapse. It experienced a rise of 71% since the start of 2013. Its performance can be said to be average.

ADT has an industry-leading 25% share of the home security market in the US and Canada, but has faltered since its spin-off in the year 2012, owing partly to high costs to acquire customers and new competition from cable TV and phone service providers. It depicts a negative performance.

Smartly, it sold the dog business of Flow Control system, relocated itself into Ireland for tax purposes, and eventually sold it to Johnson Controls. It had performed well immediately after the last break-up but have been faltering last year.

This case represents a complete demerger saga. It depicts the performers, middles, and underperformers and how to make virtue of businesses by selling them at control premium and realizing complete shareholder value.

Case Study 7.6: DuPont and Dow to Combine in Merger of Equals

(Source: Press release)

"Will Create Highly Focused Leading Businesses inAgriculture, Material Science and Specialty Products; Intend to Subsequently, Spin Into Three Independent, Publicly Traded Companies"

Wilmington, De and Midland—December 11, 2015

DuPont (NYSE:DD) and the Dow Chemical Company (NYSE:DOW) announced that their boards of directors unanimously approved a definitive agreement under which the companies will combine in an all-stock merger of equals. The combined company will be named Dow–DuPont. The parties intend to subsequently pursue a separation of Dow–DuPont into three independent, publicly traded companies through tax-free spin-offs. This would occur as soon as feasible, which was expected to be 18–24 months following the closing of the merger, subject to regulatory and board approval.

The companies will include a leading global pure-play Agriculture company, a leading global pure-play Material Science company, and a leading technology and innovation-driven Specialty Products company. Each of the businesses will have clear focus, an appropriate capital structure, a distinct and compelling investment thesis, scale advantages, and focused investments in innovation to deliver better superior solutions and choices for customers.

Intended Separation into Three Independent, Publicly Traded Companies

It was the intention of boards of directors of both the companies that following the merger, Dow–DuPont would pursue a tax-free separation into three independent, publicly traded companies, with each targeting an investment grade credit rating.

Each would be a strong, focused business with powerful innovation capabilities, enhanced global scale and product portfolios, focused capital allocation, and a distinct competitive position.

The three businesses that the boards intend to separate were:

- **Agriculture Company:** Leading global pure-play Agriculture Company that unites DuPont's and Dow's seed and crop protection businesses. The combined entity will have the most comprehensive and diverse portfolio and a robust pipeline with exceptional growth opportunities in the near, mid-, and long term. The complementary offerings of the two companies will provide growers across geographies with a broad portfolio of solutions and greater choice. The combined pro forma 2014 revenue for Agriculture was approximately $19 billion.
- **Material Science Company:** It consists of pure-play industrial leader, consisting of DuPont's Performance Materials segment as along with Dow's Performance Plastics, Performance Materials and Chemicals, Infrastructure Solutions, and Consumer Solutions (excluding the Dow Electronic Materials business) operating segments. The combination of complementary capabilities will create a low-cost, innovation-driven leader that can provide customers in high-growth, high-value industry segments in packaging, transportation, and infrastructure solutions, among others with a broad and deep portfolio of cost-effective offerings. Combined pro forma 2014 revenue for Material Science was approximately $51 billion.
- **Specialty Products Company:** A technology-driven innovative leader focused on unique businesses that share similar investment characteristics and specialty market focus. The businesses will include DuPont's Nutrition & Health, Industrial Biosciences, Safety & Protection, and Electronics & Communications along with Dow Electronic Materials business. Together, their complementary offerings create a new global leader in the range of Electronics products and each business will benefit from more targeted investment methods in their productive technology development and innovation capabilities. Combined pro forma 2014 revenue for Specialty Products was approximately $13 billion.

Questions

a. State the rationale for break-up of the conglomerate from Demerger point of view.
b. According to you, in the above case study which divisions will perform and which will not based on the principle discussed?
c. Referring to comparable companies in each of the space, can you ascribe possible market value to each of the divisions?
d. According to the Tyco case study and best possible value creation, what strategic advice will you provide for value creation?

Case Study 7.7: Piramal Enterprises to Demerge Healthcare & Financial Services Business

Details

Piramal Enterprises engaged in healthcare, financial services, and information technology is planning to demerge its healthcare and financial services businesses to grow the unrelated divisions separately.

The Piramal Group, which was primarily a pharmaceutical business pursuant willing to sell its formulation division to Abott Inc. for US $4 billion, has used larger part of the sale consideration to diversify into areas such as finance, private equity, and real estate funding in the past 5 years.

Apart from making investment in Vodafone India, it has invested Rs. 4583 crores in Shriram Group, the South India's largest financial services group. In 2014, Piramal Enterprises tied up with Dutch pension fund APG Asset Management to invest $1 billion in Indian infrastructure companies over 3 years and with Canada Pension Plan Investment Board to provide structured debt financing of $500 million to residential projects in India's major urban centres. The company is floating a $1 billion stressed asset fund.

The company's third-quarter results showed healthcare growing at 16.7%, healthcare information management at 13%, and financial services at 131.3%. More than half of the revenue comes from the healthcare business, but financial service is a faster growing business.

Financial highlights						
	201503	201403	201303	201203	201103	201003
Net sales	5122	4502	3520	2158	1673	3624
Other income	3295	239	179	472	16,875	152
PBIT	3545	614	382	336	16652	683
PBT	3035	−434	−192	120	16563	499
PAT	444	−497	−220	79	264	501
Cash flow from operating activities	−2331	−1604	−1570	−684	−4537	432
Cash flow from investing activities	6193	1535	−1494	−1581	9162	−172
Cash flow from financing activities	−3864	125	3280	640	−2984	−313

(Continued)

ROCE (%)	4.3	3.2	2.5	2.1	5.4	24.2
RONW (%)	2.7	−4.9	−1.9	0.7	3.9	32.0
Price (Rs)	920					
Lat. P/E	17.9					
Mkt. Cap.(Rs Cr)	15,880					
Lat. BV(Rs)	680					

Profile of Piramal Enterprises

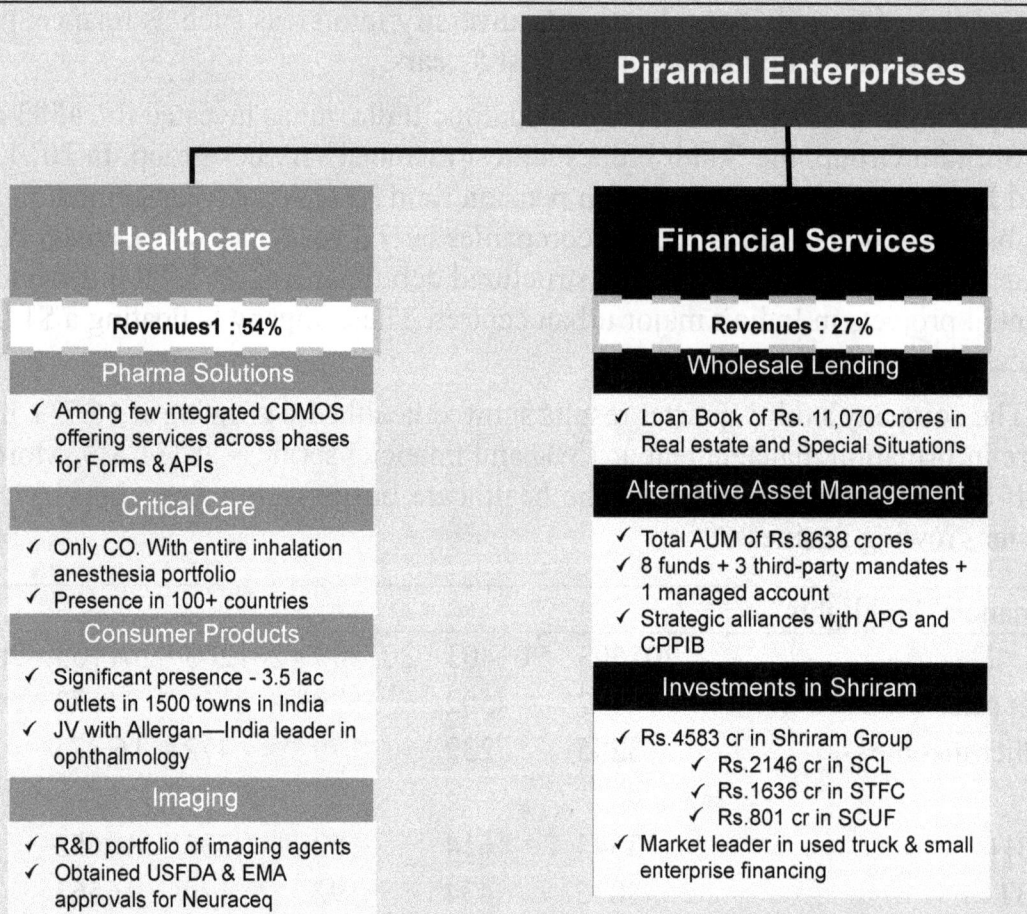

Piramal Enterprises

Healthcare

Revenues1 : 54%

Pharma Solutions

✓ Among few integrated CDMOS offering services across phases for Forms & APIs

Critical Care

✓ Only CO. With entire inhalation anesthesia portfolio
✓ Presence in 100+ countries

Consumer Products

✓ Significant presence - 3.5 lac outlets in 1500 towns in India
✓ JV with Allergan—India leader in ophthalmology

Imaging

✓ R&D portfolio of imaging agents
✓ Obtained USFDA & EMA approvals for Neuraceq

Financial Services

Revenues : 27%

Wholesale Lending

✓ Loan Book of Rs. 11,070 Crores in Real estate and Special Situations

Alternative Asset Management

✓ Total AUM of Rs.8638 crores
✓ 8 funds + 3 third-party mandates + 1 managed account
✓ Strategic alliances with APG and CPPIB

Investments in Shriram

✓ Rs.4583 cr in Shriram Group
    ✓ Rs.2146 cr in SCL
    ✓ Rs.1636 cr in STFC
    ✓ Rs.801 cr in SCUF
✓ Market leader in used truck & small enterprise financing

FEB 2016   PIRAMAL ENTERPRISES LIMITED - INVESTOR PRESENTATION

The rationale for demerger being when two unconnected businesses are demerged, value is created for shareholders.

Questions to be Considered

a. Will demerger as stated above will create value or unlock value? Why and Why not?

b. Is Piramal Enterprises having a conglomerate discount? Why and Why not?

c. Discuss the characteristics of the financial services business from risk profile and the attendant cost of equity for the business.
d. Trace out valuation of fund management business (e.g., Berkshire Hathway which trades at 1.3× book value) to determine value unlocking.

7.3 Valuation of Demergers

The valuation of demergers is not a complicated issue unlike other valuations. The only principal methodology is multiple basis.

As long as segmental or divisional results are available for the divisions involved in the demerger, based on such results and using the comparable multiples of comparable listed companies can give a fair estimate of the value of the divisions that are part of the demerger.

If there is sectoral index present, it can also be used to value the individual divisions.

For example: A company has an engineering division (Division A) and consumer division (Division B). The combined EPS of the company is say 2 and trading at multiple of 10×. Thus, share price will be20.

Let's take another example in which Division A has EPS of 0.5 and Division B of 1.5. The individual multiple are 6× and 15×, respectively, according to which the value of each will be 9 and 22.5. Thus, the combined price will be31.5 giving a 50% rise over the pre-demerger value.

Thus, the post-demerger value of Division A shall not fall as much that it offsets the gain in the price of Division B.

Thus,

Division A + Division B > Division (A+B)

The range of best to worst possible outcome includes:

a. Share prices of both divisions perform as demonstrated in demerger of Reliance.
b. Share price of Division B performs and Division A is sold at control premium as in case of L&T demerger.
c. Share price of Division B performs but little offset by fall in the price of Division A. The aforementioned scenario can be understood through Sun Pharma demerger.
d. Share price of B performs but fall in share price of A makes it loss making proposition. The above can be elucidated through Orient Paper demerger, wherein Orient Paper suffered an 80% drop in price, while Orient Cement share price performed.
e. Share price of both divisions do not perform because of ill-structured demerger. The above can be elucidated through Bajaj auto demerger.

7.4 Executive Summary

The current chapter illustrates the various types of spin-offs and demergers, the objectives, and process involved in each one of them and the impact on shareholder value creation.

In terms of shareholder value creation, vertical demergers that have the characteristics depicted in this chapter will achieve the highest value creation when the dog business is sold at a control premium. In fact, the route of demergers is being more used for selling one of the divisions as in case of SAB Miller acquiring Fosters after demerging Treasury Wine business or the acquisition of Pantaloon retail business by Aditya Birla De Novo through the demerger route.

The other forms of spin-offs or demergers are carried out with objectives other than value creation. Thus, the reasons for them are separate, but from taxation and shareholder value creation point of view, they are least inefficient.

8

Restructuring

Contents

8.1 Introduction

Restructuring can be defined as the rearrangement of the assets or liabilities of the company, which could involve selling-off or consolidating assets or interchanging the liabilities.

Restructuring is generally an internal affair that involves the company only or companies within the group. Restructuring, as we see by the above definition, has a wide scope and takes various dimensions. In the current chapter, we have made an attempt to explore this concept through these case studies to highlight the reasons and modes of restructuring.

These cases will help you to understand the novel ways adapted in the process of restructuring so that the end objectives can be met by cutting through the legal maze and the opposition of minority shareholders.

8.2 Holding Companies and Valuations

It is very common in corporate structure to have holding companies. There are various value dynamics involved in the holding companies. The case studies below explore and explain the value dynamics to enable students of corporate finance to provide a better understand while deciding their corporate structure.

Case Study 8.1: Google Restructures to Create "Alphabet"

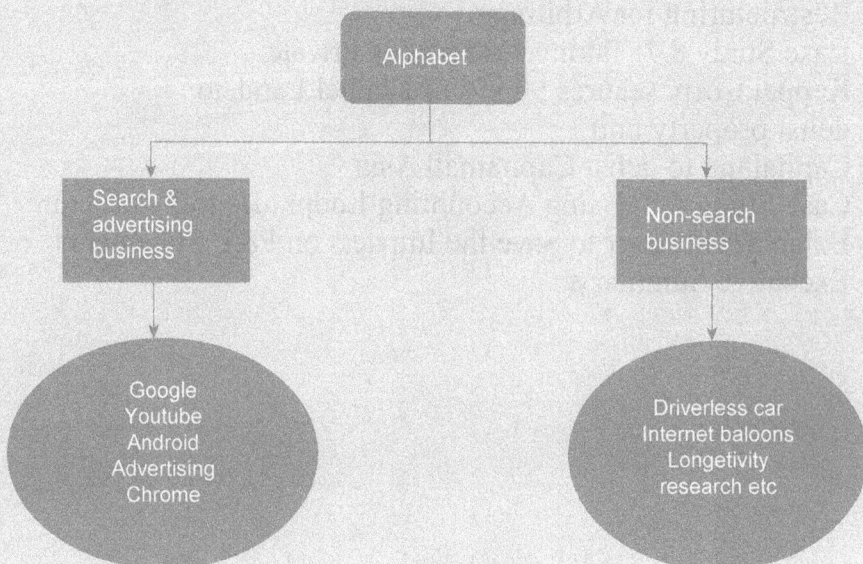

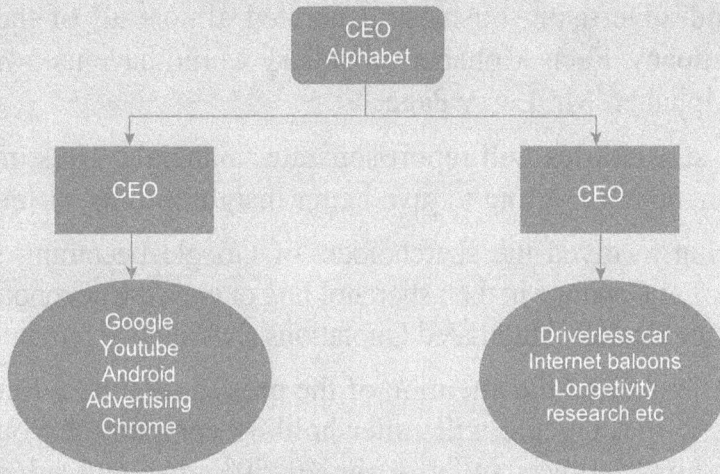

Share Price Performance

Details

Recently, Google has restructured its business and created a holding company named Alphabet. The holding company Alphabet will have two entirely owned subsidiaries.

One of the subsidiaries will hold its highly profitable search advertising business consisting of the Google, You tube, Android, Chrome, and the other subsidiary holding the so-called "Moonshots" consisting of driverless cars, scientific research, home networking, etc.

The search and advertising business generated almost all of the revenues and profits of the company. Each Alphabet subsidiary would have its own CEO, reporting to CEO of Alphabet, Mr. Larry Page.

Each of these subsidiaries will report separate financials. Thus, there will transparency in the financial reporting to give better insight into its various businesses.

The restructuring involved the shareholders of Google becoming shareholders of Alphabet. There was no change in their shareholding or even the ticker on National Association of Securities Dealers Automated Quotations (NASDAQ) remained the same.

The restructuring gained the attention of the press and quite a few of the analyst presented the view that Google will suffer holding company discount in a similar manner as Berkshire Hathway suffer or the 40–50% discount suffered by holding companies relative to their net asset value (NAV).

Issues

The issue was whether restructuring would result in Google suffering value loss due to the holding company structure.

Assuming, the holding A is holding two entirely owned investments "B" and "C," which are trading at 50 each. Theoretically, the value of "A" should be 100, but, in practice, it will range from 50 to 70 suffering a valuation discount of 50–30%.

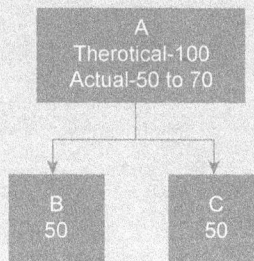

Generally, the holding company structure results in the valuation discount for several reasons. The chief among them are:

- Lack of control over the underlying holdings or the assets of the holding company.
- There is lack of clarity over the future direction the company is likely to undertake. Whether there will be monetization of the underlying assets or not.
- The leakage in the proceeds due to taxes and operational expenses.
- The holding company structure skews the balance of control to the one section of shareholder, generally to the majority shareholder. The risk of being subjected to the decision-making of such shareholders leads, valuation discount.
- The risk of investing in non-related businesses, which may lead to capital loss or funding of businesses which may not necessarily be capital optil.

Thus, it was predicted that Google will face the similar fate as all other holding companies. However, contrary to general market expectations, there has not been any discount. In fact, the shares have risen nearly 25% since the restructuring took effect on the back of strong results and has gone onto become most valuable company in the world

Let us have a look at a case, where in a holding company trades at a discount exist. This will give us so as to better the understanding of holding companies and reasons for discount valuations.

Case Study 8.2: Porsche Valuations

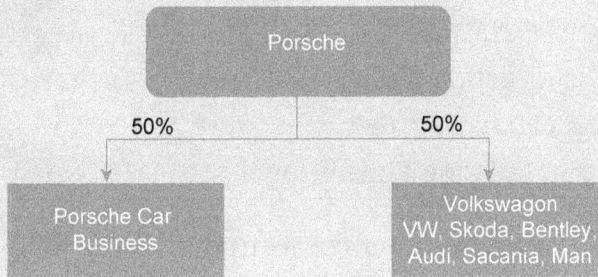

In the above case, Prosche has generally suffered a valuation discount of 25–35%.

The reasons for suffering valuation discount are listed below.

- There are dual class shares giving the controlling families more control than the economic ownership.
- Two families control 70% of the VW stock and skews the alignment of interest between the majority and minority owners.
- Porsche has been guilty of trying to takeover Volkswagen through leverage and surreptitiously through use of derivative contracts.
- Thus, the opacity and the lack of alignment has resulted in heavy holding company discount.

Why Alphabet has suffered no holding company discount despite the empirical holding company discounts?

The reasons for the same can be stated as:

- It was genuine organizational revamp. There was no change in the economic or controlling ownership.
- No dividend was paid by Google, so no leakage in the proceeds.
- The life in Google with investments remained the same pre and post-restructuring.
- The restructuring brought in more financial information transparency for the investors to evaluate "search" and "non-search business."
- There was more accountability stepped up with CEO's for both the business. Thus, giving more ownership for stewardship and freeing the managerial resources for Larry Page, Eric Schmidt, and the Group CFO.

Therefore, from the above observations, it is evident that Google holding company structure brought in more transparency even with the non-search business, thereby creating no holding company discount.

The above case studies highlight the contrasting valuations in different types of holding companies. The below parameters can be to evaluated for the reasons as why discounts exists in one case and not in the other.

	Alphabet	Porsche
Holding company discount	No	Yes
Incrementally increased transparency in financial evaluation	Yes	No
Incrementally strategic direction clarity	Yes	No
Better management reporting structure	Yes	No
Transactional cost for liquidating underlying assets	No	Yes

Next, we will see case study wherein the restrucuring was undertaken to weed out the holding company discount.

Case Study 8.2: Cheung Kong and Hutchison to be Reorganized to Eliminate Holding Company Discount

Details

A restructuring proposal was made for shareholder value creation by elimination of the holding company discount in Cheung Kong holding 49.97% Hutchison of Li-Ka Shing group. The below depicts the holding company discount and the objective of restructuring.

The restructuring entailed creating two new leading Hong Kong listed companies Cheung Kong and Hutchison Shareholders will be offered shares in both CKH Holdings and CK Property in exchange with their existing Cheung Kong or Hutchison shares through a series of transactions.

- Cheung Kong shareholders will receive 1 CKH Holdings share per 1 Cheung Kong share.
- Hutchison shareholders will receive 0.684 CKH Holdings share per 1 Hutchison share.
- After completion of the proposals, all eligible CKH Holdings shareholders will receive 1 CK Property share per 1 CKH Holdings share.
- The exchange ratios have been determined using the average closing price of Cheung Kong and Hutchison shares for the five trading days up to and including January 7, 2015, with no premium.

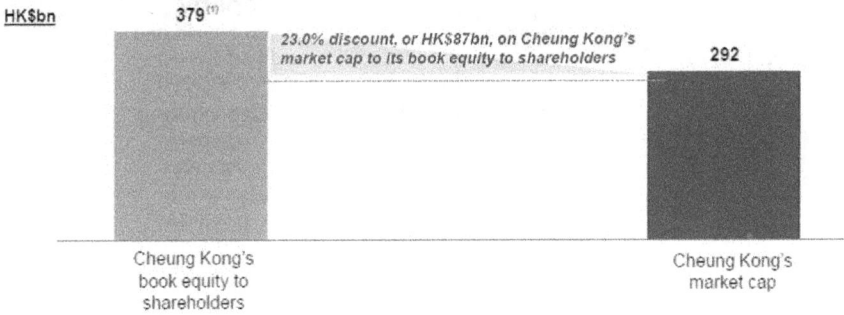

1 Shareholder value creation: Elimination of holding company discount of Cheung Kong's stake in Hutchison

- Eliminates tiered holding structure on Cheung Kong's 49.97% stake in Hutchison as no Hutchison shares will be held indirectly
- Value creation shared by Cheung Kong and Hutchison shareholders

Value creation

- Cheung Kong's market capitalisation is at a 23.0% discount to, or HK$87bn less than, its book equity to shareholders, which includes its 49.97% stake in Hutchison

- A part of this is attributable to the holding company discount on Cheung Kong's stake in Hutchison, which could be eliminated through the proposed transactions as shareholders will hold the two company shares directly

HK$bn

379[1]

23.0% discount, or HK$87bn, on Cheung Kong's market cap to its book equity to shareholders

292

Cheung Kong's book equity to shareholders

Cheung Kong's market cap

Notes:
Market cap as at 7 January 2015
(1) Book value of equity to shareholders of Cheung Kong as at 30 June 2014

5

(Source:Cheung Kong website)

Pre-transaction structure.

Pre-transaction

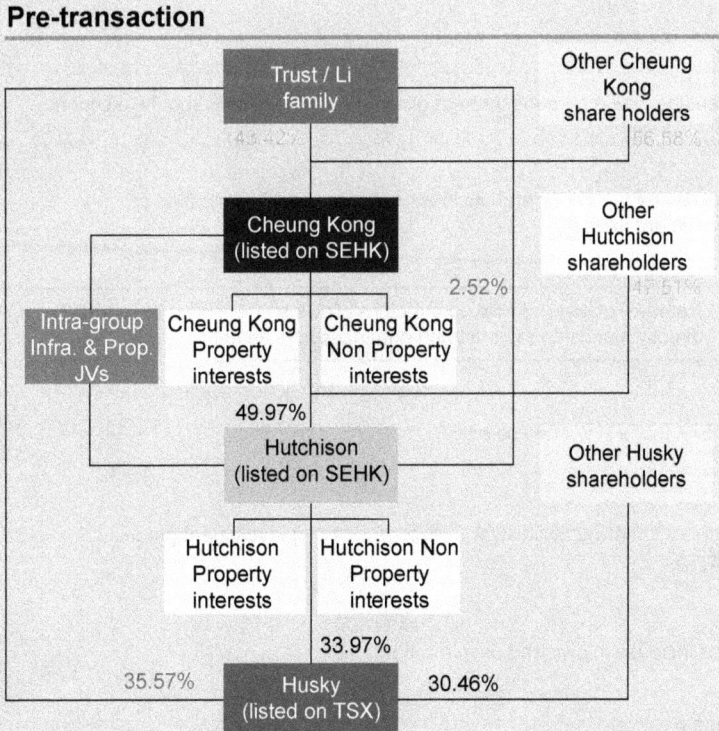

The below slide depicts the restructuring aimed at building clear and direct structure of property and non-property businesses.

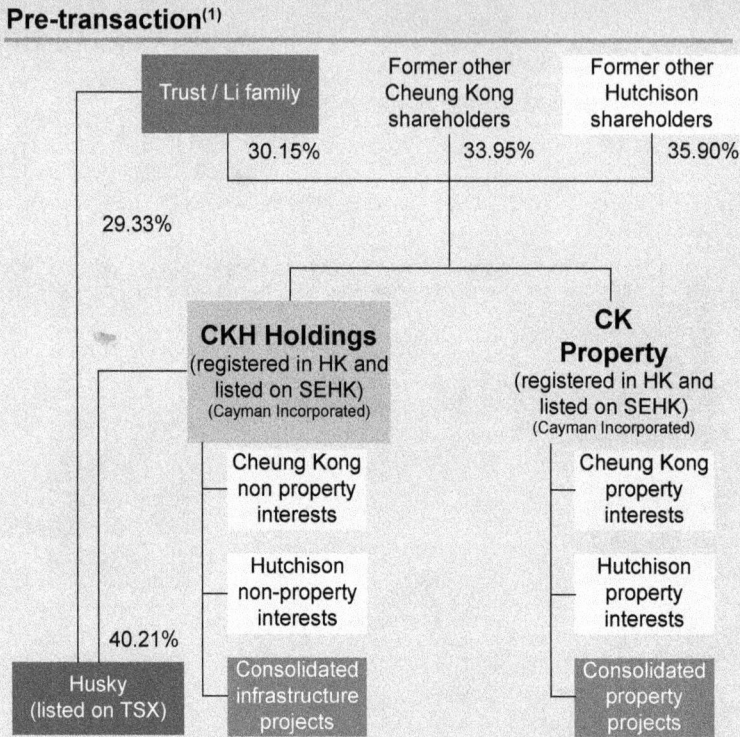

Pre-transaction[1]

	Trust / Li family	Former other Cheung Kong shareholders	Former other Hutchison shareholders
		30.15%	33.95%	35.90%

29.33%

CKH Holdings
(registered in HK and listed on SEHK)
(Cayman Incorporated)

CK Property
(registered in HK and listed on SEHK)
(Cayman Incorporated)

- Cheung Kong non property interests
- Hutchison non-property interests
- Consolidated infrastructure projects

- Cheung Kong property interests
- Hutchison property interests
- Consolidated property projects

40.21%

Husky (listed on TSX)

The strategic benefit outlined by Cheung Kong are as under:

Strategic benefits to all stakeholders

1. Shareholder value creation through elimination of holiding company discount

2. Greater transparency and business coherence and elimination of investment arbitrage

3. Removal of layered holding structure allows shareholders to invest directly alongside the trust and enhances investment flexibility

4. Enhanced size and scale

5. Greater financing flexibility with expected strong investment grade ratings

6. Expected increase in dividend payout ratios

(Source: Cheung kong website)

Market Cap Change Pre and Post-Transaction

	Cheung Kong	Hutchison	Total
Market cap (announcement)	292	372	664
Market cap (effectiveness)	392	490	882
Increase			33%

Key learnings

Thus, we see the benefits of delineation of assets, and the transparency presented to investors would result in the elimination of discounts and increase in the shareholder value.

The key aspect to be noted here is two disparate OPERATING businesses being separated out. This is not involving separation of investments/holding companies from operating business.

Case Study 8.3: Reorganization of Group Companies — Softbank

Details

SoftBank Group Corp.

100% — Domestic operations management company

CEO: Ken Miyauchi
(Director of SBG)

Shares planned for transfer from SBG:
SoftBank Corp., Yahoo Japan Corporation, etc.

100% — Global operations management company

CEO: Nikesh Arora
(Representative director,
president & COO of SBG)

Shares planned for transfer from SBG:
Starburst I, Inc., Alibaba Group Holding Limited, etc.

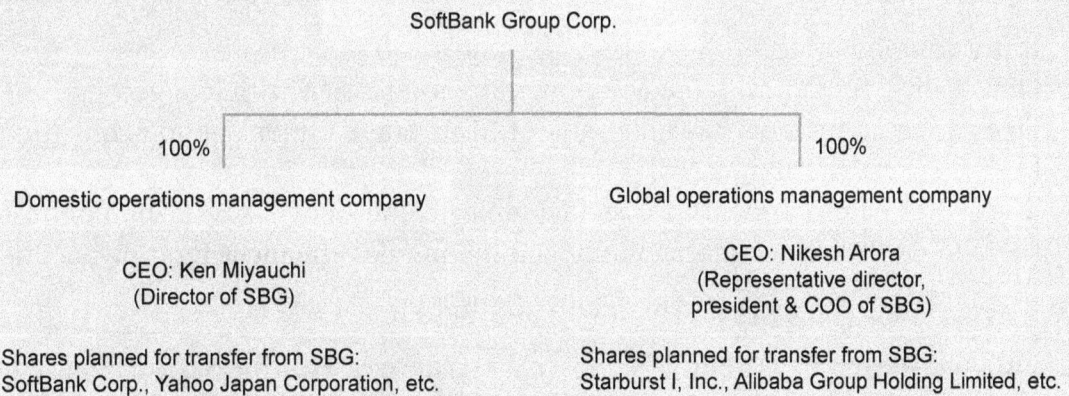

Softbank has been one of the prolific investor in the Internet ventures.

Japan's Softbank Group Corp plans to separate its domestic and overseas businesses. The overseas division of the Japanese telecoms conglomerate would include stakes in loss-making US wireless carrier Sprint Corp and Alibaba Group Holding Ltd, while the domestic unit would include its holdings in Yahoo Japan.

The restructuring is aimed at increasing shareholder value by separation of businesses.

The reorganization is aimed not to separate earnings of the domestic and overseas units, as SoftBank remains the single listed company which controls 100 pct of both units.

Questions

a. Comment on the reorganization. Whether it will or will not have impact on shareholder value.

We will now move on to another restructring from the same group which did not pass the muster of shareholders and we will analyze the reasons for shareholder not seeing it as a value creation exercise.

8.3 Restructuring Among Group Centred Around the Cash

In the corporate world, there is pursuit of strategy which involves pursuing growth and entailing risk taking. This leads to either risk or return and when only risk materializes, there is need for restructuring. The case studies mentioned below highlight such restructuring.

Case Study 8.4: Restructuring Group Companies to Utilize Cash Pile

Details

This type of restructuring is preceded by one or more of the following conditions:

- It is a conglomerate.
- One of the companies in the conglomerate is cash rich with low gearing.
- One of the companies has taken up lot of leverage either due to acquisition or because it is suffering losses.
- The merger ratio appears to be favorable to the entity where the controlling shareholder has more shareholding and the merger enhances their ownership.

We will look into three cases which will highlight the above issues.

- **Failed Merger of Cheung Kong Infrastructure Holdings Ltd. and Power Assets Holdings Ltd.**

Li Ka-Shing's conglomerate had proposed the merger of Cheung Kong Infrastructure Holdings Ltd. with the cash-rich Power Assets Holdings Ltd. where its shareholding was 38.9%.

It was offering 1.04 CKI share for each Power Assets share and all shareholders of the merged company will receive a special dividend of 5 Hong Kong dollars (US $0.65) after restructuring. CK Hutchison Holdings Ltd. will remain the biggest shareholder of the merged company with a 49.2% stake. However, the merger required minority to vote at a very high threshold, while the merger ratio was revised to 1.066 and dividend boosted to US $0.75, the merger was rejected by the minority shareholders as the proxy firms were of the opinion that the swap ratio of 1.09 to 1.12 appeared fair. However, merger valuations are always subjective and they appear to be always skewed in the favor of controlling shareholder.

The key financial features of both the companies are as under:

	Cheung Kong Infrastructure Holdings Ltd.	Power Assets Holdings Ltd.
Shareholding of controlling shareholders	30%	38.9%
Flagship company	Yes	No
Assets	HKD $126 billion	HKD $136 billion
Debt	HKD $24 billion	HKD $10 billion
Cash	HKD $7 billion	HKD $62 billion
Market cap	HKD $179.02 billion	HKD $146.41 billion
Balance of valuation	√	×

In such cases, generally the rationale is that the merger will strengthen the balance sheet and cash balance to pursue better opportunities. However, the underlying cause results in the cash pile of the merged company.

Sesa Goa, Sterite Merger

Vedanta Resources acquired 58.5% shareholding in Cairn India for $8.67 billion. Vedanta acquired directly 38.5% and Sesa Goa, one of its cash-rich company, acquired 20%. The acqusition was estimated to be funded 50% through the internal resources and the rest through debt. Thereby, approximately $5 billion of debt was taken up on the balance sheet.

Given this acqusition and funded largely by debt, a merger was proposed between Sesa Goa, Sterlite, and Vedanta Aluminium which had $4 billion of debt. Sesa Goa had cash pile of $7.7 billion on its balance sheet. Vedanta Resources interest burden was lessened by INR 1000 crore, due to the transfer of debt from Vedanata to the merged entity.

After the merger, Vedanta's resources direct holding of 38.8%in Cairn India were supposed to be transferred to Sesa Goa, along with its associated debt of $5.9 billion.

The Sterlite shareholders got three shares of Sesa Goa for every five shares held, according to the swap ratio. Malco shareholders got 7 shares of Sesa Goa for their every 10 share of Rs. 2 each.

The merger ratio here also appeared to be favoring Sterlite, where the level of ownership was higher although the balance sheet strength of Sesa Goa was much stronger.

Cairn India's Merger with Vedanta

After the aforementioned merger, there was another proposed merger between Vedanta (earlier known as Sesa Sterlite) with Cairn India at swap ratio of 1:1. The underlying reason seems to be the INR 17,000 crore cash accumulated in Cairn India. The merger was a hanging balance because the swap ratio seems to be in the favor of Vedanta; hence Cairn India minority objected to the proposed ratio.

Here, it is evident that the restrucuring was carried out among the group companies to consolidate balance sheets and use cash sitting in the other companies.

8.4 Restructuring for Return of Cash

This type of restructuring involves rewarding the shareholders with minimal impact on the balance sheet of the corporate. The case studies below give insight into the innovative ways to return cash back to the shareholders.

Case Study 8.5: Restructuring to Return Cash Back to the Shareholders

Hindustan Lever Proposes Bonus Debentures to Shareholders

Details

Hindustan lever had huge cash pile.

The return of this cash through dividend had restriction in terms of the quantum. Also, it requires cash to be paid as soon as dividend is declared. It could also not affect buyback again due to restriction on quantum and buyback would have been affected at much higher multiple.

Hence, Hindustan lever came up with the novel instrument called bonus debentures.

The advantages and features of the bonus debentures include:

a. It is same as bonus shares issued from accumulated profits of the company viz. capitalizing them.
b. There is no quantum restriction on the size of bonus.
c. The cash reserves got out of reserves and were moved toward debt, thereby increasing the ROE.
d. The coupon on the debentures is tax deductible unlike dividends which are not tax deductible.

e. The debentures were redeemable only after 2 years, but the cash will still be there with the company.

f. The debentures could be listed and traded for shareholders to monetize their holdings.

g. Cash flow was managed better as only current year interest was the outflow.

h. Unlike bonus shares which expand the equity base and dilutes the EPS, there was no expansion of shareholding base, due to issue of bonus debentures.

Companies such as Coromandel International, AstraZeneca, Dr Reddy's Laboratories, and Britannia Industries have, thereafter, adopted the bonus debentures to return cash to shareholders.

8.5 Restructuring for Arbitrage

It is again common trend to take companies public and private. It is more common with private equity-funded companies, but there are other instances of the companies arbitraging within the capital markets. The reasons for them are explored below.

Case Study 8.6: Taking Companies Private

- **Keppel Corp. secures 90.9% of Keppel Land, to delist property unit**
- **Capitaland to delist Capitamall Asia**

Details

SINGAPORE RESIDENTIAL PROPERTY PRICE INDEX

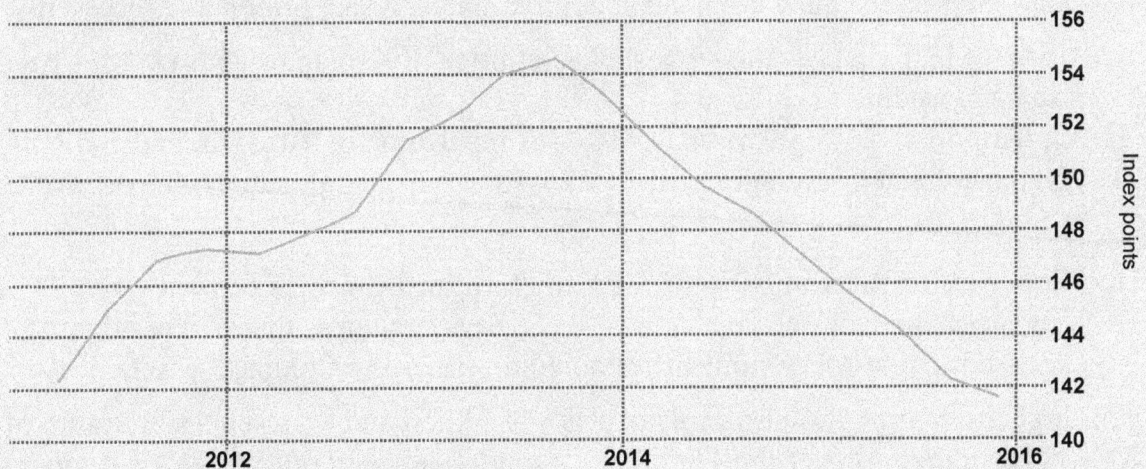

Taking companies private is also one of the many restructuring methods. The reason for taking private is the prevailing low valuations in the market. Further, the parent can have lot of flexibility with the operations.

Parent companies with deep pockets can bear the valuation risk and can arbitrage over the current valuations. They have the option to re-issue the shares and list it again when the market conditions improve. Thus, there are operational and strategic angle in such restructuring. The graph given below depicts the Singapore residential property index.The commerical index will also depict the similar trend.

Keppel Corp. is one of the large Singapore listed Companies (SGD 9.7 bn) having interest in off-shore and marine business and engaged in property business through Keppel Land.

Given the state of property market, the parent Keppel Corp decided to take private Keppel Land.

(*Press release*: Keppel Land)

January 23, 2015

Keppel Corporation limited launches voluntary unconditional cash offer for Keppel Land Limited

Two-tier price approach of:

- Base offer price of S$4.38* per share; and
- Higher offer price of S$4.60* per share, to be paid if Kepcorp is entitled to exercise its rights of compulsory acquisition.

Kepcorp is adopting a two-tier offer price approach with the intent to privatize Kepland as follows:

i. Base Offer Price of S$4.38* foz each Kepland share.

This base offer price values Kepland at approximately S$6.8 billion and represents:

a. A price which exceeds the highest closing price of Kepland shares over the past 3 years preceding the offer and

b. A premium of 25%, 29%, and 28% over the 1-month, 3-month, and 6-month volume-weighted average price (VWAP) of Kepland shares, respectively, preceding the offer.

ii. Higher Offer Price of S$4.60* for each Kepland share, to be paid when Kepcorp acquires Kepland shares or receives acceptances that will entitle it to exercise its rights of compulsory acquisition under the Companies Act.

This higher offer price values Kepland at S$7.1 billion and represents a premium of 31%, 35%, and 35% over the 1-month, 3-month, and 6-month VWAP of Kepland shares, respectively, preceding the offer.

Key Learning

The above case depicts the ongoing private transaction. The premiums offered on the trough market conditions allowing a strong parent to offer premium as well as ride the trough market along with the risk of market downturn, but with the upside of market upturn as and when the property market recovers.

Case Study 8.7: Using Accounting Loopholes to Restructure Balance Sheets or to Save the Impacts on Income Statements

This type of restructuring involves using accounting rules to restructure the balance sheetssuch as in case of Hindalco restructuring in the year 2009.

In 2008, Hindalco had made the big bang acquisition of Novelis Inc. in USA funded largely through debt. There was huge premium paid resulting in the enormous goodwill as well as subsequent impairments as credit crisis took its toll on the company and acquisition.

These would have created tremendous loss for Hindalco and affected its ratings. To get over these losses, they prosposed the scheme of arrangements where costs were charged to the share premium account and not the profit and loss account, thereby, avoiding the losses on profit and loss (P&L) reducing the accumulated reserves and the size of the balance sheet.

The above loophole of being able to charge loss to share premium account directly was subsequently closed. However, still there are such rules in USA where acquisition costs are written-off against the reserves.

8.6 Executive Summary

The case studies in this chapter highlight the various restructuring objectives. It also illustrates the contrasting results observed in the restructuring of Google and Porsche that highlights how restructuring needs to be structured keeping the basic tenet of the governance in mind with respect to transparency and how that can help in getting over issues of holding company discount.

While, the Li-ka Shing group case studies highlight the contrasting value creation objectives resulting in one working and other failing to work.

The case studies of Vedanta Group highlight the cash-oriented restructuring and the precedence of conditions leading to that restructuring.

Restructuring leads to novel methods and use of loopholes that is best exemplified by the Hindustan Lever and Hindalco case.

The going private transactions highlights the arbitrage restructuring.

Thus, restructursing done with the aim of good governance principles leads to the value creation, while skewed objectives lead to not so desired effect from the value perspective.

9

Regulatory Considerations in M&A

Contents

9.1 Introduction

The regulations in the securities market are ever-evolving, because there is always confluence of multiple types of regulations or law impinging on them along with multiple regulatory authorities administering them.

Thus, we would have security laws administered by Security and Exchange Board of India (SEBI), corporate law being administered by the Ministry of Company affairs, and taxation by tax authorities and foreign investments by the Reserve Bank of India. They tend to move at their own pace, thereby not being in sync with each other leading to arbitrage and opportunities for structuring the deals, whichever suits the best for the initiator.

In this chapter, we will discuss the various arbitrage opportunities that exist under the existing regulatory framework and the readers can use them best as per their needs.

9.2 Regulatory Arbitrage

Before the introduction of the New Companies Act, there existed huge arbitrage in terms of the Companies Act and Securities Law. The most important distinction between the two was that in the Companies Act, the majority rules while in the case of securities law, the minority rules. This distinction still exists but has narrowed the arbitrage among the two laws to a large extent.

Thus, we had Sterlite doing buybacks under the Indian Companies Act over-riding the SEBI provisions on buyback and delisting. Few other companies achieved delisting from the stock exchanges circumventing the strict SEBI rules on delisting.

The scheme of arrangement provisions under the Companies Act provided huge arbitrage opportunities. This scheme of arrangement provisions were used to bless all the things that are disallowed under other laws as long as it was approved by majority and blessed by the Courts. Thus, we had companies carrying out restructuring of their balance sheets under the scheme of arrangement by using the share premium reserves to wipe off accumulated losses or similar situations that were not allowed accounting by standards. The accounting standards required it to be wiped off only through profits.

Despite the narrowing of arbitrage between the two set of laws that govern the Indian Companies, they do provide arbitrage opportunities over one another depending on the relative positioning of the acquirer.

The Companies Act presents the following arbitrage opportunities:

a. Majority rules unlike securities law in which a single shareholder can ask for grievance redressal.

b. Valuation is still subject to the discretion of the valuer. Under the securities law, there are specific rules and less scope for discretion.

c. The disclosures required under merger scheme of the Companies Act is less onerous than required under the securities law, which are further scrutinized by SEBI, before the transaction can proceed. While the current SEBI rules require the scheme to be filed with SEBI, it is just a check to see the violation of the SEBI laws rather than going into adequacy of the disclosures under the scheme of arrangement.

d. Asset sale can be carried out under the Companies Act, without specific valuation rules. Although, the rules have become more specific but only with respect to approvals.

e. Mergers and demergers are exempted from the SEBI takeover code. In fact, after a bruised takeover attempt by Grasim of L&T under the takeover code, they proceeded with the Companies Act in the year 2004. The SEBI had exempted Grasim Ltd. from making an open offer for CemCo., the cement company proposed to be demerged from L&T whose majority stake was to be acquired by Grasim, under the scheme of arrangement between Grasim and L&T. Thus, merger under the Companies Act takes you away from strict disclosures, timelines, escrow, and payment mechanisms specified under the SEBI takeover code.

f. Last but not the least, the Companies Act provide the ability to carry out merger under the pooling of interest method rather than purchase method. The pooling of interest method is an aggregation of assets and liabilities against the recording of the assets at a fair value stipulated under the purchase method. This leads to avoidance of goodwill kind of issues. It also provides the ability to report higher earnings on lower cost of assets as against purchase method.

The existing laws lag the changes in the corporate warfare and hence contain loopholes which are exploited by the players in a takeover battle. This leads to them coming in focus transform laws. The understanding of this arbitrage helps in making clinical attacks or defenses in takeover and optimizing the resources.

Case Study 9.1: Karft-Cadbury Acquisition Impact on UK Takeover Code

Details

This case highlights the use of the slackness in the UK takeover code that was exploited by Kraft to hug Cadbury into submission to its takeover. Few of the slackness that could be highlighted state that there was virtually no time period until which the bid continued. The level of disclosures required in the bid by the acquirer was bare. The threshold required for the acceptance of the bid was 51%. Kraft went onto close quite a bit of its UK operations, which were not a part of the disclosures made in the offer.

There was hue and cry after the Cadbury acquisition, which led to immediate changes in UK takeover code, which are stated as under with objective and their implications. Such kind of changes are driven by the public sentiments and we observe the balance of power shifting to target board, because of the target in question being locally domiciled. We will probably see the next round of changes in the favor of acquirer, when the target exploits the balance of power it currently has to thwart a genuine takeover bid.

The commentary for the changes include:

The objectives of the proposed changes:

- To increase the protection for target companies against protracted "virtual bid" periods.
- To strengthen the position of the target company.
- To increase transparency and improve the quality of disclosure.
- To provide greater recognition of the interests of target company employees.

It is proposed that these objectives are to be achieved by amending the Code:

- To require potential offeror to clarify their position within a short period of time.
- To prohibit deal protection measures and inducement fees other than in certain limited cases.
- To clarify that target company boards are not limited in the factors that they may take into account in giving their opinion and recommendation on the offer.
- Requirement of the disclosure of offer-related fees.
- Requirement of the disclosure of the same financial information regarding an offeror and the financing of an offer irrespective of the nature of the offer.
- To improve the quality of disclosure by offeror and target companies in relation to the offeror's intention regarding the target company and its employees; and
- To improve the ability of employee representatives to make their views known.

The shift in balance of power in the favor of the target board was completely exploited by the UK-based Astra Zeneca when Pfizer came calling and the level of disclosures required by Pfizer were used by the politicians and media to raise anti-takeover sentiment.

One of the biggest obstacles that thwarted the attempt for Pfizer was the limited offer period and cool-off period of one year after the closure of first bid that led to successful defense by Astra.

Key Learning

The present case study elucidates the need to have knowledge and understanding of the regulatory framework and the slackness in it to push the envelope in a bid. It also presents the need for airtight case in regulatory matters. This would mean engaging quality advisors with deep knowledge is paramount in sensitive takeovers.

Case Study 9.2: Arbitraging Within Indian Takeover Code

- Sterlite bid for Indian Aluminum
- Non-compete fees

Details

In the 1990s, Sterlite Industries was involved in a hostile takeover bid for Indian Aluminum. The bid by Sterlite offered shares of Sterlite as offer consideration. The issue of shares required the approval of the shareholders of Sterlite as per the Companies Act.

The offer was made on the contingent of receipt of statutory approvals including the above shareholder approval. The Sterlite bid was attractive enough and quite a few shareholders ended up taking their offer.

However, the bid was lost by Sterlite and its shareholders went on to reject the issue of shares, thereby denying the shareholder of Indian Aluminum their due consideration for having taken up the Sterlite offer.

This went on to become one of the biggest controversies under the takeover code and SEBI went on to state that the reasons for withdrawal of an offer under the takeover code for non-receipt of statutory approvals was meant to be from Government or Statutory authorities and not the shareholder resolutions required under the Companies Act.

It became a matter of litigation, which went for very long time. However, as a consequence of this, the takeover code was amended to clarify the kind of statutory approval that can be made contingent to make an offer.

The same is the case with non-compete fees. The takeover code was amended to make a provision of non-compete fees to the extent of 25% of the offer price that can be paid to the controlling shareholder.

The amendment did not specify the circumstances and justification that was required to pay the non-compete fee. Thus, quite a few takeovers happened wherein the controlling shareholder got a 25% higher price than the minority shareholders. Some of the cases in which non-compete fee was paid involved loss-making companies, which had no reason to justify the payment of the non-compete fees. This led to hue and cry leading to drop of non-compete clause.

Key Learning

The above case study accentuates the need to attain knowledge and improve the understanding of the regulatory framework and the slackness in it to push the envelope in a bid. It also presents the importance of a airtight case with the regulations and quality advisors having a deep knowledge to be the paramount in sensitive takeovers.

9.3 Exploiting Regulatory Arbitrage within Jurisdictions

Case Study 9.3: Mylan Inc. USA

Details

Mylan Inc. which was based in USA had recently conducted a tax inversion deal to relocate itself to Netherlands and save on the US taxes having a high rate. More importantly, the Dutch laws had provision called as Stitching Rule, introduced during the World War II to prevent acquisition of Dutch assets by the German companies. The Stitching Rule involved the issue of preferred stock to a trust and the trustees can act on the preferred stock in the vent in which they adverse takeover and seize the control of the company.

In case of Mylan Inc., it had offered a call option to such a stitching trust which gave it a 51% voting control in the event of takeover bid. The trustees could be anybody, connected or dependent persons as well.

Further, as per the prevalent Securities and Exchange Commission (SEC) Law, the proposed inversion deal required only one resolution to be voted upon encompassing all the changes including the poison pill like the stitching rule.

Thus, when Teva Pharma made an attempt to takeover Mylan, it showed them the Stitching rule which led to uproar about the corporate governance, non-disclosures, etc.

Subsequently, SEC went on to make change which required separate resolution for such material changes in the governance structure.

The US laws prohibit such anti-dilutive laws; thus the transfer to Netherlands allowed Mylan Inc. arbitrage on tax as well as takeover laws.

Key Learning

Same as highlighted in the Section 9.2

9.4 Alternating between the Companies Act and SEBI takeover code/Securities laws

Merger/demerger route is helpful over SEBI takeover code if there are minority shareholder issue or valuation issue or there is need to take tax advantage. Likewise, if there is a need for speed, it is feasible to deal with single-agency SEBI or avoid getting target company's shareholder or creditor votes then, it is better to move ahead through the SEBI tender offer route than merger/demerger.

```
          Speed / Dealing with SEBI / Avoid shareholder
                         Y │ N
              ┌──────────────┴──────────────┐
        Tender Offer                  Merger/Demerger


          Minority/Valuation/Tax Issue
                    Y │ N
           ┌──────────┴──────────┐
        Merger/              Tender
        Demerger             Offer
```

9.5 Triggering SEBI Takeover Code or Exercising Flexibility to Trigger the SEBI Takeover Code

The SEBI takeover code can be triggered only on acquisition of voting rights and not mere on the acquisition of shares. Thus, if the acquirer wishes to delay the trigger but is certain of acquisition of the desired voting rights percentage, they can acquire various instruments such as GDR/FCCBs/Warrants or convertible bonds or convertible preference shares and convert them into voting rights depending on the objective of the acquirer.

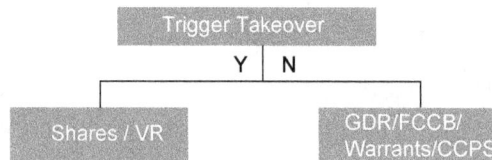

```
                Trigger Takeover
                     Y │ N
          ┌───────────┴───────────┐
      Shares / VR           GDR/FCCB/
                            Warrants/CCPS
```

Case Study 9.4: Reliance Buy Out of Network18

Details & Learning

The below case study highlights the regulatory arbitrage between various acts and sequencing of the events that can allow good planning along with minimal cost to the acquirer.

Reliance

Reliance extends funds to trust

Companies Act deals with the companies. Trust represents arbitrage with respect to such act including no need to consolidate Trust into the holding company. Thus, Reliance doesn't need to consolidate the Reliance Trust in its financial statements. Thus, the investments of Reliance Trust in Network 18 will not reflect in its financial statements

Reliance Trust

Reliance Trust extends funds in form of optionally convertible debentures to Network 18. If converted, it will be near ownership of Network 18

Optionally, convertible debenturesare exempted from the Takeover code unless, converted into voting shares.

Network18

TV18 does rights issues. Network 18 raises stake to ~70% through under subscription in rights issue.

Stake increase through rights issue is exempted from Takeover code by persons already in control of the Company. Network 18 is person in control of TV18.

TV 18

Reliance Trust converts optionally convertible debentures into voting rights and makes an open offer for Network 18 and TV18 at price computed as per the SEBI pricing regulations. The market price was above the Open offer price making the Open offer a regulatory formality, without any financial implication.

Takeover complete, control enhanced and companies stay listed by making best of each legal entity and arbitrage between various regulations.

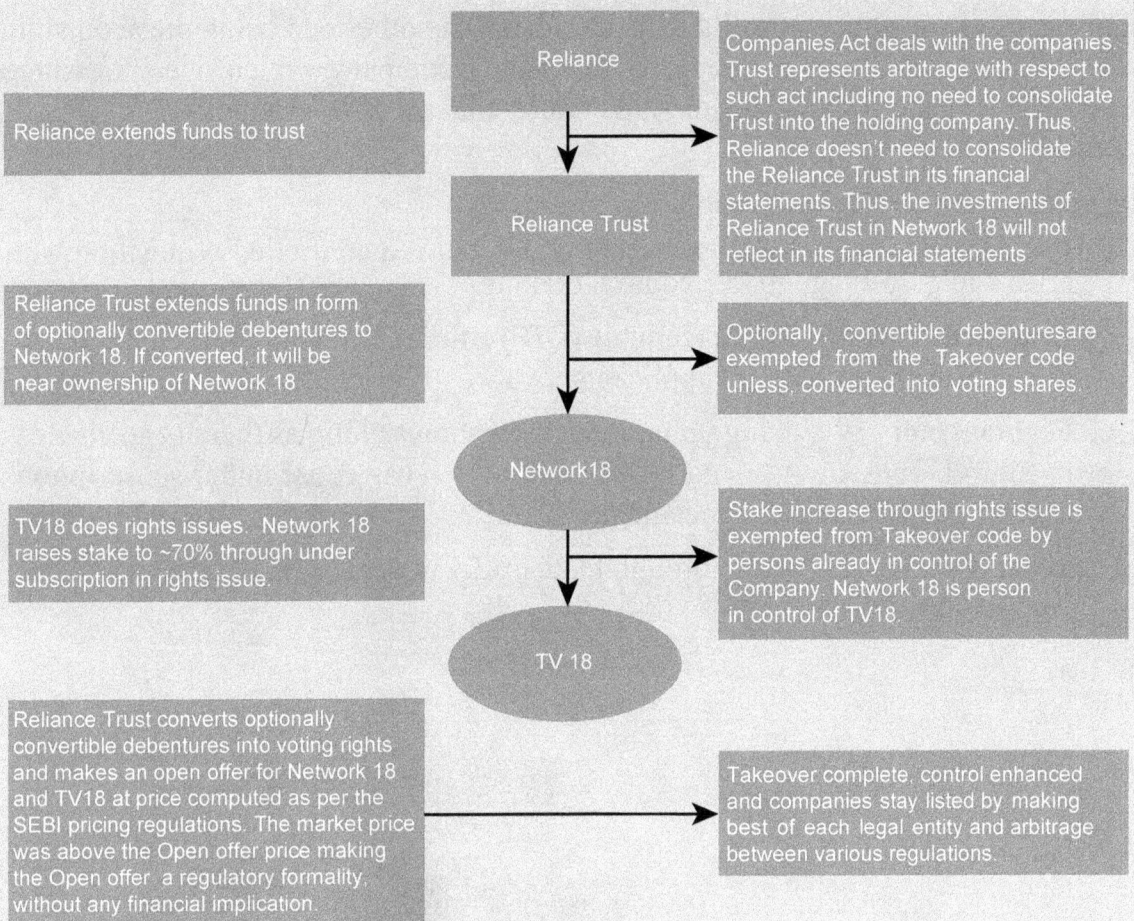

9.6 Stake Enhancement through Various Routeswith or without Triggering the Takeover Code

There are various ways of stake enhancement with or without triggering the takeover code. There is also provision to do creeping acquisition of 5% voting rights in a financial year. Thus, a preferential issue which allows warrant with tenure of 18 months can be used to creep 5% every financial year. For example: An acquirer can acquire 5% in March of a particular year followed by Company resolving to issue warrant representing 10% voting rights which can be converted into shares in April and the next 5% in the march next year. Thus, 15% shares can be creeped at a predetermined price over a span of 13 months without triggering the takeover code.

The other way to enhance stake could be through indirect way. The first being through buyback of shares, this essentially involves the use of company's cash to enhance stake for the controlling shareholders. The other one being the acquisition of stake by controlling shareholders in holding company, which does not trigger the takeover code and at the same time it also enhances the economic right over the underlying target company.

The other primary routes to acquire are:

a. **Preferential issue:** Results in the lock-up, but is a controlled acquisition with price and percentage to be acquired definite.

b. **Qualified Institutional Placement (QIP) route:** No lock-up but the acquisition is proportionate to all applicants.

c. **Rights issue:** By picking up under-subscription as long as there is no change in control. Thus, high-priced rights issue, which can cause under-subscription, can be used for stake enhancement without any lock up.

The other route is acquisition through tender offer under the SEBI takeover code.

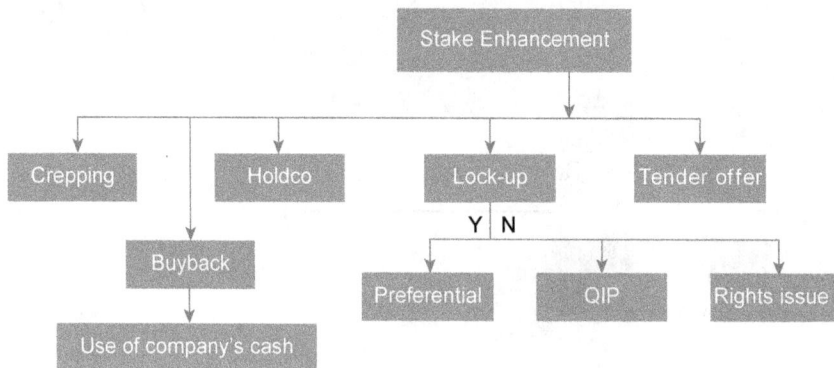

9.7 Arbitraging between Foreign Investment Regulations

There are two regimes for the foreign acquirers. First is the FII rechristened as Foreign Portfolio Investor (Regulations), which permits foreign portfolio investors to acquire shares on the stock exchange like any other investor subject to a certain percent. The second regime is FDI *viz.* Foreign Direct Investment, which is not as seamless as the FII regime and at times requires approvals to invest from the Company, the Foreign Investment Promotion Board, and at times, Reserve Bank of India as well. Further, the FDI regime in most cases does not allow investments to be done directly through purchase on the stock exchange. Further, there are sectors where FII can invest but FDI is not allowed to invest. Thus, depending on various objectives, either of the routes or combination of the routes can be used.

The above is a perfect example of how two laws on same subject matter can create room to maneuver and create arbitrage opportunities for shrewd acquirers.

9.8 Incognito Routes to Takeover

There are certain reporting rules and there are ways to avoid reporting as well. Acquisitions of holding companies as discussed above or through p-notes or acquisition of GDRs /ADRs or acquiring until 4.9% and then make a large acquisition so that the market does not get a whiff of the acquisition.

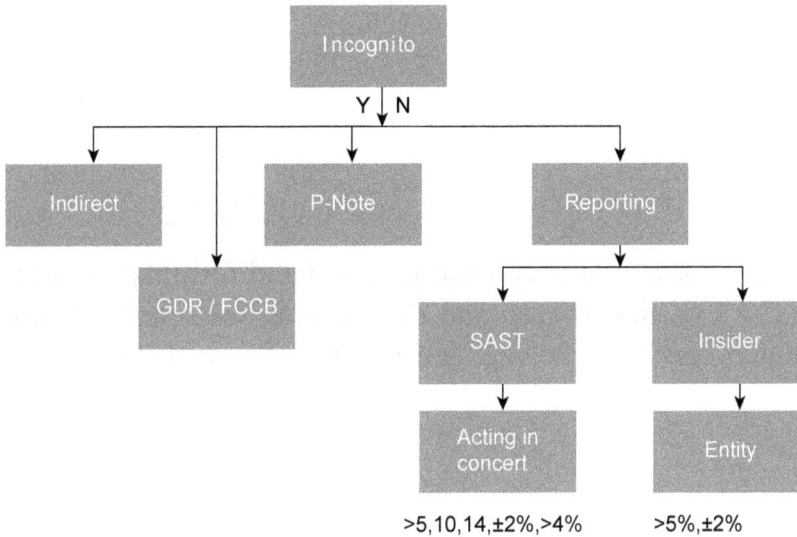

```
                        Incognito
                         Y │ N
         ┌───────────────┬─┴──────────────┐
      Indirect         P-Note          Reporting
         │                          ┌──────┴──────┐
      GDR / FCCB                  SAST          Insider
                                    │              │
                               Acting in        Entity
                               concert
                          >5,10,14,±2%,>4%    >5%,±2%
```

9.9 Pricing Arbitrage

If the objective is to exploit the pricing arbitrage, then acquisition through holding company creates holding company discount (refer to Chapter on demerger) but with the same economic rights. We have already discussed how long-dated warrants or convertible instruments can give a time discounted arbitrage along with the option value. There are other ways such as non-compete or paying for assets held by the controlling shareholder and not the company as well. If there is no need for pricing arbitrage, then the direct route refers to the acquisition of shares.

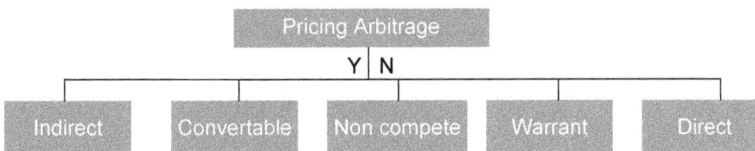

```
                    Pricing Arbitrage
                         Y │ N
     ┌──────────┬──────────┼──────────┬──────────┐
  Indirect  Convertable  Non compete  Warrant   Direct
```

9.10 Tax Arbitrage in Indian Tax Laws

Acquisition of shares through merger with the help of the scheme of arrangement and also through stock market or through acquisition of shares using Double Tax

Avoidance Agreement (DTAA) treaties are ways to plan the acquisition and save on paying taxes in a legal manner.

If tax is not a major issue, then direct acquisition can be used. The Merrill Lynch acquisition of $500 million stake of Mr. Kothari's stake in DSP Merrill Lynch was carried out through stock exchange resulting in saving for the seller.

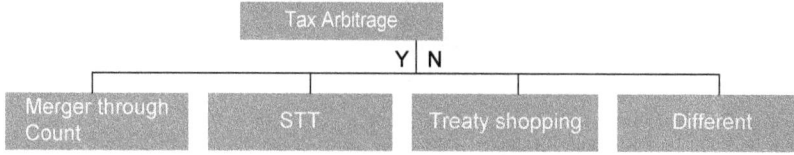

9.11 Tax Arbitrage with Structures

Many times, the tax laws are very strait jacketed and formulated in response to tax planning done in a particular case and thus leaving the other side uncovered. The below case studies highlight the vagueness of the aforesaid statement.

Case Study 9.5: Yahoo Plans to Spin-off Alibaba Stake

Earlier proposed structure

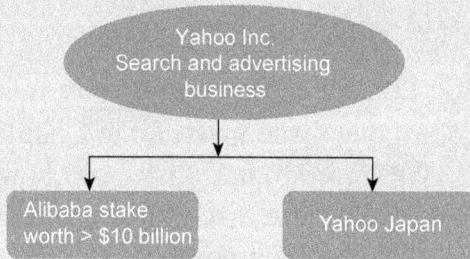

Revised Structure

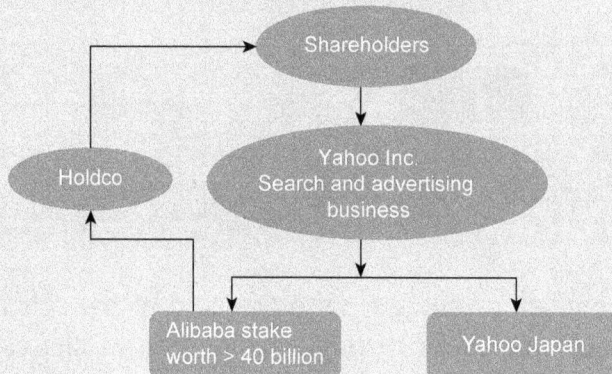

This structure involved significant taxes for spinning-off Alibaba stake to the shareholders.

This involved separating Alibaba from the Yahoo group.

The Revised Structure

The revised structure of separation of Alibaba includes the separation of the Alibaba investment from the rest of Yahoo by reversing the direction of the transaction.

The resulting Yahoo will comprise of two companies: One containing 15% stake in Alibaba and the other will have everything else, including search, email, the Tumbler social media service, various sites like Yahoo Finance, and Yahoo's $8.7 billion stake in Yahoo Japan.

The above structure will result in a very low tax bill.

Key Learning

From the above case study, it is evident that sometimes, just by reversing the direction of the transaction can result in significant tax arbitrage.

9.12 SEBI or NON-SEBI

Below is a brief illustration of SEBI and non-SEBI routes to either raise capital or acquisition or disposal of shares/assets. Each one of them has different set of rules and objectives. These can be used by the acquirer depending on their needs and objectives.

As we have discussed earlier, the securities laws are minority shareholder oriented, while the Companies Act is for majority.

Thus, routes such as the following will have to follow the securities law laid down by SEBI:

a. Initial Public Offering ("IPO") for purpose of listing,
b. Issue of further shares through preferential issue, Qualified Institutional placement, rights issue,
c. Open offer for the acquisition of shares under the takeover code or Buyback of shares or delisting of shares

While the routes such as the following will have to follow the Companies law:

a. Scheme of arrangement for merger or demerger or capital reduction or for sale of division
b. Reverse listing through merger

On the other hand, routes such as foreign currency convertible bond ("FCCB") or Depository receipts ("GDR" or "ADR") will be subject to only Reserve Bank of

India regulations and foreign securities laws which may be less onerous than SEBI laws.

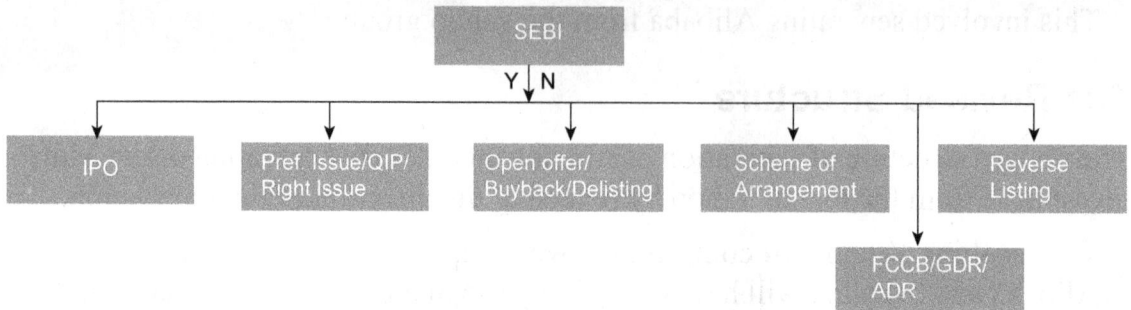

9.13 Accounting Considerations

Why is Accounting Important in M&A?

The accounting consideration is an important part of the M&A and should not be taken lightly. The accountant should be taken on job very early in the deal. While in India the purchase accounting is not mandatory, but the US GAAP and IFRS prescribes purchase accounting only for acquisitions, being the right method for accounting for the acquisition.

The method of accounting presents the correct picture in the financial statements. The use of accounting methodology and the allocation of purchase price will also reflect the quality of acquisition made.

Apart, from the above, the choice of accounting method will impact certain tax issues as well including whether the acquisition will be tax neutral or not. In the current chapter, we will first deal with the accounting consideration and then with the tax consideration arising out of the same.

Type of Accounting Methods

Purchase accounting

The purchase accounting methodology involves incorporating the assets and liabilities at their existing amounts or by allocating the consideration to individual identifiable assets and liabilities of the transferor company on the basis of their fair values at the date of amalgamation. The identifiable assets and liabilities may include assets and liabilities not recorded in the financial statements of the transferor company.

Any additional amount of the consideration over the value of the net assets of the transferor company acquired by the transferee company should be recognized in the transferee company's financial statements **as goodwill** arising on amalgamation. If the amount of the consideration is lower than the value of the net assets acquired, the difference should be treated as Capital Reserve.

The goodwill arising due to amalgamation should be amortized to income in a systematic manner over its useful life. The amortization period should not exceed five years unless a somewhat longer period can be justified.

Pooling of interest accounting

Under this method, the assets, liabilities, and reserves of the acquiree are recorded by the acquirer at their existing carrying amounts.

Thus, in the above methodology, the acquisition has neutral impact on the acquirer's financial statement.

Significance of Accounting Methods

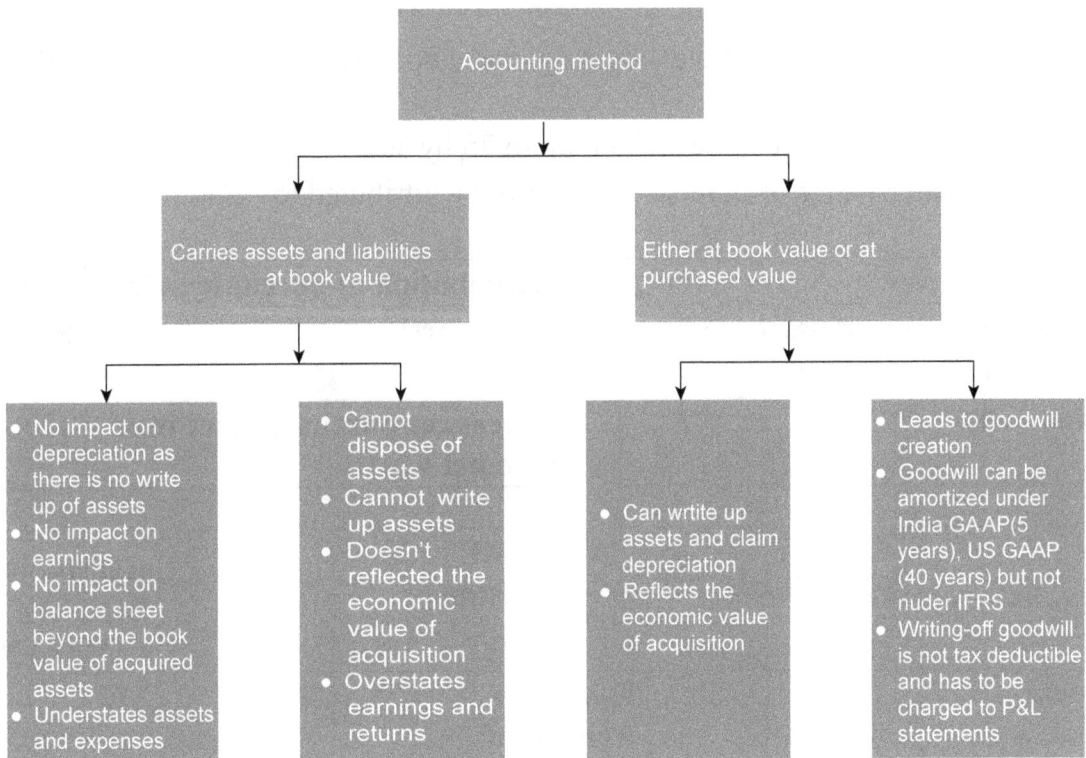

```
                        ┌─────────────────────┐
                        │  Accounting method  │
                        └──────────┬──────────┘
              ┌────────────────────┴────────────────────┐
   ┌──────────────────────┐              ┌──────────────────────┐
   │ Carries assets and   │              │ Either at book value │
   │ liabilities at book  │              │ or at purchased value│
   │ value                │              │                      │
   └──────────┬───────────┘              └──────────┬───────────┘
```

- No impact on depreciation as there is no write up of assets
- No impact on earnings
- No impact on balance sheet beyond the book value of acquired assets
- Understates assets and expenses

- Cannot dispose of assets
- Cannot write up assets
- Doesn't reflected the economic value of acquisition
- Overstates earnings and returns

- Can wrtite up assets and claim depreciation
- Reflects the economic value of acquisition

- Leads to goodwill creation
- Goodwill can be amortized under India GAAP(5 years), US GAAP (40 years) but not nuder IFRS
- Writing-off goodwill is not tax deductible and has to be charged to P&L statements

Impact of Accounting Methods on Balance Sheet and Profit/Loss

Let's explain the above scenario with help of an example:

Impact on balance sheet:

Pooling method			
	Acquirer	**Target**	**Acquirer + Target**
Asset	100	50	150
Net worth (Liabilities)	100	50	150
	200	**100**	**300**

Purchase method		
	Acquirer Target	
Asset	100	50
Net worth (Liabilities)	100	50
	200	**100**

The target was purchased for 150 against a net-worth of 50.

Assumption

The Plant and equipment of the Target against a book value has a fair value of 75.

Then, the asset will have to be written up to 75 by adding 25.

Therefore, the balance of purchase price will be attributed to "Goodwill."

Purchase price	150	**Attribution of purchase price**	150
Less: Fair value of asset and liability of target	75	**Net-worth**	50
Goodwill	**75**	**Excess of purchase price over the net worth**	100

	Acquirer (a)	Target (b)	ATTRIBUTION Adjustment (c)			COM-BINED COMPANY
Asset	100	50	Fair value write up of asset	25	Asset	175 (a+b+c)
			Goodwill	75	Goodwill	75 (c)
Net worth (Liabilities)	100	50	Acquisition financing (equity + debt)	150	Net worth (Liabilities)	250 (a+c)

Rules of Purchase Accounting

1. The fair value of both asset and liabilities is assessed and can be written up or down.
2. The purchase price is first allocated to the book value of assets net of liabilities.
3. The excess of the purchase price over the book value of asset net of liabilities will be either goodwill and/or intangible assets.
4. In case the purchase price is lower than that of the book value of asset net of liabilities, then it will be accounted in the capital reserves.
5. Goodwill can or cannot be amortized depending on the GAAP followed.

Impact on Profit And Loss

	Method	
	Pooling	Purchase
Revenue	100,000	100,000
Less:		
Cost of goods sold	75,000	75,000
Depreciation	2000	3500
Amortization		7000
SG&A	10,000	10,000 0
Miscellaneous	5000	5000 0
Profit	8000	−500

Increased depreciation due to write-up on Plant and machinery.

Amortization of goodwill and intangible assets.

Thus, we see the impact of accounting method on the profit and loss of the acquirer as a resultant of choice of accounting method. Under pooling method, there will be profit while under purchase method, there is loss.

Further, under Indian GAAP, the goodwill is allowed to amortized while the IFRS and US GAAP does not allow amortization except under impairment of goodwill. Thus, acquirers wanting to either have lesser goodwill or amortization may choose to allocate the purchase consideration to "intangible assets."

For example: If 100 is the excess value over the book value of net assets, it can be split into goodwill and intangible assets.

Therefore, the students of M&A should be able to decipher EPS accretive nature of the transaction, whether it is driven by choice of accounting method or allocation of purchase price between goodwill and intangible asset.

Impairment of Goodwill

Under the U.S. GAAP and IFRS, since the goodwill is no longer amortized, there is temptation of acquirer to allocate the excess value to goodwill as the impact is minimal on profit and loss at the time of transaction. However, each year the goodwill needs to be tested for impairment and if, it is impaired it will result in non-tax deductible charge to profit and loss account and equity written down consequentially.

Thus, resulting in double whammy on the balance sheet also profit and loss statement.

For example, having a sizeable goodwill created at the time of acquisition results in big write-off due to impairment. In such case, the equity may get wiped off or the debt/equity ratio may go for a toss forcing the creditors to liquidate or trigger call on their loans.

At times, due to loop hole in accounting standards and tax rules, the impairment can actually be done without charging the profit and loss statement but, directly to balance sheet, which results in the company returns increasing as the equity has reduced in denominator but the profit figure is not impacted.

Case Study 9.6: Microsoft Restructuring

Microsoft announces restructuring of phone hardware business

Redmond, Wash: Microsoft Corp. announced plans to restructure the company's phone hardware business to improve focus and align resources. Microsoft also announced the reduction of up to 7800 positions, primarily in the phone business. As a result, the company will record an impairment charge of approximately $7.6 billion related to assets associated with the acquisition of the Nokia Devices and Services (NDS) business in addition to a restructuring charge of approximately $750 million to $850 million.

This charge has no impact on the cash flow from operations and is non-deductible for income tax purposes. Based on the new plans, the future prospects for the Phone Hardware segment are below original expectations. Accordingly, the company concluded that an impairment adjustment of its Phone Hardware segment assets and goodwill of approximately $7.6 billion is required.

Thus, we see that within a year of acquisition of Nokia, Microsoft had to write-off the entire acquisition. Although, the sum was huge, but given the balance sheet of Microsoft, it was able to take the impairment.

Accounting standards comparative

	Indian	US	IFRS
Pooling Method	YES	NO	NO
Purchase Method	YES	YES	YES
Goodwill Amortization	5 years	NO	NO
Intangible Asset Amortization	YES	YES	YES

Accounting Standards and Impact on Stock Price

Earning quality of company has a big influence on the stock price. Thus, the use of accounting methods reflects economic reality that seeks greater positive influence on the stock price.

Thus, purchase method along with measured goodwill and allocation justifiable toward intangible assets can reflect a good earning quality. As also being upfront on the impairment and taking once and for all hit rather than recurring hit will provide positive influence. The repeated acquisitions and impairment may leave a bad taste in the mouth for stock price.

9.14 Tax Considerations in M&A

The tax neutral transactions in Indian context are as under:

a. Sale of shares carried out on the stock exchange where the holding period of the seller is greater than one year.
b. Merger or amalgamation carried out through a High Court approved scheme of arrangement subject under certain conditions.
c. Demerger carried out through a high court approved scheme of arrangement subject to certain conditions.

Itemized sale or slump sale where business undertakings sold are taxable depending upon the holding period. Apart from the above, indirect transfers are also taxable, but the jurisprudence on the same is not yet settled. Depending on what needs to be optimized in a transaction, the parties to the transaction may decide the route to execute the transaction.

The comparative across various routes are stated below. However, there is trade-off between buyer and seller, where the buyer likes to get tax deductions for purchase while the seller likes to minimize or defer taxes. The below table will be a useful guide in this regard.

Tax Implications under Various Routes

	Tax neutral	Holding period	Value write-up	Trigger takeover code	Speed	Carry forward of tax incentives	Cherry Picking of Assets	Valuation
Itemized sale	No	36 months	Possible	No	Fast	No	Yes	Valuer report
Slump Sale	No	36 months	Possible	No	Fast	No	Yes	Valuer report
Share Sale	Yes, if done on stock exchange	12 months	Not possible	Yes, if acquired in excess of 25% voting rights	Fastest	No	No	Market
Merger	Yes, if income tax conditions met	NA	Possible with purchase method	No	Slow	Yes	No	Valuer report
Demerger	Yes, if income tax conditions met	NA	Not possible	No	Slow	Yes	No	Valuer report

9.15 Corporate Law Considerations

Corporate law considerations come into play from a tactical point of view. Few of the corporate actions that require shareholder approval are listed below. If these corporate actions are part of the transaction, they are required to be assessed and strategized for improved execution.

Corporate Actions	Type of approval
Issue of shares to persons other than members of the company	Special
Buyback of shares	Special
To sell, lease, or otherwise dispose of the whole or substantially the whole of the undertaking of the company	Special
Alteration of memorandum or articles of the company	Special
Merger or demerger	Special
Appointment or removal of directors including alternate and additional	Ordinary

These days the additional challenge with respect to electronic voting and resolutions require the interested parties to opt out of the voting process. Thus, there are elements that need to be considered while planning for acquisition.

The special resolutions are the ones which require 3/4th approval while the ordinary resolutions require simple majority. Thus, acquisition of 25% shareholding also presents an opportunity to wield significant influence on the corporate actions of the company. The importance of the threshold of 25%, 50%, and 75% is highlighted in the below case studies.

Case Study 9.7: Tale of Two Takeovers Fame India and Great Off-shore

Fame India

Fame India used to operate multiplexes in India along with competitors such as Inox Leisure, Reliance ADAG, and PVR Cinemas.

In February 2010, Inox Leisure acquired 43% stake of Fame India. It went on to make purchase of additional 7.2% stake in the open market to have simple majority stake of 50.2%.

Reliance ADAG launched a counterbid at 44% premium to Inox Leisure acquisition price. Although Inox Leisure had already acquired 50% stake in the company, Reliance ADAG went on to acquire 35% stake in Fame India.

Having set itself up comfortably with 50% majority and having another dominant shareholder having 35% stake, the question arises how will Inox Leisure deal with this situation?

Fame India launched rights issue at price substantially less that the Reliance ADAG price that made it a disincentive for Reliance ADAG to subscribe to rights issue.

Rights issue needs only a board approval and Inox had the voting power to appoint the majority of the board.

Inox Leisure shareholding rose to ~73% due to subscription of additional shares in the rights issue which was not subscribed by Reliance ADAG. As a result, Reliance ADAG stake fell to 22%.

This brought Inox Leisure stake close to 75%, comfortable enough for it to pass a special resolution to merger Fame India with itself.

The merger led to the falling of Reliance ADAG stake to shade below 10% and being outwitted by Inox Leisure.

Great Off-shore

Great Off-shore dealt with oil rigging and drilling services. The promoters of Great Off-shore had defaulted on its loan given to it by Bharti Shipyard, which lead to

Bharti Shipyard acquiring ~15% stake in great Off-shore and triggering the takeover code at INR 344 per share.

ABG Ship yard entered into fray and made a counterbid at 410 per share. This led to a bidding match. Bharti Ship yard continued to acquire shares in the market and finally acquired a block deal to reach 26% stake in the company.

The 26% stake proved to be a deterrent for ABG and while they had sought control, they ended up selling their stake before the offer opened at 575 per share making a profit of INR 50 crores.

Thus, in the above cases, we see the criticality of 26% and how that made the counter-bidder throw in the towel and make handsome profit in contrast to the Fame India battle which resulted in loss for Reliance ADAG.

9.16 Securities Law Considerations

The SEBI takeover regulations are the principle regulations which deal with the acquisition and have been dealt separately in the chapter on takeover code.

The other main regulations which need to be considered are:

Insider Trading Regulations

This act is critical from the point of view of sensitivity of leakage on unpublished price sensitive information which may cause run up in price and scupper the transaction.

The recently amended insider trading regulations have expanded the scope to prohibit trading in shares by any person having "Unpublished Price Sensitive Information" ("UPSI"). Thus, the run up to M&A will enable a lot of persons in the possession of UPSI. Therefore, the need emerges to maintain track of persons who are in the possession of UPSI.

The criticality of Insider Trading regulation in M&A comes in two forms:

- **Due-Diligence**: It is a critical part of making a bid for the company. The Inside Trading Regulations permits it in two situations which are:
    - Leading to open offer under the SEBI takeover regulations.
    - If not leading to an open offer, the board had considered it to be in the best interest of the company and the UPSI is disclosed, at least two trading days in advance of the transaction being consummated.

- Acquisitions starting from 5% onward require disclosures and can affect hostile situations or surreptitious bids.

Listing Regulations

- Listing regulations require disclosure of material price sensitive information to the stock exchanges. Thus, entering into discussion for an M&A transaction is something that is a ticklish issue in terms of disclosure to the stock exchange because it is a confidential process but at the same time it may need to be disclosed to the stock exchanges.

In the Indian context, it has not yet reached a situation where the companies have been following it very strictly and the first breakout is generally around the time the takeover is announced.

Market rumors published in the newspapers are rebutted as against media policy by the companies. Although, down the line, announcement of M&A transaction is made.

While a few acquirers or targets have disclosed the information as having arrived at Memorandum of Understanding and disclosed that the talks are in progress, the aforesaid governance has not yet taken shape in the Indian takeover firmament.

The disclosure can be helped by amending the takeover regulations to state the price that will be calculated with reference to such date else, the run up in price will scupper the deal. Intangible governance issues, however, are not a priority for all stakeholders alike.

- Another issue that requires consideration is maintaining the public shareholding of minimum 25%. This provides tricky situation, wherein the acquisition plus an open offer will lead to breach of public shareholding limit.

Delisting Regulations

This regulation deals with acquirers who aspire to take the target companies private. Unfortunately, the regulations are not conducive for acquires wishing to take companies private as delisting mechanism is conducted as a reverse auction where in the shareholders bid for the price at which the acquirer can take it private and there is a delisting premium that comes into play especially given the fact that a very small section of shareholders will determine the outcome.

The price at which such number of shares can be acquired that enable the acquirer to reach at least 90% shareholding is the delisting price.

As a consequence, delisting is a very monumental task that has not been taken by many acquirers.

Corporate Governance

We have already discussed the shades of corporate governance in the disclosure requirement under the listing regulations. However, corporate governance has not yet taken the center stage in the Indian takeover battles.

Under the takeover regulations, there is certain mandatory disclosures that are required to be done as per the standard format and the disclosures have remained standard over nearly 20 years of the regulations existence.

For example, the disclosure around futures plans with respect to the target company is paid lip service with at the best two paragraphs which at the best ambiguous about the future plans that are critical for the minorities to decide about the offer.

After the Kraft-Cadbury saga, according to the UK takeover, the acquirer is required to provide much more detailed information about the plans with respect to the target company. We may probably need to take leaf out of the UK takeover regulations.

The other broader aspect has been the role of the board of directors of the target company. Unlike the practise in the western world where it is incumbent on the board of the target to recommend offer to the shareholders, the role of board in Indian context has remained passive. The boards are not required to solicit alternate offers or have sought justified valuations or spoken against anti-minority provisions of the offer such as non-compete fee. Hopefully, we will see much more active boards in the future.

While, we speak of the takeover regulations requiring some mandatory information in the takeover offers. Such is not the case with the scheme of arrangement required to carry out mergers or demergers. There is no qualitative or quantitative disclosure in such schemes for shareholders to evaluate the merger or demerger. It is presumed that the courts are the best arbiters in this matter but, that is not what the courts do and hopefully we see much disclosures in the future.

Foreign Exchange Management Regulations

Most sectors are now liberalized and there is no need for permissions from the Foreign Investment Promotion Board (FIPB) or the Reserve Bank of India (RBI). The valuation norms are also now streamlined. In case of listed company, SEBI pricing norms are considered while in case of unlisted company, it requires to have Discounted Cash Flow (DCF) valuation for inbound transfer. In case of outbound transfer, there is no prescribed norm but in both cases, it is required to be certified by Merchant banker.

Disclosure Norms

Under SEBI Takeover Regulations

(Regulation 29)		
Particulars	**Disclosure to**	**Time Limit**
Acquirer together with Political Action Committee (PAC) acquires **5% or more** voting rights of the target company	Stock Exchange & Target Company	Within 2 working days
Acquirer together with PAC holding **5% or more** in the target company shall disclose every acquisition or disposal of shares representing **2% or more** of the shares or voting rights. [Regulation 29(2)]	Stock Exchange & Target Company	Within 2 working days

(Regulation 30):		
Particulars	**Disclosure to**	**Time Limit**
Every person together with PAC holding shares or voting rights aggregating to **25% or more**	Stock Exchange & Target Company	Within 7 working days from March 31
A promoter together with PAC holding shares or voting rights in a target company shall disclose their aggregate shareholding.	Stock Exchange & Target Company	Within 7 working days from March 31

Under SEBI Insider Trading Regulations

The disclosures under the SEBI Insider trading regulations more or less mimics the disclosures required to be done as per Regulation 29 of the SEBI takeover regulations for the purpose of acquirers. There are different norms for insiders which is not germane for this book.

Under Stock Exchange Rules

Bulk deal

In case of transaction involving trading of more than 0.5% of the shares of a company through a single broker on a single exchange needs to be reported.

Block deal

In case of transaction involving trading in special window called the block window if the value of securities traded exceeds INR 5 crores, it needs to be reported.

Thus, we can conclude that there are various reporting norms. Some apply to entity as in insider regulations or as a group under the takeover regulations or some are required to be reported by the broker.

This maze presents an opportunity to arbitrage between them if the acquirer wishes to play around with the disclosures.

9.17 Anti-Trust Issues

The requirement to notify the Competition Commission in any merger or takeover arises when they relate to either

i. the acquirer and the target (the "Parties") or
ii. the group to which the target/merged entity will belong post-acquisition (the "Group") and are as follows:

- The Parties have combined assets in India of Rupees 1500 crores (approximately $333 million) or combined turnover in India of Rupees 4500 crores (approximately $1000 million); or
- The Parties have combined worldwide assets of $750 million or combined worldwide turnover of $2250 million and combined assets in India of Rupees 750 crores (approximately $166 million) or combined turnover in India of Rupees 2250 crores (approximately $500 million); or
- The Group has assets in India of Rupees 6000 crores (approximately $1300 million) or turnover in India of Rupees 18,000 crores (approximately $4000 million); or The Group has worldwide assets of $3000 million or worldwide turnover of $9000 million and assets in India of Rupees 750 crores (approximately $166 million) or turnover in India of Rupees 2250 crores (approximately $500 million).

The above is only the requirement under the Indian laws, while there are significant different laws not only in terms of threshold but, having qualitative impact on competition as well. Anti-trust approvals today are huge part of risk assessment in terms of getting the requisite approvals for the purpose of completing the takeover.

The recent proposed spin-off and sale by GE of its home appliances business to Electrolux failed to get past the competition laws and had to be called-off.

Thus, the risk of not getting an antitrust approval is one of the potent anti-takeover tools being used by the companies to thwart takeover bids such as what we observed in case of Mylan Inc., the biggest pharmaceutical giant thwarted the takeover attempt from Teva of Israel citing risk of not getting anti-trust approval.

9.18 Executive Summary

In the current chapter, we have made an attempt to present a variety of opportunities created by various laws and allow for value creation by legal planning through regulatory framework. We have already explored the way to read various regulations in the chapter on the takeover code. The other way is to look upside down, think options, think arbitrage, and craft a deal which fits through regulatory framework in a legal manner.

10

Joint Ventures—Design and Considerations

Contents

10.1 Introduction

Joint venture is one of the very effective Merger&Acquisition (M&A) tools that are effectively used by entities, apt at playing this game in the name of joint venture (JV). The concept of "Joint" makes it sound similar to a partnership approach to the venture wherein the spoils of the venture are shared equitably between the venture partners. However, in reality, parties to the venture are so unsure of their partners that the ventures fail to take-off or they take-off, but the winning party is either one of them. Win–win ventures have been very rare.

Heavily negotiated JV agreements are doomed for failure the moment they are inked. Inadequately negotiated ventures end up having mismatched expectation and doomed. Cleverly negotiated JV agreements include Trojan house allowing the foreigner to enter, learn, seize, and venture on their own. Thus, careful consideration needs to be done while designing a JV.

This chapter will dwell into the key considerations for designing the JV.

10.2 Reasons for Joint Ventures

The most common reasons for entering into JV can be stated as under:

1. *Entry strategy into new area or foreign market*: It is generally a result of tentativeness of the partner, and thus, they want to test water before going headlong. It may also be a case where the local laws or regulations would not allow 100% ownership. Therefore, there is no other way but to strike alliance or partnership. The other reason may include leveraging on the partner's expertise in the form of network, brand, distribution, employees, licenses, etc. This strategy helps to reduce the burden and the time to enter in the market.

2. *Increased revenue and market share*: In some cases, it allows the partners to roll out their existing products on partner's network and allow them to consolidate.

3. *Diversification of risk*: JV and alliances are excellent devices to diversify risk of an enterprise. It can be used as a platform for rolling out concepts, products, and test case for future strategies without taking the undue risk as resource Commitment. Partnering with a local firm, especially in less-developed countries where a foreign firm may be less familiar or comfortable with, may limit its exposure to risk.

4. *Combining to deliver scale, synergy, and intellectual property*: It is a way to combine complementary skillsets for optimal use of each other's resources and skillsets. It aims to deliver operating leverage through better use of scale and

scope. It can also be used by smaller firm to compete against a bigger firm, thereby trying to optimize cost to battle the big shark. Sometimes, the nature of industry is such that the combination is the only way the firms can survive and make profits like in airlines, commodities, etc. Sometimes, it is a flavour of the industry to follow alliance mode following the footsteps of leader in the industry. Media or advertising is one such industry in which the size matters for competitive position vis-à-vis the clients of the industry.

10.3 Partner Considerations in Joint Ventures

Choice of partner is a key consideration to achieve successful alliance. Taking a partner who can provide complementary skillsets is essential for success of the JV.

Maruti-Suzuki-Government: In this alliance, the government aided to provide the infrastructure while Suzuki brought in the required expertise.

Hero-Honda: In this case, Hero provided the local expertise and Honda used its technology and brand to increase the productivity.

DSP-Merrill Lynch: DSP providing local expertise while Merrill bringing the foreign.

JVs having unequal partners improved success rate as they have possibility to attain a win–win situation due to the complementary nature of the partners. JVs between equal partners have failed due to lack of complementary skills or resources.

   50:50 ventures are more likely to fail as the returns are even, although the resource commitments are skewed between partners. In more extreme cases, the minority partner is providing more resources, but, taking less returns or minority partner holds back his resources because returns are not commensurate. In some situations, one partner does not want to increase the value of JV if he intends taking control of the venture at a later date.

10.4 Designing of Joint Ventures

We can state JVs as misnomer. There is more misaligned alliance that leads to disjoint ventures as compared to successfully aligned joint ventures. JV by name itself presents an equitable notion of parties coming together for common good for the purpose of extracting each other's competencies. A JV may present a Trojan horse kind of device in which a shrewd negotiator of venture may benefit disproportionately compared to the other party and would have been better off without the JV than with a JV.

Thus, negotiating a JV is critical.

The key areas that need to be clearly defined and negotiated form the basis of a successful JV. They can be stated as under:

a. Nature and purpose of JV

Whether the JV would be carried out for:

- Equity
- Technology royalty based
- Alliance
- Local market expertise
- Legal necessity (insurance)

b. Structure of JV

- Equal
- Majority–minority
- Majority–minority at shareholding level but equal at board level
- Majority with minority protection

c. Key aspects

i. **Valuation of JV and induction of partner** through transfer of shares or injection of funds into the company.

ii. **Control of JV** including board composition and whether the equity holding and returns are in line with the control or not.

iii. **Key personnel appointments and reporting.**

iv. **Resource contribution** to the JVs including branding, intellectual property, etc.

v. Future **equity infusion** includes put and call options and termination clauses.

vi. **Royalty**, if any, and term of the JV.

The above are key aspects that determine whether the DNA of the JV is in order or not.

A carefully thought JV with both the parties being aware of each other's resources kept on table and the equitable return on the same ensures the profitability of the JV.

Let us move ahead with the analysis of some of the JV to learn the designing of the same. These lessons are especially critical if the party is minority or the underdog in the JV.

10.5 Equity Consideration in Joint Ventures

An entrepreneur inducting a JV partner makes a big trade-off on account of equity dilution. Thus, there is a need to use equity sparingly. Things which can be bought by other means should not be bought through issuing equity. Buying through issuing equity represents a lazy way to grow business, frittering away the equity of the business.

The key element to figure out is the value flow and creation and do not get foxed by the cash flow and premium valuations being paid by the incoming partner.

The intellectual property of the businesses should not be traded for equity swayed by the premium valuations paid by the incoming partner. It has to be a last resort instrument as the value of venture is enshrined in equity. Dilution should be done only in a situation where there is a fundamental need for the JV.

Thus, the key questions with respect to equity dilution in JV include:

a. Is it needed absolutely?
b. What is the trade-off for the same?
c. What is the quantum and what is the end use of the dilution?
d. How much control you retain on that equity through put/call, non-compete, etc?
e. Will raising equity create value or thwart value creation because of two party decision-making?
f. The intent of other party making equity infusion? Is it a small change or serious money for the infuser?

The above considerations and criticality is taken into account through case studies described below.

Case study 10.1: Hero-Honda and Bajaj-Kawasaki

Hero Honda

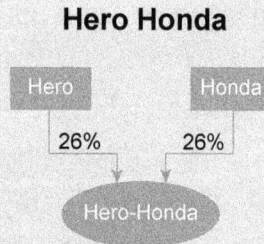

- Hero-Honda was a 26:26 equity JV between Hero Motors and Honda Japan.
- The alliance was formed in 1984 and limited to India, when India was opened up for foreign investment and there was restriction in foreigners owning 100% ventures.
- Hero-Honda is constrained by its agreement with partner Honda Motor Co., which restricts exports of bikes. Hero Honda cannot export out of India. It is bounded by brand and technology restrictions.
- Heavy reliance on partner (Honda Motor Company) for technology and branding.

- The new agreement between Honda Japan and Hero Honda does not have a "no-compete clause." This means increased competition from its own collaborator and technology provider.
- The JV was terminated in 2010 at the peak of the market value by Honda.

Key Learning

The above case study demonstrates one of the successful JVs as the partners possessed complementary skillsets. Honda had the expertise while Hero provided the Indian platform.

Many see this venture as Hero needed partner like Honda. However, the point to be noted is that it was Honda that needed a complementary partner like Hero who would be underdog at the negotiating table. This in turn allowed Honda to dictate terms with respect to:

- The kind of technology that the JV will roll out. The JV ultimately did not roll out the latest bikes from Honda.
- The bikes were limited to lower range engines only.
- The branding was of equal weightage but not at any stage of JV was Hero allowed to roll out "Hero" branded vehicles.
- The JV was not allowed to export. Not even to countries where Honda was not interested or present.
- Honda having wetted their feet in Indian market went onto launch scooters in the Indian market.
- Having tested success with the scooters, they went on to terminate the alliance and launched their own branded motor-cycles. The JV was terminated at peak of the market value with discount that hardly matters due to peak valuation.
- Hero subsequently had to spent more resources in branding and R&D of its vehicles and the market reports suggested that the absence of "Honda" in brand was a major setback.
- Hero at subsequent times of JV negotiation could have prepared for life beyond Honda. This case study highlights JV as a device utilized as entry strategy by Honda.

Bajaj + Kawasaki:

Technology Alliance

Bajaj – – – – – – – – – Kawaski

- Bajaj had no equity JV rather a technical collaboration with Kawasaki for a brief period.

- The mobikes were sold initially under the brand name Kawasaki-Bajaj. After experiencing success, they were sold under Bajaj own brand.
- Bajaj possessed nearly half of the sales coming from exports (Latin America, Africa, and Indonesia).
- Bajaj had no restrictions and operates without any fear of JV agreement review.
- Bajaj was present in all segments of two wheelers and planning four-wheeler entries.

Key Learning

- Bajaj, unlike Hero, relied on technology alliance and pay-off for it through royalty rather than equity dilution.
- It got the right to use Kawasaki brand as well as technology for initial launch but invested a larger chunk in R&D of its own.
- On achieving expertise, it terminated the alliance and launched its bikes under its own brand and its in-house developed technology.
- There was no JV restriction that further allowed it to develop export markets and ~15–20% of the revenue and profitability was generated from the export markets. In most of those markets, it was either ranked #1 or #2.

Compare and Contrast

Hero/Honda and Bajaj/Kawasaki

- Hero was not doing well and needed Honda, whereas Bajaj was a market leader. The deal was much better for Bajaj as compared to Hero. It depends on the bargaining power.
- What clauses could Hero have put to make the deal more lucrative? Although Hero needed Honda, we have to find out how Hero would be a value proposition to Honda and sell that point to extract benefit out of the deal. By taking a JV route, Honda is taking an option and minimizing its losses and building roads to enter the Indian motor market.
- When Bajaj got into a deal with Kawasaki, the single most important decision they took was in terms of price they put on equity. In any JV, it is the most important decision. It is recommended to never dilute equity unless it is the last resort that you have to take.
- More than a proper M&A, a JV is an important decision for a company, depending on its growth goals.
- Work on your weaknesses and play to your strength is the key to success in an alliance.

- It is very much evident that how careful decision-making and focusing on the value creation in near and longer term helps one to draw up a successful JV.

Case Study 10.2: Cyient (Infotech Enterprise)/Pratt & Whitney

Details:

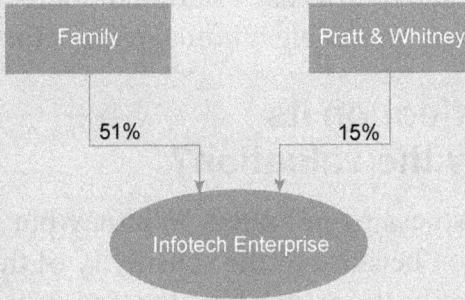

For 15% stake P&W committed certain business to Infotech.

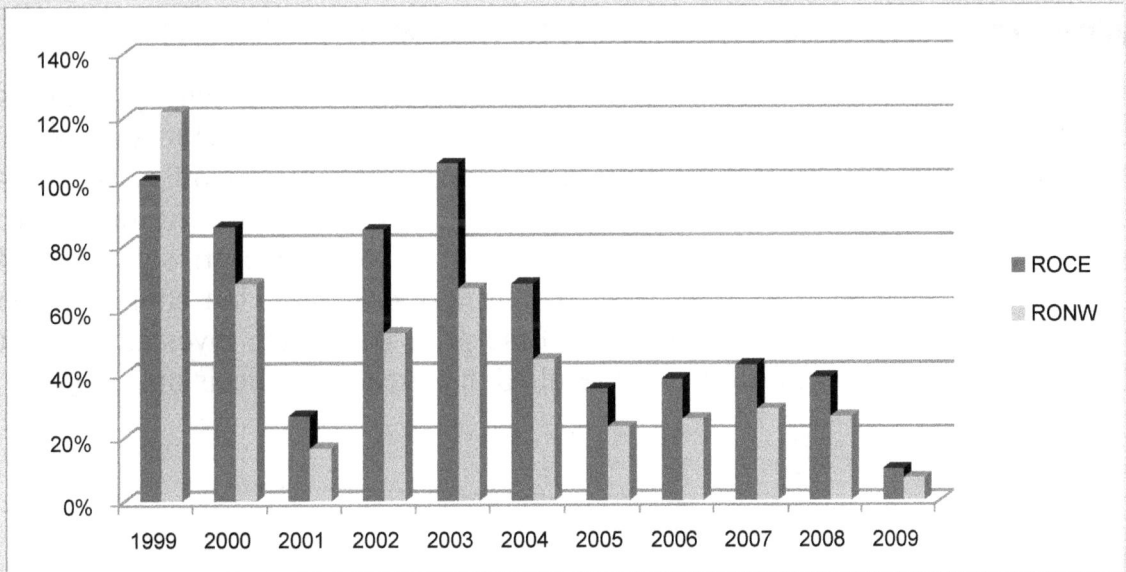

* ROCE—Return on capital employed, RONW—return on net-worth

Infotech enterprises, now renamed as Cyient, is an IT company with proficiency in aviation technology.

Pratt & Whitney is a United Technology Corporation, a Fortune 500 company. In the year 2004, it had taken 15% stake in Infotech in lieu of Infotech acting as preferred vendor for it. Infotech Enterprises made preferential issue of shares to Pratt & Whitney.

Key Learning

The above case will be driven by the following questions:

Given the financial performance of Infotech, **was it justified in issuing 15% stake to Pratt & Whitney?**

Infotech Enterprise dealt with information technology business which is knowledge and not capital intensive. Information technology business is generally free cash flow and high return business. Thus, the need for capital on face of it is not clear and as we see the capital ratios, the returns have started dipping because of the surplus cash sitting on the balance sheet producing minimal returns for the investors.

What has been the likely effect on its business and consequently the valuation?

Infotech enterprises had assured business from Pratt & Whitney but that limits its business with other players in aviation because of the sensitivity of the technology. Furthermore, this limits client diversification, and thus the concentration of Pratt &Whitney in the business increases leading to valuation discount.

Why was Pratt & Whitney keen to invest in Infotech?

The Pratt &Whintey investment in Infotech enterprise was driven by business objective rather than any investment consideration. Once its competitors saw their rival sitting with a 15% shareholding, it was very unlikely that Infotech Enterprises will get business from its competitors. Thus, a small investment for Pratt & Whitney but big decision for Infotech Enterprise. Infotech Enterprise got swayed by premium valuations, cash and assured business prospects, but could not see through the impact on value of Infotech Enterprise due to the investment. Pratt &Whitney got a preferred vendor and resulted in a great value decision.

Case Study 10.3: Balaji/Star

Details:

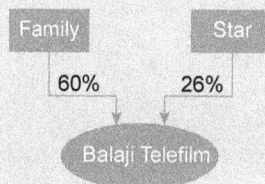

Balaji Telefilms, a successful TV serial production house, issued 26% stake to Rupert Mudroch, promoter of Star TV. In return, Star TV will have the first right over all serials produced by Balaji. In the year 2007, Star TV broke the alliance when the genre of serial produced by Balaji lost public favor then. Promoters of Balaji who had first right of refusal over the 26% stake decided to exercise the same, as per the JV agreement at a price of Rs. 300.

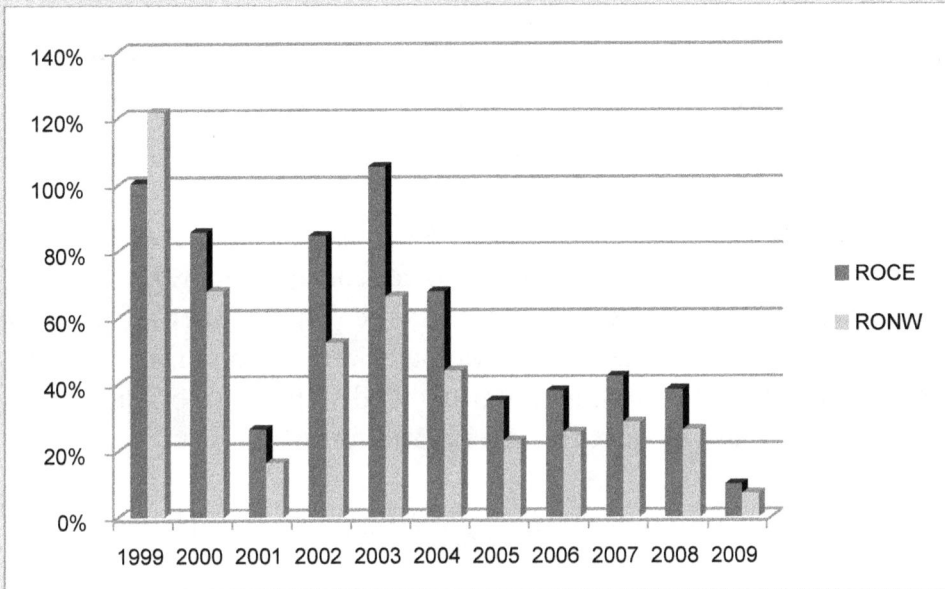

* ROCE- Return on Capital Employed, RONW- Return on Net-Worth

On the announcement of the break-off, the stock has been plummeted and the promoters of Balaji have not been able to buy the 26% stake.

Key Learning

From the above case study, the following questions emerge:

Given the financial performance of Balaji, was it justified to issue 26% stake to Star?

Balaji deals with the media content business which is again knowledge intensive and not capital intensive. Media content business is generally free cash flow and high return business. Therefore, the need for capital is not clear and as we see the capital ratios, the returns have started dipping due to accumulation of cash on the balance sheet producing minimal returns for the investors.

What were the other mistakes committed by Balaji?

The mistakes include providing the first right of refusal to Star on its content. During this time, they had complete sway over the prime TV and could very well have sold content to the highest bidder or could have given Star the right to match the highest bid.

Unfortunately, they increased the business concentration in the process, thereby affecting valuation discount. The markets were justified in valuation discount due to the concentration of Star. Pull out by Star affected the Balaji business justifying the discount.

Additionally, they could have put cap on the exit price for Star or they could have controlled the exit of Star as single end bloc but only to financial investors of its choice.

Why did Star TV take a keen interest to invest in Balaji?

The objective of the deal for star was to gain the control over content. They hardly cared about the valuation. The deal helped them rocket to number 1 spot in TRPs, allowing them the liberty to indulge in new genre. They started off by introducing reality shows such as "Kaun Banega Crorepati" which was an instant hit. Family genre lost out and as a consequence, Star decided to pull out of Balaji. Thus, they gained at the expense of Balaji with clever equity infusion.

Case Study 10.4: NTT Docomo—Tata Tele

Details:

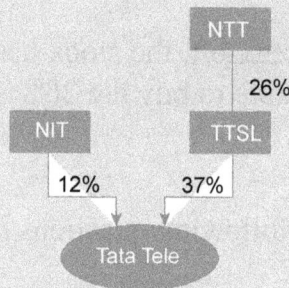

Nippon Telegraph and Telephone (NTT): NTT Docomo

Tata Teleservices Limited (TTSL): Is holding company of the Tata

Tata-Tele is the telecom operating company

a. Justify the structure of the above Transaction

TTSL is the holding company of Tata-Tele. NTT Docomo went through TTSL and got stake in Tata-Tele through TTSL. The operational work was done in Tata-Tele and the strategic decisions were taken in TTSL. Hence, NTT acquired stake in both the parties to be a part of both processes.

Thus, it requires careful consideration as to where to infuse the funds and where to take stake to establish control over the JV.

b. NTT paid a good premium to acquire the above stake. How they mitigated the risk?

NTT has put option on Tata Sons, in the event Tata Tele was unable to meet the operational parameters. However, NTT had achieved significant control over the company, they were still able to negotiate put option with the JV partner in case, JV does not meet the operational parameters. Thus, this resulted in a no-risk situation for NTT but did not make them work hard to come out as winner out of the JV.

Case Study 10.4: Microsoft-Nokia

Details and Learning

Nokia which was losing market share in the mobile handset with not so popular operating system opted to join hands with bigger partner wishing to make entry in mobile handset market. Microsoft being the larger and deep-pocketed partner could negotiate the JV much better due to the following terms:

- Win–lose JV as the value of JV would never have been increased so that it would become difficult for Microsoft to buy out stake of Nokia.
- Nokia increased its dependence on Microsoft in the process. It ended up paying license fee to Microsoft, whereas other competitors are having free Android.
- Microsoft got an efficient eye view of Nokia.
- Eventually, leading to buyout of Nokia and integration will no longer be a challenge.

Case Study 10.5: Valuation Dispute in McDonald's Case with Indian Franchisee

Details and Learning

McDonald entered India through JVs with local Indian partners. One of the franchisee agreements got terminated and led to buyout of the Indian partner by McDonalds. The valuation of the buyout became the reason for dispute between the two. It further demonstrates how well a dominant and well-bred partner protects its interest through agreements.

- Valuation basis provided in the JV agreement for exiting partner is book value rather than current market value method.

- The valuation model was selected by McDonalds as it was the dominant partner. This should have been raised as a concern at the time of deal initiation by the Indian partner.
- Raising concerns at the time of exit would be of no use as the details had already been inked earlier and cannot be changed.
- The exit offering to Indian partner also seems fair because of the fact that it was the brand that led to the success of McDonald's in India and therefore, the benefits should also go to McDonalds and not Indian partner who just acted as the local agent for McDonalds.

The above reflects the negotiation expertise of companies such as McDonalds in protecting its value and intellectual property.

Case Study 10.6: Nokia-Siemens

Details and Learning

Nokia-Siemens formed a 50:50 JV in the telecom enterprise business, being the industry trend for alliances. The partners thought to combine their businesses on 50:50 basis. The results are as under:

- There was no driver of the JV. Risk and return both diversified. No clear line of control.
- JV partners hold back bringing in technology/IP to the JV as they do not want to increase the value of JV which may become roadblock for buying out the partner at inflated value.
- 50% JV stake made it difficult for Siemens to sell its stake to the other companies. The main reason being the fact that 50% does not allow you to have the complete control over the JV and therefore, you are at the mercy of the continuing partner.
- Also, Siemens made the mistake of making their intention of selling the stake public. They had already approached TPG, Blackstone Group, and KKR & Co. and were refused by them. This was known to Nokia and hence, it was able to get itself a cheap deal (just paying 1.7 Billion Euros for the stake). Rather, nobody would buy 50% because they have to deal with other 50% partner.
- Thus, a 50:50 JV between strong partners is a difficult proposition to operate due to lack of clear driver of JV. JV itself is conflicting because increase in value will be shooting oneself in foot as the increased value will be a deterrent for other party to buy.
- Thus, well-intentioned JV will never flourish as the seeds of the failure are sowed in the structure itself.

Case Study 10.7: Contrasting Joint Venture Designs in Airline Industry

Details and Learning

	Jet-Etihad	Air-Asia & TATA
JV percentage by dominant partner	Etihad offering to buy 24% stake in Jet Airways.	Air Asia holding 49% and Tata sons holding 30% in the venture (rest was held by a private investor).
Who is in control	Jet Airways got a good deal because it was the dominant partner in the JV and was not losing out on much in terms of control. Etihad secured 24% without control but by paying control premium.	Air Asia using JV only for the reason that it cannot own majority percentage due to regulatory reason. While complying with 49% rule, it ensured it is in control by being the largest shareholder and splitting the Indian shareholders in lower percentage. In this way, it can be easy for it to buy out in future when the ownership percentage changes. They may very well have negotiated a call option at financial interest rate.
Partner strength	Strong partner. Thus, difficult to control and consolidate in future.	Tata just acted as a way for Air Asia to enter the Indian markets after the government deregulated and allowed 49% FDI in the Aviation sector. Thus, Air Asia will have free hand in operating the airlines.
Entity form	Publicly listed. Thus, buying out in future will entail open offer to minority shareholders.	Private. Thus, no open offer to minority and greater control over the entity.

Overall, Air Asia has designed the JV in a manner that meets the test of regulations at the same time, providing it an effective control over the operations of the company including the very important aspect of Branding viz. "Air Asia." Further, it had chosen the partners who have no ambition to be in the airline business as well as have the ability to buy them back based on private arrangement.

In case of Jet, the branding remains the same, the control does not seem to be there but control premium seems to have been paid for 24% stake. There cannot be private arrangement for future buyout and the partner is equally strong and in control of the operations.

Case Study 10.8: Navneet Publications Invests in K-12 Techno Services Pvt. Ltd.

Details and Learning

Navneet Publications Forays into School Management Services

Navneet Publications has forayed into school management services by investing Rs. 45 crores in Sequoia Capital-backed K-12 Techno Services Pvt. Ltd.

K-12 is a Hyderabad-based school management company servicing around 67 state board schools run by several trusts across Andhra Pradesh with over 50,000 students in the affordable education segment and run under the Gowtham Model Schools (GMS) and Orchids brands. In addition to state board schools, K-12 also manages eight junior colleges and an international school. K-12 had earlier raised capital from marquee investor-Sequoia Capital last year for expansion and consolidation of its activities in Andhra Pradesh. It was reported to sign management contracts with more than 15 schools at different locations in Andhra Pradesh. With this latest round of funding, K-12 aspires to launch its services across five different states and is targeting to manage over 200 schools in the near future.

Value Addition for Navneet

- **Access to 50,000 students** in an affordable school segment in Andhra Pradesh (AP).
- **Opportunity opened to service AP state board schools. This will lead to direct entry for Navneet and the expected sharing would be 25% while for K-12 it will 75% in Andhra Pradesh.**
- **School management co-model to be implemented in states of Maharashtra and Gujarat:** Navneet has a strong presence in the states of Maharashtra and Gujarat with good rapport with 30,000–40,000 schools. Navneet and K-12 will also work closely with schools in Maharashtra and Gujarat to extend school management services to schools in these states using Navneet's market strength and K-12's expertise in school management area. **The revenue sharing ratio in these two states is expected to be 50:50.**

- **Foray into Other States:** K-12 plans to launch its service across five different states and is targeting to manage over 200 schools in the next 3–4 years.

Is There a Value Addition for Navneet?

a. **Access to 67 schools now and 200 schools over 3–4 years?**

Navneet has been serving schools in the range of 30,000–40,000 through its educational publications. The incremental access of 67 school is very minute.

Investment of Rs. 45 crores? Controlling stake?

No controlling stake was mentioned. The business in an expansionist mode will require further capital dilution. The dilution of Navneet's stake will be higher unless it keeps reinvesting.

Alternatively, with Rs. 45 crore and control over the allocation of funds it could have spent that amount on advertising and distributors to reach a greater span of school and students.

10.6 Key Lessons in Structuring Joint Ventures

- Majority–minority JV has high degree of success. Exercise due diligence in choosing right and complementary partner.
- Equal JVs have high degree of failure unless the structure is designed in a manner to provide a driver seat to one of the partner. The pay-off is clear for the driver and the other partner.
- JVs are smart devices to create value by using the front of JV. So, one needs to be careful of the Trojan horses in JV deals.
- Equity dilution should be the last option. Always concentrate on value and not the cash flow.
- Beware of premium being paid over the market valuation.
- Understand the end game of the infuser and negotiate JV accordingly.
- Negotiate rights very carefully. Plan the scenario and negotiate terms of the JV accordingly. Always think why I am going to be a partner and why I am chosen to be a partner? What is the value being put on table? What is the pay-off for the same?
- Plan the scenario in a manner that you have a game plan and an exit plan.
- Entry premium and exit strategy. Negotiating put and call option are essential for value protection.
- Future capital requirement and maintenance of percentages will have to be negotiated well.
- Do maintain control over your the intellectual property.
- Reassess the value proposition and competitive position whenever the JV agreement comes up for re-negotiation.

The following checklist will help you understand the various legal terms and how to negotiate the same.

10.7 Designing of Joint Venture Agreement

a. Formulating JV

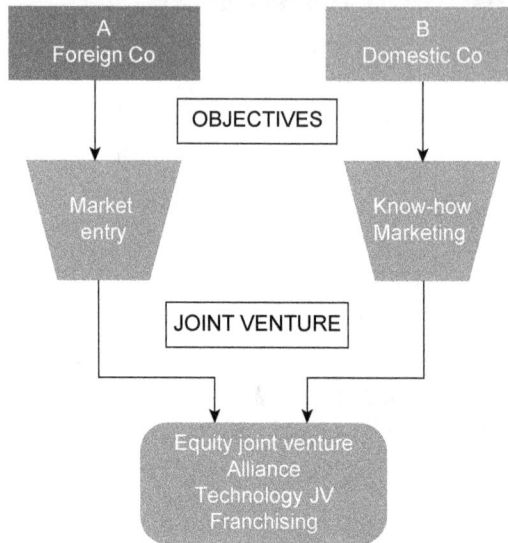

The structuring of the JV is the foundation of the JV that requires special consideration as described above. As stated above, "A" and "B" need to fill certain resources in their strategic plan. The objectives will determine what will be the structure of JV.

Equity venture: Participating in equity of JV is called as equity venture.

- Minority JV: (Coke taking minority position of 16.7% in Monster Beverage).
- Equal JV: (Wilmar Singapore and Promoters of Renuka Sugar taking 27% stake each in Renuka Sugar).
- Majority JV: Vistara in which 49% is held by Singapore and rest are held by Indian partners defines the majority JV.

Alliance

Alliance is described as the sharing of resources to share the cost of operations. Alliance is very loose and the working is also very loosely defined due to lack of ownership. Pharmaceutical companies get into alliance for drug development distribution. The best example of alliance will be the "Star Alliance" among the airlines in which they code share and share facilities for customers of alliance partners.

Technology know-how

These kinds of ventures rely on the royalty payment on peddling of technology by one partner who does not need it as much or is better off hawking its technology on royalty basis rather than taking equity risk of JV. The Bajaj and Kawasaki JV is an example of a technology know-how venture.

Franchising

This kind of venture can be referred to as the process in which the franchiser provides all the resources required to run the enterprise in form of branding, products, and the operating model. The franchisee needs to provide only the input capital and run the enterprise. These kind of models are prevalent with fast food chains such McDonalds, Starbucks, and Subway to name a few.

b. **Setting up of JV**

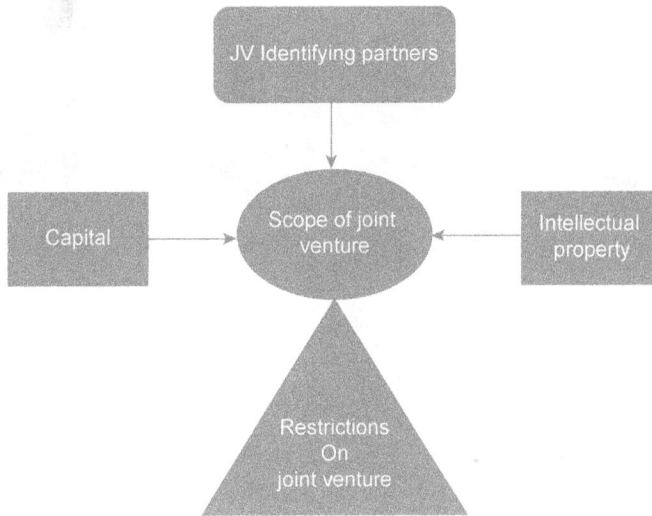

The steps involved in setting up of the JV is explained through the below case study.

Case Study 10.9: Vistara Airlines

Identifying the Partners: The JV setup initiates by finding complementary partners such as in case of "Vistara" the JV between Singapore Airlines and the Tata. Singapore Airlines was restricted by the foreign investment regulations not to hold more than 49% chose complementary partner in the form of "Tata" who can provide minority shareholding to meet the foreign investment norms and who have similar JV with Air Asia, but that will be addressed through non-conflict clause. Air Asia probably did not impose the restriction on Tata to enter into any other JV in the aviation sector.

Scope of JV: The JV is restricted to Indian domestic market and probably restricts Tata from the use of intellectual property as well as imposing strict confidentiality obligations given their similar JV with Air Asia.

Capital: The JV partners committed to invest Rs. 600 crores toward the venture.

Intellectual property: The entire intellectual property being contributed by Singapore Airlines will have had strict representations and warranties on the use of the intellectual property by the either parties.

c. **Structuring JV**

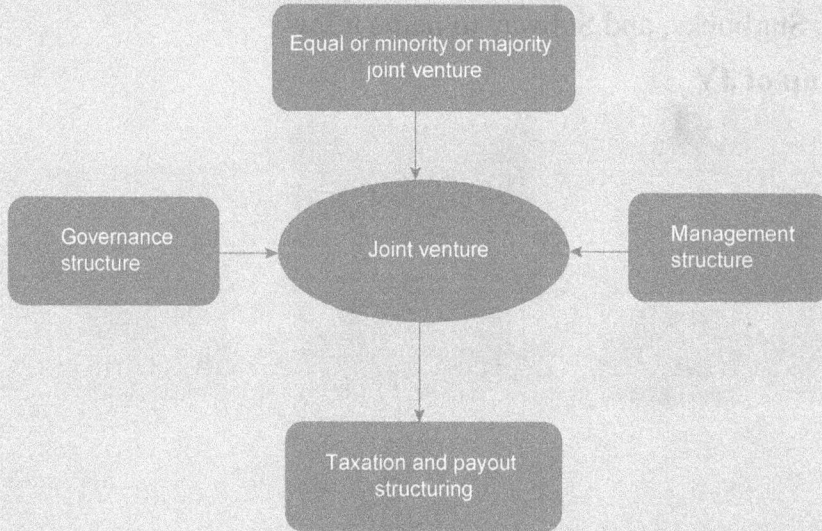

The steps involved in structuring of the JV is explained below:

Case Study 10.10: Jet-Etihad

Equal or majority or minority JV

The JV has been structured with Etihad owning 24% which was close to veto percentage of 26% but not having absolute veto as per Company Law requirement. The existing promoters of Jet own 51% and the rest was held by the public shareholders.

Governance structure

The JV governance structure was amended to meet the regulations. The existing promoters of Jet has four nominees, Ethiad having two nominees and rest six independent directors were appointed by the central governing committee.

The nomination committee comprised of five members with one each nominated by Promoters and Etihad and the remaining three members were appointed by the board.

With the above example, we can observe an elaborate structure to meet the regulations as well as trying to meet the demands of each of the JV partners to be able to have control over the decision-making body of the JV.

Illustrated by the fact that Mr. Naresh Goyal being the Chairman of the Board and the Company will not have a casting vote in case of a tie unlike the conventional role of the Chairman to break the tie.

Management structure

At least four directors are required to form the quorum for a board meeting with at least one nominee Director each of the Promoters and Etihad unless they waive their presence in writing.

Certain matters such as CEO appointment, matters related to share capital, amendment of memorandum and articles, and declaration of dividend were earlier designed to require approval of at least 3/4th of the directors. However, to meet regulatory approvals it was stipulated for approval by the simple majority.

Taxation structure

It is an important aspect especially if royalty and dividend payments are involved.

The other structural points that require attention are appointment of key managerial persons such as CEO, CFO, and other business heads including positions such as the legal head.

To have a better and independent oversight, special consideration should be taken into account for the appointment of auditors and internal auditors.

The above is further tightened by defining the role, responsibilities, and the reporting of such officers. The scope in some cases is also defined to delineate their executive powers and compensation along with the reports to be presented for evaluation at the board meetings.

The other key matters pertain to capital and assets of the JV namely the capital structure, future funding of JV, capital expenditure, and indebtedness and matters involving M&A and dividend restrictions.

a. **Legalizing JV**

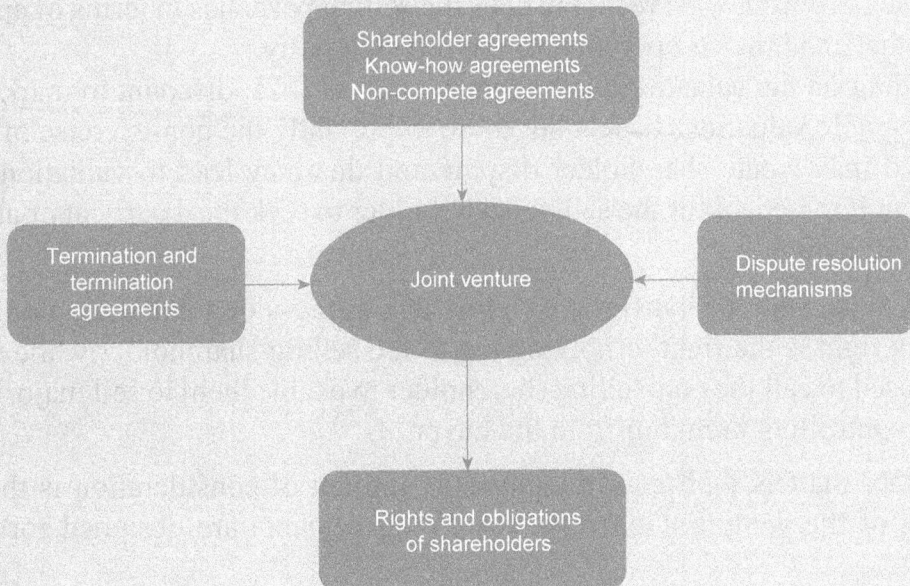

Legalizing the JV is very critical as the devil is in the detail. The key areas of the legalization are:

Agreements

There are various agreements that need to be executed and include shareholders agreement, know-how agreement, and non-compete agreement. Of all these agreements, the shareholder agreement is the most critical as that will essentially drive the JV.

The key aspects of the shareholder agreements from the point of view of operating include the JV and regulating the conduct of the shareholders inter-se. These aspects require close consideration not only from the point of view of stating the rights and obligations but also to be practical as to how they will be exercised.

For example, "Right of first refusal" although it follows the standard template one needs to be cognizant of valuation and timing, whether one of the parties have right to veto, to whom the shares can be sold in the event of non-exercise of right of first refusal etc.

Restricting the selling shareholder from creating overhang on the stock price or creating adverse effect on the stock price are some of the practical issues that arise from the intention of transfers and need careful consideration and articulation.

The key points to be kept in mind with respect to the right of first refusal are:

- The content and delivery of the notice.
- Pricing and valuation of such offer.
- The time period of exercise and the right of other party to seek valuation advise in case of non-agreement.
- Modalities on acceptance or refusal.
- In case of refusal, what recourse does the selling party has in terms of approaching others and the co-operation of the refusing party.
- Deciding on the valuation methodology such as DCF, discount to market price, comparable valuations basket but more importantly the non-exercise of right of refusal may create shareholder dispute and this may lead to valuation hit and make it impractical for the selling shareholder to seek third party at or above the same valuation.

Attached to the right of transfer are rights such as tag-along and drag-along rights. Tag-along right is the right to holding tag to the selling shareholder while the drag along is used to call the non-selling shareholder to enable them to sell majority stake and take controlling premium from the buyer.

The other matters that require equivalent amount of consideration is the future financing of the venture. Generally, the JV agreements are designed for happier times and do not take into account the scenario wherein it may enquire losses and requires constant or substantial cash infusion to keep it running. The mounting losses can make the parties dither and the JV may come to standstill. Thus, the agreements need to be designed to deal with these eventualities as well.

The other issues would be dispute resolution mechanisms viz. jurisdiction, arbitration etc., exit and termination rights and conditions alongside that non-compete and non-poaching agreements.

Case Study 10.11: Minority Investing

Wilmar to Buy stake in Shree Renuka Sugars

Details

Singapore's Wilmar International took 27% stake in the heavily indebted Shree Renuka Sugars giving it a foothold in the world's biggest sugar-consuming market.

Wilmar International is one of the large market cap Singapore company having interest in Palm plantations and sugar. On the other hand, Shree Renuka is the largest sugar refiner in India.

The other promoters of Shree Renuka Sugar hold 27% and the remaining 45% is held by public shareholders.

Shree Renuka Sugar at the peak of sugar cycle in 2008–2009 acquired sugar plantation and sugar refining companies in Brazil.

The downward trend in sugar prices left it gasping under the debt taken for acquisition and was in the need of equity infusion.

It also provided a perfect opportunity for a big player like Wilmar to set afoot in the Indian market which is the largest sugar consumption market.

Key Learning

The questions that need to be answered are:

What benefit does a minority non-controlling 27% stake bring to the table. It could have bought control or bought controlling stake in some other sugar company.

The above case highlights the need to understand pay-off from minority investing. It is certainly not the end game for Wilmar in terms of call option to take control or the ability to consolidate the results of this entity in its financial.

On the facts of the case known, it does not seem to be better alternative for investing in sugar assets in the absence of control and ability to consolidate full the financials of the underlying company.

SGX Buys 5% Stake in BSE

Details

Singapore Exchange (SGX), in 2007, acquired 5% equity for Rs. 189 crores or $42.7 million.

In return for this 5% stake, both the parties agreed to explore opportunities in various areas relating to listings and product development, while leveraging on SGX's leading position as a regional hub for derivatives and international listings and BSE's strong presence in India.

SGX got a one board seat on BSE for its 5% stake. Subsequently, in the year 2011 SGX wrote-off its investment in BSE.

Key Learning

The case highlights:

a. The perils of minority investing with no backup to consolidate the stake or exit mechanism or having suitable mechanism to pursue the investment.
b. Trading equity investment for operational business matters is not the right business approach. Business matters have their own currency and saleability that can be traded for equity reasons.

Coca-Cola's Two Step Strategy from Minority to Majority Ownership

Coca-Cola Co. has generally been buying companies in two stages that comprise of a minority stake to start with and followed by complete buyout or majority ownership in two years time.

This approach is a risk mitigation exercise due to existence of downside of valuations running up in the future due to the attractiveness of the industry that would mean a larger bill for later stake enhancement.

So, the above approach will mean:

- Less cash upfront
- Option value on investment
- Backing the option value with put and call to either exit or enhance the stake
- Mitigating financial and business risk
- Evaluate the business from close quarters

Recently, Coca Cola bought 16.7% stake in Monster Beverage Corp. for USD 2.5 billion and got two directors on Monster's board. Monster is a manufacturer of popular energy drinks.

In return, Coke will get access to Monster's non-energy brands, such as Hansen's Natural Sodas and Peace Tea. On the other hand, Monster will get Coke's energy brands, which include NOS and Full Throttle as well as access to Coke's extensive distribution system.

Energy drinks have been mired in controversies and have been object of litigation.

Thus, minority investing will give it a wait-and-watch approach with downside of investing at a later date at higher value.

Coke has made similar minority investments in companies such as Honest Tea and Zico Beverages, the maker of coconut water and bought them out later. It followed similar step increase in Keurig Green Mountain Inc., a single-service coffee brewing company by initial 10% and then raising it to 16% later.

Key Learning

Thus, it appears to have developed a calibrated strategy of minority investing approach and does not seem to be ad-hoc, unlike the other two cases discussed above.

Case Study 10.12: Joint Venture between Singapore Airline and Virgin Atlantic

Details

Singapore Airlines ("SIA") and owners of Virgin Atlantic formed a JV in 1999 by acquiring 49% stake in Virgin holding company. The owners of Virgin Atlantic retained 51% stake in the JV.

SIA paid US $965 million (SGD 1.6 billion) to acquire the 49% stake. The shareholders agreement provided for seven board seats out of which four were to be nominated by Virgin and three to by SIA. The quorum for decisions of the board shall comprise two VTL directors and one SIA director. Decisions were taken by simple majority. SIA possessed veto rights over certain decisions of the JV.

The JV was done with the intent of SIA to secure more landing rights at Heathrow and other places in Europe. The complementary nature of the business dominance of SIA (Asia) and Virgin (Europe) was supposed to be a win–win for both the parties.

After a decade of JV, eventually, in the year 2012, SIA sold its 49% stake in Virgin Atlantic for US$360 million ($440 million) to US carrier Delta Air Lines.

Thereby, taking a write down of half a billion US$ and SGD 1billion.

Questions on the above JV:

a. Comment on the design of JV
b. Why the JV was never supposed to take-off from strategic point of view.
c. Comment on the valuation of JV and the opportunity cost.
d. Can it be said that the JV was under joint control.
e. Comment on whether the valuation reflected joint control.
f. Could control or valuation have been better negotiated?

10.8 Executive Summary

The chapter explains the various nuances of JV. It goes into the academic discussions on the reasons for JVs and also the practical aspects of JVs starting from partner selection to decision-making structure of JV. The case studies also illustrate the need to ascertain the real value of JV and not necessarily the equity value. In some of the case studies, we have seen how the value flow has been contrary to the flow of cash.

Through case studies, we have discussed the designing and structuring of JVs, which will help in designing and negotiating the JVs.

Understanding of JVs is critical as it completes the number heavy side of M&A and will help the practioners to hone the other skillsets paramount to executing successful M&As.

11

The Takeover Code

Contents

11.1 Introduction

The takeover code by the name itself fascinates as a device to craft acquisitions. It is described as a skill that is needed to be known, if persons or entities aspire to transact majority stakes.

The fundamental principle on which the takeover codes rests is fair and equitable to the minority shareholders and it is the premise on which the rules and regulations of the takeover have been enacted.

It is very essential to distill this principle to the readers of this book as it has been rarely observed that buyer or seller rests their case on the basis of this principle. The entire deal is crafted around the takeover regulations to suit the needs of the buyer or majority seller and the treatment of the minority shareholders come in as last piece in the deal and for the purpose of doing bare minimum compliance with the letter of law and not the spirit behind it.

It is rare to see a law which initiates by saying that the interest of the minority is the fundamental principle based on which this law has been enacted.

However, it provides the opportunity to buy the entire stake of the promoter, but only 20% of the public shareholding or as stated in the latest amendment 26%. Thus, an open offer price is offered to the public shareholders, which is much belabored in its calculation and is never the offer price that is received by the public shareholders. This is due to the acceptance ratio being just 26% of the total public shareholding. For example: If the public shareholding is 100 shares, the open offer is for only 26 shares and if you own 10 shares then, only 2.6 shares will receive the open offer price.

The stress on the principle and the inequity in the enacted code is being accentuated to provide a perspective of the students of M&A of the turf of the takeover code and how the players are arraigned.

Depending on the degree of belief you have in corporate governance, you can craft your takeover around the takeover code for the betterment of the deal, to the betterment of the minority shareholders or to the betterment of your own self.

11.2 Key Trigger Points of the Takeover Code

As a student, it is difficult to remember the trigger points and so we will try and put it in the most simple language.

The takeover code gets triggered mainly for the acquisition of more than 25% voting rights in a company.

The above could be achieved through either direct or indirect acquisition. Voting rights is the key and for the same reason, when HSBC had made an announcement for the acquisition of UTI Bank (now Axis bank), it was asked to withdraw because nobody can acquire more than 10% voting rights in a bank as per the extant banking laws.

Another condition involves the acquisition of control over the target company. However, it is rare to observe an acquisition of control over a company without the acquisition of 25% or more voting rights in a company.

The Indian takeover code is the only one which has the "control" trigger and goes on to give a vague definition of what constitutes control.

The Jet-Etihad deal went into the above controversy. If somebody had control but lack economic right of 25% shareholding, then, it is up to the person to work hard without having economic right in the company. There could be allegation of diversion of profits through control; however, there are various ways in which this is already being done through transfer pricing, royalty arrangements, technical part-nerships, etc.

The salient features of the takeover code are discussed in the chapter later. We will use this space to understand much better the nuances of how to and how not to deal with the takeover code.

11.3 Learning the Craft of the Takeover Code

We will lay down the rules to understand the craft, which even a non-lawyer can assimilate to do the needful while facing a deal with the takeover code.

1. Understand the main triggers of the takeover code;
2. Look at rest of the regulations which follow from this main triggers;
3. Search for the exemptions given from the takeover code;
4. Find the "proviso" to main clauses which are sort of exemption from the main clause "Provided" you to meet certain conditions.

Then, the rest of the game is mix-n-match. A better understanding of the above stated rules will assist people in mastering the takeover code. Try reading from last to start or bottom to top as like pearls which lie at the bottom of the sea, the exemptions and provision lie at the bottom of the clause or the regulations.

After accomplishing the aforementioned points, the rest is just a gaming issue as how to arrange yourself to either exempt yourself from the takeover code or trigger it when you want or get the best out of these requirements.

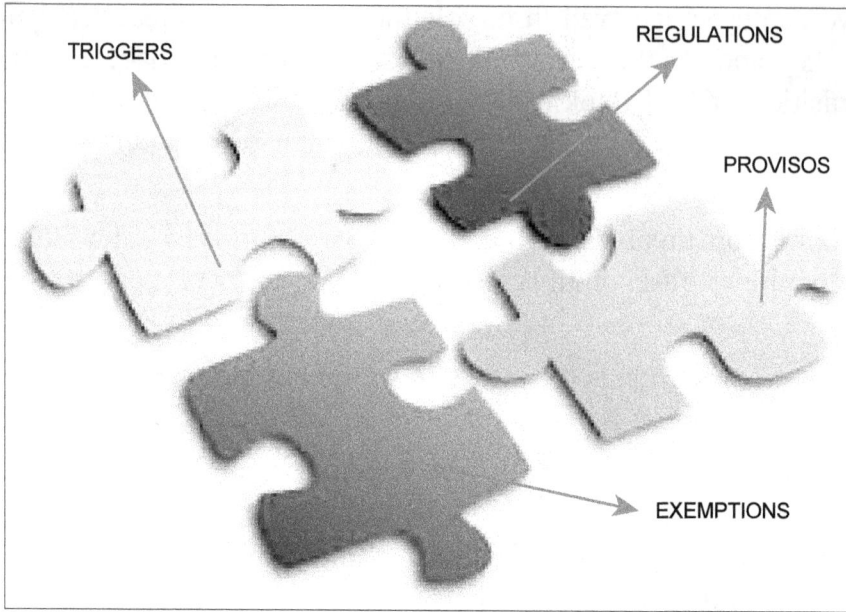

Case Study 11.1: E*Trade Acquisition of IL&FS Investsmart

Details

The below case study of acquisition of IL&FS Investsmart (which was taken over by HSBC later) highlights the use of the above rules. During this period, the take-over code exempted acquisition of GDRs from the takeover code unless they were converted into shares carrying voting rights to avoid triggering the takeover code and pay a very high price for the open offer. IL&FS Investsmart had outstanding GDR program, the acquirer being foreigner picked the majority stake in the target company through the GDRs with no open offer and reporting requirement that is required as per the takeover code from 5% onward. They waited for a period of 6 months so that, their acquisition price is not one of the factors based on which the open offer price is determined. E-trade converted its GDR into shares and made an announcement for the open offer to complete the formality of acquisition of voting rights directly in their name.

Key Learning

The given case study represents the use of exemptions provided in the code to craft the takeover of IL&FS Investsmart.

Category	30-Sep-05 % Holding	30-Dec-05 % Holding	30-Mar-06 % Holding	30-Jun-06 % Holding	30-Sep-06 % Holding	31-Dec-06 % Holding	31-Mar-07 % Holding
Indian Promoters	46.81	31.63	29.58	29.58	29.58	29.58	29.36
Foreign Promoters	0						43.85
Sub-Total	46.81	31.63	29.58	29.58	29.58	29.58	
E*Trade	11.14	7.53	7.04	7.04	7.04	7.04	0.00%
GDR	35.32	58.62	19	17.53	31.52	31.52	0

11.4 Commonly Used Exemptions

Another commonly used exemption from the takeover code is the mergers or demergers under the scheme of arrangement as per the Companies Act. It is relatively easier to get all the approvals by majority resolution at Annual General Meeting (AGM) or Extraordinary General Meeting (EGM) and the Courts, which go by the majority rule principle, then through process of takeover done under takeover code. Further, the level of disclosures required therein are comparatively less onerous.

The above is off-shoot of the stress the law makers put into drafting the main clause that by the time the drafting of exemptions and the provisions steps in, there is already fatigue and they are not well-conceived leading to exploitation of loop holes through use of provisions and exemptions.

Case Study 11.2: Sterlite v/s Alcan—Battle for INDAL

Details & Learning

One of the earliest battles in the takeover code around the exemptions was the hostile battle for Indian Aluminum Company (INDAL) between Sterlite and Alcan (Canada).

Sterlite had proposed issue of shares of Sterlite as a part of the offer consideration, which was subject to receipt of shareholders approval under the Companies Act.

As per the extant takeover code, the open offer can be withdrawn among other conditions on non-receipt of the statutory approvals. Sterlite having lost the battle for INDAL withdrew the offer, citing the non-receipt of shareholders approval being a statutory approval.

The battle went for a decade between SEBI and Sterlite. However, the point to be noticed is the efficacy of exemptions or provisions in the regulations.

Case Study 11.3: Takeover of Listed Company using Most of the Exemptions

Details & Learning

The present case highlights how exemptions can be effectively used to complete takeover without any open offer to the shareholders. The case involves one of the big corporate house and control over a listed company, which was not previously under its control but, under the control of different family within the group. The takeover virtually utilized all the exemptions provided in the takeover code to complete the acquisition and control of the listed entity with sizeable undervalued real estate as part of its assets.

Exemptions	Transaction
Inter-se transfer of shares among relatives as defined under the Companies Act.	Transfer of shares of intermediate holding company done from grandfather to grandson of below 5%. Hence, no reporting required.
Inter-se transfer of shares among group as defined under the monopolistic and restrictive trade practices MRTP Act.	The mentioned 5% shares are then transferred from the individual to one of the group companies. Hence, no reporting required.
The change of control done through special resolution vide postal ballot.	One of the group companies acquired control through the special resolution.
Acquisition through rights issue exempted for entities already in control.	Rights issue done and under subscription picked up by the Group Company and became majority owner and controller of the intermediate holding company.
All reporting done post the control having been seized to formalize the takeover.	Acquisition of control over the underlying listed company and change of board of directors carried out at the listed company level.

Case Study 11.4: Crafting Takeover Offer in Face of Heated Market: EDS Acquisition of BFL Mphasis

Details

Electronic Data System (EDS) which was later taken over by HP made an open offer for the acquisition of BFL Mphasis, now rechristened as HP-Mphasis.

The above case study represents the beautiful use of the not so often used clauses of the takeover code. The conditional offer clause is rarely used. In the given case, it was used with such a deadly effect that kept the market guessing. In a bullish market, they could conclude the offer without any rise in the share price. In fact, the market price stayed at nearly 5% discount to the offer price throughout the offer, making the offer attractive to the shareholders resulting in the offer getting over-subscribed.

Background

Generally, if there is a takeover by a multinational, there is steep rise in the market price of the target company as well as there is premium sought for control. In case of Mphasis, the control was with management shareholders having ~8% shareholding. Barings private equity although, not controlling but, was the single largest shareholder, holding 34%. This offer represents a perfect example of negotiation by controlling shareholders as well as minority shareholders in a single dimension and controlling the offer without giving too much premium and keeping the markets guessing about the outcome.

Facts of the Case

EDS made a **conditional open offer** to acquire majority stake in Mphasis BFL Limited, a leading applications and business process outsourcing (BPO) services company based in Bangalore, India, for Rs. 204.5 (approximately US $4.58) per share in cash, pursuant to Indian securities regulations. The given price represents an approximate 30% premium to the 26-week average price of Mphasis.

*The offer will be **contingent** upon EDS acquiring 83 million shares representing approximately 52% of the current outstanding shares. If at least 83 million shares are not tendered in the offer, EDS will not accept any shares tendered.*

Case Analysis

The ALL or NONE offer for control at reasonable premium of 30% kept the management shareholders happy enough not to ask for premium. It also conveyed a strict message to the market that EDS was not interested in acquiring any share if it failed to garner 52% at Rs. 205; this kept the market price in check.

Thus, the major shareholder could not demand higher price based on the market price later in the deal. This also kept the speculators or manipulators at bay and kept the price in check as there was serious risk that they would be saddled with share at high price if EDS does not increase the share price.

Thus, in the view of the above fact, the EDS offer price looked attractive as compared to the ruling Mphasis share price.

The major shareholding percentage was 42%, the conditional offer was pegged at 52%, a delta of 10%, good enough delta to keep the speculators at bay. Hence, EDS only had to bet on the additional 10% tendering out of the remaining 58% shareholders. They would have had shake hands with the major shareholders on tendering their 42% shares in the offer, otherwise, they would not have proceeded with the due diligence and the offer.

Result

The above case resulted in the largest institutional shareholder in Mphasis Baring India Pvt. Ltd. off-loading its entire stake of 34.73% in Mphasis through an open offer. Apart from Baring, a couple of key officials of Mphasis have also offered to sell their stake in the open offer. Given the premium to the market price, the offer got over-subscribed.

EDS then announced a follow-on open offer (the "Offer") to acquire an additional 20% of Mphasis BFL Limited ("Mphasis") for Rs. 204.5 per share in cash.

Earlier, EDS acquired a majority ownership stake (approximately 52%) in Mphasi through a conditional open offer for Rs. 204.5 per share. Due to the significant over-subscription of the offer, a portion of the shares tendered had to be returned pursuant to Indian securities regulations.

This offer provided a follow-on liquidity opportunity for all shareholders including those whose tendered shares were partially returned in the conditional open offer.

Therefore, the above case study elucidates the alluring design of a takeover offer at the time of adverse condition not by a mere vanilla offer but an appealing offer that treated all shareholders impartially.

Key Learning

What worked for EDS?

The biggest advantage that EDS had was the absence of competitive bid and reasonable major shareholders and the absence of financial institutions that are loathe to tender in an ambiguous offer for the fear of being scrutinized. Further, a decent premium and clear message that it would walk away if they did not show interest in the given price also worked in the favor of EDS.

Why conditional offer did not work for Bombay Dyeing in case of Ahmedabad Electric Company (AEC)?

The presence of competitive bid for AEC was one of the major factors for the above question. The offer prices were at discount and there was sizeable financial institutional shareholding.

Why should practioners of takeovers look out for clauses like the "Conditional Offer" clause?

"Conditional offer" to some extent allows conditioning of the market. It allows the offeror to pass clear unambiguous messages to the market. Further, it also allows the offeror to prescribe conditionality at certain threshold and unconditionality at higher threshold.

Open offer by ITW Signode, USA for ITW Signode India, wherein it was holding 51% prescribed 29% conditional offer and unconditional open offer for the balance 49%. Thus, allowing it to achieve at least certain minimum threshold before making it unconditional.

The conditional offer can prescribe acceptance lower than the minimum 26% open offer condition. Last, it presents the acquirer with the option to make it unconditional or revise the open offer price as well.

International credit rating agency, Moody's has revised its conditional open offer price to raise its holding in ICRA from 28.5% to up to 55% to Rs. 2400 per share, up 20% compared to its previous offer of Rs. 2000 per share made 3 months ago.

The offer is conditional upon Moody's picking a minimum number of shares which would give it at least 50% holding in India's second largest rating agency.

The point that is being stressed by the author is the latitude offered by kind of clauses to the takeover artistes to draft their takeovers. Thus, it is being urged to be innovative and make most of the exemptions, provisos, and clauses which give latitude to keep the markets within your control.

11.5 Hostile Takeovers and Defence Mechanisms Peculiar to Indian Scene

The hostile takeover in Indian turf has been far and few compared to the western geography because most of the companies are controlled by the promoters with 50% plus shareholding. Even, if not, they exercise control over the board of directors to frustrate any hostile attempt to takeover. Third, there is always a white knight in the form of financial institution which will generally side with management. Last, foreigners are not present because such purchases require approval from the government, which in a hostile environment is tough to come through. The prime example of this situation is demonstrated between Swaraj Paul and Escorts in early 1980s. Thus, virtually all battles have been between Indian parties.

Indian takeover scene has no defensive mechanisms like the poison pill, suicide pill, Pacman, greenmail, proxy war or crown jewel, etc., that exists in the western market.

Indian corporate has developed their local defensive mechanisms akin to the great Indian rope trick.

The great Indian rope trick defensive mechanism in the Indian takeover scene is as described below:

- Poking legal holes in an open offer made by the hostile bidder. The takeover regulations are loosely drafted. So, start challenging legal grounds and eligibility for the offer followed by challenging the inadequacy of disclosures or misstatements in the announcements.
- Writing open letters to SEBI, alleging irregularity and delay in the open offers. Every letter to SEBI needs response from the manager to the offer. Use the delayed time to start digging more or frustrate the bidder. This time value starts getting reflected in the share price of the target company. It may at times flag, use it to either build stake, or keep it beyond the bidder's price.
- Challenge the open offer by raising procedural issues of inequity and how the open offer price is not correctly calculated and challenge the open offer price. This is the easiest defense as the open offer calculation rests only on the market price. Therefore, they can always challenge that it does not reflect the true value and how the price by other valuation methodology is much higher. Even provided mechanisms like non-compete in the regulations fee have been successfully challenged.
- Getting injunctions from the court on the open offer, which is very easy to get from the remotest place in India.
- Raking up dirt on the bidders not connected to the open offer in question and complaining to SEBI.
- Alleging irregularity by the bidder. The most important link here is the definition of "person acting in concert" and "person deemed to be acting in concert." This brings within its ambit a large number of entities and given the splintered holdings that Indian promoters have, there is always some slip up somewhere and there are multitude of reporting requirements. This can be studied and exposed for further frustrating the bidder.
- Use all of the above with the help of media to create negative publicity and pressure on the regulators to go slow on the open offer.
- The material documents to be kept for inspection are very minimal and rarely looked into. Either there can be complaint of inadequacy of documents or match the disclosures in the announcement or offer letter with the disclosures in the documents kept for inspection.

- Last, the financial institutions or block shareholders. If you can induce them to side by you by hook or crook then, it acts as the final straw that breaks the camel back.

The above defense mechanisms are not only employed in hostile bids but also in situation in which the corporate rivalry is being settled through guerilla warfare.

The hostility results in the increased price for the bid resistor and if minority shareholders have the time and patience to withstand the delay. The bidder emerges bruised through the takeover battle.

Some of the hostile bids and the defensive mechanisms used:

Deals	Defense	Effect
Shri Vishnu Cement &Raasi Cement	• Persons acting in concert with the acquirer not disclosed by one of the bidder. • Court injunctions.	The bidder paid at least nine times higher price as compared to the fair value of the target.
Acquisition of one of the family's stake in Asian paints by ICI	• Allegation of violation of foreign investment rules by ICI, needing prior permission from FIPB.	ICI failed in its attempt to acquire the stake in Asian paints as also from there on even secondary purchase by foreigners required permission from the Target's board. Although, it was only intended for issue of shares.
Arun Bajoria (hostile bidder)-Bombay Dyeing	• Allegation of violation of reporting requirement of 5% initial stake in Bombay Dyeing.	Open offer bid for Bombay Dyeing by Arun Bajoria rejected. However, the technical requirement of reporting could have been penalized differently.
Emami- Zandu Pharma	• One of the co-major shareholder alleged violation of the joint venture agreement between the two major shareholders. Violation of SEBI takeover code and SEBI insider trading regulations. • Court filings.	The hostile major shareholder walked away with a higher price of INR 16,500 against the first seller price of INR 6,900. The takeover bill for the bidder rose from 350 to 750 crores.

Dalmiya (hostile bid)- GESCO Corporation	• Alleged violations of the takeover code and reporting requirements. • Upping the ante on the hostile bidders. • Bringing in white knight as person acting in concert to fight the hostile bid.	• Hostile bidder walking away with arbitrage gain rather than control. • White knight turns out to be not so white and walks away with the company rechristened as Mahindra Lifestyle.
Damani (hostile bid)- VST Industries	• Court injunctions. • Violations of Securities law. • Delaying the open offer by making allegation against the acquirer.	• Open offer opens by delay. • Allows BAT and ITC to step in to counter the bid. • The hostile bidder fails to wrest control.
Grasim's bid to acquire L&T	• Alleged violation of the open offer price by Grasim post- acqui-sition of the Reliance stake in L&T. • Media raked up against the bid by Grasim to acquire L&T. • Pitched battle through SEBI & media.	• Grasim drops the bid to acquire L&T. • Negotiates later through intermediaries for acquisition of only the cement division of L&T.

Likewise, there are several unchallenged clauses in the takeover code which can be exploited in a hostile bid. With the help of above examples, we have made an attempt to illustrate the effectiveness of hostility.

11.6 Hostile Takeover and Competing Bids in Indian Context

There is subtle difference in hostile takeover and competing bids. Hostile takeover are the ones in which the target company resists the acquisition, while the competing bids in other cases make the takeover hostile.

In Indian context, the competing bids have been very far and few and in most of the cases, it has resulted in an arbitrage played by the bidder initiator exploiting the undervalued asset. In Indian context, it has been mostly the value of real estate that has not been captured in the market cap. If we look at the Abhishek Dalmiya takeover of GESCO or Arun Bajoria's attempt to takeover Bombay Dyeing or the Forbes Gokak offer was the cold fallback on the real estate, if the takeover succeeded to eventually cash out through sale of real estate.

Unlike the western hostile takeovers or takeovers by activist investors, the end game in Indian context has been to sell out the acquired stake to the other bidder and make a killing in the process.

Case Study 11.4: Corporate Raiders of India Inc.—GESCO

Details

The takeover offer for GESCO presents all elements of general corporate warfare. GESCO was a company engaged in real estate. In early 2000, when the real estate market was in slumber, the market cap of the company was mere INR 23 crores having promoter holding of sheer 15%.

Abhishek Dalmiya sensing the arbitrage started accumulating the share of the Company in open market and quietly acquired around 10% stake in the company at average price of Rs. 18 per share and announced an open offer for 45% of GESCO, which will give it a majority at Rs. 23 per share and steadily increasing it Rs. 27 per share.

The prospect of losing control led the existing promoter to make a counter bid and roping in the white knight to thwart the bid. There was counter offer made by the promoters with a Mahindra group affiliate joining in as person acting in concert at Rs. 36 per share. The competing bids made the share price jump for the target that allowed the bidders to reach settlement and Abhishek Dalmiya cashed out his 10.5% stake at Rs. 54 per share a three times profit.

Eventually, the white knight swallowed GESCO and today stands christened as Mahindra Lifestyle Ltd.

Key Learning

The above case highlights the following learning:

a. The successful exploitation of arbitrage between market price and underlying asset price.
b. The successful exploitation of low promoter holding.
c. The 10% acquisition was analogous to option premium being paid and generated eventually an asymmetric return trade-off for the bidder.
d. Skilful plotting of the takeover bid. Raising the bid price and making an offer to gain majority control to get on the nerves of the counter bidder.
e. Finally, the most important lesson is that white knight is not so white.

Case Study 11.5: Corporate Raiders of India Inc.—Zandu

Details

Zandu Pharmaceutical, the maker of the well-known "Zandu balm" was being managed by two families the "Vaidyas" and the "Parikhs" roughly holding equal stake of ~23% each. The families were not getting along and the company was unable to perform well financially although they had a well-known brand.

Zandu also had a prized real estate in the heart of Mumbai. Because of the share holder in fighting the market price of the company was not reflective of the brand potential of the company.

The entry of corporate raider from the eastern India viz. Emami, buying the Vaidyas at Rs. 6900 per share setting into motion a hostile bid for Zandu.

The other shareholder Parikh's digged in and started the classical Indian defence mechanism alleging violations of various laws such as:

- The acquisition was made on two successive dates of 10% and 12%. They alleged the takeover code was triggered on the first date.
- The selling shareholder being an insider was violating the insider trading regulations.
- They had the first right of refusal over the shares sold by Vaidyas.
- The violation of corporate law by Emami.

The whole imbroglio resulted in the share price going up in the market and thwarting the bid of Emamis. They eventually bought over the Parikhs at Rs. 16,500 per share and the takeover bill going up to Rs. 750 Crore.

Key Learning

The above case highlights the following learning:

a. Successful defence by launching shark repellent technique.
b. The selling shareholder viz. Vaidya's failure to protect their value by not putting a clause that if there is eventual acquisition at a higher price; they will get the higher price also.
c. The importance of real estate in launching a hostile takeover.

11.7 The Antidote on the Great Indian Rope Trick

The antidote on the great Indian rope trick in theory is simple but difficult in practice. It requires a very holistic approach, starting with basing the takeover or response on the principles of the takeover code. This requires measured approach that would make you avoid shortcuts and be ripped apart.

The next step is to use the takeover code like an artiste uses the various clauses of it effectively to have a backup to support various positions being taken. The keystone for any takeover offer is the offer price and the trigger date. Do take time to validate and get opinion on the trigger date and the offer price. Most offers are contested on the offer price. Quite a few offerors have got the offer price wrong because of the misinterpretation of the trigger date.

After analyzing, put together the takeover code, the standard format of public announcement, and various submission forms. The forms and the formats carry the expression of the regulators intent and need to be taken seriously and read in harmony with the takeover code.

Engage good investment bankers who can engage with the regulators formally and informally. If needed, they are capable to conduct informal purchase of the regulators on the gray area.

Try and use the expertise and resources of the sellers also in dealing with the regulators and media.

Do have comprehensive media policy and competitive evaluation of the various elements involved in the transaction.

Last, but not the least, follow the spirit, try and build options and flexibility in the deal, thereby crafting a beautiful response to any hostility or launching a bid to successful completion.

11.8 Salient Features of the Takeover Code

Principles (Source: SEBI Takeover code)

The takeover regulations are premised on the principles of fairness, equity, and transparency based on the following fundamental objectives:

- To provide a transparent legal framework for facilitating takeover activities;
- To protect the interests of shareholders in securities and the securities market, taking into account that the acquirer and the other shareholders need a fair, equitable, and transparent framework to protect their interests;
- To balance the various, and at times, conflicting objectives and interests of various stakeholders in context with the substantial acquisition of shares and takeovers of listed companies;
- To provide each shareholder an opportunity to exit its investment in the target company when a substantial acquisition of shares in, or takeover of, a target company takes place, on terms that are not inferior to the terms on which substantial shareholders exit their investments;
- To provide acquirers with a transparent legal framework to acquire shares in, or control of, the target company and to make an open offer;

- To ensure that the affairs of the target company are conducted in the ordinary course when a target company is the subject matter of an open offer;
- To ensure that fair and accurate disclosure of all material information is made by persons responsible for making them to various stakeholders to enable them to take informed decisions;
- To regulate and provide for fair and effective competition among acquirers desirous of taking over the same target company; and
- To ensure that only those acquirers who are capable of actually fulfilling their obligations under the takeover regulations make open offers.

Important Definitions

- Acquirer is defined as the person acquiring either by himself or through persons acting in concert acquires directly or indirectly either through voting rights or control over the target company. The acquisition of voting rights are of the following types:

  - Wherein the acquirer by himself or persons acting in concert acquires more than 25% voting rights.
  - Wherein the acquirer by himself or persons acting in concert holding more than 25% voting rights in a financial year acquires more than 5% voting rights.

The above can be categorized as mandatory offers, offers which are triggered due to acquisition of voting rights above certain threshold or acquisition of control.

The other category of offers is "voluntary offers." These are the offers in which the existing shareholder wishes to raise his stake through open offer.

- Control is defined as the right to appoint majority of directors or control the management of the company by virtue of shareholding or agreement or management rights or in any other manner. Thus, shareholders who are single largest although not having shareholding greater than 25% can also be called to be in control of the company.

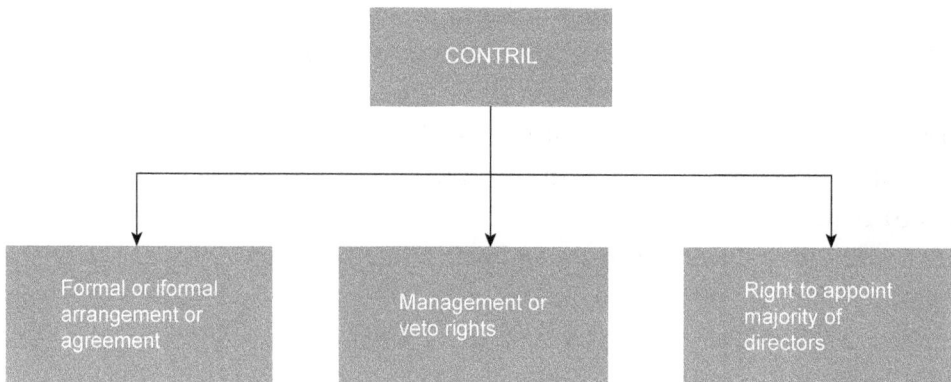

- Person acting in concert are defined as the persons who come together with a common objective of acquiring substantial share or control over the target company. The agreement to act together can be either explicit or implicit.
- There are certain categories of deemed PACs, unless proved to the contrary. Thus, directors or relatives of the acquirer or merchant bankers are also deemed as persons acting in concert. Due to the aforesaid definition, in case of the hostile takeover of INDAL. The shares were acquired by the merchant banker on behalf of the foreign promoter viz. Alcan in capacity of deemed PACs.

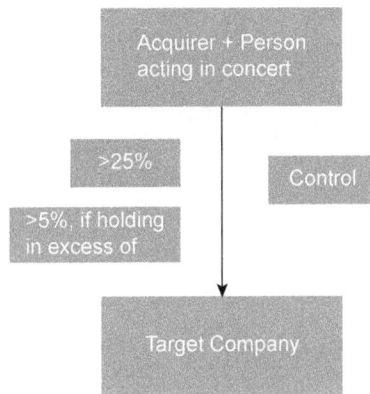

Applicability of the Code

- While we have already discussed the applicability of the takeover code to the direct acquisition there are cases where it applies to indirect acquisition as well. Indirect acquisitions are described as the acquisition in which there is either substantial acquisition or acquisition of a company holding substantial shares or control over the target company.

The above acquisition covers global acquisition as well where the target company happens to be >80% of the value of the global company it will be termed as direct acquisition.

The above refers to the qualitative and quantitative assessment of the trigger. Generally, acquiring control or greater than 50% shareholding in the holding company which is either having controlling shareholding or control will result in the trigger of the takeover code.

Thus, acquisition of 49% in holding company which is controlled by 51% shareholder exercising control over the target company may not result in the trigger of the code unless the 51% and 49% shareholder agree to control the holding company.

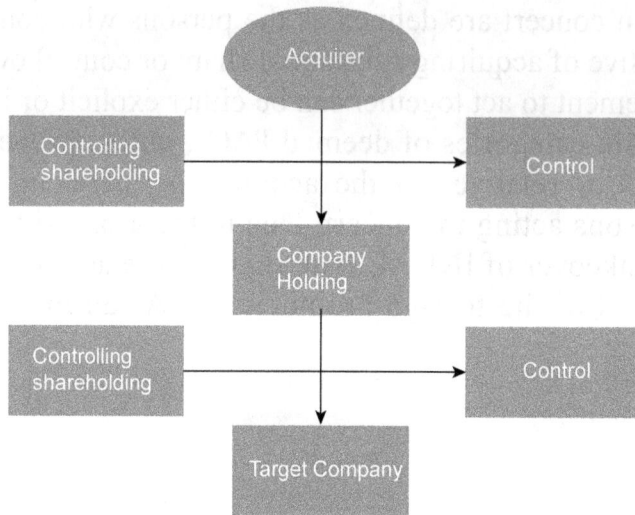

Offer Requirements

Open Offer Process

Offer Price

The offer price is generally the highest of the following:

- The negotiated price arrived at between buyer and seller;
- The volume-weighted average price paid or payable by the acquirer/ PACs during the 52 weeks immediately preceding the date of the tender offer;
- The highest price paid by the acquirer/PACs for any acquisition during the 26 weeks immediately preceding the date of the tender offer;
- If the shares are frequently traded, the volume-weighted average market price during the 60 trading days immediately preceding the date of the tender offer;
- If the shares are infrequently traded, the fair price determined on the basis of parameters which are customary for the valuation of shares of a company, such as book value and comparable trading multiples.

The above price will be affected by any acquisition made after the public announcement at a price greater than the offer price.

The offer price can be revised only till the last 7th day and in case of competing offer, they will follow the same schedule.

Exemptions from making open offer

Certain types of acquisitions are exempted from making open offer, and these are the cases which do not result in the change of control.

Thus, transfers between co-promoters, relatives, holding and subsidiary companies, and buybacks are the cases which will not require open offer.

Obligations of Merchant banker

The merchant banker is the one who is primarily responsible for compliance with the takeover code and also ensures that the acquirer meets its obligation.

The primary responsibility is to ensure the offer price is properly calculated and has been secured by escrow.

Apart from the above, it is his responsibility to ensure that the disclosures are proper and all material information is disclosed.

Obligations of Acquirer

The obligations of acquirer mirror the responsibility of the merchant banker, but they are also responsible to ensure that offer is true and fair and they sign-off on the public announcement and letter of offer.

Obligations of the Target Company

The target company is expected to be neutral providing equal access and information to bidders. They are also not supposed to make any material changes to the company including issue of shares, except through special resolution.

They are also supposed to constitute committee of independent directors to recommend on open offer.

They are supposed to make available all information to acquirer and basically be in standstill position till the offers are closed.

11.9 Executive Summary

This chapter highlights the intricacies of takeover code and their salient features. We have made an attempt to represent a few case studies which have been alluringly crafted around the takeover code. The chapter stresses on the development of ability to craft rather than know only what triggers the takeover code. It is important to know as a practitioner, how can we avoid triggering the takeover code which completes the inside view of the Takeover code.

We have also looked into defence mechanisms for the hostile offers and the relative ease of such mechanisms.

The chapter is compiled by explaining the salient features so that the readers of the book get complete picture of the art of takeover code.

12

Negotiations in M&A

Contents

12.1 Introduction

Negotiation skills are the integral part in all walks of life, but they seem to be more pronounced in the art of dealmaking. Negotiation at times may appear to be natural ability. However, one can still emerge as a successful negotiator merely by following few basic principle.

The ability to negotiate and to be successful at it is the matter of preparation and confidence to know the situation in and out to achieve your objective. The ability to negotiate impromputu situation is a matter of experience rather than skill.

Many times, there is a attribution of luck factor to the negotiation outcome, but it would reflect more of under-preparedness of one side or an overarching hurry to close deals, resulting in skewed outcome in favor of one of the parties.

Shades of above are demonstrated in the below-mentioned ill-negotiated deals where in larger burden is felt by the acquirers like Bank of America and Noumura. The distressed sellers like Merrill Lynch and Lehman Brothers could salvage much more in an hopeless situation by striking a sweet deal with the acquirers.

Still, in the end negotiating fair and square with win–win outcome probably is a better Karma than a win–lose situation.

With this, let us move onto the art, the principles, and rules to negotiate better.

12.2 The Art of Negotiation in M&A

1. Be Better Prepared:

Know all the aspects of the deal like the back of your hand. This would mean knowing the elements in the entire deal which is:

- Counter-party and its key decision-makers;
- Regulations;
- Media;
- Key stakeholders.

This will help you to anticipate the expected reactions and enable you to respond them accordingly. For example: If you are foreign buyer and there is requirement of regulatory approvals, you can pin the responsibility for the approval on the resident seller.

This will bind the seller to the deal and they will not be able to use it as an excuse to wriggle out of the deal. In the Axis-Enam deal, it was rumored that the delayed RBI approval was being used as a tool by Axis to squirm out of the deal. Thus, engaging and ensuring the skin in the game of the counter-parties is an essential factor to keep the deal tight and protected.

Case Study 12.1: Kraft Craftily Negotiates to Acquire Cadbury

Details

a. The timeline

2009

Aug 28, 2009	Irene Rosenfeld, Kraft's chairman and chief executive meets Cadbury's chairman Roger Carr to outline a takeover deal in cash and shares which valued Cadbury's shares at 755 pence each but Carr dismissed the approach. The Kraft bid was worth 300p in cash and 0.2589 new Kraft shares for each Cadbury share.
Sept 7, 2009	Kraft goes public with the bid but by this time the value of the same offer had slipped to 745p per Cadbury share or £10.2 billion. Cadbury promptly rejects the bid.
Sept 12, 2009	Cadbury's Carr, in a letter to Rosenfeld, again rejects the bid saying it was an "unappealing prospect" being absorbed into Kraft's "low growth conglomerate business."
Sept 16, 2009	Warren Buffett, the world's second richest man and a leading shareholder in Kraft with a 9.4% stake, warned the U.S. food group not to overpay for Cadbury.
Nov 9, 2009	Kraft formalizes its bid at the same terms for Cadbury as the original approach—300p in cash and 0.2589 new Kraft share for each Cadbury share valued at 717p.
Nov 18, 2009	Both, Italy's Ferrero and Hershey separately said that they were reviewing a possible bid for Cadbury but gave no assurance that either of them would make an offer.
Nov 23, 2009	Cadbury shares hit all-time high of 819-1/2 pence on the speculation of a battle between Kraft and rivals for the British chocolate maker.
Dec 4, 2009	Kraft posts its offer document to Cadbury shareholders starting-off a 2-month fight for the British group under UK takeover rules. Kraft says its bid is now worth 713 pence a share or 10.1 billion pounds.
Dec 14, 2009	Cadbury issues its official defense document promising bigger dividends and strong growth as Cadbury reminds its shareholders that Hershey and Ferrero may bid.
Dec 18, 2009	Cadbury CEO Todd Stitzer told Reuters in an interview that a significant number of its major shareholders do not believe Kraft's bid reflects Cadbury stand-alone value.

2010

Jan 5, 2010	Kraft sweetens bid with 60p more cash but cuts shares on offer to keep offer price unchanged.

First Fortnight of January 10

Berkshire Hathaway, the holding firm of US billionaire Warren Buffett, said it had voted against Kraft's plans to sell new shares to help fund the takeover.

It claimed that the share sale gave Kraft a blank cheque allowing it to change its offer "in any way, it wishes."

However, the company said that it may change its vote if the "final bid does not destroy value for Kraft shareholders."

Based on the above, the News agencies reports claimed Kraft's plans to buy Cadbury were now in jeopardy.

Cadbury shares fell on the news, closing 3.2% lower in London at 779 pence.

Jan 19, 2010: Cadbury accepts raised Kraft bid valued at 850 pence a share, or GBP11.9 billion ($19.5 billion) and recommends the deal to shareholders.

Despite his view that Kraft paid too much, Mr Buffett said he won't be selling his stake in the company, best known for its cheese slices and Maxwell House coffee.

Cadbury shareholders will get 500p in cash and 0.1874 Kraft shares for each Cadbury share. Mr Buffett called Kraft's original offer of around 771p a share a "pretty full price."

Key Learning

The US company sealed the deal after increasing its bid three times from the *771p-a-share offer made in September to 830p, 840p and finally, 840p plus dividend.* Irene Rosenfeld, Kraft chairman and chief executive, hailed the takeover, which will create the world's largest confectionery group with sales of nearly $60 billion (£37 billion), as "transformational."

Thus, we observe a cleverly crafted and negotiated deal, in which to achieve a transformational deal, the price offered was controlled in a spectacular fashion. Key stake holder like Berkshire hathway was used to signal to Cadbury Board that there is no way that the offer price is going to be revised.

"Roger Carr, chairman of Cadbury, quoted: 'In essence, Kraft's offer is limited by powerful Kraft shareholders restricting what they can offer."

Therefore, we see the negative influence of powerful Kraft shareholder on the Chairman of Cadbury. He had started seeing the deal from the buyers' perspective rather than the sellers' perspective.

The stock price ran ahead of the Kraft offer and subsequently dropped below the Kraft offer and the Cadbury Board which had been stubborn threw in the towel and had to agree to the takeover offer.

2. Don't Take Undue Burden to Make Deal

Let us note down the key or basic objectives to be achieved by the buyer and seller. So, we know the battle lines and the need to cross them needs to have a strong rationale:

For the buyer

a. To offer lowest possible price
b. To secure the deal with appropriate representations/warranties and minimum possible pre-conditions for the buyer
c. To close the deal as soon as possible

For the seller

a. To get best possible price
b. To ensure the buyer has the resources to deliver the consideration
c. To provide minimum reps and warranties plus indemnities

Beyond this, there has to be strong rationale to take the burden traded-off for equal and opposite balancing condition. Else, there may be case of missing the woods for the trees.

This is what happened, in the case of Vodafone–Hutch deal. In the need to close the deal, the buyer ended up taking the tax liability of the seller. For the price premium being paid by the buyer, they should have negotiated for indemnity on the tax.

The same holds true for Daiichi–Sankyo and Ranbaxy deal. Once the price being paid is as per seller, do ask for all the things required to protect that price.

In case of Gujarat Ambuja–Holcim deal, wherein the promoter held ~20%, the acquirer negotiated for 14.9% (takeover code limit) acquired and took control and for balance 5% locked in the escrow effectively with the buyer, preventing the seller from falling to the temptation of competing offer. The seller in return also asked for money to be put on the table.

3. Follow Principle Approach, Be Reasonable but, Firm

This allows a much guided approach to negotiations. It allows the person to be credible in the process and permits practicality to the points being made.

Let us consider the Arcellor–Mittal deal. As the controversy panned out, Arcellor raised several principle based issues including the management of Mittal (Aditya Mittal, son of L.N. Mittal is on the board), family ownership, corporate governance, safety record of Mittal, which eventually helped it to secure one share one vote capital structure, Mittal's holding came down to 45% and composition of Board of Directors was made more broad based.

Mittal's were unable to answer the principle issues and had to appear credible to the French government, eventually paying a higher price but had to give a lot away along side the price.

Mittal Steel Paid a Huge Premium for the Deal

As the deal was initially rejected by the board of Arcelor, Mittal Steel was forced to make a revised offer. Mittal Steel had to pay almost double the price planned initially. This deal demonstrated the biggest premium ever paid for acquiring a steel company.

The principle stand is also essential in discussing valuation. Good preparation around the basis for valuation and being firm around the value makes the person to cross the bridge more than half way.

We have seen the shades of it in the Kraft–Cadbury deal as well as in Abott–Piramal deal, wherein Abott ended up paying $3.72 billion for the acquisition of Piramal's CRM business as a slump sale (business acquisition).

The payee was the company being a slump sale and not its shareholders. If the shareholders had to realize the consideration, it would have involved demerger of the CRM business, which has long timeline structure. Hence, in lieu of the acquirer paying premium price demanded a most suitable structure. It staggered the payment of the purchase consideration over the next four years without any explicit guarantee. So, effectively lowering its acquisition price by staggering the payments and using the CRM business cashflow for the said purpose.

4. Lookout for the Weak Link in the Chain

Similar to how Sonny Corleone turned out to be the weak link in Don Corleone's team of negotiators. Try to look out for the weak links, which have weak body language and would give out the game plan or blurt out impatiently some hint of where the other party stands. Just like Sonny, look out for the young kid of the patriarch as they have more emotions blurting than seasoned negotiatior.

5. Do Not Over Promise—Missing the Woods For the Trees

Case Study 12.2: NTT DoCoMo-Tata Tele

Details and Learnings

Tata-Docomo is a classic case of over-promise to secure the deal. NTT, in return, paid a premium to buy Tata's telecom asset to secure guarantee on Put option from Tata Son's that they will receive atleast 50% of its purchase price.

NTT DoCoMo wants to unload its investment in India's seventh-largest cellular carrier, Tata Teleservices (TTSL), in a retreat from India's challenging market.

Japan's largest mobile telecommunications firm by subscribers said it wants to sell the entire 26.5% stake acquired in 2009, citing a range of negative factors.

"Intense price competition with many carriers, slow growth of 3G services, confusion in the licensing policies and regulations made it difficult for DoCoMo to use its know-how in the carrier business for the growth of TTSL and we couldn't generate business synergies with them," a DoCoMo spokesman said on Friday.

The Japanese company has yet to find a potential buyer but it has decided to exercise its option to sell the stake if TTSL did not meet performance targets in the fiscal year to March 31, 2014.

Under a deal struck with Tata Sons, the holding company of the Tata Group, DoCoMo, will receive at least 50% of what it paid for the stake in TTSL, which would be AY=125.4 billion (US $1.2 billion), DoCoMo said.

Thus, despite being in the management, NTT Docomo could secure performance and guarantee. This completely erodes the equity value of the Tata's telecom assets.

Another case that justifies the criteria of over—promise is Bharti-MTN.

6. How Much Empowered is the Negotiator in Chief ? Is there Agency Problem which Can Be Exploited?

There are teams led by the principal or by their agent, which maybe CEO/CFO/Banker/Lawyer or family man. One should always look at how empowered they are and whether they enjoy the confidence of their bosses. Weakly empowered teams can be pressurized by putting up strong demands or building up pressure as they delay decision-making due to their constant to and fro with their bosses.

In such situation, the CEO will be politically inclined to close the deal to keep the local happy. This inclination can be exploited by the counter-party.

We also face super-empowered negotiators, who run amok at the negotiation table. The only way to deal with such negotiation is to have firm and reasonable stand, try to open battles on many fronts to engage him in dousing flames. Especially, if it is second or third time that the deal is being negotiated, it is easy to cage the tiger by subtly threatening to walk out.

7. Negotiating graceful exit, to protect sellers reputation

In such cases, the seller is looking for honorable exit or the seller does not want to be seen as undersold or as seller especially, in Asian context.

Sometimes, it is easy to propose the terms which take care of their big egos and make them appear a winner but, essentially it is a tactic to make the other person feel the "emperor without clothes." In the process, seek the core of the deal.

Generally, in leveraged situations, it is preferred to give exit to the seller through infusion in the company rather than through direct purchase from the seller. Aditya Birla's acquisition of Pantaloon stresses the above point. Further, the deals are then touted as partnership or friendly takeovers. For example:

Kingfisher Buys Stake In Air Deccan

The flamboyant billionaire who controls UB, Vijay Mallya, became the Vice-Chairman of Deccan Aviation, while Gopinath a former army captain became the Executive Chairman.

8. Don't declare victory until done. Don't be impulsive but pragmatic

Case Study 12.3: Fortis' Parkway Battle: The Khazanah Story

Fortis to acquire strategic stake in Parkway Holdings, Singapore.

Fortis has entered into a definitive agreement with TPG Capital, one of the world's leading private investment firms, to acquire its 23.9% stake in Parkway. Fortis intends to seek four seats in the Board of Directors of Parkway and also to nominate Mr. Malvinder Mohan Singh (current Chairman of Fortis Healthcare) as the Chairman of the Board of Directors of Parkway.

Khazanah which held approximately 24% was having two seats an the board. On seeing that Fortis is planning to acquire 4 board seats despite same ownership percentage, Khazanah also sought equal number of board seats. Fortis, rejected the demand. Although pragmatism would have meant in view of equal shareholding and the fact that sovereign fund will be egoistic, giving up on the softer issue of board members, would have been easier option than battling a counter bid by deep pocketed Khazanah.

Eventually, Khazanah launched counter bid and wrested control of Parkway from Fortis.

9. Do Not Build the Deal Edifice Around Far- Fetched Conditions

It is generally observed in case of mega-acquisitions that the deal is conditional on events, which require major approvals or changes in law. It requires several things to fall in place for the deal to go through. Additionally, there are business rivalries and vested interests who would scuttle the deal. It is suggested to try and build the deal around the existing framework and not make transformational deal which requires changes in the regulatory framework or requires transformational conditions to be met.

Case Study 12.4: Bharti-MTN Deal – Far Fetched Conditions

Bharti–MTN had agreed for a merger structure. Bharti, telecom company listed on Indian stock exchange offered shares to the shareholders of MTN listed on South African exchanges, The shares of the combined entity will be tradeable in both the exchanges meaning that non-Indians will be able to move money in and out over-riding the convertibility restrictions of the Reserve Bank of India.

India could not have accepted the demand of the South African government for dual listing of shares in the absence of full convertibility of rupee which ultimately led to the collapse of the $23 billion merger deal between Bharti Airtel and MTN.

"As the Indian rupee is not fully convertible, it is not possible to go in for dual listing of shares which allows people to buy shares in the stock exchanges of one country and sell in the bourses of the other country".

Bharti called-off discussions with telecom giant MTN, citing the South African government's rejection of the proposed merger structure.

10. Do Not Stitch in deal conditions that Can Be Easily Brought Down by Competition

Case Study 12.5: MTN Deal Scuppered

Low probability–high impact conditions are easy pickings for the rivals to scupper the deal especially if it involves high-profile assets.

Below are two listed cases, wherein they were low probability events but had high impact of calling-off the deal.

In the Bharti–MTN deal, they had to issue receipts of Depository and at the time of deal, the acquisition of Depository receipt was exempted from provision of the takeover code. Bharti had obtained the SEBI guidance as well on the point of law. But, the closing of deal took some time, which gave SEBI time to amend the law that scuppered the deal.

In another case, the Reliance–MTN deal was built around the assumption that there would be no need for any NOC from Reliance industries. However,

Reliance Industries claimed to have the first right of refusal on any shares that Reliance Communications sell. It was enough to scare away MTN and that low probability event led to the cancellation of the deal.

11. Never Reveal your Hand in the Deal

Case Study 12.6: Tata-Corus

When the Tata–Corus deal took place, the inextricable link between the nationbuilding and commerce came to fore in a surge of nationalism as congratulatory messages powed into media.

Terms like "we are proud of you," "inspirational," "watershed deal," "spirit of India, "keep it up," even, " *lage raho* ..." fast became cliches as readers shed trademark cynicism to celebrate what everyone seemed to agree was a golden moment in the history of Indian business.

Ratan Tata stated that the takeover "is the first step in showing that Indian industry can step outside its shores into an international market place as a global player."

The newspapers reflected the euphoric "Five Pence Gives India A Pound of UK," *TheEconomic Times* exclaimed, "Corus, the erstwhile British Steel and one of the icons of Her Majesty's Empire will now fly the [Indian] Tricolour." *The Financial Express* reported the merger using the headline "World's No. 5, India's No. 1," while *The Hindustan Times* used the headline "Signed, steeled."

The clear-cut intentions of acquiring Corus by Tatas was seen and exploited by CSN by making a counter bid.

The key points to be noted are:

a. False assumption of Tata to have already acquired and completed the deal at the time of bidding.

b. The deal was so much touted and reams of newsprint on euologising the deal and the Tata that the intention's of Tata's to acquire Corus was clearly apparent.

c. When CSN made the bid for Corus, it was no-loss deal for CSN as they had two options available to them (a) acquiring Corus at a price they wanted or (b) make a cool profit on its existing holding in Corus.

d. CSN would have known that Tata's will never let Corus go as there was no way after 9 months of bidding war where they were hailed, as visionary would make cool calculation and lose out on the bid.

e. Thus, the bidding war which started at 455 pence, got topped up by CSN at 475 pence. This pushed Tata's to overbid at 608 pence allowing cool exit to CSN.

12. Use Signaling Effect:

Case Study 12.7: HCL Tech Makes Counter Bid for Axon of U.K.

HCL Technologies made a counter bid to Infosys bid for UK-based software company Axon by raising the offer by 8.3% to seal the biggest overseas deal by an Indian firm in this space.

HCL Technologies on Friday made an offer of 650 pence per share as compared to Infosys' offer of 600 pence announced late last month.

HCL technologies has arranged a 400-million pound loan for the deal with balance of the money to be paid from internal accruals, HCL Technologies CEO Vineet Nayar told reporters, announcing the counter bid.

"We, hereby see that HCL signaling it has money bags to fight Infosys bid was enough for Infosys conservative management to take bow out of the deal."

13. Never Quote First

This brings us to the story of a shopkeeper and a kid who had come to shop. The shopkeeper seeing the lovely kid asked him to pick candies from the candy jar. The kid refused. The shopkeeper again forced him to take candies but he refused. Finally, infuriated, the shopkeeper dipped his hand and thrust the candies in the kids" hands. The kid laughed at the shopkeeper and said "see now I have more candies and ran away."

In real life negotiation as well, never quote first and give away your gameplan as we never know what is there in counterparty's mind. Unless, you are sure enough that it is a number that gives you asymmetric positive pay-off and back by cold assessment and calculation. It can signal the counterparties of your cold-blooded intentions.

Overzealous buyers, at time, quote price much higher than the seller has in mind that helps to take economic advantage by not quoting first or vice versa. Sellers who have faced repeated failures to sell may end up frustrated and quote a real good price to get rid of the assets that the buyer would have budgeted.

As a buyer, you are advised to look more deeper whether it suits you to buy at that price and do not get influence by competitor and competiton. Discipline to walk away and not engage in ego game is the best strategy. As a seller, always put oneself in the buyers' shoes and work out the price the seller is desiorous of paying especially checking out as elucidated in the strategy chapter as the sellers' over desire to buy.

14. Avoid Falling in Love with the Asset as a Buyer and Don't Act like a Jilted Lover if the Bid is Spurned

We already spoke about not revealing your hand. A bit of its not being overtly desirous to buy. Once it is known that the buyer is in love with the deal, it is most unlikely that the seller will reduce his asking price and make the buyer step up. The story is very akin to girl's family having it easy when they know the boy has fallen for the girl.

Second, don't behave like a jilted lover. If somebody says no, don't become overaggressive to possess the asset. So keep cool and walk away.

Case Study 12.8: Negotiations Brew Over in the Takeover of SAB Miller

Details

SAB Miller has agreed to sell itself to Anheuser-Busch InBev for $104 billion (£68 billion). The takeover is accalimed to be one of the top 5 takeovers in the M&A history.

AB InBev is backed by Brazil's richest man, the financier Jorge Paulo Lemann, who is behind the big private equity firm 3i Capital. AB InBev had a reputation to be serial acquirer and making aggressive bid. It bought "Brahma," the Brazilian brewer, to become the largest brewer in Brazil, combining with Interbrew, the maker of Stella Artois, in 2004 and buying the US Budweiser brewer, Anheuser-Busch, 4 years later.

The £44 cash offer values SAB Miller at 50% premium to the unaffected price. The takeover will secure AB InBev, a target it has long coveted.

The deal took place after repeated attempts by Inbev of £38, £40, and £42 per share in private before AB InBev tried to force board's hand by going public with a £42.15 proposal to pressurize them.

SAB's top managers will share a potential $2.1 billion payout of shares and options if the deal is completed. Alan Clark, SAB Miller's chief executive, was likely to receive more than £80 million.

SAB Miller's had the two biggest shareholders, Altria 27%, the maker of Philip Morris cigarettes, and BevCo (14%) owned by Colombia's billionaire Santo Domingo brewing family. Altria was in the favor of the deal at the earlier lower price proposed but the other shareholder was not in the favor of the deal.

At SAB Miller's request, the takeover panel has extended its deadline for AB InBev to make a firm offer until 28 October. Chairman of SAB Miller had the backing of the board and the big shareholders as he had conveyed that AB InBev needs them more than they need AB InBev. However, it was also apparent that they would not want to lose such an attractive bid.

SAB Miller negotiated a $3 billion break-fee payable by AB InBev if the deal falls through because of competition hurdles or opposition by the latter shareholders.

The Timeline

Carlos Brito, CEO of AB InBev, called Jan du Plessis, the Chairman of SAB Miller on Sunday evening prior to the deadline that was about to expire in 24 hours to arrange an urgent meeting the following day as he wanted to make a last-ditch attempt to negotiate the acquisition.

The reason for making the call to SAB chairman was obvious. The time to make formal deal was Monday 5 pm; hence, the acquirer was running out under the UK takeover code, which would have precluded Ab InBev from making another bid for more than a year.

AB InBev bosses proposed an offer £67 billion, or £43.50-a-share, to buy SAB Miller.

Earlier bids made in private of £38-a-share and £40 had already failed. On Monday to hammer in a bid, AB InBev went public with the suggested potential bid of £42.15-a-share.

Tobacco Company, Altria, which is the biggest shareholder of SAB with 27% stake and three directors in its board, indicated the British company it would accept such an offer.

However, SAB Board of Directors resisted the offer and ramped up the pressure by proposing a trading update and future business plan for SAB Miller by suggesting billion dollars of cost reductions, thereby suggesting AB InBev to bid higher.

On Monday morning, sweetened takeover proposal of £43.50 was made setting in motion the revised bid of £44. It is believed that it was Goudet, the AB InBev Chairman, who made the crucial decision to lift the bid to £44-a-share on Monday evening, sealing the £68 billion deal.

Key Learning

Thus, from the above case, we see that SAB Miller has successfully negotiated the deal. The points in favor of SAB Miller are stated as below:

- 50% premium to the unaffected price. Raising the bid from £38 to £44, a 20% increase.
- Realizing that AB InBev needed it more than they needed AB InBev.
- SAB Miller realized the penchant that AB InBev had for the deal and would not like to be seen as loser.

- Exploited the high octane deal machine of AB InBev.
- SAB Miller was tactful and not stubborn. It did not allow the ego to interfere the deal.
- Despite having two dominant shareholders with only one in the favor of deal, the chairman successfully kept its flock together.
- Used the takeover deadline tactfully.
- Used signaling and pressure tactics by giving trading update.
- Never revealed its hand or showed desperateness for the deal even on the face of potential huge employee compensation.
- Negotiated a handsome breakaway fee.
- NNot a single misstep in negotiation despite having all the weaknesses viz. lack lustre share price, not so great prospects in the immediate future, emerging markets were already under pressure.

Thus, we see from the above that AB InBev weakly negotiated the deal. The principles violated by them include:

- **Not to reveal your hand in the deal.**
- **To avoid falling in love with the asset as a buyer and don't act like a jilted lover if the bid is spurned.**

The 50% premium would have been good enough for the board of the seller to fall in line. It got frustrated by the stubbornness of the seller. It never used any signaling to suggest they would walk away from the deal. It failed to exploit the weak links such as the 27% shareholder, who was willing to sell, and the executives, who were going to receive bonanza for the takeover along with the weak performance of SAB Miller.

The jury is still out on the eventual success of the acquisition but more crafty negotiation could have brought in better price.

15. Taming the Tiger (To rethink)

The above point can be justified by stating that as tigers prefer to hunt large prey by ambush. If you look at a tiger, it is less likely to attack, as it has lost the element of surprise.

Thus, when confronted by counterparty carrying big reputation, the best way to tackle their unjust demands is to just say NO if you have courage of conviction and the tiger will get tamed.

16. Runaway Bride (Sellers who have Failed Transaction)

Case Study 12.8: Axis Bank Acquisition of Enam

Japan's Nomura Holdings backed-off from the negotiations to take a stake in Indian financial services group Enam on differences over valuations. Nomura was not willing to pay more than USD400 million for acquiring Enam, while the Indian firm had stuck to a minimum valuation of USD500 million.

Morgan Stanley paid a net USD425 million to split from its Indian partner, while Merrill Lynch paid USD500 million to raise its stake in its local joint venture to 90% from 40%.

Thereafter, initially in the year 2010, Axis buys Enam Sec. in a Rs. 2067Cr deal and slashed the valuation further in the year 2012 to Rs. 1400 crore.

Thus, in such cases, it is buyers' delight in terms of getting the best from the seller. The above case study highlights the change in valuation. It substantially declined from $500 million to ~$300 million. Also, from all cash deal, it became all stock deal with lock in of the shares.

Case Study 12.9: Sun Microsystem Acquisition by Oracle

Sun Microsystem, the makers of Java, was on the selling block as it was unable to sustain in the technology world which was integrating fast with clients demanding integrated offerings. They were looking forward to a white knight due to heavy cash losses.

IBM appeared on the scene and after months of negotitation offered a price of $7.55 per share which was later scaled down to $7.40 per share citing the clause of change of control in the contract of Sun Microsystem. The reduction in price became the sole reason for the rejection of offer by the board members of Sun Microsystem.

The situtaion left both IBM and Sun Microsystem high and dry. Especially, Sun Microsystem is in a vulnerable position due to its urgent need to find a whte knight. Meanwhile, Oracle without much effort and a bid of $7.50 made Sun Microsystem to agree to their conditions.

Therefore, in the above case study, it is evident that Oracle was able to achieve the deal with much ease and the slugfest of IBM-Sun yielded nothing.

12.3 Key Tactics to Negotiate

- **Do not Burn the Bridge**

The Dow–Dupont deal exemplifies the above maxim. Both the companies had acitivst investors on their shareholding. Dow made overtures to Dupont quite a number of times. Despite the rebuffs, between the activist shareholders and their respective boards or between Dow and Dupont,the bridge was never burnt and resulted in the announcement of a $30 billion merger.

- **Do not Vacillate**

The Kraft–Cadbury case study in this chapter highlights the consistency of pitch maintained by Kraft. This consistency made the other party *viz.* Cadbury to vacillate and give into Kraft. Hence, prepare, know, and be consistent.

- **Use Pressure Groups**

Astra Zeneca–Pfizer case study accentuates on the use of the pressure groups such as politicians, media, and markets to create pressure on the either parites to fend-off the bid or ask for better price or terms.

- **Always Keep Bargaining Chip on Shoulder**

The above signifies heavily negotiated agreements. At times, becoming a mindless tit for tat specially in merger of equals such as the Lafarge–Holcim or Dow–Dupont. Both the deal had identical give and take. For example: If one is CEO, the other is the Executive Chairman.

If a bidder wants exclusivity, it should be balanced with termination fee or breakway fee. It is the art of negotiation that a M&A practiner needs to develop, and if one ends up as a buyer giving a higher price in return, they should negotiate other softer things in return. It could be used to extend time period or mode of payment or right to put.

Especially, in a situation where the buyer is ending up paying high price, they should ensure that they are getting what they are buying by ring fencing key areas seeking reps and warranties, options, liabilities, etc. The seller should not get carried away with the high price being offered and make sure there is no concurrent financial liability or reputational liability being created. Reps and warranties should be restricted to what is possible within their scope and ability to do so. In the enthusiasim to do the deal lured by the carrot of the price, sellers may end up taking up onerous liabilities which may be improbable but have turned probable in quite a number of deals.

- **Frustrate Single Track Negotiator's**

Sometimes, the sellers are single track with expectation of a particular price. This often leads to single track negotitation. It is an opportunity to extract sizeable concession in return for the price. The impact can also be tapered by changing the mode or time of the payments.

- **Use Law as a Shield**

Mylan rejected Teva Pharmaceuticals $40 billion bid citing Global Anti-trust disapproval risk. The anti-trust risk has created a defense shield for companies to reject bids. Ask for opinions to support the counterparty position.

- **Create Hostility**

By raising legal and ethical issues, the Astra Zeneca–Pfizer case study highlights the issues of job losses, losing R&D positioning, tax inversion issue to fend-off hostility.

- **Bring Competitive Element**

The Hutchison case study discussed in Chapter III highlights the competitve element in the deal and how it helps to negotiate.

- **Keep Ego Outside**

It is part of the folklore that L N Mittal, the CEO of Mittal, gave a call to Arcelor CEO on his cell phone announcing his intention to bid for Arcelor.

The things that we need to introspect is why would a CEO give a telephonic call to another CEO instead of dealing through the advisors. It is an example of keeping ego outside the table and try to strike a friendly note so that the bid does not transform into a hostile one which means more struggle and higher price.

12.4 Negotiating with Short Sellers and Activist Investors

Short Sellers

The key to understand and negotiate lies in undertanding the motivations. Generally, the short sellers will attack companies which have the following chinks in the armor.

- Accounting aggressiveness in terms of revenue recognition or asset valuations.
- Leveraged balance sheet and nowhere to go.
- Masking growth by using series of M&As and mostly leveraged bets.

The cases of short selling in Olam International, the Singapore listed commodity player by Muddy Waters, Noble Group Ltd. by Iceberg and Valeant Pharmaceutical had all the above three elements.

The conventional response to short sellers has been typical:

- Disputing the accusations
- Threatening litigation
- Getting auditors or entities which are not supposeldy indepeent to rebut the accusations
- Launching buybacks to arrest stock price

Unfortuanely, all of these issues do not address the thoroughly researched issues raised by the short sellers, creating a further decline in the market.

Thus, effective negotitations would mean looking the short sellers into eyes and coming up with the actual response to the issues raised by the short seller such as raising capital backed by the anchor investor or causing asset sale or taking fundamental steps to address the isues raised rather than converting it into a battle.

Thus, the Olam could escape the brunt of short selling because of the Temasek picking up $750 million rights issue, thereby thwarting the short sellers. But, that is not always the luxury as in case of Noble Group, the Noble Group went on to announce a buyback which would eat up 75% of its cash balance to shore up the stock price. It is akin to subjecting patient to surgery even though he has high sugar levels or blood pressure.

The above means that companies have to be much more proactive if the above-mentioned elements are present. The risk management of short selling is paramount here and be able to look into eyes of short seller and negotiate is comparable to take the bitter pill than going for painful surgeries.

Acitivist Investors

The advent and success of acitivst investors has made activism a reality and no company today is immune against the attacks of the activist investors.

The activist investors, who had low-profits approach and are patient were able to create much more value than the aggressive ones.

The key activist are as can be stated as centered around:

• Financial strategy centered around the change in capital structure of return of capital. For example: Apple Inc. raising its buyback and dividend in respone to Icahn, the activist.
• Business strategy involving dropping of high cost pursuits and consolidating operations and cutting costs.
For example: Microsoft writing-off Nokia handset business in response to value investor demands.
• Execuitve compensation.
For example: Daniel Loebe making pitch for cutting compensations at Sothbheys.
• Pursuing M&A or spinning-off.

The Dow–Dupont deal highlights the issue of the pressure created by the activist investors on both sides.

In most cases, the acitivist investors would have a point of view which makes sense. However, in most situations, because they are investors and not owners, the suggestions from acitivist are looking for creation of value in the near term rather than in longer term.

The above is the single most important point based on which an attack of acitivist can be thwarted. The key to success in this matters can be seen in the Pepsico case wherein CEO Indira Nooyi could have the confidence of the entire board making a persuasive pitch to look long term rather than the short term.

Hence, we could observe today the success of Pepsicos capital expenditure and strategy bearing fruit over the suggestion of breakup by the activist investors.

The above case would again highlight the following:

- Being prepared to deal with such a situation.
- Keeping the Board abreast of plans and rationale.
- Building a strong shareholder base and keeping the large shareholders abreast of longer term vision.
- Do not allow slack in the balance sheet by excess cash or capital structure that can be attacked.
- Last, always negotiate with the acitivsit, the least of their demand is Board seat and if, it is frustrated, they would generally back track or if, they are constructive, they can be taken on board in return for certain quid pro quo.

This brings us to famous maxim in both the above cases. Let us not fear to negotiate but let us not negotiate out of fear.

12.5 Executive Summary

The chapter has touched the dynamic aspect of negotiations in M&A. Apart from the rules of negotiations, the case studies have been brought in to illustrate the flow and aspects of negotiations. The following golden rules summarize the art of negotitation.

The Art of Negotiation

- Never say NO
- Be better prepared
- Agree to disagree bridge
- Do not reveal your hand in the deal
- Never quote first
- Talk less observe more
- Be ready to walk away
- Keep ego out of the negotiating table
- Be focused on goal

13

Interpreting M&A Press Releases

Contents

13.1 Introduction

This chapter helps discern M&A announcements/press releases, which are made to suit the issuer rather than the readers of the press release. The few guiding points here are threads that can be picked up for judging the M&A's as to stated whether they will create value for the acquirer or the seller.

The chapter aims to help finance and non-finance professionals to understand the announcements, without doing much financial computation or they need not be finance wizard to understand the contents of the announcements.

The chapter states down some qualitative and quantitative criteria that readers can assimilate and take a better view of the corporate action to judge, where the value is being created, and for whom.

13.2 Criteria

The default start to any press release is to know whether it is EPS accretive for the buyer. These are buttressed by a set of assumptions and numbers that are difficult for outsider to understand. The criteria below will help in cutting through the maze of numbers and the verbose press release.

a. Qualitative Criteria

The first and foremost criteria is to see the business area of the target company, whether it complements the existing business of the acquirer or whether it is incidental to the business of the acquirer company.

Next is the size of the acquisition. what is the size of the acquisition relative to the assets or the revenue of the buyers. If the percentage starts trending up from 10%, one need to be careful of M&As, as it may saddle the buyer with assets which may not produce commiserate growth in profitability. Acquisitions that are 50% or higher could generally be destructive for the buyer reflecting a case of overeating by the acquire unless it has a good appetite to digest a heavy meal. Even python goes into slumber after a big catch.

Another question that emerges is how many acquisitions the buyer has done in the recent past or whether the acquirer need to set its house in order, before attempting acquisitions. It has a very cohesive M&A strategy.

Whether the acquirer is resorting to buy stuff and being lazy to bend its back to build business in the organic manner. Is it buying stuff which ordinarily could have been built at lesser cost but taken little bit more time to build.

If the acquisition is being done to shore up the sluggish revenue growth, then the problem is with the acquirer and not the acquisition.

Whether the acquisition is cross-border or domestic also needs consideration. Domestic acquisition projects lower risk than the cross-border. If it is cross-border, does it possess geography that has similar characteristics as the buyer's geography. Whether they have experience of running business in that geography or similar geography.

A very important point to note is whether the target company or asset has been bought in an auction process. The press celebrates the winner much akin to war type celebration. The same is true in hostile battle with the target company. A buyout after hostility could mean the winner's curse as the seller has walked away with economic gains.

Another vital note is whether the target company has been passed by several buyers. There has to be sound reason as to why a company which has been rejected by others makes an economic sense to the buyer and whether the buyer has paid a right price for the desperate seller.

Many times, acquisitions are justified for forward or backward integration. Forward integrations may be good for progressing ahead on the value curve, while the backward integration would add to operating leverage. Larger asset base being acquired without corresponding top up in the revenue or profits needs a closer look.

An acquisition which is subject to a large number of approvals and longer timelines essentially junks the excel sheet-based model, which are built on the assumption that synergy will kick in from day 0.

There is also compounding effect based on at what point of the business cycle has the acquisition been carried out. Acquisition done in boom times with deal frenzy means that the acquirer has paid a premium price and prone to suffer low profits or losses on such acquisition. On contrary, the acquisition carried out at trough of the cycle means the acquirer has paid a discounted price for the target which result in asymmetric pay-off.

We will deal with the price aspect in the quantitative criteria but essentially whether the price discounts the risk of acquisition.

Further, whether the price paid is leading to substantial goodwill or intangibles being created in the acquisition. EPS accretion will standout if there is goodwill created in acquisition as goodwill need not be amortized.

Last but not the least, acquisition funded through cash on the balance sheet or the internal accrual indicates that the company is investing the cash surplus generated for further value creation in the best suitable manner. Acquisition funded through debt is trickier as that would imply that the acquirer is relying on steroids to punch above its weight. Large acquisitions funded largely through debt means marriage of operating leverage and financial leverage creating potency for train wreck down the line. Further, given the cost of debt, it is easy to take debt and justify EPS accretion due to lack of dilution of equity and the denominator stays constant with numerator going up. As a consequence, mathematical EPS accretion is easy to demonstrate.

Further, we need to understand the use of shares as currency to pay for the acquisition. The higher the value of acquirer shares, the lesser would be the dilution. Further, the earnings would have to outpace the dilution to justify the EPS accretion.

b. Quantitative Criteria

Enterprise value

Assuming existence of debt in the target company, there would be equity and the enterprise value of the acquisition. Let us assume equity value to be 100 and debt 50. Then, the enterprise value will be 150. Further, based on the last EBIT or EBIDTA or PAT achieved by the target, calculate the ROCE or ROE and judge the return being made. Then, add the synergies being proposed to the EBIT or EBIDTA or PAT of the target or by the acquirer or take acquirers projected combined EBIT or EBIDTA or PAT. Then, figure out the delta between the pre-acquisition ROCE or ROE to the post-acquisition ROCE or ROE . The size of delta will give the idea whether they are achievable or unachievable and whether it requires marginal effort or transformational effort to reach that number.

		TARGET (EXISTING)					
Equity value	Assumed debt	Enterprise value	EBIDTA	EBIT	PAT	ROCE	ROE
100	50	150	15	12	10	**5%**	**10%**
		TARGET (PROJECTED)					
			EBIDTA	EBIT	PAT	ROCE	ROE
			30	24	20	16%	20%
					DELTA	**233%**	**100%**

The transformation in numbers would look stupendous based ONLY on the superlative effort.

c. Play between Debt and Equity Funding of the Acquisition

We have already discussed in the qualitative criteria about the debt financed acquisition and how they help punch above your weight while acquiring companies. The below example depicts how to achieve it as well as how debt finance acquisition would contribute to EPS accretion and how equity financing would dilute the EPS.

Thus, EPS accretion justified on the basis of debt financing is something that needs to be viewed with a pinch of salt.

Cost of debt Financing	Tax rate (given)	Cost of debt financing net of tax	Implied PE = (1/0.035)	Existing PAT of acquirer	Existing number of shares	Acqui-sition share price	EPS
5%	30%	3.5	28.6	50	10	100	5
PAT	After tax Synergy	PAT+ Synergy	Equity value (28.6×25)				
20	5	25	714				

Sensitivity analysis for debt financing

Interest rate	6%	7%	8%
Equity value	595	510	446

EPS accretion analysis

Due to dilution	Number of new shares to be issued based on equity value and current share price	Total number of shares	PAT + PAT (target)	Revised EPS	EPS accretion
Equity financed	7.14	17.14	75	4.4	-0.6
Debt financed	0	10	75	7.5	2.5

The above example depicts financially engineered accretion to EPS, by debt financing. However, it doesn't show the risk accretion to the acquirer and drop in the PE multiple of the company.

d. Bootstrap Effect

Bootstrap effect arises when a high PE company acquires a low PE company. Let us assume the PE of acquired and target is 20 and 10, respectively.

On the simple basis, the yield on both the PEs is as under:

Acquiring company = 1/20 = 5% target company = 1/10 = 10%.

Thus, the acquisition of target company would provide yield of 10% to the acquirer.

Assuming the PAT of target company to be 10, at a multiple of 10, the value of that profit will be 100, while if we apply the acquirer multiple of 20, the value of the target company will be 200. Thus, the value accretion is 100.

Effectively, meaning 10 worth of profits have been acquired at 5% financing and yielding 10% return with differential of 5% to the acquirer.

e. Synergy

The press releases at times provide synergy number to be achieved over 2–3 years. Discount the synergy with cost of capital back and compare the discounted numbers relative to the size of profit of the acquirer company. If its 5–10% of the profit of the acquiring company, then it a palatable number, anything above that will be in most cases be overestimation.

Case study 13.1: Apollo Tyres to Acquire Cooper Tire & Rubber Company

Press Release

Combination Creates World's Seventh-Largest. Tire Company with $6.6 Billion in Revenue

Gurgaon, India and Findlay, Ohio, USA–June 12, 2013: Apollo Tyres Ltd. (NSE: Apollo TYRE) and Cooper Tire & Rubber Company (NYSE: CTB) today announced the execution of a definitive merger agreement under which a wholly-owned subsidiary **of Apollo will acquire Cooper in an all-cash transaction valued at approximately $2.5 billion.** Under the terms of the agreement, which has been unanimously approved by the boards of directors of both the companies, Cooper stockholders will receive $35.00 per share in cash. **The transaction represents 40% premium to Cooper's 30-day volume-weighted average price.**

This strategic combination will bring together two companies with highly complementary brands, geographic presence, and technological expertise to create a global leader in tire manufacturing and distribution. Apollo, founded in 1972, has an international reputation for high-performance tyres across a portfolio of well-known premium and mid-tier brands, including the flagship Apollo brand and Vredestein. Cooper, the 11th-largest tire company in the world by revenue, was founded in 1914 and today supplies premium and mid-tier tires worldwide through renowned brands such as Cooper, Mastercraft, Starfire, Chengshan, Roadmaster, and Avon.

The combined company will be the seventh-largest tire company in the world and will have a strong presence in the high-growth end-markets across four continents. With a combined $6.6 billion in total sales in 2012, the combined company will have a complete range of brands and greater ability to satisfy the customer needs worldwide.

The combination is expected to deliver value creation benefits of approximately $80–120 million per annum at the EBITDA level. These ongoing benefits are expected to be fully achieved after 3 years and derived from operating scale, sourcing benefits, technology, product optimization, and manufacturing improvements. The transaction is expected to be immediately accretive to Apollo's earnings.

About Apollo Tyres Ltd

Apollo Tyres Ltd. is a high-performance tire manufacturer headquartered in India. It is built around the core principles of creating stakeholder value through reliability in its products and dependability in its relationships. The company has manufacturing units in India, Netherlands, and South Africa and exports its products around the world. In each of its market, the company operates through a vast network of branded, exclusive, and multi-product outlets.

About Cooper Tire & Rubber Company

Cooper Tire & Rubber Company (NYSE: CTB) is the parent company of a global family of companies that specializes in the design, manufacture, marketing, and sales of passenger car and light truck tires. Cooper has joint ventures, affiliates, and subsidiaries that also specialize in medium truck, motorcycle, and racing tires. Coopers headquartered in Findlay, Ohio, with manufacturing, sales, distribution, technical, and design facilities within its family of companies located in 11 countries around the world. For more information on Cooper Tire, visit www.coopertire.com, www.facebook.com/coopertire or www.twitter.com/coopertire.

Key Statements of the Press Release

a. Apollo will acquire Cooper in an all-cash transaction valued at approximately $2.5 billion.
b. The transaction represents a 40% premium to Cooper's 30-day volume-weighted average price.
c. A combined $6.6 billion in total sales in 2012.
d. The combination is expected to deliver value creation benefits of approximately $80–120 million per annum at the EBITDA level. These ongoing benefits are expected to be fully achieved after 3 years.

Looking Through the Press Release

Metrics	Disclosure	Remarks
Enterprise value	×	Non-disclosure of enterprise value probably means the debt being assumed is on higher side. Also, important to understand the EV/EBIDTA multiple.
Equity value	$2.5 billion	Important to analyze the equity value and acquisition multiple.
Premium	40%	Important to analyze the valuation.
Combined revenue	$6.6 billion	Important for pro-forma analysis.
Combined EBIDTA	×	Important to find out the EBIDTA margins being assumed and its relativeness to the industry.
Combined EBIT	×	Important to find out the operating profit margins being assumed and its relativeness as compared to industry.
Combined PAT	×	EBIDTA is given but, not PAT essentially means the interest or depreciation cost may depress the PAT.
Synergy	$80–120 million	To be generated after 3 years. Important to analyze the IRR on synergy to justify the acquisition. The figure and time to achieve is important. In this context, the figure and the timeline to achieve looks conservative.
Financing	×	Silent on financing does not provide the benefit to analyze the cost of financing and expected return.
Internal accruals	×	Important to know the cash flow financing of the acquisition.
Leverage	×	Important to understand the financial risk.
Equity	×	Important to understand the dilution impact.
Time to close	√	To determine the effect of combination.
Number of approvals	√	To determine the effect of combination.
Goodwill	×	Probably on the higher side, given the premium being paid relative to price.

Intangibles	×	Probably on the higher side, given the premium being paid relative to price as EBIDT is mentioned not, the EBIT. As intangibles will have to take depreciation.
Trading multiples for acquirer	×	Generally not mentioned in the press release but need to be checked for the purpose of quantitative analysis.
Trading multiples for target	×	Generally not mentioned in the press release but need to be checked for quantitative analysis.
EPS accretive	×	Not mentioned means does not seem to be rosy on accretive.
Same or similar business	√	To determine the probability of success.
Similar geography	√	To determine the probability of success.
Size of target bigger to acquirer	×	Not mentioned means relatively higher and signifies operating risk.
Acquisition multiple vis-à-vis historical industry multiple	×	Generally not mentioned in the press release but important to understand the point in business cycle that acquisition is being made.

Analysis

Thus, we see the key numbers to understand the value creation to be absent meaning that the financials are challenging. However, on the basis of the synergy figure of $80–100 million per annum after 3 years, the present value of which will be $50–65 million at capital cost of 15% which will be 5–6% return on the incremental value of $1 billion paid as premium to ruling price (40% of $2.5 billion).

Given the size of the transaction, different geography, and marriage of operating and financial risk, it is evident that it hardly covers the cost of capital and is very unlikely to be EPS accretive.

Case study 13.2 : Valeant to Acquire Salix Pharmaceuticals

Press Release

Valeant to Acquire Salix Pharmaceuticals For $158.00 Per Share In CashLaval, Quebec and Raleigh, N.C., Feb. 22, 2015 /PRNewswire/--

- Salix is the leader in the growing US gastrointestinal market.
- Transaction creates a new specialty platform for growth.
  - Key promoted products showing strong, double-digit volume growth, far exceeding the market.
  - Expected near-term approval for IBS-D indication of Xifaxan additional catalyst for the future growth.
  - Additional upside from expected approval of Relistor oral as well as strong near-term pipeline.
- **Transaction represents total enterprise value of approximately $14.5 billion**
  - Fully committed financing from a syndicate of banks led by Deutsche Bank and HSBC
- **Expected to achieve run rate cost synergies of greater than $500 million from combined company cost base within 6 months**
  - Synergy estimate does not include any benefit of Valeant's corporate structure
  - No planned reductions to Salix's specialty sales forces or hospital, key account, and field reimbursement teams; optimal size of primary care sales force to be determined.
- Transaction expected to close in the second quarter of 2015.
- **Expected to be over 20% accretive to cash EPS in 2016.**
  - Due to reduction of wholesaler inventory levels, modest accretion expected to cash EPS by 2015.
- No change expected to Valeant's credit ratings.
- Valeant to hold conference call to discuss Salix transaction and fourth quarter and full year 2014 earnings at 8:00 am ET on Monday, February 23.

Valeant Pharmaceuticals International, Inc. (NYSE: VRX) (TSX: VRX) and Salix Pharmaceuticals, Ltd. (NASDAQ: SLXP) today announced that they have entered into a definitive agreement, under which Valeant will acquire all of the outstanding common stock of Salix for $158.00 per share in cash, or a total enterprise value of approximately $14.5 billion. The transaction was approved by the Board of Directors of both the companies.

Salix Pharmaceuticals is a widely recognized gastrointestinal market leader with a portfolio of total 22 products including well-known prescription brands Xifaxan, Uceris, Relistor, and Apriso, as well as a strong near-term pipeline of innovative, new assets.

"Salix's market-leading gastrointestinal franchise is an ideal strategic fit for Valeant's diversified portfolio of specialty products," said J. Michael Pearson, Valeant's chairman and chief executive officer. "The growing GI market has attractive fundamentals, and Salix has a portfolio of terrific products that are outpacing the market in terms of volume growth and a promising near-term pipeline of innovative products. With strong brand recognition among the specialist GI prescribers, a highly rated specialty sales force and a significant product and commercial presence across the undertreated and underserved gastrointestinal market, this acquisition offers a compelling opportunity for Valeant to create a strong platform for growth and business development."

Thomas W. D'Alonzo, Chairman of the Board and Acting Chief Executive Officer of Salix, stated, "We are pleased to have reached an agreement with Valeant, which is a logical partner and importantly, creates immediate value for our shareholders. Combining Salix's leading market position in gastroenterology with Valeant's scale and resources will create a stronger and more diverse business committed to providing better health solutions to health care providers and their patients. We are proud of the accomplishments of our Salix team. Together, we have built our company into the leading gastrointestinal specialty pharmaceutical company providing solutions for patients and healthcare providers. We look forward to work with the Valeant team to ensure a smooth transition."

The combination is expected to yield greater than $500 million in annual cost savings from the cost base of the combined company. Synergies are expected to be achieved within 6 months of close, primarily from reductions in the corporate overhead and R&D rationalization, with the cost to achieve these synergies to be approximately 65%. Valeant and Salix will determine how best to integrate the two companies to leverage the combined strengths of both while ensuring a smooth and orderly transition. Consistent with Valeant's approach to integrating Bausch & Lomb, there are no planned reductions to Salix's highly rated specialty sales forces or hospital, key account, and field reimbursement teams and we will determine the optimal size of Primary Care Sales Force through the integration process.

On November 6, 2014, Salix reported 5- to 9-month wholesaler inventory levels for its top four products. Valeant has conducted extensive due diligence on Salix's stand-alone wholesaler inventory levels, stand-alone inventory work down plan, and associated potential litigation and regulatory exposure. Valeant expects to work down wholesale inventory and plans to target 2 months or less of wholesale inventory by year-end 2015. The net impact of the excess inventory on 2015 revenues is expected to be greater than $500 million.

Transaction Details

The acquisition is structured as an all-cash tender offer for all of the outstanding shares of Salix common stock at a price of $158.00 per share followed by the merger in which each remaining untendered share of Salix common stock would be converted into the right to receive the same $158.00 cash per share consideration as mentioned in the tender offer.

The all-cash offer will be financed through a combination of bank debt and bonds. As a result of the need to draw down inventories, EBITDA will be artificially low in 2014 and 2015 resulting in the initial net leverage ratio of approximately 5.6. Valeant is committed to reduce its net leverage ratio to be below 4.0 by the second half of 2016. As a result of the plan to reduce wholesaler inventory levels in 2015, the transaction is expected to be modestly accretive to 2015 cash EPS but over 20% accretive to 2016 cash EPS.

Valeant does not expect any change in its credit ratings as a result of the transaction.

The transaction, which is expected to close in the second quarter of 2015, is subject to customary closing conditions and regulatory approval.

About Valeant

Valeant Pharmaceuticals International, Inc. (NYSE/TSX:VRX) is a multinational specialty pharmaceutical company that develops, manufactures, and markets a broad range of pharmaceutical products primarily in the domain of dermatology, ophthalmic, neurology, and branded generics. More information about Valeant can be found at www.valeant.com.

About Salix

Salix Pharmaceuticals, Ltd., headquartered in Raleigh, North Carolina, develops and markets prescription pharmaceutical products and medical devices for the prevention and treatment of gastrointestinal diseases. Salix's strategy is to in-license late-stage or marketed proprietary therapeutic products, complete any required development and regulatory submission of these products, and commercialize them through the Company's 500-member specialty sales force.

Salix trades on the NASDAQ Global Select Market under the ticker symbol "SLXP."

Key Statements of the Press Release

- Transaction depicts the total enterprise value of approximately $14.5 billion
  - Fully committed financing from a syndicate of banks led by Deutsche Bank and HSBC.
- Expected to achieve run rate cost synergies of greater than $500 million from combined company cost base within 6 months.
- Expected to be over 20% accretive to cash EPS in 2016.
  - Due to reduction of wholesaler inventory levels, modest accretion expected to 2015 cash EPS.

- Salix for $158.00 per share in cash, or a total enterprise value of approximately $14.5 billion.
- On November 6, 2014, Salix reported 5- to 9-month wholesaler inventory levels for its top four products. Valeant has conducted extensive due diligence on Salix's stand-alone wholesaler inventory levels, stand-alone inventory work down plan, and associated potential litigation and regulatory exposure. Valeant expects to work down wholesale inventory and plans to target 2 months or less of wholesale inventory by year-end 2015. The net impact of the excess inventory on 2015 revenues is expected to be greater than $500 million.
- The all-cash offer will be financed through a combination of bank debt and bonds.

Look Through the Press Release

Metrics	Disclosure	Remarks
Enterprise value	$14.5 billion	Important to understand the EV/EBIDTA multiple.
Equity value	×	Important to analyze the equity value and acquisition multiple. Only price per share mentioned.
Premium	×	Not mentioned means a high cost acquisition.
Combined revenue	$6.6 billion	Important for pro-forma analysis.
Combined EBIDTA	×	Important to find the EBIDTA margins being assumed and its relativeness compared to the industry
Combined EBIT	×	Important to find out the operating profit margins being assumed and its relativeness compared to the industry
Combined PAT	×	EBIDTA is given but not PAT essentially means the interest or depreciation cost may depress the PAT.
Synergy	$500 million	Expected within 6 months and based on inventory levels being brought down from 9 to 2 months.
Financing		
Internal accruals	×	Important to know the cash flow financing of the acquisition.

Leverage	100%	Important to understand the financial risk.
Equity	×	Important to understand the dilution impact.
Time to close	√	To determine the effect of combination.
Number of approvals	√	To determine the effect of combination.
Goodwill	×	Probably on the higher side given, the premium being paid relative to price.
Intangibles	×	Probably on the higher side given, the premium being paid relative to price as EBIDT is mentioned not the EBIT. As intangibles will have to take depreciation.
Trading multiples for acquirer	×	Generally, not mentioned in the press release but is needed to be checked for quantitative analysis.
Trading multiples for target	×	Generally, not mentioned in the press release but is needed to be checked for the purpose of quantitative analysis.
EPS accretive	√	Mentioned as 20% in 2016.
Same or similar business	√	To determine the probability of success.
Similar geography	√	To determine the probability of success.
Size of target bigger to acquirer	√	Appears to be inline.
Acquisition multiple vis-à-vis historical industry multiple	×	Generally, not mentioned in the press release but important to understand the point in business cycle that acquisition is being made.

Analysis

The numbers represent a mixed bag. Equity value and the premium paid are not mentioned. So, also the resultant goodwill and intangibles created due to the premium.

The key numbers here to analyze are the financing, the enterprise value, the resultant leverage due to acquisition financing, and the synergy with the timeline to achieve it. The above is important in backdrop of it being EPS accretive.

The leverage is too high compared with the operating size. The EPS accretion is coming against backdrop of leverage financing.

Case study 13.3: Lupin Acquires GAVIS to Expand US Generic Business

Press Release: Lupin Acquires GAVIS to Expand US Generic Business

Mumbai, July 23, 2015: Pharma Major Lupin Limited (Lupin) has entered into a definitive agreement to acquire privately held GAVIS Pharmaceuticals LLC and Novel Laboratories Inc. (GAVIS), subject to certain closing conditions in a **transaction valued at USD 880 million, cash and debt-free.** The transaction has been unanimously approved by the Board of Directors of Lupin and GAVIS. The acquisition enhances Lupin's scale in the US generic market and also broadens Lupin's pipeline in dermatology, controlled substance products, and other high-value and niche generics. GAVIS brings to Lupin a highly skilled US-based R & D organization which would complement Lupin's Coral Springs, Florida, inhalation R&D center. GAVIS's New Jersey-based manufacturing facility will become Lupin's first manufacturing site in the US.

New Jersey-based GAVIS is a privately held company specialized in the formulation development, manufacturing, packaging, sales, marketing, and distribution of pharmaceuticals products. **GAVIS recorded sales of $96 million in FY 2014** and has over 250 New Jersey-based employees. GAVIS currently has 66 ANDA filings pending approval with the US-FDA and a pipeline of over 65+ representing niche dosage forms. To date, GAVIS has filed 25 Para IVs and 8 FTFs products. GAVIS's pending filings address a market value of about USD 9 billion. The combined company will have a portfolio of 101 in-market products, 164 cumulative filings pending approval, and a deep pipeline of products under development for US. The acquisition creates the fifth largest portfolio of ANDA filings with the US FDA, addressing USD 63.8 billion market products under development. 72% of these filings have pending approvals.

Commenting on the acquisition, Ms. Vinita Gupta, Chief Executive Officer of Lupin Limited, said, "This is a pivotal acquisition for Lupin as it aligns with our goal to expand and deepen our US presence. GAVIS has a strong track record of delivering highly differentiated products in a short time and is poised for continued strong growth as it delivers on its existing pipeline. GAVIS's capabilities and pipeline are an excellent complement to Lupin. The acquisition accelerates Lupin's entry into niche areas like controlled substances and dermatology. We are confident that Lupin's proven commercialization capabilities, vertically integrated manufacturing operations and supply chain strengths will accelerate GAVIS's growth. The acquisition is expected to be accretive to the earnings from the first full year of operations. In addition to the compelling strategic fit, there is a strong cultural fit between GAVIS and Lupin's entrepreneurial spirit and values."

Dr. Veerappan Subramanian, Founder and CEO of GAVIS, commented, "This is a time of globalization for the specialty pharmaceutical industry and GAVIS is well positioned to capitalize on this exciting opportunity. Joining forces with Lupin, a truly global player, will help realize our vision of building a broader, research-based high value, specialty business through organic growth. I am confident that the combined entity will be a powerhouse in the US specialty space and will significantly enhance Lupin's US platform."

About Lupin Limited

Headquartered in Mumbai, Lupin is an innovation-led transnational pharmaceutical company producing and developing a wide range of branded and generic formulations as well as biotechnology products and APIs, globally. The company is a significant player in Cardiovascular, Diabetology, Asthma, Pediatric, CNS, GI, Anti-Infective, and NSAID space and holds global leadership positions in the Anti-TB and Cephalosporin segment.

Lupin is the fifth largest and fastest growing top five generics player in the US (5.3% market share by prescriptions, IMS Health) and the third largest Indian pharmaceutical company by sales. The company is also amongst the top 10 generic pharmaceutical players in Japan and South Africa (IMS). For the financial year ended on March 31, 2015, Lupin's consolidated turnover and profit after tax were 125,997 million (USD 2.06 billion) and 24,032 million (USD 393 million), respectively. Please visit http://www.lupin.com for more information.

You could also follow Lupin on Twitter—www.twitter.com/lupinlimited

CIN: L24100MH1983PLC029442 Registered Office: 159, C.S.T. Road, Kalina, Santacruz (East), Mumbai—400 098.

About GAVIS

Somerset, New Jersey-based GAVIS, specializes in developing and marketing niche pharmaceutical products in a variety of dosage forms. Since its inception in 2007, GAVIS has compiled an impressive portfolio of niche marketed products and a formidable ANDA pipeline, along with a talented scientific, business, and regulatory team comprised of some of the foremost professionals in the generic pharmaceutical industry. GAVIS has also amassed an extensive, state-of-the-art facilities portfolio, which includes 45,000 square feet of R&D and manufacturing space with an additional 105,000 square feet of newly constructed space coming online by the end of 2015, complemented by 124,000 square feet of packaging and distribution operations.

Look Through the Press Release

Metrics	Disclosure	Remarks
Enterprise value	$880 million	Enterprise value is nearly 10 times the sales.
Equity value	$880 million	Important to analyze the equity value and acquisition multiple.
Premium	×	Unlisted.
target revenue	$96 million	Important for pro-forma analysis
Target EBIDTA	×	Important to find out the EBIDTA margins being assumed and its relativeness compared to the industry.
Target EBIT	×	Important to find out the operating profit margins being assumed and its relativeness compared to the industry.
Target PAT	×	EBIDTA is given but not PAT essentially means the interest or depreciation cost may depress the PAT.
Synergy	×	Not mentioned in quantitative terms but potential market for the targets ANDA filing is given.
Financing		
Internal accruals	×	Important to know the cash flow financing of the acquisition.
Leverage	×	Important to understand the financial risk.
Equity	×	Important to understand the dilution impact.
Time to close	√	To determine the effect of combination.
Number of approvals	√	To determine the effect of combination.
Goodwill	×	Probably on the higher side given, the premium being paid relative to price.
Intangibles	×	Probably on the higher side given, the premium being paid relative to price as neither EBIDTA nor EBIT is mentioned. As intangibles will have to take depreciation.
Trading multiples for acquirer	×	Generally, not mentioned in the press release but need to be checked for quantitative analysis.

Trading multiples for target	×	Generally, not mentioned in the press release but need to be checked for quantitative analysis.
EPS accretive	×	Not mentioned.
Same or similar business	√	To determine the probability of success.
Similar geography	√	To determine the probability of success.
Size of target bigger to acquirer	√	Smaller than the acquirer.
Acquisition multiple vis-à-vis historical industry multiple	×	Generally, not mentioned in the press release but important to understand the point in business cycle that acquisition is being made,

Analysis of the Press Release

From the above press release, it is evident that the details are sketchy. The valuation multiple is high relative to the revenue as profitability figures are absent. The acquisition is small as compared to the market cap of the company. Nevertheless, it is still 5% of the market cap and the profit figures may be low given the revenue size.

Thus, larger bet has been put on the future profitability at high multiple.

13.3 Executive Summary

The current topic highlights the general criteria that can be used by all to make an intelligent guess of the value creation in M&A.

Although, above is only a set of criteria not an exhaustion of criteria but good enough for you to understand the dynamics of M&A.